PRENTICE HALL

Complete
BUSINESS
ETIQUETTE
Handbook

BARBARA PACHTER & MARJORIE BRODY
with Betsy Anderson

PRENTICE HALL
Englewood Cliffs, New Jersey 07632

Prentice-Hall International (UK) Limited, *London*
Prentice-Hall of Australia Pty. Limited, *Sydney*
Prentice-Hall Canada, Inc., *Toronto*
Prentice-Hall Hispanoamericana, S.A., *Mexico*
Prentice-Hall of India Private Limited, *New Delhi*
Prentice-Hall of Japan, Inc., *Tokyo*
Simon & Schuster Asia Pte. Ltd., *Singapore*
Editora Prentice-Hall do Brasil, Ltda., *Rio de Janeiro*

©1995 *by*
PRENTICE HALL

10   9   8   7   6   5   4   3

Library of Congress Cataloging-in Publication Data

Pachter, Barbara.
    Prentice-Hall complete business etiquette handbook / by Barbara
Pachter and Marjorie Brody, with Betsy Anderson.
      p. cm.
    Includes index.
    ISBN 0-13-156951-1
    1. Business etiquette—Handbooks, manuals, etc.   I. Brody,
Marjorie, 1946–   . II. Anderson, Betsy. III. Title. IV. Title:
Complete business etiquette handbook.
HF5389.P33   1995
395'.52—dc20   94-32896
                                                   CIP

ISBN 0-13-156951-1

PRENTICE HALL
Career & Personal Development
A Division of Simon & Schuster
Englewood Cliffs, New Jersey 07632

Printed in the United States of America

*We dedicate this book with love and gratitude to our parents,
Mr. and Mrs. Victor Pachter and Mr. and Mrs. Donald Brody,
our role models and early etiquette teachers.*

ACKNOWLEDGMENTS

For their editing and advice: John Bing, President of ITAP International; Josephina Calzada; Denise Cowie; Edward Oxford; Robert Pimental; Robert Radway, President of Vector International; Hang Bo Tan; and author Susan Roane.

Ellen Coleman, our editor; Betsy Anderson, writer of good words; Michele Remey for research assistance; Aren Alfaro for creative ideas.

Our clients and the participants in our seminars for their interest and desire to learn.

And our families, particularly Alan R. Frieman, Jacob Pachter Oxford, Amy Brody and Julie Muchnick for their support and patience.

CONTENTS

Chapter 3
BIG TECHNIQUES FOR SMALL TALK 24

Chapter 4
PROFESSIONAL PRESENCE:
How to Make Your Appearance Work for You 42

Chapter 5
OFFICE COURTESIES THAT INCREASE YOUR CLOUT 66

Chapter 6
COURTESY CHALLENGE:
The True Test of Diplomacy 87

Chapter 7
WHAT TO SAY WHEN
YOU DON'T KNOW WHAT TO SAY 100

Chapter 8
THE TELEPHONE:
Your Voice to the World 114

Chapter 9
WRITTEN COMMUNICATION:
Write It Right! 134

Chapter 10
MUST WE MEET LIKE THIS?
The Protocol of Meetings 158

Chapter 11
DINING FOR FUN AND PROFIT:
The Business Lunch 194

Chapter 12
BUSINESS OUT OF THE OFFICE 218

Chapter 13
GIFTS THAT PACKAGE YOU WELL 233

Chapter 14
BUSINESS TRAVEL:
Skillful Manners in Motion 249

Chapter 18
THE WAY WORK WORKS OUTSIDE THE USA 318

Chapter 19
INTERNATIONAL BUSINESS OUTSIDE THE OFFICE 338

Chapter 20
A GLOBAL GUIDE TO GIFT-GIVING 355

Part 3
THE ETIQUETTE GAME 365

Chapter 21
FIND THE FAUX PAS 367

MANNERS MATTER
NOW MORE THAN EVER

Should a man always open the door?

Should you keep a notebook on the table during a business dinner?

Should you wear a nametag on the right side of your jacket?

These questions and their answers (see the end of this Introduction) are part of the growing field called business etiquette—putting to work in business those social skills which provide us with the confidence to handle people and situations with tact, diplomacy and respect.

Think of a time when you were uncomfortable.

Think of the worst faux pas you've ever witnessed.

Now think of someone who handled a difficult situation well. Chances are, he or she applied some business etiquette basics—apologizing for an error, treating the person's concern with respect, demonstrating a professional demeanor.

In today's business world, knowing a lot about your area of expertise isn't always enough. The ability to get along with others, demonstrate good manners and make others feel comfortable is increasingly important. Without these skills, business can be lost. Because our goods and services don't differ that much, the way we treat our customers often determines whether they'll choose our company instead of another. A polite, professional manner is a key component of quality.

But since we already know how to eat, to dress, to say hello or talk on the telephone, why do we need to study these things any further? For three reasons:

So that we present ourselves to our best advantage. Manners impact on how others perceive you, whatever your company position may be. Your attire may be holding you back from a promotion; you may be embarrassed or afraid to take clients out to lunch; your lack of grace in business gift-giving situations may cost you a return invitation to the boss's house.

Because many of us were not taught the proper rules. Maybe your school never offered "Business Etiquette 101." Perhaps your parents didn't know the rules or didn't stress their importance. In fact, you may be missing the "fork gene"—you didn't learn where to put the fork or where to place the bread and butter plate. As a result, you function, but not as well as you could. And sometimes, you end up eating your neighbor's bread!

Because the world is changing and the rules of behavior have changed as a result. While we often associate good manners with behavior in social situations, those rules don't always apply in modern business settings. For instance, some women were taught to curtsy upon being introduced—obviously not appropriate in today's work environment!

What's more, today's business setting, vastly different from the workplace of twenty or even ten years ago, necessitates an update of the manners you learned earlier. Women, minorities and people with disabilities have joined work environments that previously were the exclusive domain of white males. Good manners can help you demonstrate sensitivity and eliminate behavior that might be considered sexist, racist or discriminatory.

Manners also can assist people with technical backgrounds who move into positions requiring strong interpersonal skills. In today's hectic, bottom-line oriented business environment, manners can soften the high-pressure demands we place on our co-workers and forestall explosive outbursts.

Manners need updating for another reason—to keep pace with technology. We frequently communicate by fax or voice mail—useful, but often impersonal tools that actually increase the need for politeness.

For those who do business internationally, etiquette awareness can help distinguish between behavior that is proper in one culture and offensive in another.

Even if your office environment is quite casual and laid-back, etiquette is appropriate. Being friendly and polite is a significant asset in all business situations.

THE POWER OF POLITENESS

As a child, you probably grew tired of hearing your mother say:
   "Did you write a thank-you note?"
   "Put your napkin on your lap."
   "Don't interrupt when others are talking."
   And, the ever-popular:
   "Don't speak with your mouth full!"
   But Mom, who knew the importance and power of politeness, also knew that someday it would help us make our way through the world if our good manners were like natural reflexes. When most of us find ourselves in formal situations and don't know how to behave, we may "freeze"—losing our focus and becoming even less

effective. This can be particularly disastrous in business, when missed opportunity becomes a lost opportunity.

You might think that the emphasis on etiquette is frivolous when compared with a company's financial concerns. However, good manners do enhance the corporate life of an organization from three perspectives.

Graciousness will help you get clients and keep you from losing the ones you have, since customers and clients will be more likely to do repeat business with a company that makes them feel comfortable and valued. Within the organization, etiquette skills will improve morale and the quality of life, reducing turnover and heightening efficiency. Employees who are treated politely will feel valued and so may be willing to contribute more. On an individual basis, a courteous demeanor can advance your career and enhance your reputation as a professional, while poor manners can place a ceiling on your advancement.

Manners are both practical and pertinent in today's business world.

HOW THIS BOOK WILL HELP YOU AVOID THE TEN MOST COMMON ETIQUETTE BLUNDERS

We've designed this book to be a reader-friendly guide to the etiquette dilemmas that most employees encounter. That's why you'll find plenty of checklists and quizzes for quick reference and review. We've tested these materials for effectiveness in the workshops we've conducted. We'll show you, through anecdotes, the concrete impact of our suggestions in real-life situations. You might be surprised at what you already know, and this book could serve as a review or help you polish skills you possess but which have become rusty.

The first part of this book will take you through typical work situations in the United States. In Part Two, we will deal with international etiquette. Part Three is a game that reinforces the information presented throughout the book.

THE TEN MOST COMMON ETIQUETTE BLUNDERS

What are the ten most common etiquette errors?

1. *Inappropriate language.* This includes using demeaning salutations or diminutive names, employing vulgar, tasteless humor and spreading gossip. In fact, using diminutive forms of actual names can be downright dangerous. One woman, repeatedly called "Little Annie," retaliated one day in a crowded elevator. She addressed the male perpetrator, whose name was Richard, as "Big Dickie."

We address these problems in Chapter Three, "Big Techniques for Small Talk," in Chapter Six, "Courtesy Challenge: The True Test of Diplomacy" and in Chapter Seven, "What To Say When You Don't Know What to Say."

2. *Disregard of others' time.* It's rude to arrive late or unprepared for meetings or appointments. Barging into someone's office is a breach of protocol. Turning in an assignment late demonstrates disrespect. Interrupting a business meeting to answer non-emergency calls or to take care of unrelated business shows bad manners.

One corporate client was kept waiting for a meeting with a company director for a half-hour, never notified that the director was detained. The client complained. The president was furious. The client eventually took his business elsewhere.

You'll discover how to handle these deadline situations in Chapter Five, "Office Courtesies That Increase Your Clout," in Chapter Nine, "Written Communication: Write it Right!" and Chapter Ten, "Must We Meet Like This? The Protocol of Meetings." International views on office procedures are discussed in Chapter Eighteen, "The Way Work Works Outside the USA."

3. *Inappropriate dress and poor grooming.* We've all heard horror stories about people who committed etiquette blunders in the wardrobe and hygiene departments. Such mistakes are addressed in Chapter Four, "Professional Presence: How to Make Your Appearance Work For You." Appropriate appearance and behavior while overseas will be discussed in Chapter Seventeen, "Communicating Across Borders—Verbal and Nonverbal Communication."

4. *Misuse of the telephone.* This category includes keeping people on "hold" too long, not returning calls, not giving messages, slamming down the phone, not identifying who is speaking, and eating while speaking.

A consultant dialed the wrong client's number twice, each time hanging up without apologizing. After the second hang-up, he received an irate call from the client who had used technology to trace the call and identify the embarrassed culprit. Needless to say, that consultant's services were never used.

In Chapter Eight, "The Telephone: Your Voice to the World" you'll find out how to handle calls correctly.

5. *Failure to greet someone appropriately.* Greeting someone with no handshake, a limp handshake, or a death grip is an etiquette error. Introductions can be difficult, but they're essential. You'll uncover techniques for effective introductions in Chapter Two, "Powerful First Impressions: How to Meet and Greet." International introductions have their own set of rules, found in Chapter Sixteen, "Greetings With A Foreign Flair."

6. *Poor listening skills.* Cutting people off or interrupting others, avoiding eye contact, asking a question and not waiting for an answer—these are all wrong moves.

A junior member of a department finally got enough nerve to speak up at a departmental staff meeting. As he started to talk, he was cut off by a more senior person. It was a long time before the junior man felt comfortable contributing again. The company suffered for lack of his input.

We explore effective listening techniques in Chapter Three, "Big Techniques for Small Talk," and in Chapter Seventeen, "Communicating Across Borders—Verbal and Nonverbal Communication."

7. *Disregard of shared property and others' space.* It's rude to invade someone's privacy. Misuse of office equipment such as the fax machine, the copier, the coffee pot, can cause tempers to flare. Somehow people figure out if you're the one who never adds paper to the copier or who never makes more coffee after drinking the last cup.

Chapter Five, Office Courtesies That Increase Your Clout," offers practical suggestions for polite sharing of office space and equipment.

8. *Embarrassing others.* While constructive feedback is a necessary component of any efficient business, it can be humiliating when it is not properly delivered. Put-downs are just plain inconsiderate; rudeness, of course, is never tolerable.

Chapter Six, "Courtesy Challenge: The True Test of Diplomacy," explains how to handle conflicts graciously and how to provide feedback. Chapter Seven, "What to Say When You Don't Know What to Say," provides appropriate responses to rude remarks. In Chapter Twelve, "Business Out of the Office," you'll receive tips on discussing your personal life.

9. *Poor table manners.* Business meals require appropriate table etiquette which is often sadly lacking.

Poor manners can cost you lunch partners, and that's just for starters. We'll review gracious table manners in Chapter Eleven, "Dining for Fun and Profit: The Business Lunch." International dining manners are discussed in Chapter Nineteen, "International Business Outside the Office."

10. *Inappropriate or inconsistent recognition of others.* This most frequently occurs when undue attention is paid to someone's gender, such as asking the only woman to make coffee or commenting on a man's physical strength. Of course, inappropriate recognition also can have a non-gender basis as well. For example: A number of departments were working on a major project. Once the project was complete, the director acknowledged the contributions of three out of four departments. When the head of the unacknowledged department complained about being left out, the director simply said, "I forgot. Just forget it." But the damage was done—the group was hurt, embarrassed and less inclined to invest effort in the next project.

Giving and receiving praise is addressed in Chapter Six, "Courtesy Challenge: The True Test of Diplomacy" while Chapter Seven, "What to Say When You Don't Know What to Say," explains how to deal with out-of-bounds remarks. In Chapter Thirteen, "Gifts That Package You Well," we discuss tangible recognition of your co-workers.

***P.S. The answers to those questions asked earlier in the Introduction are:

No, a man doesn't always open the door. Whoever gets to the door first opens it. (Chapter Five)

No, don't keep a notebook on the table unless it's been approved by your dining companion. (Chapter Eleven)

Yes, wear your nametag on the right side of your jacket. It makes it easier for someone to read your name as you extend your right hand to shake. (Chapter Two)

Part 1

BUSINESS
IN THE U.S.A.

Chapter 1

TEST YOUR ETIQUETTE AWARENESS

A person should be allowed to have a few redeeming vices,
but never bad manners.

—MARK TWAIN
Pudd'nhead Wilson

Etiquette is a set of traditions, based on kindness, efficiency, and logic that have evolved over time. They give you a structure in which to operate. Think of them as rules of the game. Would you play golf or football without knowing the rules? And even if you would, do you think you'd be asked to play again?

WHAT ETIQUETTE IS NOT:
Myths About Manners

There are many myths about manners. Some people think manners make you a wimp or a snob or that manners prevent you from acting in a "natural" way. Others believe that manners are time-consuming or complicated. None of these things is true.

You can be both powerful and polite. You don't have to be mean to be strong. In fact, someone who motivates from fear actually has less power than someone who leads through respect. Aren't you more inclined to go the extra mile for someone who treats you with dignity?

Unfortunately, some people think of etiquette as snobbery. Too often, people do use their knowledge of protocol as a badge of superiority over others. These self-appointed protocol police are constantly monitoring others to determine if they demonstrate "appropriate" behavior. But the reality is that snobbery is bad manners. A well-mannered person uses his or her knowledge to make everyone feel at ease.

3

Manners don't stifle self-expression. You don't have to change your personality to be polite (unless, of course, you see rudeness as an integral part of your character). You can still joke without hurting anyone. You can have a wry attitude on life without treating others inconsiderately. You can be honest without being crude. Business etiquette allows for a wide range of behavior.

Does it take more time to do things politely? No. While learning to apply manners may take time—just as it takes time to incorporate any new behavior into your routine—good manners will save you time because you won't have to soothe over hurt feelings or make up for damaging mistakes. Etiquette requires only a small investment for a large return.

Best of all, once you understand the basics of etiquette and some of the reasons for the rules, good manners are not all that complicated. Once you become familiar with the guidelines, they're easy to apply, and they free you from the discomfort of uncertainty and the fear of offending someone.

CASE STUDIES FOR FAILURE

What impact can bad manners have on a career? They can place a ceiling on advancement and, in the worst-case scenarios, lead to dismissal. Consider these Case Studies for Failure. As you read them, remember that the person involved may have been the company's most knowledgeable, highly skilled employee or the best qualified job applicant, but bad manners mattered more.

The Case of The Missing Grip—An administrative assistant extended her hand when the job applicant entered the room. Not only did the applicant fail to extend his own hand, but he said, "I don't shake hands with women."

When the assistant brought the applicant's file to her boss, she told him what had happened. The candidate did not get the job, which involved frequent interaction with people. The applicant called the following day to apologize for his behavior, but it was too late.

The Terminal Typo—A female business owner receives numerous resumés each week. Any with the salutation "Dear Sir," or with typos end up in the trash.

The Vanishing Person—A woman went to a gathering of a networking association dressed for an evening cocktail party. No one bothered to talk with her. She sent such an unprofessional message that she was effectively invisible.

The Airport Snafu—A sales representative went to pick up the district manager. But he didn't offer to help with the luggage, even though his car was parked in a remote parking lot. When they finally reached the car, it was dirty and littered; moreover he had a spot on his tie. He was not put on the promotion list.

The Man Who Drank Too Much—A management trainee in an accounting firm went to a company outing at a country club and treated it as a social event. He drank too much, and became loud and obnoxious. He did not get an offer to join the firm.

The Woman In a Hurry—Because a meeting was running late, a participant became impatient. She pulled a cellular phone from her briefcase and called her voice mail, taking notes on the messages while the meeting was still under way. Her action was noisy, distracting, and rude. Her call managed to put her own professional advancement on hold.

ETIQUETTE AWARENESS QUIZ

Perhaps you wouldn't make those mistakes, but you may fall prey to others. How's your etiquette know-how? Take this quiz to find out.

1. True or False? It is appropriate to keep a double-breasted jacket open.

? 2. True or False? If you are disconnected, it's the caller's responsibility to redial.

3. True or False? To signify that you do not want any more wine, turn your wine glass upside down.

4. True or False? The following is a proper introduction: "Ms. Boss, I'd like you to meet our client, Mr. Smith."

5. True or False? Bread should be cut into small pieces with a knife.

6. True or False? Climate should be considered when choosing clothing.

? 7. True or False? "Dear Sir/Ms." should be avoided as a salutation.

? 8. True or False? In handshaking, a man should wait for the woman to extend her hand.

9. True or False? Photo-grey glasses are a good choice because you don't need to carry two pairs.

10. True or False? It is rude for a company to use an answering machine.

11. True or False? Thank-you notes should be typed.

12. True or False? In a modest restaurant, you can use your fingers to eat french fries.

13. True or False? It's not acceptable to twirl your spaghetti against a spoon to gather the strands.

14. When meeting someone new, it is appropriate to discuss:

   a. Your health   b. Controversial issues   c. Current events

15. What percentage of the message that you communicate to someone is conveyed through your visual appearance?

   a. 30%   b. 55%   c. 75%

16. Important mail should be answered within:

   a. 48 hours   b. Four days   c. One week

17. When two American businesspersons are communicating, the distance they should stand apart is approximately:

   a. 1 1/2 feet   b. 3 feet   c. 7 feet

18. Who goes through the revolving door first?

    a. Host   b. Visitor

19. True or False? When meeting a blind person who uses a Seeing Eye dog, it's polite to pet the dog.

20. True or False? The best seating arrangement at a meeting for people with opposite points of view is across the table from each other.

    Here are the answers:

1. False. A double-breasted jacket doesn't hang well unless it is buttoned. This also includes buttoning the inside button.

2. True. The caller knows where the caller is and so should call you back if you are disconnected.

3. False. To indicate you do not want any more wine, you can say "no thank you" if the conversation permits, or indicate your wishes non-verbally by shaking your head "no," or you can put your fingers over the rim of the glass.

4. False. It's actually the reverse. The proper introduction is: "Mr. Smith (the client), I'd like you to meet Ms. Boss."

5. False. Break your bread with your hands.

6. True. It makes sense to consider climate when selecting clothing.

7. True. You want to use the person's name in the salutation.

8. False. In handshaking, men should not wait for the woman to extend her hand. The only exceptions are in the case of an elderly woman or the Queen!

9. False. Photo-grey glasses usually do not lighten up enough inside. When people cannot see your eyes you may seem deceptive.

10. False. An answering machine is acceptable because it prevents your phone from going unanswered.

11. False. Thank-you notes should be handwritten, excepting possibly one for a job interview.

12. False. Use your fork to cut french fries into bite-sized pieces.

13. True. Twirling spaghetti against a spoon is not the most acceptable way because the spaghetti often is lifted and the guest has to observe messy hanging strands. Using the side of the plate avoids this problem.

14. c. Current events provide appropriate topics for a new acquaintance.

15. b. 55% of the message you communicate is conveyed visually.

16. a. 48 hours is the deadline for answering important mail.

17. b. 3 feet is the appropriate distance between two communicating American businesspersons.

18. a. The host goes through the revolving door first, because he knows where you are going.

19. False. Petting a Seeing Eye dog without first receiving permission is impolite.

20. False. If opponents are seated opposite one another, the situation can become more confrontational. Seating opponents on the same side of the table lessens the hostility.

WHEN TO BREAK THE RULES

We know that etiquette in the real business world isn't a true-false, multiple-choice test. It's more like a never-ending story problem and sometimes there is more than one possible answer. We will, though, provide you with guidelines to help you come up with your own answers. The rules we will give you are flexible—not cast in stone. Following them will make your life easier, but the final decision on when to do so is yours.

It's been said, "A gentleman or lady never does anything rude unintentionally." What we want to do is to make sure that any blunders you commit will be on purpose and not out of ignorance.

The question, then, is not "Should I break the rule?" but "What do I gain by breaking the rule? Does it work for me or against me?" We want you to consider the consequences of stepping beyond the boundaries of protocol.

OK, we'll admit it: We're not slaves to etiquette ourselves. For instance, we caution women against using bright red nail polish, suggesting instead a pale color, because red draws attention to your hands and can convey a "party" image. However, we've been known to have red fingernails. Our rationale: We speak to large groups, make large gestures and have received feedback that it works for us.

Before you can determine when to break the rules, though, you need to know what they are. That's what this book is all about—equipping you with etiquette guidelines that will see you through your business day and even beyond office hours. We're sure you'll find that good manners make for good business.

Chapter 2

POWERFUL FIRST IMPRESSIONS
How to Meet and Greet

A good beginning makes a good ending.

—ENGLISH PROVERB

First impressions really are important, but you already know that. The way you greet people can set the tone for the entire interaction that follows. If you make a poor initial impression, you may spend the rest of your meeting trying to overcome it. But how do you make sure that your first impression (which often is a lasting one) is positive? Since you want to put your best foot forward with the right handshake, effective introductions and gracious greetings, how can you avoid embarrassing and potentially costly mistakes?

In this chapter, you'll discover:

- What's most important about introductions and learn how to make them in a courteous, complimentary style.
- The keys to a good handshake and find out when it's appropriate to offer one.
- What to do in those awkward moments when you have forgotten someone's name or have received a death-grip handshake.
- How to treat the disabled and make them feel immediately welcome and comfortable.
- How to present and request business cards with appropriate flair.

INTRODUCTIONS THAT NEVER FAIL

Have you ever NOT been introduced while a business colleague chats with someone who's a stranger to you? It's awkward. It's embarrassing. Sometimes it's even insulting. It doesn't matter why it happens—perhaps your mutual acquaintance forgets to introduce you, thinks you already know the other person, or is trying to avoid an uncomfortable social situation. But the bottom line is, if someone hasn't been introduced, he or she is, socially speaking, invisible. Your impulse (which of course shouldn't be indulged) might even be to nudge your co-worker with your elbow, to say, in effect, "Hey, remember me?"

When introductions aren't made, both strangers will be distracted from the content of the conversation as they try to determine who the other person is or wait for a break in the discussion to introduce themselves. As soon as introductions are made, everyone feels more comfortable. The person who makes the introductions appears well-mannered and considerate. The process creates rapport and establishes some openings for conversation. Plus, you learn the other person's name! Once people know who the players are, they can focus on their roles in the game.

So, the main thing to remember about introductions is to make them! Introducing people is one of the most important protocols in business etiquette. And doing it correctly really isn't all that complicated.

Introductions at a Glance

WHAT TO SAY

1. Mention the name of the person of authority or importance first.
2. You only have to say each person's name once.
3. If you can, add some information about each person.

HOW TO RESPOND

1. Stand up.
2. Move toward the person, establish eye contact, look pleasant or smile.
3. Shake hands.
4. Greet the other person and repeat his or her name.
5. When the conversation ends, say goodbye.

Three Time-Tested Tips for Making Introductions

A properly performed introduction does more than make the person being introduced feel flattered and the new acquaintance feel included. Introductions can be a subtle acknowledgment of someone's professional status or rank. It will reflect favorably on you, the person performing the introductions, when you show that you are aware of the protocol and act in a manner consistent with it.

Three guidelines will get you through most situations requiring introductions:

1. *Name first the person who holds the position of most authority or importance.* This applies *regardless of gender.* Here are some examples:

   "President Lincoln, I'd like you to meet Ms. Brody."

   "Ms. Dole (the boss, or the division head), may I present Mr. Gardner (the sales associate)?"

2. *Say each person's name clearly once.* You do not *need* to go back and forth. If you do, it may seem like a ping-pong game, especially if more than two introductions are needed. Nevertheless, we should note that some etiquette advisors, and we as well, recommend this back-and-forth approach in certain circumstances. It offers a chance to catch a name that was missed the first time, and also makes it easy to provide additional information about each person.

3. *Add some information about each person.* This is not always possible, but whenever it is, you should do so. An example:

   "Anne Davis, I'd like you to meet the new sales manager, Bill Smith. He just joined us from XYZ Corporation, where he was the assistant manager of sales. Bill, Anne Davis is the company's director of finance."

Status Solutions

The person-of-authority or person-of-importance rule applies in most situations. (A client may not have authority, but she certainly has importance!)

For instance, you can:

Introduce a colleague to a customer or client.

"Mr. Client, I'd like you to meet my colleague, Ms. Brody."

Introduce a non-official person to an official person.

"Senator Smith may I present Mr. Williams."

If you don't know which person holds the position of most authority or importance, or if everyone's position is equal, pick the person whom you wish to compliment and mention that person first. Introduce the others to him or her.

If both are equal in status and you are unsure of whom you wish to flatter, you can fall back on the traditional rules, introducing a younger person to an older person.

"Mr. Fifty, I'd like you to meet my assistant, Ms. Thirty."

or the man to the woman

"Mary, this is Bill."

In combined business-social situations, such as an office cocktail party which might include spouses, partners, roommates and special friends, business rules apply. But who's more important? Your boss or your spouse? Whom do you wish to flatter?

The answer depends on knowing both your boss and your spouse, and gauging the situation accordingly. Perhaps your spouse will be understanding enough to agree to be "slighted." Perhaps your boss is the sort who will appreciate an acknowledgment of the importance of family.

We tend to introduce our boss first in settings that have been selected by the company, even those outside the office, since our spouses likely will acknowledge the importance of the supervisor in this sphere. If we were at a party in our home or if it was a chance social encounter outside the office, we'd introduce our spouses first.

Why You Should Use First Names Last

Should you use first names? It is always better to call people by their honorary title (Mr., Ms., Mrs., Dr.) and last name until you are asked to use first names or are sure that first names are appropriate. Ms. is usually the preferred title for women. However, the informal rules of your company's corporate culture will apply here—in some places, the chairman of the board is known as "Joe Smith," while elsewhere, it's always "Mr. Smith." *When in doubt, don't use first names.*

Providing Appropriate Introductory Information

The information that you provide about the person being introduced should be either neutral or positive. For example,

> "Mr. Nesmith is the one to see when your computer won't cooperate—he can find files no matter where they hide."

Introducing someone by providing ambiguous information, such as "Bill is the one I told you about yesterday," will make Bill uncomfortable. He can't help but wonder, "What did you say about me?" Try saying instead, "Bill is the person I mentioned to you yesterday. He's the one who came to this conference from Wyoming." Everyone will be more at ease.

When you introduce people, you are casting them in a temporary role, and protocol requires that the conversation continue, at least briefly, in the same direction. Bill, for instance, probably will explain why he came from Wyoming to the conference. Make sure that the role that you select for the person who is being introduced is appropriate. If you introduce a co-worker by saying, "Jake goes hang-gliding every weekend," you are not calling attention to his professional accomplishments. If you say that about him as you introduce him for the first time to a prospective client, you are de-emphasizing his business skills and qualifications—unless the client manufactures hang-gliders.

Also remember that the introductory information you provide says something about you. It indicates what you consider to be significant or interesting about the person being introduced. If you introduce the accounts payable manager by saying, "Linda has the most organized records in the building," it shows that you have noticed Linda's efficient filing system. If, however, you say, "Linda has the most beautiful eyes in the building," it shows that you are not relating to her on a professional level. While this remark might embarrass or flatter Linda, it will make you appear to be sexist, superficial, and insensitive.

A common mistake is an introduction that lasts too long. You want to provide just enough information to get the conversation started. One or two sentences usually are enough—you can always provide additional information later. If you bring a date to the company's holiday party, for instance, you need only say, "This is my friend Jennyse (or Jared)."

Five Impressive Responses to an Introduction

At least half the time, of course, you will be the one who is being introduced. And just because you are not the one making the introductions doesn't mean you don't have an important role to play. In fact, once the person makes the introduction, the spotlight shifts to you and your performance. Follow these five steps for the best presentation:

1. *Stand up.* Men stand, and, despite what your grandmother may have taught you, women stand too. If you are trapped in a chair or otherwise unable to stand, indicate that you would if you could or rise as much as you can. Failing to stand up can send a message that you are not of equal status with the person to whom you are being introduced.

2. *Move toward the person, establish eye contact, look pleasant or smile.* Don't be distracted by something that is going on elsewhere in the room or be dismissive of the person being introduced. Give the person the courtesy of your polite attention.

3. *Shake hands.* This affirms the connection and is a sign of trust and respect.

4. *Greet the other person and repeat his or her name.* You can say something like:

    "Nice to meet you, Mr. Jones."

    "It's a pleasure, Mr. Jones."

    "Hello, Mr. Jones."

    or, when appropriate,

    "Hello, Tom."

5. *When the conversation ends, say goodbye.* You want to make sure you close the loop even if you are moving on relatively quickly after meeting the person. To "Goodbye," you can add something like:

    "I enjoyed meeting you."

    "I'll look forward to seeing you at the annual meeting."

Reacting Well When Introductions Go Wrong

Not all introductions, alas, go as smoothly as textbook examples. The key to handling these situations is to subtly acknowledge the problem so that it can be addressed, corrected and then forgotten.

If you realize you don't know or have forgotten the name of the person you are introducing, admit it! After all, sooner or later, this happens to everyone. It would be more embarrassing to use the wrong name.

You can say something like:

"My mind's gone blank. I don't remember your name."

"I remember meeting you, but I can't recall your name."

"How could this happen! I know your name so well."

"I'm terribly sorry, I've forgotten your name."

(while smiling) "My computer just went down. I'm sorry, but I can't access your name."

It's possible to take a gamble and say,

"Have you met my friend, Bill Jones?"

Then, it's the cue for the other person (what's-his-name) to introduce himself to Bill. Or, Bill might say,

"And your name is ...?"

If someone forgets to introduce you, take the initiative. Give your name quickly. Say:

"My name is _____. I don't believe we have met."

If someone calls you by the wrong name, mispronounces your name or provides inaccurate information about you, politely make the correction without embarrassing the other person. For example, say,

"Actually, it is pronounced 'Guf-staf-son.'"

or

"My official title is director of finance."

This is especially important in situations in which you expect to see the other person again or when the information may influence the relationship.

Introducing ... Me!

You need a self-introduction for those situations in which you are not introduced or when no one is available to introduce you. Plan and practice a self-introduction that is clear, interesting, positive and well-delivered. Your 10-second commercial, which can be tailored to the event, should provide essential information and offer something relevant to help start conversation.

"Hello. I'm Marjorie Brody. I teach Powerful Presentation skills."

"Hi. I'm Barbara Pachter. I teach business etiquette for corporations."

"Hello, Mr. Johnson. I'm Linda Preston, the office manager for the Detroit office."

A way to practice this is to write out a self-introduction for a situation you will face in the next month. Try saying it out loud, in front of the mirror, until you are comfortable with it.

HANDSHAKES THAT GRAB RESPECT

In the currency of business encounters, the handshake is the dollar—the most frequently exchanged legal tender of American business transactions. Traditionally, the handshake has been a sign of trust. In the past, extending your hand in friendship demonstrated that you were unarmed.

The handshake today is an important symbol of respect and, in the United States, it's the proper business greeting. To be taken seriously, whether you are male or female, you must shake hands appropriately. Like it or not, you often are judged by the quality of your handshake. One woman at a training seminar said she got her job because she shook hands with the interviewer at the beginning *and* at the end of the interview. And all things being equal, that's what the boss told her on her first day on the job: "You conducted yourself professionally. You got the job."

Mastering Handshake Moments

Knowing when to shake hands is mostly common sense, but *"handshake moments"* include these customary times:

- When you are introduced to someone and when you say good-bye.
- When a client, customer, vendor or any visitor from the outside enters your office. (Not, however, every time your lunch buddy walks in.)
- When you run into someone you haven't seen in a long time, such as a co-worker from another division.
- When you enter a meeting and are introduced to participants.
- When a meeting ends, to say goodbye and to help formalize any agreements that have been reached.
- Whenever you feel that it will be appropriate. You will develop a sense for it.

Three Keys to an Effective Handshake

Do you know how to shake hands? Yes, of course you do. And yet, some people provide limp handshakes or else squeeze your hand so hard that you want to cry. Many of these people think they have the proper technique and would be surprised by the negative feedback. Does your handshake give you a lightweight appearance or the respect you deserve?

A number of books on the subject make it very complex. We will make it simple. There are three keys to an effective handshake:

1. *Say your name and extend your hand.* In most situations, the higher-ranking person should extend the hand first. If he or she doesn't, you should.

2. *Extend your hand at a slight angle, with your thumb up. Touch thumb joint to thumb joint.* Put your thumb down gently once contact has been made, and wrap your fingers around the other person's palm. Many people think they already use this technique, but are amazed when they test it to find how different it feels from their usual handshake.

3. *Provide a firm handshake, but not a bone-breaking one.* Two, possibly three, pumps are enough. Then drop your hand.

How to Handle the Problem Handshakes

When you are the recipient of a poorly executed handshake, don't call attention to the other person's inappropriate behavior—that's bad manners. Instead, your goal is reducing any discomfort (physical or psychological!) that you may be feeling without passing the awkwardness back to the person who caused it.

If you receive a bone-crushing handshake, go limp. This is a self-defense technique that may allow your hand to slide through. Holding your hand at a slight angle may reduce the pressure. If you know before an event that you will encounter bone-crushers, take off your rings.

If you receive a limp handshake, aim for the thumb joint with your hand. This position will eliminate some of the limpness.

If you extend your hand and there is no response, just put your hand down and carry on. Your behavior is correct. It's the other person's problem, not yours.

If you are wearing gloves, there are two possible ways to react. Some say to take the gloves off first; others say that if you are outside, leave them on. Good manners require that you be logical: there's no point fiddling with your gloves when it's extremely cold outside!

If you receive a two-handed shake—sometimes referred to as "the handshake hug"—you shouldn't pile your free hand on top of the other person's. (In this handshake variation, the left hand of the person initiating the handshake covers the back of the other person's hand.) Most people consider this approach too intimate for business. Others call it a power struggle, even referring to it as "the power pat."

Because it can confuse or intimidate the recipient, we recommend that you do not use it.

If something is in your hand-shaking hand, put it down or use your free hand. When chances are good that you'll need to shake hands, hold items in your left hand, and put your briefcase and pocketbook on the left hand or shoulder so that the right hand is free.

If you have sweaty palms, use talcum powder or a cloth handkerchief to absorb the sweat. (Make sure you have eliminated all of the sweat and that there is no powder on your clothing.)

Answering the Gender Question

Are there different rules for men and women in handshaking situations? Not any more. It used to be considered polite for a man to wait for the woman to extend her hand. That is no longer the case unless the woman is elderly.

But people often do what they were taught, even when those rules no longer apply. For that reason, even though it is no longer correct, some men will wait for the woman to start the process. This explains why some men of higher status don't present their hands and also why women often want to say their name and extend their hands first—some men will be waiting for it. Some women, though, still hesitate to shake hands with men or with other women.

Many men think they can hug and kiss women during the greeting. (And while you know that some men can do so, not *all* men should.) Which is another good reason for the woman to say her name and extend her hand first, even though etiquette no longer requires it: she is establishing the greeting. After that, in order for a man to hug or kiss her, he must pull her in. We're not going to tell you that this will eliminate all of the unwanted hugging and kissing, but it should eliminate most of it.

For many reasons, women often hesitate to shake hands with other women. Many women in business today were taught not to shake hands and, strange as it may sound, some even were taught to curtsey. In social encounters, women remain less likely to use a handshake with other women as part of the greeting. However, in business settings women should work through any initial awkwardness and shake hands with other women both in mixed groups of men and women where a round of introductions is being made and in one-on-one situations with another woman.

SMART COURTESIES FOR THE DISABLED

How do you greet the disabled? Politely, of course, and as much as possible in the same way in which you would greet anyone else.

Unfortunately, many people become nervous or do not know what to do or say around those with disabilities. As a result, they may not include the disabled individual in daily conversations or activities. While it's always been good manners to be polite to everyone, now—following the July 16, 1992, passage of the Americans with

Disabilities Act (ADA)—it's also the law. American businesses are required to create, through reasonable accommodation, an environment in which disabled individuals can become productive parts of the workforce.

Here are nine ways to make meeting and greeting those with physical disabilities a positive experience for all involved:

1. *Don't ignore the person.* Some people unconsciously behave as if a person who cannot see or hear is not there at all. Speak to disabled persons directly, maintaining eye contact with them rather than with their interpreters. Don't refer to them in the third person (as in "Would *he* like a cup of coffee?" or "Does *she* want to hang up her coat?")

2. *When introduced, offer a greeting.* Be prepared to shake hands. If someone with limited use of his or her hands or who has an artificial limb offers a left hand, use your left hand. Ask a person who is blind, "Shall we shake hands?" and then bring your hand to hers.

3. *Be sensitive in your use of language.* Don't use "handicap" in reference to someone's condition; use "disability." Avoid mentioning the disability unless it is pertinent. Use non-judgmental, neutral descriptive terms such as "a person with cerebral palsy" (instead of "cerebral palsy victim" or "spastic"), "person who uses a wheelchair" (not "bound to a wheelchair") and "person who is blind" (not "blind woman"). However, if you use common expressions such as "Did you hear about ...?" or "I see," don't be overly embarrassed or apologetic. Address the disabled person by his or her first name only if you are being equally familiar with all others present.

4. *If the person has a visual impairment, alert the person to your approach and identify yourself.* If you just say "Hello" and the person does not use your name in return, identify yourself with a few sentences to allow your voice to become familiar. If you are part of a group, use names to make it clear to whom you are speaking, such as "Judy, have you received an update on this quarter's sales figures?" Ask permission before petting or interacting with a guide dog.

5. *If the person has a hearing impairment, place yourself within sight, wave, or gently tap the person on the shoulder.* Use short, declarative sentences. If the person is reading your lips, speak slowly and expressively (but not in an exaggerated fashion). Keep hands, papers, cigarettes, drink and food away from your lips while speaking. Face the light source so that it shines on you. If you are conversing through an interpreter, be sure to look at the person with the hearing impairment while keeping in sight of the interpreter.

6. *If the person has difficulty speaking, listen patiently, without interrupting.* Don't pretend to understand if you don't. Repeat the part that you have understood and let the person continue from there. Try to phrase your questions so that they require only short answers or a nod.

7. *If the person is in a wheelchair or motorized cart, speak in a normal voice.* Try to get on that person's eye level when communicating. Don't pat the person on

the head or shoulder—it's patronizing. And don't lean on or hang on the chair—
it's an extension of the body.

8. *If you are unsure how to proceed, take direction or guidance from the person.*
You can offer to help the person travel or sit down, but wait to assist until he
or she accepts and provides you with instructions.

9. *Consider how you would like to be treated if you had that disability.* Being disabled is a part—but not all—of who that person is. People with disabilities likely share many of your dreams, fears, and hopes. They don't want to be considered, or treated, as one-dimensional symbols of their disability.

HANDLING BUSINESS CARDS WITH FLAIR

Business cards provide an effective way for your new acquaintance to remember your
name, address and phone number. After you are introduced, shake hands, and speak
briefly, you may want to present your business card.

In the United States, while the exchange of business cards frequently takes place,
it is rarely required. There also is no hard and fast ritual associated with the
exchange. However, if you plan to do business internationally, presenting business
cards may be mandatory as well as ritualistic (see Chapter Sixteen, "Greetings With
a Foreign Flair," for more information on international greetings.)

Designing an Impressive Business Card

Your card introduces you and your company to potential customers. As a symbol of
your official and professional status, it should be well-designed.

The standard $3^1/2$ by $2^1/2$ inch size is not mandatory as long as a quality image
is provided. Odd-shaped cards attract attention, but don't fit in most wallets or card
cases and so are not as easily kept.

The paper from which the card is made must be strong enough not to tear when
fingered or extracted from a card case. The texture may be matte or shiny and of any
color, provided it can be easily read and matches your image and industry.

A two-sided card is effective for those who regularly do business in another
country. The English version can be on one side and the host country's language on
the other.

The typeface may be either printed or engraved. Some people use their printed
cards for mass mailings and save their engraved versions for personal presentations
or VIP use.

An effective business card includes the following items which can be presented
in either a horizontal or vertical format:

• A logo, trademark, or company symbol.

- Your name. In the United States, use only professional titles: "Dr.," "Ph.D.," etc. If your first name could be that of either a male or female, it's OK to use Mr., Mrs., or Ms. You can use a nickname if that is what you are really called (Michele "Muffy" Remey, Vice President," for instance). It's best, though, to be cautious with nicknames, since you may send a childlike message, especially for women. You can always have your official name "Elizabeth Westminster" on the card and explain, "Everyone calls me 'Libby'" as you present it.
- Your title.
- The company name.
- The business address.
- The telephone number.
- The fax number.
- If pertinent, the address of other offices.

Your home telephone number is optional. It can be an effective touch as you present a card to personalize it by adding your home phone number in pen. That gesture can signal that you are giving that person special access to you.

While your company may issue a standard card, you might also want to develop a personal business card to emphasize your professional, rather than your corporate, affiliations, if, for instance, you are president of the Society of Mechanical Engineers.

If your company doesn't provide a business card, develop your own card that lists your name, address and phone number. You want to be able to reciprocate when others present you with their cards. It also can be a very effective self-marketing device, a way of saying "ask for me when you call." Consult with a professional designer to create the card.

For examples of well-designed professional cards, see *Sample Business Cards* on page 20.

The Keys to Determining When to Present a Card

In America, your decision regarding when to present your card will be based on the situation and also on how well acquainted you are with the participants. You will most likely present your card during your first encounter with someone, when it is most comfortable to do so. The card exchange usually signals the end of a first or early meeting. Presenting your card indicates that you may be willing to continue the dialogue at another time.

However, presenting a card at the beginning of a sales meeting is traditional in encounters between a sales representative and a client and frequently marks the unofficial opening of the business portion. Similarly, a visitor to an office may present a card to the receptionist in order to be properly introduced or to be directed to the appropriate person. Another card may then be presented to the host. In these cases,

Sample Business Cards

CoreStates

**Philadelphia
National Bank**

Joseph A Sparacino
Vice President
Director of Training

Wholesale Bank Training
Department
FC 1-1-4-22
1345 Chestnut Street
PO Box 7618
Philadelphia PA 19101-7618
215 973 6771
Fax 215 786 7017

Alan R. Frieman, D.M.D.

3201 Morrell Avenue
Morrell Avenue at Academy Road
Philadelphia, Pennsylvania 19114
Telephone (215) 637-2000

---

ruth wreschner

authors' representative

**10 west 74th street
new york, n.y. 10023**

**tel: (212) 877-2605
fax: (212) 595-5843**

---

(215) 886-1688   •   (800) 726-7936   •   Fax: (215) 886-1699

B̲RODY COMMUNICATION̲S

Presentation and Communication Skills
Seminars, Coaching, and Keynotes

197 Linden Drive
P.O. Box 8868
Elkins Park, PA 19117

Marjorie Brody
President

SECA°

Steven L. Barsh
President

SECA, Inc.
630 Sentry Parkway • Suite 200
Blue Bell, PA 19422-2329 • USA

215-834-0400
Fax 215-834-5723

SECA°

スティーブン L. バーシュ
社 長

SECAインコーポレーテッド
米国ペンシルベニア州ブルーベル市
セントリー・パークウェイ630番地 200号

電話 215-834-0400
FAX 215-834-5723

بـريـور
سـميـث
&
وبـريـور
الخليـج

BREWER
SMITH
&
BREWER
GULF

معـاربـون
مهنـدسـون

Architects
Engineers

كريس لوكيت
دبلوم معماريون
آر.آي.بي.ايه.

CHRIS LOCKETT
Dipl. Arch.
R.I.B.A.

شـــربك

Partner

ص. ب ٥٠٦٦٧
دبـي – ا.ع.م.
هاتف: ٢٢٨٩٣٥/٦
فاكس: ٢٨٤٥٩٦
سيارة: ٠٥٠-٢٩٢٨٦

P.O. Box 50667
Dubai
U.A.E.
Tel : 971 4 228935/6
Fax: 971 4 284596
Car: 050-29286

Barbara Pachter
president

Pachter &̲Associates

THE EXPERT IN BUSINESS COMMUNICATIONS TRAINING

32 Whitby Road, Cherry Hill, NJ 08003 USA
609.751.6141 • fax 609.751.6857

the business card functions somewhat as social calling cards once did—announcing both your identity, your presence and your intention to conduct business.

In group situations, receiving business cards at the beginning can help keep the cast of characters straight. If there are a number of people in the meeting or if you are unsure of someone's correct name or title, you can ask for cards before the meeting starts. When you receive a number of cards, you can adopt the Japanese custom of spreading them out on the table as a sort of seating chart.

During an office visit, if the host does not offer a business card, the guest should request one before leaving. If the business cards are in a desk holder, ask before taking one. You can give two business cards—one for the secretary. You also can request two cards—one for your rolodex and one to staple in a client file.

Don't hand out your card during a meal; wait until it's over. Don't give out cards during a private dinner party unless you are asked to do so—it blurs the business/social lines of the situation. Carry your cards with you to social events in case the opportunity to network presents itself, but don't turn a garden party into a sales presentation!

When you are not physically present, you can let your card "represent" you. For instance, enclose it when forwarding material with a brief note, or when you send a business letter to someone you plan to contact in the future.

The Subtle, Sophisticated Way to Present a Card

Be selective in distributing your cards. Your policy should fall somewhere between handing out your cards indiscriminately, which devalues them, and hoarding them. Ask yourself whether the person might actually want the card in order to reach you in the future. It's best to err slightly on the side of over-distribution.

The protocol of exchanging business cards parallels that of the handshake: usually the senior, or higher-ranking, person starts the process. Wait for the senior executive to ask for your card first. However, if she does not, you should present yours and then also ask for hers.

In a group or party situation, the card exchange should be private. People sometimes pass out their business cards as if they were dealing at a poker game, and this is unprofessional. You want your card to be respected and valued, which it can't be if it is randomly distributed. An appropriate card exchange most often occurs between just two individuals at a time.

Make sure your cards are readily available—in a pocket or briefcase. A good card case is a worthwhile investment. Not only does a quality case keep the cards neat, but it adds to your professional demeanor. To avoid fumbling in pockets or purses, always keep the cards in the same place. A good location is the inside pocket of your suit or jacket.

The card that you present should be in good shape—not tattered or folded.

What to Say When You Swap Cards

Requesting someone's business card is a straightforward process. You need only say,

"Do you have a business card?"

or

"May I have your business card?"

When you want to present your own card, you can say,

"Here's my card. Please feel free to call me if you have any other questions."

Or, you might say,

"Please send the information to this address. I look forward to hearing from you soon."

If you wish to offer your card to a long-time associate, you can say,

"Did I ever give you my card?"

or

"I've been meaning to give you my card."

Presenting your card and saying,

"Here's my new card."

can help inform someone that your position has changed.

It's not polite to directly refuse a request from someone for your business card. Instead, you can say,

"I'm afraid I'm all out at the moment."

or

"I neglected to bring them with me."

Giving someone your card, of course, does not obligate you to continue contact, nor does accepting someone else's card. Accept politely any card that is offered, and then, later, throw it away.

When you do receive a card, say "Thank you" and examine it briefly before putting it away. A short observational comment may be in order, for example:

"You're located in Grand Blanc, Michigan—isn't that where the Buick Open is held?"

You can use a business card that you have received to refresh your memory about someone's name and title before your next meeting. You can record notes about the meeting on the back of the card, or place it in your telephone file.

STARTING OFF ON THE RIGHT FOOT

By this point, you should be off to a very good start in your new business relationship. You know to whom you are speaking and they know who you are, because you've been introduced. You've established yourself as a professional by your use of a handshake that commands respect. You have presented a business card, allowing the individual to follow up on the fine impression you have just made. Now you're ready to proceed on to the lost art of conversation, particularly small talk, in business situations.

BIG TECHNIQUES
FOR SMALL TALK

One always speaks badly when one has nothing to say.

—VOLTAIRE

"Small talk" is the chitchat that comes before contract negotiations, the banter exchanged by smiling heads of state before they disappear behind closed doors, the light conversation that takes place between people who are casually mingling or just passing time.

In a business setting, it can occur immediately following introductions or through chance encounters in the elevator, at the water fountain, and before a meeting. The amount of small talk varies with the corporate culture as well as with the geographical location.

Although it may seem insignificant, small talk has potentially enormous consequences. Someone who talks too much will be seen as nervous or insensitive, while someone who ignores others will be considered snobbish. Those who discuss only work may come across as limited. Every encounter offers an etiquette opportunity: a chance to impress the other person with your gracious demeanor.

The ability to make small talk about non-business topics is an essential part of establishing any business relationship, contributing significantly to both an employee's rapport and credibility within the company. It also performs the important function of setting clients at ease. One study by a Midwestern university found that a lack of communication skills—rather than technical ability or business know-how—was cited 80 percent of the time as the reason people do not get ahead in their jobs. Mastering small talk is a significant part of the protocol of interpersonal communications.

For some people—sales representatives, public relations representatives and managers, to name a few—the ability to make small talk is an unwritten component of their job description and a determinant of their success.

In a large company, an executive may know your work only by reputation or through written communiques, and chance encounters may be the only other opportunity you have to make an impression. Yet, the situations in which small talk occurs do not offer the time and certainly are not the place for meaningful, in-depth work-related discussions.

Whatever the circumstances, you want this conversational opportunity to work for you. You don't want a co-worker to leave thinking you are awkward, pompous or stand-offish.

Of course, not everyone is naturally at ease making small talk. Perhaps you're shy by nature or just shy around strangers or supervisors. Maybe you're overly serious and never learned how to perform the passing-time pleasantries of social conversation. The good news is that you can learn to be more comfortable making small talk.

INGREDIENTS OF A GOOD CONVERSATION

Conversation is an art, not a science. Like a recipe, it's a formula subject to individual interpretation through the chef's skill. If small talk has the right flavor, it may even whet the appetite for a more prolonged conversation. But as you will see, small talk requires a blend of three key ingredients—*attending skills, listening manners* and, of course, *your conversational contribution.*

We'll begin our discussion by focusing on attending skills, those "tuning in" techniques that establish a communication connection with the speaker—an essential of good etiquette. Then, we'll explain listening skills that make the other person feel heard and ensure that you get the actual message. Finally, we'll provide ideas on what to say and how to say it. You'll find out how to:

- maximize small talk opportunities;
- prepare for "spontaneous" conversations;
- use suggested topics to keep business chatter light;
- select reliable opening lines;
- establish guidelines for humor (the spice of small talk);
- learn the ABCs of handling questions, and words and phrases to eliminate from and include in your vocabulary.

TUNING IN TECHNIQUES THAT CREATE A CONVERSATION CONNECTION

When someone makes an announcement by saying "May I have your attention please?" or opens a business session by saying "Let's get started," he or she is actually saying, "Listen up." Implied is a polite request to cease other conversations, stop other activities and focus on what comes next.

The same steps are required for etiquette success in small talk. The first, often overlooked, step is to get ready to listen and let the other person know you will indeed be paying attention. Positive Attending = Paying Attention. You are, in effect, making a commitment to engage in conversation.

SOFTEN: The Key to Gaining and Giving Attention

The acronym SOFTEN explains the six most significant attending skills.

S mile
O pen Posture
F orward Lean
T one
E ye Communication
N od

What ties these behaviors together is that they make the other person feel comfortable or important. Here's why:

Smiling isn't as simple as it seems. Many listeners forget to do it and, surprisingly, expect someone to talk with them despite the distracted, indifferent or even hostile expressions on their faces. A smile is a sign of friendliness and receptivity. Men often need to smile more, because they usually aren't in the habit of doing so. Women shouldn't over-smile, a habit they may have fallen into as children. The smile should be consistent with the message being presented. If someone is giving you bad news, don't stand there and smile!

Open posture also communicates non-verbally that you are open to the ideas being presented and to the person expressing them. Face the speaker. Sit or stand in an attentive position. If you're standing, your feet should be parallel, with your weight evenly balanced, indicating that you're grounded and are not ready to run out. Don't cross your arms or legs—that can send out a hostile or defensive message. In the United States, a good distance for business communicating is approximately three feet between the speaker and listener. Anything too close can become stressful for the other person, and when the stress level goes up, the ability to listen goes down.

Forward Lean. While you do not want to invade the speaker's space, you also don't want to make him shout or feel as if you are being distant. Don't touch the person or his wheelchair, which is an extension of his body. During the conversation, occasionally lean slightly forward to emphasize your attention. Remain alert but comfortable.

Tone of voice communicates interest. If you mumble, shout, or whisper, you're making communication more complicated. Don't yell at a blind person. Research into both men's and women's voices indicates that the deeper the voice, the longer people will listen to it. If you are concerned about your voice—its pitch, modulation, rate, volume, etc.—get feedback and consider using professional help. Do you have an accent that interferes with comprehension? You may benefit from audiotaping yourself, consulting a speech coach, using an audio program or attending a presentation skills class.

Eye contact is one of the best ways to say "I'm listening" without opening your mouth. In fact, in the United States, unless you are looking at the speaker, she'll assume you are not listening. "Let me put on my glasses—so I can *hear* you," one woman told us. One shy man had to learn from friends that he was undermining his credibility and trustworthiness by averting his gaze during conversations. Behind his back, a colleague called him, "Old Shifty Eyes." Most people feel that if you are looking across the room, at papers on the desk, and, especially, at a watch or clock, you are not giving them your full attention. You may need to sit down to get at the same eye level as a person in a wheelchair.

Take care to accomplish this direct eye contact without staring down the speaker—too direct a stare can be considered threatening or harassing.

Nod occasionally and positively to indicate acceptance or interest, but don't overdo it so that you look like a yo-yo.

It's important to get feedback on your SOFTEN skills and practice and improve them whenever you can. Watch a videotape of yourself in conversation and then go through the *Conversation Checklist* to see how you did.

Conversation Checklist

Did I smile at appropriate times?

Was my smile genuine?

Was my body language open?

Was I careful not to cross my arms in a defensive posture?

Did I move and lean toward people rather than backing away?

Was my voice enthusiastic?

Did I sound interested in others?

Did I look at people approximately 80 percent of the time?

Did I avoid eye jumping or staring?

Did I periodically nod or look as if I agreed?

Ready, Set, Listen

Like a fax machine that has to be plugged in, turned on, and warmed up in order to receive data, you too need to get prepared to receive auditory input during small talk and other conversations. These steps require you to:

CREATE A SETTING. Get yourself into a non-distracting situation. Eliminate the extra noise by closing the door and holding all telephone calls. If you have an answering machine, turn down the volume. Also eliminate the physical barriers to communication: put a visitor's chair at the side of the desk; take a seat next to the speaker, instead of across from her. If, despite these measures, you are having trouble picking up the words the person is saying, have your hearing checked.

TUNE OUT THE DISTRACTIONS. During conversation is not the time to be thinking about the afternoon meeting or a car maintenance appointment. Internal distractions such as headaches, hunger, fatigue, or your current emotional state should be on "hold" for the duration of the conversation.

BE AWARE OF YOUR NON-VERBAL SIGNALS. Make sure you are signaling that you are ready to listen. Don't fidget. Avoid shifting in your seat. Stop yourself from blinking, biting your lip, doodling, frowning deeply, as well as from playing with your hair, tie, or jewelry.

Be aware that changes in eye contact or in posture (such as tensing up, turning away or backing off) will indicate that you no longer are receptive to what is being said.

LISTENING:
It's More Than Hearing

Conversation: A vocal competition in which the one who is catching his breath is called the listener.

—UNKNOWN

Listening, of course, is far more than just pausing for breath while the other person talks. It involves actively tuning in to what he or she is saying.

It's been said that we hear half of what is said, we listen to half of that, we understand half of that, we believe half of that, and we remember half of that! That's not very much (about three percent of what was said). And most of us make more than one listening mistake each week, whether it's transposing digits in a telephone number or misinterpreting instructions.

"You're not listening," a woman accused her husband. He smugly repeated back everything she had said, word-for-word. But she responded, "I didn't say, 'You're not hearing me.' I said, 'You're not listening.' There's a big difference."

Hearing is essentially a physical response to a stimulus. The only way to really avoid hearing something is to cover your ears or get out of range. Listening, though, involves not only having the sound come in contact with the ears, but interpreting, understanding, and responding to the sound. Listening is both an intellectual and emotional act.

Unfortunately, today many of us have become accustomed to tuning things out and fall quickly into poor listening habits. We don't really hear background music, we talk over other conversations, we shut out noises so we can hear ourselves think. But like any other skill, listening needs to be learned and practiced. Toddlers, for instance, have to be taught not to interrupt conversations with random remarks—they haven't learned to take turns talking or to stick to the topic.

Listening Losers

Can you spot yourself among these listening losers? What do you do when you encounter one?

Wandering Wendy—You frequently allow your mind to wander, especially when the person is speaking slowly. This happens because we can think faster than we can speak. People can speak between 120 and 160 words per minute, but they can think at speeds between 400 and 600 words per minute. Although Wendy is physically present, she's mentally miles away.

The solution: Be patient and force yourself to concentrate. Someone speaking to Wendy should use short sentences and make the conversation as interactive as possible, asking a lot of open-ended questions.

Visual Victor—You get overly influenced by visual stimuli—facial expressions, gestures, dress, posture—and don't listen to the actual message.

The solution: Shift your focus to the verbal, temporarily putting on "blinders" to other data. Someone speaking to Victor can make sure that his or her visual appearance is as effective and professional as possible. The speaker should also use visual language—such as "Picture this" or "I see what you mean"—and where possible, diagram the discussion on paper.

"Technophobic" Tom—You shut down and stop listening if you think the information is too difficult or technical to understand.

The solution: Tell yourself you can comprehend and then concentrate on the information rather than your fear. Someone speaking to Tom should use simple language and short sentences, make the conversation interactive and employ hands-on demonstrations and visual illustrations to reinforce key points.

Sam Stage Hog—You are very interested in expressing your ideas and not as interested in what the other person has to say. This is the classic non-listener.

The solution: Take turns. You'll get your chance. Besides, by listening carefully to the speaker, you can make yourself sound even better by addressing what he has brought up. Someone speaking to Sam should politely but firmly make his or her own point. Use phrases such as, "That's interesting. I see it differently," or "Let me finish," or "As I was trying to say ..." Or the speaker may choose not to bother to try conversing with Sam and just listen instead.

Anita Ambusher—You listen critically only to find fault. You collect information you will use against the speaker and counterattack what has been said. This is a good skill to have as a courtroom lawyer, but in most other situations, you will try people's patience.

The solution: Make yourself find something to agree with for each point on which you take issue. Someone speaking to Anita can ask, "Why did you say that?"

Insensitive Ira—You get hung up on words and are seldom able to look beyond them and understand feelings. You take all remarks at face value. If a person with tears running down his cheeks says, "I'm fine," you believe him.

The solution: Improve your listening literacy by expanding your interpretation. A passage in a novel that describes a dark and stormy night isn't merely issuing a weather report—it's establishing a mood. So, too, do the many nonverbal cues that you can learn to read—facial expressions, posture, body language. Someone speaking to Ira should be specific and say directly what is meant, rather than relying on nonverbal language.

At times, we have all found ourselves among this cast of characters. But when these behaviors become a pattern, it's time to make a change. To get the full meaning of what someone is saying requires energy and discipline. You need to be both physiologically and psychologically ready to listen with your ears, eyes, heart and head.

Four Benefits of Listening

Listening is, of course, the polite thing to do. There are, though, four specific reasons to listen:

1. *To better understand people and problems.* Relatively little of our communication is done in writing. When we want to repair our office equipment, to order dinner, to explain a problem to our boss, or to give directions for a project, in most cases, it's done verbally. We rely on the other party to listen carefully so he or she understands what we want done.

2. *To learn more.* We use conversation not only to express requests but to conduct research. If we want to find out something, we usually ask someone. Listening enables us to get and retain information.

3. *To improve working relationships and the work itself.* Redoing work because of miscommunication can strain a business relationship. Sending a shipment to Camden, N.J. instead of Camden, Maine, can be a costly mistake. Listening carefully is crucial to satisfying a customer who can say, "They heard me. They responded to my needs."

4. *To reduce tension.* Listening improves understanding between people. It saves the company time and money spent resolving disputes based on misunderstandings. It's frustrating when you think someone doesn't understand you. Listening skills let you get closer to people, making you a more compassionate person.

How effective a listener are you? You can find out by placing a tape-recorder on the table during a family dinner or tape-recording part of a lunch discussion with a friend (who grants permission). Let the machine run long enough so that you can "forget" it is there. Assess your performance according to our *Do's and Don'ts of Listening* guidelines.

Do's and Don'ts of Listening

Do	Don't
Paraphrase the speaker to indicate understanding.	Interrupt.

Do	Don't
Use positive listening skills (SOFTEN).	Tune out and daydream.
Ask appropriate and relevant questions.	Switch subjects midstream.
Make statements that reflect similar situations to keep the conversation flowing.	Finish other people's sentences.

Effective Listening: A Two-Way Street

I know that you believe that you understand what you think I said, but I am not sure you realize that what you heard is not what I meant.

—Unknown

Our *Do's and Don'ts of Listening* are part of a technique known as "Active Listening"—a two-way process between the speaker and listener.

Active Listening involves three main steps. We've already discussed the first one—attending skills, the readiness to receive information. The other two steps are letting the speaker speak and reflecting back what you've heard.

Let the speaker speak. We have two ears and one mouth for a reason—we should listen more than we speak. In this step you just let the speaker talk while you remain quiet. Let him finish his sentences. Do not interrupt. Do not assume you know what the speaker will say next. Do not think about what you are going to say next. Your job at this time is two-fold:

1. *Be aware of your own filters.* Your values, beliefs, perceptions, expectations and assumptions may stop you from really listening to what the speaker has to say. Warning symptoms include thinking to yourself, "There he goes again!" or "What else do you expect her to say!" Substitute instead thinking about ways that you could apply this speaker's information. Your speaker's lack of organization, use of language, delivery, appearance, gender and cultural differences may make listening more difficult for you. Her nonverbal signals and tone of voice may even reveal underlying feelings that hinder communication. Even so, listen and monitor your own response. The point here is to understand the speaker's point of view.

2. *Ask questions and use verbal prompts occasionally for clarification and to encourage the speaker.*

   Clarifying questions include:

   "I'm not sure I understand. Could you be more specific?"

   "What other aspects should be considered?"

   "Could you elaborate on what you mean by _____?"

   Note that these only request information, without comment on or assessment of what has already been said.

It's also especially important if someone has a speech impediment or accent that you be honest about your comprehension of his remarks. It's insulting to pretend to understand someone when you don't. You're not doing either of you a favor—the speaker wants to communicate, to be understood. You might want to paraphrase ("So you're saying that...") or repeat a word you didn't quite "get." Allow yourself time to "digest" the information. You will understand more if you go with the flow and let yourself become accustomed to that person's speech patterns.

Questions or comments to encourage the speaker:

"You've been given several suggestions. Which one do you think is best?"

"Tell me about it."

Prompts are encouragements to continue, while acknowledging what you have heard so far:

"I see."

"That's interesting. Tell me more."

"Really!"

"Uh huh!"

Reflect back. The last step in Active Listening is to restate in your own words what you understand the speaker to have communicated, both the ideas and the feelings. This provides feedback to the speaker to complete the listening process so he can know that the message was heard and understood.

There are three ways to reflect:

1. *Repeat what the speaker said word for word.*
   Speaker: The computer went down last night.
   Listener: Oh, the computer went down last night!
2. *Repeat what the speaker said, but change the "I" to "you."*
   Speaker: I'm looking for a new job.
   Listener: You're looking for a new job.
3. *Paraphrase what the speaker said in your own words.*
   Speaker: I don't like my boss and the work is boring.
   Listener: You're unhappy with your job.

You also can use a confirming question or statement to judge your understanding of the message and anticipate the next step. Some examples:

"Can we conclude that this is the next step?"

"Is this the situation: You feel that if I don't call the customer immediately, we will lose the sale?"

"So what you're saying is ...."

Avoid saying, "What you're *trying* to say is ..." They are saying it. You are trying to understand it.

Five More Tips to Make You a Conversation Winner

1. *Establish rapport by mirroring* some of the speaker's behaviors such as gestures, breathing, voice rate, vocabulary, favorite phrases, and facial expressions. Of course, you don't want to do it so much that you appear to mock or mimic the speaker.

   Some specific ways to do mirroring:

   • Match your voice pitch to the speakers.

   • Change your voice volume to match the speaker's.

   • Notice and use some of the same words and phrases as the speaker.

   • Approximate the speaker's gestures.

   • Sit forward or back, hand on or off the desk, as the speaker is.

   • Breathe at the same rate, without being obvious.

2. *Avoid negative responses* that would shut the speaker down, such as "We already tried that" or "Why bring that up again?"

3. *Pause before you speak,* to avoid blurting out something inappropriate or interrupting.

4. *Listen for a purpose.* Develop a genuine interest in the person or the topic. Plan to report on what you hear (if only to your cat). If you know you are going to share it, you'll listen more carefully.

5. *Take notes on what's being said* (if appropriate). Keep in mind, though, that some speakers get nervous or start to just watch you write, so note-taking can become a distraction. It might help to explain, "That's a good idea—I don't want to forget it." As the Chinese proverb notes, "The palest ink is better than the best memory."

YOUR ROLE:
When to Speak, What to Say

To talk or not to talk is not the question. Just as it's impolite to monopolize a conversation, it's rude to stay silent. People may interpret silence as hostility or disapproval. The key is knowing both when to speak and what to say.

Maximizing Small Talk Opportunities

What makes small talk small is both its duration and its focus. Small talk is a brief discussion of a neutral and relatively insignificant topic.

Some locations—such as office hallways, elevator corridors, and equipment rooms—easily lend themselves to small talk. Certain times of day—such as arrival or departure from the office or the time before a meeting begins—provide small talk opportunities as well.

While you want to recognize and take advantage of these opportunities, you also need to be sensitive to the specific situation. What looks like an ideal small talk opportunity can be deceiving. For instance, some people like to settle into their work in peace and are only receptive to conversation after their coats are hung up and their briefcases unloaded. Or, someone who seems to be standing idly waiting for an elevator may be actually reviewing a checklist mentally as he dashes off to an appointment. You're not out of line to initiate small talk in these circumstances, but if the other person doesn't follow through on the conversation, take the hint and move on.

Even if the setting and time of day are conducive and the person is willing to talk, make sure that you don't overstay your conversational welcome. Being a polite professional means that you should be willing to engage in small talk, but people's levels of tolerance vary. When the talk goes on too long, even if the discussion is pleasant, people become uncomfortable. Remember, small talk should not get in the way of business. (In Chapter Seventeen, we discuss the role of small talk in the international arena.)

If you are in a group setting where small talk is appropriate, such as a conference or office party, work the room. Go up to someone, introduce yourself and initiate conversation. Don't stay with one person too long. A good average is four to seven minutes, depending on the situation and the people involved. Don't just find someone you know and talk only to that person the entire time.

If you are engaging in small talk in a small office setting, you need to be aware of the impact of the conversation on others who are present. Few things are quite so distracting as having to pretend not to listen to a conversation that you can't help overhearing! Speaking softly is at best only a temporary solution—it heightens curiosity and creates the appearance that you are gossiping about someone. Although your colleague may be quite content to keep chatting with you, be aware of the body language of others around you. It may be advisable to continue the discussion during a break or lunch.

It can be difficult to tell when a small talk conversation is over, since it often is a free-flowing, unstructured discussion. The simplest strategy is to politely announce when you are stepping out of the dialogue, such as, "Well, I'd better get back to work" or "Time for me to see about those financial statements." Leaving the group when you have finished saying something rather than when someone else has stopped talking provides for a smoother exit.

If someone else talks too long, you can disentangle yourself from the conversation in the same way. In a group setting, you can say, "It's been nice speaking with you. I just noticed the time and I really need to speak with Dana before I leave" or "I enjoyed meeting you. I'm going to get a refill on my coffee."

If a chatty person interrupts your work with small talk, you can suggest another time for the conversation. You can say, "I'd talk more with you, but this report is due at noon," or "You've caught me at a bad time. Why don't we touch base after the sales meeting?"

Preparing for a Conversation

Real life, unlike reel life, has no script. You can't predict when you will be called upon to speak. But just because you'll be ad-libbing doesn't mean you can't prepare in advance for your role.

When you are meeting someone for the first time or are attending a meeting, you can come prepared with ideas for topics. Conversational readiness helps put you, and others, at ease by eliminating awkward silences. It doesn't take long—you can think on the drive to the airport what you want to say when you pick up your district manager. And the more you do it, the more naturally it comes. When you later face a similar situation, you may even be able to borrow a few lines from an old script.

Here's how to find things to talk about:

Read at least one newspaper a day and several magazines a month to keep abreast of current events. It's an especially good idea to read the local newspapers of any cities you visit.

Observe the world around you. You will be able to talk about community events, weather, cultural happenings. A traffic jam, new buildings under construction and the opening of an art exhibit are all possible topics.

Read your professional journals. These magazines give you up-to-date information on your profession. One man who has changed companies four times in ten years keeps track of all his former colleagues through the promotions and transfers columns. When he meets someone who now works at one of his previous firms, he uses his former colleagues as a way to establish a new connection. "Do you know Max Patel?" he'll ask. By doing so, he not only creates a link with the person he's just met, but finds out the latest information about Max.

Maintain a written log of interesting stories, statistics, and situations. It can include newspaper and magazine clippings, something about the main industry of a particular town, the city's slogan, or its claim to fame. Marjorie Brody will often say that she grew up in Indiana, Pa., and will elaborate that it is the hometown of Jimmy Stewart as well as the Christmas tree capital of the world. You can check the log before encountering a difficult situation.

Safe Topics

We've developed a *Topic-ographical Map* (see page 36)—a list of generally safe topics as well as conversational territories to avoid. You of course need to know your audience. Current events with widespread appeal like the Oscars or the Superbowl are better topics than less closely followed matters like Congressional budget deliberations.

A Topic-ographical Map

Safe Topics	Topics to Avoid
Weather	Your Health
Traffic	Other's Health
Sports	Cost of Items, Income
Non-Controversial Current Events, Such As The Oscars	Personal Misfortunes
Travel	Stories of Questionable Taste
Environmental Issues	Dirty Jokes
Favorable Comments Regarding the Meeting Place or City	Gossip
Common Experiences	Religion
Books	Highly Controversial Issues such as Abortion or Flag-Burning
The Arts	Intimate Details About Your Personal Life

If you have many brief encounters with several people during the day and so must make a lot of small talk—a sales representative or a personnel manager, for instance—you can select a "topic of the day." As long as you are dealing with different people, it doesn't matter if you repeat yourself. Think about the topic on the way to work.

For practice, come up with a "Topic of the Day" each day for a week and try each one on a friend or acquaintance (waitress, store clerk, garage attendant). Which ones worked best? Why?

Limits on Business Banter

Small talk situations particularly require that you avoid the minefields of office politics. You probably know which are safe small talk topics within your business environment—and which are not. Office personality feuds and simmering controversies about decisions, for instance, may be what is on everyone's mind, but they are not good subjects for brief, polite conversation.

Small talk situations also are not the time to press your point about the need for additional staff or to request an update on the findings of the audit. Serious topics deserve serious discussion, with the appropriate time allotted. An opportunity is not necessarily an opportune time.

Take into consideration whether what you are saying requires a response. If you are passing someone in the hall and say, "It felt like spring today," both parties can keep moving. However, if you say, "We aren't going to make the deadline for the Perez contract," you might stop someone in her tracks.

If you bump into your elusive supervisor in the hallway and have been meaning to talk with her about a work-related problem, you have to weigh whether the setting is actually conducive to the conversation. Depending on your office environment, it could be advisable merely to mention that you have been wanting to speak to her and ask if you could set up a time. That then leaves the decision about engaging in a more prolonged conversation up to her.

Sports-Speak, Baby Talk, and Topics That Exclude

For many men, small talk *is* sports talk. In the communications code of Sports-Speak, "How 'bout those Phillies!" may even substitute for "How are you?"

Similarly, many parents center their small talk around their families. Women who are pregnant may share stories about their ultrasound examinations, while fathers of teenagers may seek strategies for coping with rebellion.

On their face, these topics meet the criteria for small talk subjects: they are light discussions about matters of mutual interest. When all the parties in the conversation share an understanding and appreciation for a topic, it becomes fair game.

However, it's equally important that small talk be inclusive. Small talk often occurs in gatherings of three or more. When the conversation about any topic becomes so specific that a casual observer cannot participate, it's impolite to continue in that manner. Whether you are discussing sports, children, music or movies, you need to make sure everyone can contribute. It's simply good manners to make everyone feel valued.

Of course, it helps to be conversant with many topics in order to be a small talk success. You don't have to be an expert in child development to ask, "How's Drew doing?" If small talk in your office tends to center around new movies, you should at least read the movie reviews. Rather than saying, "I don't follow professional golf," you can say, "I missed that. Was it exciting?" Small talk can provide an opportunity for you to broaden your horizons.

Opening Lines That Work

Starting conversations can be the most difficult part of small talk. The longer you wait, the more difficult it is. Of course, it's worthwhile to persevere. Opening lines can get you past the initial awkward moments when you first meet someone.

You want to make a connection, so it's more important that you be clear than clever. If you use a fancy or witty remark and it falls flat, you've lost some momentum. Make sure to introduce yourself first if the person doesn't know who you are.

Your opening line should be no longer than most bumper stickers. Some suggestions:

If you are observing what is going on around you, keep it upbeat.

"This is a wonderful party. Everyone is having a good time."

Or:

"This conference is well-attended. It seems to draw from a large geographical area."

Use an open-ended question to encourage a response.

"How did you manage dealing with the traffic today?"
"What type of work do you do?"
"How do you know our host?"

Offer a pleasant self-revelation.

"I just started going to graduate school."
"This is my first time at an annual conference."
"I just returned from attending an interesting seminar on Business Etiquette."

Ask general questions.

"Where are you from?"
"Do you have a long commute?"
"Have you ever tried to play golf?"

For practice, you can role-play a one-line opening suitable for a business lunch with a friend. You are meeting a vendor. Use one of the four options (upbeat observation, open-ended question, pleasant self-revelation, general question). Then, switch roles.

When you start a conversation with someone and your opening line does not work, try another one. How much effort you invest in continuing the conversation depends on how crucial that particular conversation is. An open-ended question should generate a response if someone is reluctant or shy. If not, and if you are in a group situation, it might be an appropriate time to move on to the next person.

Breaking the Ice with Laughter

Tasteful humorous stories can be effective ice-breakers. When you laugh, endorphins—chemical substances that make you feel good—are released into your bloodstream. Laughter bonds people, serving as a bridge to understanding.

We offer these four guidelines:

1. *Remember the punch line.* A little girl once made a riddle book and, confident that she could never, ever, forget the punch lines, included only the questions. Years later, when she rediscovered the book, it did indeed make her laugh, but not for the reason she had intended—she had forgotten all the punch lines. As the comic Steve Allen notes, "The best ad-lib is one that is written down."

2. *Practice your timing.* The material is only part of an effective joke—it also demands good delivery. Make appropriate use of pauses. Let the comment sink in. Take the time you need to tell the joke—a rushed presentation of a good joke is unsatisfying.

3. *Make it pertinent.* You may have a hilarious tale of an incident that occurred on a fishing trip, but how do you work it into a conversation? Transitions do matter—people want to feel that even though you are taking them on a fun detour,

you haven't completely switched directions. You can, of course, make up appropriate tie-ins if you think about it. "I understand the next executive meeting will be in the lake region," you might say. "When I was there last summer ..."

4. *Make sure the humor is at no one's expense.* That means *no* ethnic, racial, or gender-based humor. These jokes are not funny—they're painful, and often reinforce unfounded stereotypes. Most important, it's not nice. Be careful, too, about naming names, insulting other companies, or attacking causes. You never know who is married to whom, whose grandfather worked where, or what the listener's values are.

What if the person you're mocking is yourself? There's a fine line here—you want to make sure the joke doesn't turn out to be on you.

Laughing at yourself can show that you are secure, confident, willing to admit human failings and even able to turn a "bad" circumstance into useful material. For instance, Barbara Pachter once went to the bathroom with her cordless microphone still turned on. Her audience could hear every flush and gurgle, and she had to go back out and face them. Although she was embarrassed at the time, she has since used the incident as an example of the double-edged sword of technology, the importance of honing presentation skills and the necessity of rebounding from difficult situations. She's almost glad it happened—although she has no plans to repeat the event. Now she says each situation you face can become good material for your next presentation!

However, in a business setting, you certainly don't want to tell a joke that makes a negative general statement about your abilities. Someone who is listening may innocently or intentionally tell the boss, who will then have a seed of doubt planted about you. You also don't want to tell a joke that would reinforce your status as an outsider—for instance, if you are the only woman in a group of men, or the only non-engineer on the long-range planning committee. When in doubt, don't.

The ABCs of Questions

Because they require a response, questions can be an effective tool for conversation as long as they do not put the other person on the spot. For instance, never ask a listener, "Did you understand?" Chances are, she'll say "yes," either because she thinks she does or she doesn't want to be embarrassed by admitting she doesn't.

Direct questions, particularly about finances, also often are considered rude. It's better to ask "Was that printer expensive?" than "How much did that printer cost?"

Part of being a good conversationalist means being prepared to handle questions that are asked of you. In a small-talk situation, the questions will not be as probing or public as they would be at the end of a formal presentation, but your response is still important.

Remember that people don't always ask questions just to get information. They may be trying to challenge you, show off what they know, impress friends and colleagues or just participate. These techniques can help you handle the situation:

Anticipate. Think in advance about whom you're speaking to, what they might ask and why they might be asking it. Consider questions to be a compliment. If someone is bored, confused, or overwhelmed, he will change the topic or move on. The fact that someone may feel comfortable asking you a "dumb question" means you have put that person at ease. When someone asks a question, don't withdraw or tense up—let her know you're glad she asked.

Be brief, clear, and to the point. A short response is sweet. If someone wants to know more, he'll ask. You don't want to turn off a genuine curiosity with a haranguing lecture.

Be controlled. You have the power to turn even a hostile question to your advantage. Politicians are masters at this. Some of the tricks they use:

Rephrasing the question before answering it. This allows you to respond to the question in a more positive, uplifting manner. The question may be, "Don't you think that's an expensive alteration?" Your answer could be, "You're questioning the cost of the product. We are quite excited about providing all these additional services for that amount of money."

Defusing hostility with humor or a short anecdote rather than going on the defensive. At a tense news conference following the arrest of suspects in the World Trade Center bombing, one reporter asked James M. Fox, the head of the FBI in New York, "You arrested these guys, but what if you didn't? What if the whole city had started exploding?" In a deadpan manner, Fox responded, "It certainly would have ruined my day." The room broke up with laughter.

If you don't know the exact answer, either talk about what you *do* know or admit you just don't know. Don't apologize or make up answers that can be proven wrong. You can sometimes acknowledge, "I'm glad you asked that."

If someone's getting to you, don't let it show. Maintain a calm demeanor. Suggest a change of topic, or excuse yourself. Don't let the situation get out of hand.

Words and Phrases to Avoid

There are words and phrases that are "conversation killers"—statements that leave others groping desperately for an appropriate response, often leaving them in stunned silence. If someone blurts out, "Today on the way to work, I ran over a cat," there's no appealing direction in which the conversation can go.

Similarly, certain words (not just topics) can be offensive or misunderstood and so are usually inappropriate. Using these words can diminish your professional credibility. Avoid them.

Vocabulary dangers fall into these categories:

Slang: "main man," "yucky," and "creep." These words are too casual for a business setting. In most cases, use of nicknames, such as referring to someone as "Slugger," should be avoided for the same reason.

Foul language: You know what we mean. And bear in mind that if you don't use the actual word but a euphemism or abbreviation that conveys the same meaning, it reduces but doesn't eliminate the offensiveness.

Jargon: "News hole," "ROP," "J shoot." It excludes people.

Pretentious language: Boasting to impress or using over-complicated language. "I communicated my displeasure regarding the preponderance of accumulated refuse in numerous receptacles to the sanitation engineer" instead of "I told the janitor the wastebaskets were full."

Sexist language: Whether you call a woman, "girl" or a man "babe" (as one man said his female boss did to him), it's a very bad idea. We've talked with a number of people of both genders who, long after the incident occurred, were angry, humiliated, and resentful. Such language draws attention to the gender rather than the individual. It could also get you in serious legal trouble.

Statements of disagreement that are rudely expressed: "You're wrong." "What a stupid idea!" It's possible to disagree without being disagreeable or insulting. For instance, you can say, "I'm not sure I see it that way" or "That's a possibility I hadn't considered."

References to someone's race, class, ethnic background, or disability: These are just not appropriate. They indicate that you are conscious of—and perhaps preoccupied with—something that historically has been used as a basis for discrimination. It reinforces an "us vs. them" mentality.

Words and Phrases that Should Not Be Forgotten

You'll be considered a more effective and courteous communicator if you include these words and phrases in your conversation:

The name of the person to whom you are speaking. It's easy to fall into the habit of just using "you" or skipping names altogether, but it is much more gracious to call someone by name. Try to interject the person's name into the conversation at least once. It reinforces that you are talking to a specific individual. Of course, avoid overuse.

Statements of agreement, such as "You're right" or "You've hit the nail on the head."

Requests for advice or assistance, such as "Is there a good restaurant near here?" or "Have you figured out how to use the new software program?" It's a compliment to be asked for guidance, and most people will be flattered.

Statements or questions that refer to a previous conversation or event. "Did you like the afternoon speech as much as you did the morning program?" "Is this tax season as hectic as last year's was?" These show that you have paid attention to what the person said or did in the interval since you last saw him.

THE CONVERSATION CONNECTION

The ultimate purpose of small talk is to get to know someone a little better on an informal basis. You not only discover something about that person, but he or she gets better acquainted with you—perceiving you as someone who is friendly, social, and "easy to talk to." In this case, as in so many other situations, good manners make good sense.

PROFESSIONAL PRESENCE
How to Make Your Appearance Work for You

We never get a second chance to make a good first impression.

—Unknown

Good manners include how we look and how we carry ourselves. Although most people haven't stopped to consider it, etiquette does include professional presence, or the way we come across to others. An appropriate appearance demonstrates respect for yourself, for others, and for the situation.

Society has established rules—now considerably more relaxed than in the past—about appropriate attire and proper presentation for various situations. Wet hair and casual clothing are perfectly acceptable at the beach, but not in the boardroom. It's impolite to dress inappropriately—it can be interpreted as a sign of disrespect, for instance, if your clothing is less formal than the situation requires. Failure to heed these guidelines is just as much of an etiquette gaffe as not introducing someone or failing to make small talk.

APPEARANCE COUNTS:
It Pays to Pay Attention

What's more, packaging does make a difference: Ask anyone involved in product design. Consider your own consumer choices. Would you buy a product with a torn, dirty wrapper? Such choices are not just human vanity—in the animal world, appropriate appearances can be a matter of survival. Animals instinctively know to hide any evidence that they are wounded or weakened to fool their predators. Your peers and your supervisors similarly size you up, based on how you look and move. You are, in fact, trying to fit in. If your clothing or mannerisms are out-of-sync, outdated or outlandish, you won't be a full member of the team, whatever your professional talents may be.

We know of one very tall engineer whose expertise was highly valued but who, behind his back, was called, "The Giant Cabbage Patch Doll." His clothing was always too short, giving him an unprofessional image. He was unaware that he needed to buy custom-designed shirts and extra long suits to achieve the proper fit. If an image consultant hadn't told him, he might still be better known for his weird wardrobe than for his work.

You do, of course, always have a choice on this issue. And you're free to make choices that don't conform to accepted standards, provided you are aware of their consequences. Yet why would you choose to be held back for cosmetic reasons? As consultants, we often are hired by corporations to personally coach their high-potential people who, despite their technical expertise, will not advance because they lack professional presence. It's a problem that affects all levels of personnel, including top executives who have fallen into poor habits.

One situation in which we recommend that you always choose to conform to professional appearance standards is a job interview. First impressions usually are made within the first five seconds. First impressions will not get you a job, but they could make you lose the opportunity for getting one. You may consider your frugality an asset, but an interviewer may be turned off by your worn-out pockets and suit jacket with shiny elbows. One personnel manager at a large pharmaceutical firm told us that if an applicant came to an interview with unpolished shoes, he wouldn't hire him. To the interviewer, it meant the applicant did not pay attention to detail, a trait that would be reflected in his work.

WHAT MESSAGE DOES YOUR APPEARANCE SEND?

So what does professional presence mean to you? Perhaps it's someone who is well-groomed, dresses appropriately for the role and conducts himself or herself with assurance. You can make sure this is the message you are sending by focusing on the components of a professional presence.

The communication signals that we send to other people fall into three main areas. Dr. Albert Marhabion of UCLA called them the three V's—visual, vocal, and verbal. Together, they make up our professional presence.

The visual is what can be seen—dress, body language, facial expressions, etc. The vocal component is how a person uses his or her voice. The verbal aspect is the words we choose.

We've discussed the vocal and verbal components in Chapter Three, "Big Techniques for Small Talk." This chapter focuses on the visual aspect, the silent but significant signals you send just by walking into a room.

How much of the overall impression that you make is based solely on the visual component? Most people are surprised to learn it accounts for 55 percent of the impression! Contrast that with 38 percent for the vocal part and only 7 percent for the verbal aspect. Clearly, if more than half of the way people size you up is based on a glance, it's important to become fluent in the language of visual signals. The three important visual areas that affect etiquette are body language, grooming, and clothing. In this chapter, you'll find out the keys to success in each of these areas.

BODY LANGUAGE THAT SPEAKS WELL OF YOU

Body language is how you carry yourself. It's your posture, body position, gestures, and facial expressions.

Try turning off the sound on your television set and see how much of the plot and characterizations you can figure out just by watching. Who looks tough and who looks frumpy? Who seems polished and in control? Part of any actor's training, of course, is learning how to physically "become" the person he or she is portraying. He may style his hair in an unflattering manner to indicate a lack of sophistication. She may hang her head to indicate shyness or awkwardness, be animated to indicate confidence, or hold her head up and have eyes look askance to portray someone who is haughty. In business, you want to make sure that if, for some reason, people focus only on the visual stimuli that you present, they will see a polished professional.

Visual signals are culturally based. For instance, co-workers from another country may be showing respect by averting their gaze (see Chapter Seventeen, "Communicating Across Borders" for more information on international body language). We urge tolerance and respect by all parties for these customs. In this chapter, we focus on behaviors that bring success in U.S. business environments.

Does demeanor really make a difference? Of course it does. Consider the health care provider who set up an interview with the best qualified candidate, on paper, for the position of head nurse/nurse manager. During the session, the candidate pounded on the table, clicked her shoes on the floor and was constantly moving and shifting her body. When asked "Tell us about yourself," she spoke for 45 minutes. The job was hers to lose—and she did. Her body betrayed her unprofessionalism.

Do's And Don'ts of Body Language
STANDING POSTURE

Do	Don't
Stand straight	Slouch
Keep feet still	Shift feet
Keep shoulders relaxed	Sway
Keep arms at your side	Cross arms
Keep head and chin up	Hang head

SEATED POSTURE

DO	DON'T
Sit up straight.	Slouch, fidget or shift in your seat.
Cross legs at ankles.	Sit with knees spread or crossed.
Lean forward slightly.	Tap your feet.

MOVEMENT

DO	DON'T
Move purposefully.	Drag your feet.
Maintain a deliberate stride.	Clomp or shuffle.
Bend from the knees when picking up an object	Angle feet ("duck walk").

Think of your own behaviors. Does your body communicate the message you want it to convey?

Powerful Posture

One woman who thought of herself as fairly optimistic and cheerful was surprised that co-workers continually asked her, "What's wrong?" or suggested she "cheer up." She was unaware that her slumped stance communicated sadness. She soon learned that "chin up" was advice that could be taken literally to communicate a more positive self-image.

Slouching indicates that you lack confidence and makes you look tired, sloppy, or indifferent. Stand up straight, and you'll not only look better, but you'll feel more assured. Picture yourself being pulled up from your abdominal area by a silk cord that goes through the top of your head.

Keep your feet approximately four to eight inches apart, under your hips and parallel to your shoulders, with your weight on the balls of the feet. Women have a tendency to stand with their legs crossed at their ankles, which makes them unstable. Men tend to get into the "John Wayne" (feet wide apart) stance or do the "jock dance" (shifting from side to side).

Keep your shoulders relaxed and your arms at your side—crossed arms signal defensiveness or even hostility. Don't keep your hands in your pockets; you might play with change or keys, which is distracting. Just keep your hands loosely at your side.

When sitting, be careful not to get "too" comfortable. Many people get into the habit of slouching, a difficult habit to break. Tapping your feet or otherwise fidgeting by shifting in your seat implies impatience.

When you bend, bend from the knees. It's not only good manners (your derrière doesn't stick out in the air), but good sense—it's better for your back.

Remember, your posture speaks before you do. It sends messages which create impressions. It indicates if you are interested in others and in their perceptions of you, an attitude which is important for etiquette excellence and overall success.

Confident Movement

Experts say that street criminals often select as their victims those people who move slowly, tentatively, and awkwardly. They know their chances of snatching a purse or briefcase from those people and getting away are better than if the subject moves purposefully and deliberately. Criminals understand that the way people move is a powerful indication of their overall coping abilities.

Political candidates and those in the media are keenly aware of movement too. If, for example, a candidate moves toward the podium with a purposeful stride and open posture or enthusiastically walks toward the crowd to shake hands, he is thought to be confident and relaxed. Voters, viewers—and co-workers—often are subconsciously influenced by someone who moves smoothly.

Correctly accomplished, movement can be graceful, natural, and simple. Watch yourself on a videotape or practice by watching yourself moving toward a full-length mirror. Ask yourself what you would think about someone who moved as you do.

Effective Gestures

Your use of gestures, like your use of language, is heavily influenced by the patterns that you observed during your formative years. They also can be an expression of culture and personality—Italian people often gesture more than German people do. Demonstrative, outgoing people are more likely to use gestures than are quiet, reserved people. But even if gestures aren't part of your natural body language, you can learn a few "expressions" to help you communicate your views.

The first rule is to avoid gestures that make others uncomfortable. Hands on the hips, pounding fists, or crossed arms can indicate annoyance, while finger-pointing implies accusation. Playing with items in your pocket is unattractive, distracting, and rude (it signals you are restless). Wringing your hands signals nervousness. These and other gestures send implied negative messages, but most people don't even realize they are using them. One woman approached us after a seminar and announced that she never pointed a finger when speaking—until we, in turn, pointed out that she was doing so even as she spoke. Watch yourself on videotape. What you do when you practice, you do in real life.

Gestures

Do	Don't
Gesture with open palms with fingers together.	Put hands on hips.

Do	Don't
Use gestures to reinforce your message.	Over-gesture.
Vary your gestures.	Play with things in your pocket.
	Cross arms.
	Point a finger.

On the other hand, gestures can be effective when used correctly, especially when making a presentation before a large group. Make sure that the movement is natural to you and that it is consistent with your message (don't hold up three fingers when discussing four points). Open palms with fingers together indicates openness; a closed fist the opposite, sometimes even menace.

We suggest you use gestures above the waist that flow out to the audience. For a large group, use bigger gestures than you would for a small group, when the same gestures would be overpowering and make certain you vary them to avoid repetitiveness.

Gestures are, after all, a form of sign language. You want to make sure that you communicate effectively and politely even if you never utter a word.

Dynamic Facial Expressions

People consider facial expressions to be the best indication of a person's mood, and with good cause. From infancy, we learn that a smile brings one result, a pout another. If someone smiles while delivering bad news about a colleague, we consider him strange, at best. If someone frowns when asked how work on a project is progressing but insists, "Everything's fine," the message becomes mixed.

The best way to gauge your normal facial expression is to look in the mirror. If you saw someone with that look on his face, what judgment would you make about his mood or personality? People don't usually realize what their normal facial expression is.

Effective people—whether male or female—smile in a friendly fashion, nod to show their understanding, and are appropriately animated to indicate interest. When the situation requires it, they camouflage their feelings by masking their expressions of fear, envy, or disappointment.

In the United States, eye contact is extremely important: we don't really trust anyone who won't look us in the eye. The significance of eye contact in determining credibility is acknowledged in the courtroom, where jurors are positioned so that they can look at both the witness and the accused. In one murder trial we heard about, the judge instructed the witness to remove his photogrey glasses, so that the jury could see his eyes.

If possible, you want to be at the same eye level as the person to whom you are speaking. The expressions "look down on someone" and "look up to someone" underscore just how significant height differences can be.

One female manager at a seminar told us it took a long time before she realized why all her family fights occurred in the hallway. Whenever she felt a fight coming on, she'd drag her husband to the hallway and she would stand on the second step.

She is 4′9″, her husband 6′1″. "I didn't know why I did it," she admitted, "but it felt better."

Facial Expressions

Do	Don't
Smile	Frown
Have direct eye contact	Stare
Be animated	Have shifty eyes
Nod positively (without yo-yo-ing)	Yawn without closing mouth

How to Detect Your Distracting Mannerisms

We once had a director in a presentation skills training program who had a terrible twitch—he blinked both eyes while squirreling up his face. He did this as a program participant and when he gave his presentations. After seeing himself on videotape, he said, "I never knew I had a twitch." We gently let him know that the twitch was constant—that it occurred not only when he was speaking.

Many of us have unconscious behavior patterns that create negative impressions. These distracting mannerisms can be difficult to detect in yourself, but very apparent to others. Below is a list of distracting mannerisms. Do any of them apply to you?

- Scratching or picking at yourself.
- Tugging or playing with hair.
- Combing hair in public.
- Drumming fingers.
- Playing with, picking, or biting fingernails.
- Tapping feet.
- Applying makeup or nail polish in public.
- Picking teeth.
- Moving tongue around inside cheek or in front of teeth.
- Fidgeting.
- Yawning.
- Straightening up paper/paper clips.
- Clicking pens.
- Chewing gum.
- Crowding other people's space.

No matter what your position may be, don't say you don't do these things until you get feedback. Remember, you don't know what you don't know! If you think you might have some of these mannerisms, get feedback from trusted friends or, as we've previously suggested, videotape yourself. Then work to eliminate the behaviors by being aware and "catching" yourself in the act.

Distracting mannerisms not only affect people's impressions of you, but can actually intimidate others. Pounding a table, for one example, makes people fear you are enraged. Most important, you should rarely, if ever, touch a person in a business setting. That is an intimacy that is subject to misinterpretation, even if you do it playfully. People have widely varied tolerances for physical contact, and the best rule of thumb is to avoid it altogether. Innocent, supportive pats on the shoulder can be considered harassment. One man developed a habit of "playfully" pulling on a woman's ponytail. She was angered, not amused, and correctly insisted that he stop.

Even getting too close to someone—crowding other people's space—can have negative consequences. A comfortable distance in a business setting is approximately three feet, or about an arm's distance. If you move in closer, you can enter intimate space (which is 0 to 18 inches and is usually reserved for family and loved ones) or personal space (18 to 36 inches, which is designated for friends). Keeping your distance can keep your professional reputation intact.

GROOMING THAT BRINGS OUT YOUR BEST

Grooming means paying attention to the all-important little details that add polish to your professional presence.

Most of us attend to our grooming needs without even thinking about them. But it is important to occasionally stop and reevaluate your routine. Are you doing all that you can? Often it's the little things—perhaps the one item you forgot or are unaware of—that stand out like a sore thumb. A well-dressed woman can still have runs in her stockings or lipstick on her teeth. A well-dressed man can still have perspiration stains in the armpits of his shirt or food stains on his tie.

Since grooming is a habit, it's easy to get locked into a pattern. Things that once worked may not work as well as they previously did. As we get older, our bodies change, and what was effective ten or even five years ago may no longer be appropriate. For instance, some men are surprised to discover a "five o'clock shadow" when one shave a day used to be sufficient. And some women, who over time have grown accustomed to the smell of their perfume, may be surprised to learn that they are overdoing it because they have gradually been applying more and more.

Good Grooming Checklist

Hair out of face and well styled.

Hair is clean and free of dandruff.

Nose and ear hairs are clipped.

(Continued on next page)

Ears are clean.

Glasses fit, and are clean.

No glasses hanging on chains.

Polished, straight, white teeth.

Fresh breath. (Avoid onion and garlic.)

Fingernails are clean.

Amount of perfume, aftershave, cologne, is limited.

MEN	WOMEN
Trimmed mustache and beard.	No facial hairs.
No five-o'clock shadow.	Lipstick blotted (not on teeth).
Fly zipped.	Well-designed makeup, not over-done.
	Fresh, conservative unchipped nail polish.

Fair or not, it seems that there are more potential grooming pitfalls for women than for men. Behavior or style for women that is considered acceptable or even encouraged in non-work arenas can undermine a professional image.

For instance, women should be careful about the presentation of their nails: designer nails or nails that are too long can be distracting and detract from your credibility. One bank professional noticed that her team seemed to focus on her long, decorated fingernails, although no one said so to her. She changed her nails and noticed a big difference in her reception. She was recently chosen for a highly selective management director's program.

Very long hair also may send an unprofessional message. If your hair is very long, pull it back for work. Any hair style that is too extreme or exaggerated, whether it makes you appear too sexy or "little girlish," will detract from your professional image and should be avoided.

Fashion has more of an impact on women's grooming routines than on men's. Acceptable colors for eyeshadow, nail polish, and lipstick change over time. Hair styles are revised every few years. Rather than trying to be totally trendy, though, we recommend that women develop a classic, timeless—and therefore perpetually professional—appearance.

Allow enough time for your daily grooming routine. It's dangerous for either men or women to get dressed in the dark: you may find yourself taking off your overcoat only to discover you grabbed the wrong suit jacket or have mismatched socks. It's also all too easy to miss the fact that your collar has become frayed or that a button is missing. Make it a point to check yourself in front of a mirror in a well-lit room before you head out each morning.

You should also check for grooming gaffes at intervals throughout the day. You can start the day well-presented, only to acquire food between your teeth, blotchy makeup, or food stains as the day goes on.

One supervisor told us a story about how she unwittingly emerged from the bathroom with her skirt stuck up in back at the waistband. Fortunately, she was standing facing her boss. Unfortunately, *his* boss had a clear view of her from his office.

A new college graduate who was going for a first job interview bought a new shirt and unwrapped it on the day of his interview. He wasn't worried about the creases, since they would be under his jacket. During the interview, though, the interviewer told him to take off his jacket and get comfortable. Of course, he was distracted since all he could think about was the creases.

It is good manners to point out discreetly a gaffe of which someone may be unaware—a slip is showing, a button unbuttoned, a fly unzipped. Find a private time to do so, and just state the situation. You can say, "You might want to check a mirror—your lipstick is smeared" or "Your slip is showing" or "Your fly is down" or "You might want to check your fly." The other person will be as grateful as you would be if the situation were reversed.

The situation is more tricky to handle if the gaffe cannot be immediately remedied or if it signifies an ongoing physical problem, such as dandruff or bad breath. In general, we recommend you be cautious about commenting in those instances, because it can prove risky to a relationship to point out that a co-worker has such problems. However, if you are a supervisor, you can take your employee aside privately and present your observation as part of your desire to see him succeed. You can say something like, "As your boss, I care about your doing well here. I notice you have bad breath. Some people have commented on it to me. It's usually easily remedied and that will significantly improve your ability to get along well with clients."

Mishaps do occur, and part of having professional presence is knowing how to handle them. We like the story one woman told us about the time she was walking down a hallway with a female colleague and a male co-worker, and the other woman's half-slip fell off. The woman stepped out of the slip, picked it up and put it in her pocket without missing a beat. That's presence!

Giving Yourself The Once-Over

Developing a professional demeanor requires that you combine all the components of body language and grooming in one package. To assess your skills, videotape yourself and then consult our *Body Language and Grooming Self-Test*. Your answers can help pinpoint areas that need improvement.

Body Language and Grooming Self-test

	Yes	No
Is there anything about your appearance that is overdone?		
Too much jewelry?		
Cologne/perfume too strong?		

(Continued on next page)

Y<small>ES</small>   N<small>O</small>

Is hair well styled?

Is your posture too relaxed? too rigid?

    Is your chin down?

    Are your shoulders up?

    Are your knees locked?

Is your facial expression inconsistent with what you are saying?

    Do you smile too much? too little?

Do you avoid eye contact or stare at people when speaking?

Are your gestures overdone when communicating?

    Do you play with your hair, glasses, tie, or jewelry?

    Do you tap your feet, crack your knuckles, or play with change in your pockets?

Do you touch acquaintances when you speak to them?

Do you invade people's space when you communicate?

Does your voice call attention to itself?

    Is it too loud? Too soft? Too fast? Too slow?

    Does it lack variety in pitch and tone?

CLOTHING THAT ADDS TO YOUR CLOUT

In matters of principle, stand like a rock.
In matters of taste, swim like the current.

—T<small>HOMAS</small> J<small>EFFERSON</small>

Look at the people in any lunch-time crowd. Based on what they're wearing, can you guess what position they hold? Does their choice indicate their attitudes? Does the way their clothing fits flatter them—showing they know how they look and care about the impression they make? Without knowing anything about their abilities, whom would you trust with an important project?

In one sense, judging ourselves and others based on what we wear seems superficial, because what really matters is who we are and our abilities, not what we wear. For good or ill, however, a large part of any first impression is based on clothing. We use clothing as clues to a person's personality, attitude, and professionalism.

Clothing can either enhance your professional reputation or detract from your credibility. Anything that is exaggerated or overdone, whether it is your jewelry, make-up, hairstyle, or the clothes themselves, will detract from your image. Business clothes are a sort of uniform that we wear to signal that we have "put on" our professional, work-oriented mentality. In fact, most people carry themselves differently when dressed professionally; they may stand straighter or be more serious in their demeanor.

At the beginning of each work week, we make the transition from weekend to week-day by getting into our career "costumes" and dressing for our working roles.

We're sure you can come up with an example of how your clothing has influenced the way people have treated or perceived you.

Some companies are reinstating dress codes to avoid the lack of good judgment demonstrated by employees, specifically, clothing that is too informal, too sloppy, too tight, too sexy. An experienced employee who had recently joined the staff of a large, national consulting firm wore a blue shirt on his first day and a striped shirt on his second day. That afternoon, he was told, "In our company, we wear white shirts."

Appropriate clothing may not only impact on how you do your job, but may negatively influence customers and co-workers. We know of one company in which mail room personnel received a new dress code prohibiting jeans and T-shirts. They had to wear ties and jackets. The delivery of the mail improved.

You can learn a lot by watching people's eyes as they first meet you. Does their expression indicate that they are favorably impressed or do they suppress a smile? Listen to what co-workers say about your clothes. "Why are you all dressed up?" or "What's the occasion?" may mean that you have noticeably altered your usual appearance. Such comments could imply that you are signaling the importance of a special meeting with a client, or they could be an indication that you look more like you're ready for a social event than work. If your clothing frequently draws comments, it could mean it is distracting.

Drawing attention to your physical attributes also can detract from the business at hand. You want people to see you as a professional so that they will treat you like one.

Pregnant women should emphasize a professional appearance by purchasing maternity wear at stores that cater to professional women. Whether or not you plan to continue work after your maternity leave, you want clothing that communicates, "As long as I'm here, I'm focused on my job."

One way to determine what to wear is to watch for clues in what others wear—co-workers you believe are successful and doing well. You want to emulate them, while setting your own style based on what makes you feel comfortable. When choosing a business wardrobe, the rule of thumb is to dress for the position you would like to have and the image you want to create.

Cultivate sales personnel at department stores. Learn which departments stock the kind of career clothes that are right for you. Some stores have personal shopping services that can assist you on an ongoing basis. Explain that you want to upgrade your business wardrobe and when you try an outfit on, consult with the sales staff about the fit, as well as whether it is flattering and appropriate.

The *Clothing Checklist*, on page 54, outlines minimum standards for dress. In addition, each time you select something for your business wardrobe, ask yourself these three questions:

1. Is it appropriate (for the job, the company, the season, region, and climate)?
2. Does it fit?

3. What message am I sending?

We will discuss each of these considerations.

Clothing Checklist

Clean, unspotted, lint-free, well-fitting.
Well-pressed, including collar.
Not frayed at collar or cuffs.
All buttons attached and hems and seams sewn.
Polished, well-heeled and soled shoes.
Double-breasted jackets must be buttoned when standing.

MEN	WOMEN
No undershirt showing.	Hide slip and bra straps; make sure slip and panty lines don't show.
Well-knotted tie that ends in middle of belt.	Avoid clothes with designer labels that show.
Mid-calf length socks with good elastic.	Check for hosiery runs, snags or sags.
Jewelry limited to a good watch and a ring.	Jewelry limited to a good watch, necklace, earrings, and one ring per hand. Nothing noisy, flashy or distracting.
	Make sure skirt hem does not show below coat.
	Avoid running shoes. Use flats.

Safe Selections

A Suit: The jacket can be removed to make it less formal. It's more formal than a blazer and slacks for men and than a dress, blazer, or pantsuit for women.

Darker Shades and Cool Tones: They project authority. Lighter colors or warmer tones have less power.

Quality: It shows, is recognized and lasts. Buy fewer and better. Select clothes by asking, "What is the image I want to convey and to whom?"

Appropriate Attire: What to Wear When

Many factors affect whether an outfit is appropriate for your work setting: your type of job, the area in which you live, the climate, and the specific situation for which you are dressing.

Your job, naturally, will dictate much of what is appropriate. Jobs that require client contact usually require more professional attire. Bankers, insurance representatives, and stockbrokers are usually more conservative in clothing choices than those in ad agencies, software design companies, or the entertainment field. Conversely, wearing a pin-striped suit while working on a production line is inappropriate. Your clothing should allow you to perform comfortably and safely whatever physical chores are required, whether using a flip-chart to present an ad campaign or designing graphics for a new label.

Regional differences in dress also persist. The standards of attire are casual in Florida. Chicago is more conservative than Los Angeles. In Washington, D.C., employees need a "power" look. Some colors, such as pastels, may be more acceptable in the South than in the Northeast.

The local climate determines appropriateness in many instances. The fabrics should be practical for the weather, since your common sense will be called into question if you wear only cotton in the dead of winter in Minnesota. The climate affects not only clothing, but footwear and outerwear. Men in northern climates often wear wing tips, which are heavier shoes than people would wear elsewhere. An appropriate raincoat is essential in Seattle.

The setting has an impact on appropriateness as well. If you wear your power suit on a Saturday afternoon during inventory review, for instance, you'll be out of place. A partner in an accounting firm clearly recalls the day he wore tasseled shoes to the office. People kept asking him, "Are you on your way to play golf?" Later, we'll discuss in more detail the type of attire we call "Business Casual" as well as the separate standards for dressing when entertaining away from the office.

Finally, accessories and small details also need to be appropriate for your position. We recently coached an engineer who had just been promoted to management. He wore braces, a tie, and a handkerchief that all matched, and he wasn't sure this was the image he wanted. We agreed with his assessment and helped him discover tie and handkerchief patterns that weren't identical but that coordinated well together.

Whether you are trying to fit into a new work environment or are relocating to a new area, take your cues about appropriateness from the people around you.

Finding the Fit That Flatters

You need to pay particular attention to the fit of any garment you select to make sure that it not only is the correct size, but that it flatters you. We often forget to think about some of these common-sense considerations.

If you are short, wearing an oversized blazer could "swallow you up." If you are tall, pants or sleeves that are too short could make you look (and feel) ungainly.

If something is too tight, don't wear it. Painful as it may be to admit it to yourself, get the correct size—the one that fits, not "your" size. Bulges, popping buttons, and bursting seams only accentuate what you are trying to hide. If you are overweight, it is unflattering to wear horizontal stripes or clothing or accessories that divide the body rather than create a "long" look. Buy something that looks good on you now, not something you hope to fit into when you've lost the weight you've been trying to lose for the past five years.

Don't buy anything without trying it on. Can you sit down and not have the buttons pull in the front? Are the button holes sewn tightly? Can you move around in the garment? Check for pulls, bulges, or bunching material. Use a three-way mirror to check the front, back, and side views.

Men particularly should make sure that the pants and shirt are not too short. Is the suit jacket long enough to cover the buttocks? You should be able to button that double-breasted jacket, without any pulling, when you are standing. Long-sleeve shirt cuffs should show 3/5 to 5/8 of an inch below the jacket, even in summer. The tip of the tie should end at the middle of the belt, or no shorter than the top of the belt. The trouser legs should break at the front of the shoe and taper down in back.

Women need to avoid any clothing that is too tight, too short, low-cut, or sexy as well as too frilly or girlish. This doesn't mean that suits and dresses can't flatter your figure—they can and they should. But the fit should be one that allows you to be attractive without overemphasizing any particular part of your body, especially the breasts or the legs. The hem of your skirt should not show below your coat hemline.

Clothing Communication: Sending a Professional Message

Whether clothes work for you or against you depends on the message they send. In business, it is important that the message people receive from your attire is both intentional and professional. Think of yourself as a member of a team. You want to play by the rules. The uniform is part of the game. If you show up without your uniform, they might not let you play.

We want to reiterate here, though, something we said earlier—people can choose to break the rules, provided they are prepared to accept the consequences. You just don't want to break them out of ignorance.

Depending on where you work, a non-conforming wardrobe can signal rebellion. In one company, an attractive young administrative assistant gradually changed her conservative attire and her professional-looking hairstyle as she began dating someone who was in a rock band. The change in her appearance allowed her to leave work and meet her boyfriend without having to change clothes. Unfortunately, just as she was becoming more professionally competent, she undermined her career image. Her appearance left no doubt as to her priorities.

Breaking the rules outright can be interpreted as challenging authority. Whether it is a woman who wears extremely short skirts and too much jewelry or a man who always wears an open shirt and a sports jacket, the message they convey may be: "I don't take my career seriously." Even being known as the best-dressed person in the building can be a double-edged sword: you have to work to overcome the impression that you are interested exclusively in your clothes.

You want clothes that communicate "I belong," "I'm a professional" and "I have judgment and taste."

Wardrobe Economics: Spending With Style

Money inevitably affects your clothing choices. It only makes sense that you should spend the greater percentage of your wardrobe budget on the kind of clothing you wear the most. Research shows that most people spend far more time at work than at leisure. If that is true for you, then professional attire should be a significant part of your clothing budget.

You should buy the most expensive merchandise that you can reasonably afford. A fad item is not a good investment. Genuine quality never really goes out of style.

Cost is not just a function of price. To determine the real cost of an outfit, use this time-tested formula:

$$\frac{\text{Cost}}{\text{Total number of wearings}} = \text{Cost per wearing}$$

Using this equation, a wool-blend navy suit that costs $300 and is worn 10 months of the year, once a week, for four years is a bargain:

4 wearings per month x 10 months x 4 years = 160 wearings

$$\frac{\$300}{160} = \$1.88 \text{ per wearing.}$$

By contrast, a trendy outfit that costs $150, is worn nine months of the year, once a month, for two years, actually is four times more expensive:

1 wearing x 9 months x 2 years = 18 wearings.

$$\frac{\$150}{18} = \$8.33 \text{ per wearing.}$$

We once complimented a doctor on her coat, only to learn she had bought it in Switzerland. It had been expensive, she admitted, but she felt the cost had been worth it. She'd had it ten years, and it still looked brand new.

Some fashion experts recommend shopping in February/March and August/September, when new selections come out. July and January are the best times to catch sales, but you shouldn't buy something just because it is on sale. Buy it on sale only if you would have paid full price for it.

Shopping at a quality discount store can help stretch your wardrobe dollars. Comparison-shopping through catalogs and newspaper advertisements can help you recognize a good value.

Do you hate to shop? The reality is that you must acquire clothes somehow. You might schedule for yourself some seasonal "shopping expeditions" that you plan just as you would any other aspect of your business preparation. Pick a deadline at the start of each season. First, go through your closet to weed out what is too worn, does not fit, or what you haven't worn for whatever reason. Decide what you need by familiarizing yourself with what you already have. Go shopping armed with information on your size, needs and the mistakes you may have made with past purchases.

How to Choose a Wardrobe That Delivers

Clothing is, ultimately, a highly personal decision. The selections you make are, and ought to be, a reflection of your personality. Many people mistakenly assume that assembling a career wardrobe is boring and uncreative. In reality, there are hundreds of choices within the boundaries of professional attire.

Start with an assessment of what colors best flatter you. Your hair color and skin color make a big difference in your choices. One woman who changed her hair from brunette to blonde found that she had to redesign her wardrobe and makeup to accompany the change.

Keep it simple. If you buy most of your clothing in similar color tones, it can limit your mistakes and cut your costs. Barbara, a brunette, has black as her basic wardrobe color. Marjorie, on the other hand, is a blonde and so wears softly cool tones. Her accessories, including purses, shoes, and stockings, coordinate with shades of gray.

We offer these guidelines with the reminder that your clothing must be tailored to you, your personality, and business situation. Because men and women dress differently, we will discuss each wardrobe separately.

Smart Strategies for Women

Women's business clothing is still far more individual than men's, but there are certain guidelines all women should follow. Each woman needs to develop a style that best reflects her own personality and individual taste.

There are three basic clothing styles for professional women: the skirt suit, the blazer or unconstructed jacket, and the one- or two-piece dress. Pantsuits—a combination of slacks and a jacket—are not recommended for most corporate environments, even though they are increasingly common. Each choice involves considerations of color and fabric.

THE SKIRT SUIT. The skirt suit is a recommended standard for your career wardrobe. It conveys a powerful image. A single-breasted jacket can be left unbuttoned, while a double-breasted suit should always be buttoned (that includes the inside button). To appear taller and thinner, wear a solid-color suit. Two types of skirt suits are the matched suit, where the jacket and skirt are the same fabric and color, and the unmatched suit that features a contrasting jacket.

Color choices: The best colors for business suits are black, navy, taupe, grey, and burgundy. Subtle plaids, prints, and stripes are acceptable. Be careful about purchasing two-piece red, yellow, or lavender suits. They can shout.

Fabric selections: Some wools, such as gabardine, can be worn year-round and are long-lasting. Wrinkles fall out if the garment is hung up overnight. Cotton can be effective in warm climates. Linen should be purchased only if it is blended with manmade fabrics such as polyester, rayon, or acrylic. Alone, it wrinkles easily and should be avoided. Be careful about silk which can wrinkle and appear too dressy. One way to test whether a fabric is wrinkle-resistant is to squeeze the material in your hand. If it wrinkles, think twice before buying it—it won't make it through the day.

THE BLAZER. This is a casual jacket that can be used to mix and match with skirts to extend your wardrobe. It usually has a more informal look.

Color choices: We suggest the same choices as for a suit—black, navy, taupe, grey, and burgundy. Be careful about purchasing plaids, tweeds, prints, and other patterns that do not easily match with multiple outfits.

Fabric selections: Like a suit, wool gabardine and wool blends are safe choices, with silk and blended linen also possibilities. Avoid leather, suede, ultrasuede, corduroy, velvet, velour, denim, and satin. They give less than a professional appearance.

BLOUSES: Blouses come in a wide variety of color options. Coordinate them with your suits. White, off-white, and beige will work with most suits.

Silk is the best fabric choice for blouses, but it can be expensive to dry clean. Check the label, since some silk is now washable. Another choice is 100 percent cotton, provided it is starched and carefully pressed. Polyester, which can be either hand- or machine-washed and will not wrinkle, should look like a natural fabric.

THE ONE- OR TWO-PIECE DRESS. The one- or two-piece dress can be worn alone or with a jacket. This look is not as powerful as a suit, although it is very appropriate in certain situations. A coat-dress style, a tailored dress with buttons all the way down the front, usually is more powerful and professional than a cotton shirt-dress style, in which buttons extend only to the waist.

Color choices: We suggest grey, navy, burgundy, beige, camel, tan, red, and rose. Discreet prints and patterns are permissible. Bright patterns and designs shout.

Fabric selections: Silk works best, although 100 percent rayon also can be effective. Linen can be used only if it is combined with man-made fabrics; unblended linen wrinkles easily and should not be selected. Avoid cotton, as it usually is too casual for business wear.

JEWELRY. Purchase fourteen-karat gold, sterling silver, or quality costume pieces. Wear the best watch that you can afford.

Avoid jewelry that dangles or makes noise. Don't overdo. Limit rings to one per hand. Make sure that you are wearing both earrings whenever you leave your desk, especially if you have a habit of taking one earring off to answer the phone. We have both started seminars wearing only one earring, only to find ourselves announcing, "This is not a fashion statement!"

Pearls add elegance to any business outfit.

BELTS. Belts should be leather, have a discreet buckle and should coordinate with your shoes.

SCARVES. Select scarves that include colors in the suit. The only fabric choice is 100 percent silk, since others do not knot or tie well.

HOSIERY. You can't go wrong with neutral tones—sheer nude and taupe colors—or one shade darker than your skin tone. Pale grey and bone also are good neutral colors.

Do not wear dark stockings with light shoes. Dark stockings show runs easily and sometimes look like tights, something you want to avoid. Pure white stockings frequently imply health care professionals.

Do not wear stockings with patterns. They draw attention to your legs.

Carry an extra pair of sheer stockings so that you are prepared for snags or runs. (In a pinch, clear nail polish can stop runs from growing!)

SHOES. Classic leather pumps are the best-selling business shoe—they are both comfortable and attractive. One- to two-inch heels are recommended. Avoid sandals, sling backs, and open-toed shoes.

The color of your shoes should be the color of your hemline or darker. Continuing the look from the hemline down makes most people look taller. If you introduce another color, you will draw people's eyes downward. Some people do this for accent purposes, but you need to make sure it is effective.

We recommend neutral colors, such as black, navy, burgundy, grey, and taupe. Avoid red, pink, rose, and yellow. White, even in summer, can have a social rather than a business connotation.

To preserve shoes while driving, keep a pair of old flats in the car or use "driving shoes." Trying to drive without wearing shoes runs your stockings.

When walking distances, use flats rather than sneakers. You never know whom you will meet, and flats look more professional.

However, if you must walk through five inches of snow or across glare ice or through deep water to get to the office, shoes can be impractical. Wear boots that allow you to travel easily and carry appropriate shoes for office wear.

HANDBAG/BRIEFCASE. Leather is preferred for both briefcases and handbags. Avoid designer labels on handbags. Women can carry either a hardsided or a softsided briefcase.

The most practical colors are black, brown, and burgundy. Purses should match shoes, while briefcases need not.

MISCELLANEOUS. Make sure your undergarments fit properly.

Glasses can add credibility to your look. Since you may wear these all day, every day, invest in a professional-looking pair. Avoid tinted or photogrey glasses. They hide your eyes.

Read over the list entitled *Women's Basic Business Wardrobe* and note where you may have gaps to determine what you need to buy.

Remember, these guidelines are flexible, depending on your location, your position and your industry.

Women's Basic Business Wardrobe

Black or Grey Suit

Navy Suit

Scarf that picks up colors from the suit (optional)

Pair of Black Pumps

Three coordinating jackets and skirts.

One- or Two-Piece Dress

Three Solid-Color Blouses

Two Pastel or Print Blouses

Gold, Silver and Good Costume Earrings, Necklace, Bracelet, and Pin

A Good Quality Watch

Pair of Navy or Taupe Pumps

Black, Navy, or Taupe Leather Bag

Black Belt, Navy Belt

Black, Brown, or Burgundy Briefcase

All-Weather Coat

Smart Strategies for Men

Men usually have fewer clothing choices than women, but that doesn't mean they don't have to think about their wardrobe. In fact, for men, subtle variations can have a large impact on the signals clothes send. You should develop a style that reflects your own personality and individual taste.

For men, there are two different kinds of clothing appropriate for business—the two-pieced suit and the sport coat with trousers.

TWO-PIECED SUIT. The two-pieced suit usually is the best choice for most businesses. At least five two-button, three-button, or double-breasted suits should be the basis of your business wardrobe. Double-breasted jackets are always buttoned, including the inside button. Suit buttons should match the color of the fabric.

We recommend lapel widths of three- to three-and-a-half inches, which are less likely to become outdated than wider or narrower lapels. Trouser cuffs are a matter of personal preference, although they are usually found on less formal suits.

The jackets should not be worn with other trousers. Vests add a more formal note and more expense to the suit.

Color choices: Navy, grey, and charcoal are power colors. Be careful with brown, since many people have a negative reaction to it. Be careful, too, with black, because it can be intimidating. Medium blue is friendly. A pinstripe in a subtle pattern can add interest and variety to your wardrobe.

Fabric selections: Wool and wool blends can be worn all year and do not wrinkle easily. A cotton pincord or poplin can be worn during warm weather. One way to test whether a fabric is wrinkle-resistant is to squeeze the material in your hand. If it wrinkles, think twice before buying it—it won't make it through the day without wrinkling.

SPORT COAT AND TROUSERS. Sports coats and trousers should always contrast in keeping with their more casual look. Plaid sports coats are usually too casual for business.

Color choices: The power colors of navy, grey, and charcoal blend easily with a wide range of contrasting colors. Brown and camel can be more acceptable in a sports coat than in a suit if they are paired with blue trousers and are blended with an appropriate shirt and tie. Medium blue is versatile since it can be paired with navy or grey.

The darker color of the jacket allows lighter color choices for the trousers, including tan or beige.

Fabric selections: As is the case with suits, jackets should be wool or wool blends, or cotton or silk blends. Trousers should be wool gabardine, wool blends, or permanent press blends.

SHIRTS. Men's dress shirts should always be long-sleeved, even in summer, so that the cuffs show 3/5 to 5/8 of an inch below the jacket. Be thankful that you live in an era in which office air-conditioning is standard.

Color choices: Solid colors are preferred; white is the best and safest choice. Pale blue is also acceptable. Light blue, taupe, and red pinstripes are acceptable alternatives in some organizations. Avoid lavender, peach, plaids, dots, and broad stripes.

Fabric selections: The best choice is 100 percent cotton, but it needs professional laundering to ensure that it is starched and well-pressed.

TIES. The tip of the tie should end at the middle of the belt, or no shorter than the top of the belt. Be cautious with bow-ties—you can be labeled as an eccentric. The tie should be approximately three inches wide, although tie width does change with the times.

Color choices: The tie and the suit color should complement each other, but not match. Burgundy, red, and navy work as background colors. Accent colors and patterns generally should be subtle, or not shout.

Fabric selection: The preferred choice is 100 percent silk. It's elegant and can be worn all year in any climate.

Small geometric prints and stripes are good choices. Paisleys with subdued patterns are alternatives.

When combining a suit, shirt, and tie, choose: one solid and two patterns or two solids and one pattern. Coordinating three patterns, while requiring skill and experience, can look outstanding if it is well done.

The tie and handkerchief should coordinate, but not be identical patterns.

JEWELRY. Men should wear no more than one ring per hand.

Men also can wear a good quality watch in sterling silver, gold, or stainless steel.

Leave the earring at home, unless you work in an organization where it is accepted.

BELTS. Belts should be either leather or reptile skin in black, brown, or burgundy. The belt color should match the shoes and have a discreet buckle.

Braces are acceptable.

SOCKS. Socks should fit over-the-calf in either nylon or thin cotton.

They should be black, brown, or navy. Selecting socks that are white, beige, brightly colored or large patterned, including argyle, could draw undue attention to your legs. Choose the color to match or blend with trousers. The exception is with tan trousers, when socks should match the shoes.

SHOES. Footwear is very noticeable. Many men assume they can experiment in this area. They're wrong.

Select leather shoes in either a lace-up or a slip-on style. Tasseled loafers are less conservative and may even be considered non-serious "slip-on bedroom slippers" in some industries. Heavy wingtips are for colder climates.

The shoe color should not be lighter than the trouser color. Wear black shoes with grey, navy, or black suits. Wear dark brown shoes with tan or beige suits.

BRIEFCASE/WALLET. The briefcase should be brown, black, or burgundy leather.

It's preferable to carry your wallet in the front inside pocket of your suit jacket. When the wallet is carried in a back pants pocket, it affects the look of the suit.

Read over the list entitled *Men's Basic Business Wardrobe* and note where you may have gaps to determine what you need to buy. Remember, these guidelines are flexible, depending on your location, your position and your industry.

Men's Basic Business Wardrobe

One Navy Suit	Five to Eight Solid, Striped, or Patterned Silk Ties
One Charcoal Grey Suit	Two Black Leather Belts
One Medium Blue or Gray Suit	Leather Briefcase
Two to Three Pinstriped or other subtle pattern Suits	One Pair Black Lace-up Shoes
Six White Cotton Shirts, Long-Sleeved	One Pair Black Slip-on Shoes
Blue or Pinstriped Shirt	All-Weather Coat
A Good Quality Watch	

Practical Wardrobe Maintenance Tips

Store your clothes properly. Avoid wire hangers. Hang clothes with one inch of space between the garments to allow breathing room.

Don't overdo dry cleaning. Dry cleaning only about once for every four or five wearings will extend the life of your clothes. One casino professional was thrilled to learn this information: He always dry-cleaned his clothes after one wearing, whether they needed it or not. As a result of our advice, he realized a significant savings. Of course, if your clothes become soiled or spotted, they should be cleaned right away.

You also can just press your clothes periodically, without the cleaning.

A competent tailor or seamstress and even a professional shoe-polisher can help you make a good impression.

Business Casual: Effective Informality

A variation on the basic business wardrobe is often used when attending conferences and seminars, for office "Dress Down Days" or corporate-sponsored picnics or golf tournaments. This is called "Business Casual," which used to be a contradiction in terms. The key point is that this is not the same as a purely casual or leisure look. You are still conducting business, even though the clothing may be less formal than the standard business attire. Because the clothing will still be a reflection on you and your professionalism, it should meet all the standards for traditional business clothing: that is, be flattering, well-fitted, clean, and pressed.

Particularly for "Dress Down Days" at the office, the business casual look requires flair which may actually be more difficult to achieve successfully than with traditional business wear. Because business casual outfits usually can't be purchased as an ensemble, you need to attend to accessorizing and the coordinating of separate pieces. It also may be more expensive to buy items piece by piece than to purchase a tailored suit. Some manufacturers, sensing a growing demand for this type of clothing, have introduced lines specifically intended to meet this need.

For women, the business casual look can include blouses with skirts, split skirts (skorts) or well-fitting slacks, or a blouse/jacket combination. Wear flat shoes, not sneakers or sandals, unless it is a sporting event. If bathing suits are called for, a tasteful one-piece suit is more appropriate than a bikini, regardless of how great your figure may be. Bermuda shorts also can be acceptable.

Men can wear slacks with just a shirt, a collared cotton T-shirt or sweater. Be cautious with jeans—if you do wear them, make sure they are not tattered, and that they are acceptable in the environment. In this setting, loafers and slip-on shoes are OK. Men should wear trunks instead of bikini bathing suits. Well-fitting shorts also are acceptable.

Business Dress: Dynamic Dress-Up

Business Dress guidelines usually apply when conducting business out of the office in the evening, such as attending the theater or a symphony concert with a client. In some organizations, Business Dress may apply to holiday parties as well. (For more information about situations in which you should wear this wardrobe, see Chapter Twelve, "Business Out of the Office.")

Again, the basic standards for professionalism prevail. Cocktail dresses should not be too low-cut or slinky. Black tie events require appropriate dress. Your mentor or a colleague who is attending the event with you may be able to provide some guidance. If you need help finding an outfit for this situation, admit it in advance! Rather than displaying weakness, this shows that you take the situation seriously and want to be a success.

Questions to Ask *Before* You Buy

Whether you are male or female, the final decision as to whether you should add a particular item to your wardrobe depends on whether it meets the criteria we've just discussed.

Before making any purchase, ask yourself these seven questions:

Is it appropriate?

Does the garment fit?

Does the garment feel comfortable?

Will you be able to wear the garment often?

Does it complete your wardrobe?

Does the garment look good?

Do you like it?

You need a "yes" to all the questions. If you are in doubt, don't buy it. And don't remove the price tags until you try the garment on one more time at home, just to be sure.

You want to buy clothes that look and feel good and that you love to wear. Your wardrobe should show that you respect yourself and in doing so, generate the respect from others that you deserve.

LOOKING THE PART:
Success with Style

Projecting a professional presence can sometimes feel like an uncompensated second job. It does require time, some planning, on a regular, repetitive basis, and perhaps even new routines. The rewards can seem intangible, because the consequences of *not* looking and acting like a professional are more readily apparent.

However, there are benefits to looking the part of a professional, including the satisfaction and self-confidence it instills. Part of staying competitive is portraying an image that both co-workers and clients respect. It makes everyone feel more comfortable, and that, as we've said before, is the essence of good manners.

Chapter 5

OFFICE COURTESIES THAT INCREASE YOUR CLOUT

All doors open to courtesy.

—THOMAS FULLER, M.D.

You didn't choose your co-workers, and, with the possible exceptions of your boss and/or the personnel department, they didn't choose you. Yet, somehow, despite possible clashes in personalities and in working styles, you must all manage to get along for the major part of your day. Deadlines and work pressures can make people irritable, but they are no excuse for poor manners. The need to respect a person's territory and privacy does not diminish in a corporate climate. Thinking of others and their needs enhances the work flow and your work relationships, making everyone more productive and content. Manners can make the difference between a cooperative and a combative office environment.

In this chapter, you'll find:

- Etiquette hints for entrances and exits—such as elevators and revolving doors—and ways to greet visitors to your office graciously. Tips on timing—ways of showing respect for other people by honoring their schedules.

- Special courtesy concerns for specific types of rooms within the building, from private offices to the company cafeteria.

- Etiquette for office equipment—manners for computers, copiers, fax machines and coffee pots.

- How to handle the hot topic of smoking.

66

HOW TO MANAGE INS AND OUTS AND UPS AND DOWNS

We once knew a man who always took the elevator up to his office in the morning, but always took the stairs down on the way home at night. He was quite serious, he admitted, about making sure that in case of a malfunction, he would only get stuck "on company time."

Many of us get stuck when it comes to handling entrances and exits, not because we're caught between floors but because we're caught between old and new manners as to what is appropriate behavior. Do we hold the door? Get off the elevator in reverse order of the way we entered it? Wait for the revolving door to stop?

When it comes to such matters, polite behavior today places more emphasis than ever before on what's practical. Courtesy has become increasingly gender-blind. When in doubt, do what makes the most sense, and most of the time, you will be acting appropriately. Our *Guide to Gracious Entrances and Exits* summarizes the points we'll discuss in detail.

Guide to Gracious Entrances and Exits

REVOLVING DOORS

Who Goes First: First to arrive. Host leads way for guests, pushing gently and meeting them at the other side.

Yield To: People with disabilities, old people, slow travelers, those with bulky packages, your host.

Other Considerations: Maintain the pace. Do not stop or suddenly change speed.

ELEVATORS

Who Goes First: First arrivals. Guest enters before host. Host can leave first, holding door for guest while providing directions.

Yield To: People with disabilities, people getting off.

Other Considerations: Hold the door or door button for people who are entering, exiting or on their way to the elevator. Make room for those who are entering or exiting. Don't crowd. Don't push. Don't gossip. Greet those you recognize. Announce your floor before arriving there.

STAIRS AND ESCALATORS

Who Goes First: The host. Otherwise, first arrivals.

Yield To: People with disabilities, people in a hurry.

Other Considerations: Don't rush people on stairs—instead, go around them.

(Continued on next page)

Doors

Who Goes First: Whoever gets there first.

Yield To: People with disabilities, someone whose hands are full.

Other Considerations: Hold door for the person behind you. If someone holds the door for you, say "Thank you."

Revolving Doors: Making Turnabout Fair Play

Revolving doors were originally designed to speed traffic flow in two directions through a small space. However, their effectiveness depends on whether those entering and leaving can adopt the same pace and rhythm. Getting synchronized requires courteous cooperation. Abrupt stops and sudden changes in speed can be both rude and dangerous. The key point for anyone using a revolving door is to be alert and accommodating.

If someone is disabled, revolving door traffic should yield to him or her. A doorman can adjust a revolving door to remain stationary and open it wide enough to allow people through. If there is no other entrance available, this should be done for anyone with a cane, on crutches, or carrying an especially bulky package. In some instances, if the opening is sufficiently wide, a wheelchair may be able to fit through.

If someone is just a slow walker or fearful about entering a revolving door, that person should wait until most of the other traffic has cleared. He can then proceed at his own pace. Of course, if you happen to arrive immediately after such a person has entered the door, it's polite to either wait until he has exited or adjust your speed to avoid "pushing" him through.

When you are the host who is bringing someone in or out of a building with a revolving door, you lead the way by going first so that you can meet the person on the other side and help direct him. As you enter the door, you might want to say, "I'll meet you at the other side" or "See you at the sidewalk." Push the door, but not too fast. Once you have exited, wait for your party to join you and then continue. If more than one person is following you, wait until all have left the revolving door.

Elevators: The Basics of Riding in a Box

Not so long ago, most elevators had human operators to make sure that the equipment functioned properly. Elevator operators were also "transportation moderators," encouraging people to "step to the back please" or announcing "Sixth floor." Today, we rely on elevator riders to politely police themselves.

Alas, not all elevator riders know or practice courteous behavior. It's a measure of the fast and sometimes frantic pace of business that we may find elevators to be too slow! Ironically, the more crowded and the slower elevators are, the greater the need for courteous behavior. Polite riders adopt a group mentality, acknowledging that the elevator is not their own personal conveyance.

When the elevator door opens, pause briefly to see who needs to exit. If you try to go in as others go out, it can result in a collision or just delay things as you dance around each other. It is acceptable to put your hand on the rubber strip along the door to make sure the door stays open long enough for you to enter. If others are entering with you and you will exit on a nearby floor, hold back and enter late, so that you are in the front of the elevator for an easier exit.

Don't push your way in. If someone else does, it's OK to be assertive. You can say, "The elevator is full. Please wait for the next one." If that person doesn't respect your request, *you* can always wait for the next one.

Once you are inside, make room for others and hold the door, or "door open" button, for anyone who appears headed for the elevator. It's acceptable etiquette for the first arrivals to stand along the walls just inside the door; others may then line the side and back walls; final arrivals fill the middle. Hogging the space in the middle so that you can make a quick exit exhibits a "me first" mentality, not considerate behavior. In addition to being impolite, it defeats your purpose by slowing things up as people have to step around one another.

People with disabilities should be allowed to place themselves near the elevator door. If someone is blind, uses a cane, or is in a wheelchair, maneuvering in and out can be complicated enough without having to move around others to get to the door. It is polite to hold the door as a disabled person enters or exits, since elevator doors open and close according to their own schedule.

As a host escorting someone in your building, hold the elevator door and allow the guest to enter first. When leaving the elevator, depending upon where you are positioned, you should exit and hold the door for your guest, giving your guest directions where to go next. "My office is down the hall and to the left," you might say. If you are the host of someone who is leaving the building, walk that person to the elevator and wait with him until it arrives.

If you can't reach the button for your floor, ask politely that someone else do so, then thank him or her.

If you bump someone, say "Excuse me."

As the elevator stops at floors that are not yours, move to allow people in. If you are in the front of a very crowded elevator, move out when people in the back need to get out, holding the door so that you don't get left behind.

If you are in the back, indicate when you are about to reach your floor. You can say, "Excuse me, I'm getting out next," so that people can begin to maneuver to make room. Indicating this before your floor actually arrives saves time for others, and so is considerate.

If the elevator is not crowded and you recognize the person who just got on, it's polite to greet the person and engage in brief small talk. If someone you know joins you and another colleague on the elevator, introduce everyone.

Don't speak loudly on controversial or private topics. You never know who is standing in the back of the elevator or who came in when you weren't paying attention. This is a public conveyance in a confined space—not the place for intense conversations. We're all titillated by snatches of overheard chatter. Providing grist for the gossip mill is not smart and not polite.

Stairs and Escalators: Motion Without Commotion

Using stairs and escalators requires that you display courtesy while you move.

When traveling with someone who may have difficulty using stairs—perhaps because of a heart problem, breathing difficulties, or because a leg is in a cast—take the elevator or escalator, if one is available. When in doubt, it's always polite to ask, "Do you mind if we take the stairs?"

On stairs or escalators, the host leads the way whether you are going up or down. Once again, this allows the host to greet and lead the visitor once he arrives at the destination. You can say, "Let me show you the way." Male and female colleagues can get on stairs and escalators in the order in which they arrive; in fact, it sometimes works to travel side by side. Don't follow too closely the person in front of you.

If you are on a wide escalator, stay to the right so that someone in a hurry can pass you on the left. On stairs that are crowded, follow the traffic flow, which usually dictates that people stay to the right, whether they're going up or down. Of course, if there are handrails only on one side of the stairs and someone needs to use the rail for safety's sake, the traffic should yield to that person.

It's both dangerous and impolite to rush people on stairs. Either slow your pace or pass the other person, but don't pressure someone else to speed up. If you are the slow person, you can say, "Go ahead, I need to take my time."

Because it's difficult to carry on a conversation while climbing stairs or riding an escalator, it's better to wait until you arrive at your destination. This avoids putting someone in the awkward position of not being able to contribute to the conversation.

Doors: Getting In and Out Without Becoming Unhinged

Doorway manners aren't exactly an "open-and-shut" case, but many people have made them unnecessarily complicated. The result is that some people approach doors gingerly, hanging back, hoping that someone else will resolve the perennial dilemma of who opens and who holds. In the past, many rules about who opened the door, who held it, and who went through first were based on gender or on the relative status of the two individuals (such as supervisor vs. employee). Today, door decisions swing more toward practicality.

The basic guideline: Whoever gets to the door first opens it. Period. This applies regardless of gender, corporate status, or age.

Of course, it's always polite to hold the door for someone, especially if that person's hands are full, if he or she has difficulty moving, or if the door is a swinging one that could slam back at them. Naturally, you should never slam any door in someone's face—let the person behind you grab hold of it.

When you are escorting a visitor, try to get into position to hold the door for the guest.

If someone holds the door for you, say "Thank you." We often say, to both men and women, "Chivalry isn't dead." This always gets a chuckle.

If you are a woman, should you hang back so the man will open the door for you? If you are the junior member of the team, should you hustle to open the door for your boss? Your answer depends on your personality and on your corporate climate. In a traditional business environment the more traditional rules may work best—letting the man hold the door for the woman or the younger person open the door for the senior one.

However, we'd like to think of men and women today, as well as bosses and associates, striding down the corridors of power at approximately the same pace, arriving pretty much at the same time (depending on whose legs are the longest) and then proceeding through the door without undue fuss.

The Secrets of a Sensible, not Sex-based, Strategy. Alas, much ado has arisen about gender issues regarding doors in particular. Instead we consider this to be predominantly a courtesy question.

Don't expect others to do things for you just because of your gender, whether you are male or female.

Help anyone who needs help, regardless of gender. If, for instance, someone is carrying something and you can assist her or him, do so.

We do recommend that you allow people to save face. If we accompanied a 60-year-old man to the door and he insisted on opening it for us, we'd let him! Yes, we're aware of the possible implications of that gesture, but our interest is in making him comfortable, rather than strictly adhering to rules. The reverse is equally true: if a woman will become self-conscious while a group of men wait for her to go through a door first, the men should just walk through in order of arrival.

Appreciate gracious gestures. Don't make a to-do about small stuff. Keep a sense of humor.

Good manners also mean showing respect for those who deserve it, and some of the old rules were based on that premise. Small people struggle more with big loads, just as an older person is more likely to need a seat on a crowded bus. Barbara Pachter remains impressed that someone yielded a seat to her on the New York subway when she was eight months pregnant. When you are more concerned with the rules than with what's rational, you've lost your perspective about the importance of people, which is and always will be the main consideration for manners.

WELCOMES THAT "WOW" THEM:
Gracious Greetings for Visitors

Marjorie Brody once was kept waiting for 45 minutes by a corporate host. She found the situation both telling and ironic, given the fact that the appointment was to discuss a new training program for effective meetings. The client certainly needed the instruction!

The way you greet your visitors can affect the tone and outcome of the meeting and the subsequent relationship between that person and your company. People often are extra alert when coming to a new place or when meeting someone new, and that heightened consciousness makes every detail count. You want things to get off to a good start so you can build on a solid foundation. How you greet people initially may determine whether you have the opportunity to greet them again, as established clients. (*The Visitor Grid* summarizes appropriate behavior whether you are the visitor or the host.)

The Visitor Grid

SITUATION	VISITORS TO YOUR OFFICE	WHEN YOU VISIT
Appointment Time	Don't keep visitors waiting.	Arrive on time or a few minutes early.
Upon Arrival	You or an assistant escort visitor to your office. If taking an elevator, hold the door for the visitor. Visitor goes in first. If it's a revolving door, the host goes through first, so the host can direct the guest.	Give your name, the company name and whom you are visiting to the receptionist. Also provide a business card.
Introductions	Greet with handshake and smile. Stand and come from behind the desk and sit as equals.	Shake hands.
Coats/Hats	Hang them up.	Wait to be shown where to hang your coat.
Sitting	Indicate where the guest should sit.	Wait for the host to tell you where to sit. Put purse, briefcase on floor, but nothing on the desk. Do not take candy from the desk unless offered.
Small Talk	Just for three to four minutes, then business.	Host takes the lead unless you called the meeting.

SITUATION	VISITORS TO YOUR OFFICE	WHEN YOU VISIT
Business Cards	Offer a business card.	Ask for a card if the host does not offer one. Ask before taking one from a card holder. Also provide yours.
Smoking	Ask for guest's permission.	Refrain from smoking.
Interruptions	Don't accept calls or interruptions unless it is an emergency.	If your host takes a call, motion to ask whether you should stay. If a person enters, stand up.
Goodbyes	Walk visitor back to the reception area. Say, "I appreciate your visit." If the visitor lingers, say, "I'm sorry, I have another meeting." Or, use your assistant to remind you of your next appointment.	Stand, shake hands. Don't overstay your welcome. Depending on the meeting, write a thank-you note.

APPOINTMENT TIME: Don't make anyone wait—don't be late. Appointments are not approximations. It is incumbent on the person who determined the time of the meeting to be ready when he or she agreed to be, and it is the responsibility of the person attending the meeting to get there on time.

If you keep an executive waiting, that person will very often take his or her business someplace else. If you arrive at a location rushed and anxious, you will need even more time to settle down and focus on business. In American business, keeping anyone waiting—regardless of whether you are the visitor or the host—is just plain rude. It implies that you think your time is more valuable than the other person's. (For international views on time and appointments, see, Chapter Eighteen, "The Way Work Works Outside the USA.")

If you are the host and are running behind schedule, you must let the visitor know about the delay immediately upon his or her arrival. Depending on the length of the delay, the person may want to wait, come back, or reschedule the appointment. You need to give the visitor the option. Do not let guests just sit and stew, wondering if you've forgotten about them, are playing power games with them or are just hopelessly disorganized.

If the wait will be short, it is polite to offer visitors a beverage to help pass the time. Show them to a reception area with comfortable chairs and a few magazines to read.

If you are the visitor and are going to be more than ten minutes late, call to let your host know. Give him or her the option of canceling or rescheduling the meeting. Apologize when you arrive.

UPON ARRIVAL: You should, of course, have made it clear when you set up the appointment where your visitor should report (front desk? third floor lobby? Room 626, down the hall to the left of the elevator?). In some cases, the visitor needs to allow time to sign in and receive a visitor's pass. The host is responsible for smoothing the visitor's way through security check-ins. This includes making sure the visitor's name is on an authorized visitors' list.

If you are the visitor, you need to check in upon arrival: provide the receptionist with your name, the company name, and a business card (which lists your title), along with the name of the person you are to meet. In a large organization, it may be helpful to know the host's telephone extension. The host or an assistant should be informed of your arrival and one of them should escort you to the office.

INTRODUCTIONS: The visitor and the host need to exchange handshakes and smiles (see Chapter Two, "Powerful First Impressions: How to Meet and Greet.") If a move to another location will be necessary, the host should make sure the other room is available in advance of the visit to avoid wasting time.

COATS/HATS: The host should offer to hang up the visitor's coat or hat. Depending on the company, the coat may have been left in the reception area. If there is a wait, the coat also can be taken from the reception area and carried to the host's office.

SEATING: The host should indicate where the guest should sit and the visitor should wait for the host to indicate that before sitting down. If the host for some reason fails to indicate a chair (perhaps out of forgetfulness), it's a good idea to inquire before sitting down. You don't want to take someone else's seat by mistake. What's more, the meeting may not be in the room that you first enter.

The host should stand up and come out from behind his desk, sitting with the visitor as an equal. If office space does not permit a side-by-side seating arrangement, you can place a chair directly beside the desk, or adjourn to another room where you can talk more comfortably. The desk should not be a physical barrier between the host and the visitor. If the visitor is in a wheelchair, the host should make room for the wheelchair, preferably in advance of the visit.

The visitor should move a chair only if the host gives permission or issues an invitation to do so. If you do move the chair, replace it in its original position when you leave. If you need to get closer than the chair allows, first try leaning closer, or stand up —temporarily—so that you can see the document that is being discussed.

The visitor should put his briefcase or her purse on the floor, not the desk, which is the host's territory. Similarly, don't take any candy from the desk unless offered and don't touch or obviously appear to read any papers on the desk.

SMALL TALK: The host takes the lead in small talk, unless the visitor called for the meeting. Do engage in a few minutes of small talk before getting down to the subject. A few minutes—maybe only a few sentences—are often sufficient. As a guest, it's not courteous to drag out this portion of the meeting. Pay attention to the personality of the host. Some prefer extended conversation as part of the rapport-building; some don't. Possible topics for small talk include observations regarding the office and its accessories—pictures, awards, art objects, books. See Chapter Three, "Big Techniques for Small Talk," for additional suggestions on brief conversations.

BUSINESS CARDS: You may pass out your business card at the beginning or at the end of the meeting. There are no hard and fast rules in the United States regarding this— it flows from the conversation. If the host does not offer a business card, the guest should request one before leaving. If the business cards are in a desk holder, ask before taking one. You can give two business cards—one for the secretary. You also can request two cards—one for your Rolodex® and one to staple in a client file.

SMOKING: The visitor should refrain from smoking. The host should always ask for permission before lighting up. (We cover this subject in greater depth later on in this chapter.)

INTERRUPTIONS: No one likes interruptions, but sometimes in business they are unavoidable. A host should plan not to accept calls or interruptions, unless it is an emergency. If the host takes a call, the visitor should, through body language, offer to step outside the office so that the business can be transacted in private. If someone comes into the office, the visitor should stand and the host should make introductions.

GOODBYES: The host should escort the guest back to the reception area. Don't assume the visitor can find his or her way out—office corridors can turn into mazes for some-one who is unfamiliar with them. What's more, it's just not gracious to send a visitor away, in effect dismissing him or her without the courtesy of your company. Wait with the person for the elevator. The host should say something gracious before departing, such as "I appreciate your visit." If the visitor lingers, you can say "I have another meeting" or arrange for your assistant to remind you of your next appoint-ment. The visitor should shake hands when the host leaves and thank the host for his or her time. Later, depending on the circumstances, you can write a thank-you note.

Tips on Gracious Timing

Courteous conduct includes demonstrating respect for the other person's time. When you honor someone's schedule, you honor that person as well. As you know, you should always take the other person's schedule into consideration when scheduling appointments.

Once the appointment has been made, there are many things you can do to avoid being late. You can schedule meetings further apart so that if one runs over, the next meeting won't be delayed. You can better estimate how long something will really take instead of planning based on how long you *hope* it will take. We learned this lesson the hard way: in scheduling a meeting with a book publisher, we underestimated the amount of time the discussion would take. That meeting spilled over into a back-to-back meeting we had scheduled with a client. Fortunately, the client was flexible.

On a personal basis, you might be able to be more organized: leave earlier, assemble materials in advance, plan your route. You can schedule fewer tasks into each day, or delegate more of your work. You can even set your watch, office clock, or car clock five minutes ahead so that you can be "late" and also be on time. This is one area in which a car phone can be used to its best advantage as you let your next appointment know of an unexpected delay.

You can't schedule your illnesses, but you can react as soon as possible when it becomes apparent that they are going to interfere with an appointment. If you feel you must carry on even though you are ill, it's polite to acknowledge the situation. You can say, for instance, "I'm not my usual self today—my cold medication is making me drowsy."

Polite timing also means limiting the meeting to its stipulated length. (In Chapter Ten, "Must We Meet Like This? The Protocol of Meetings," we discuss tips for conducting effective meetings.) Whether you are visiting a co-worker's office to discuss a problem or making a sales presentation to a prospective client, don't over-stay your welcome.

If it becomes apparent that a meeting or project is going to run late, acknowledge the delay. You can say something like,

"This is taking more time than I anticipated. Should we continue, or take it up again later?" It also is courteous to acknowledge the other person's commitments:

"I know you have another meeting at 3. I think we can finish this up in five minutes."

If someone detains you, you can politely detach yourself by saying,

"I have to go now. We'll finish this later."

TERRITORIAL IMPERATIVES:
The Basics of Boundaries

A man who underwent several weeks of intensive cancer treatment was pleased when he could finally return to his office. His co-workers greeted him warmly and told him they had anxiously awaited his return. However, as he settled down at his desk, he received a different sort of message. His stapler was gone. His files had been rearranged. Cards were missing from his telephone file. It was clear, from the scavenging that took place around his desk during his absence, that some people did not expect him to come back!

People stake their claim on their allotted portions of office space and equipment, and woe to those who fail to respect those boundaries. Although we understand that the office, the desk, the file drawer aren't "ours" in the sense of private ownership, we nonetheless regard them as personal property—that is, corporately-owned property which is on loan exclusively to us for the duration of our employment. Good manners require that we respect people's needs for space and privacy. We hope that they do the same for us!

If you have a meeting scheduled in someone's office, don't walk in if the person is not there. Wait outside the door if there isn't a waiting area.

If you are visiting a co-worker, knock before entering his or her office, even if the door is open, to alert that person of your arrival. Wait to be acknowledged before entering. If the person is on the telephone, wait outside or come back later.

All of what we said regarding visitors applies to your co-workers as well: wait to be offered a seat before sitting down in someone's office. If a phone call interrupts your session, ask through body language if you should go outside. Do not put your feet, your files, or your coffee cup on the desk—it is that person's space. Ask for permission. Say, "Do you mind if I put my coffee cup here?" Move chairs only if the person gives permission, and then put things back where you found them before you leave.

If you need to use someone's office or a piece of equipment, get permission first. If the person agrees, he or she has granted you a privilege that you should not abuse. Do not rifle through drawers or files or snoop at papers on the desk. If you need to borrow something, return it promptly and in good shape. Thank the person for sharing it with you.

When space is shared by a group of people—whether it is the cafeteria, the bathroom, the boardroom, or the copy room—you are at least partially responsible for helping to keep the room in good condition. Clean up after yourself, and pitch in above and beyond the call of duty if extra help is needed. It's not courteous conduct to fail to clear your table yourself or to leave wadded up paper on the floor until the cleaning crew arrives. In fact, you may some day be inconvenienced or even embarrassed to discover the mess that someone else has left. It's especially effective when managers help clean up, because it sends a silent signal that they expect others to do so. What is no one person's responsibility is every individual's shared responsibility. Grownups don't worry about who made the mess—they just take care of it. (See *Territorial Tactics—Do's and Don'ts*).

Territorial Tactics—Do's and Don'ts

Do	Don't
Ask permission to enter an office, borrow, move, or use equipment.	Place items on someone's desk.

(Continued on next page)

Respect property and space.	Snoop through drawers or files, read papers on desk.
Return borrowed items promptly and in good condition.	
Clean up after yourself.	Leave a mess, even if you didn't make it.
Take turns when sharing office materials.	Be sloppy, disorganized or unprofessional in your office setting.

When someone fails to follow these guidelines, you can ask politely that he or she do so in the future. For instance, you can say,

"I'd like my stapler back. Please check with me before you borrow it again."

or

"Next time you arrive at my office before I do, please wait outside."

Making Your Personal Space an Impressive Place

A leading candidate with solid credentials and ample experience for a job with a major manufacturing company turned down the lucrative job offer after touring the office and manufacturing plant. Although the position, salary, and benefits were attractive, she was offended by a pin-up she saw prominently displayed during her visit. She said she didn't want to work in an environment that would allow such behavior.

Whether it's a cubicle or a corner office, your office space reflects on both you and your company. As a physical expression of your personality, you want it to make a positive impression.

Be neat and organized. Usually the less clutter, the better. You don't have to get rid of everything, provided you keep what you have mostly out of sight. Do your part to make sure the desk surface and office equipment are clean. Throw out dead flowers. Empty and clean your coffee mug. Stack papers neatly so that the housekeeping staff can dust adequately.

Respect office guidelines regarding personal decorating. Make sure personal pictures, awards, and artifacts, if allowed, are in good taste. The objects are nonverbal reflections of you. Limit the number of self-promoting paraphernalia. People in photos, including those of your children, should be properly attired. There should be no sexual connotation to any of the items. Religious mementos are generally better left at home.

Be prepared to explain anything in your office. Some people take this one step further and use items to get attention. One CEO hung a decorated 11-foot lance from his ceiling. "That's so I can deal with those things you wouldn't want to touch with a 10-foot pole," he would explain. Each Christmas, a male communications officer would bring in his "holiday ornament"—a branch with a gun shell hanging in it. "That's a cartridge in a bare tree," he said, tongue firmly in cheek. Both men used these objects as ice-breakers and to express their gentle sense of humor.

Be careful about cartoons or "clever" sayings that you post on personal bulletin boards—they should not imply a serious dislike of the job or any other unprofessional attitude. One man listed on his wall calendar what he guessed were the menstrual dates of his female employees. According to the newspaper account we read, he and his company were being sued for sexual harassment.

Keeping the Company Cafeteria an Appetizing Environment

Lunch and coffee breaks may be a welcome change of pace, but when they're held on company property in the presence of other employees, you're still on duty and should act accordingly.

You will, of course, want to use appropriate table manners (see Chapter Eleven, "Dining for Fun and Profit: The Business Lunch"). People notice who has a sloppy eating style, and it reflects negatively on an overall image. Such incidents tend to stick in the mind. We were visiting a company cafeteria when we saw a woman who used her hand to remove some alfalfa sprouts, from her salad plate. She placed them on the table next to the plate; when she finished making the rest of her salad, she picked them up with her fingers and put them back on the salad plate. We never did learn her name, but we never forgot her either.

Try not to sit with the same people every day; instead use this time to network. We can't stress this enough. We know it's all too easy to get locked into a "lunch group," but make the effort to avoid it. Invite a co-worker from a different department to join your table, or make lunch dates with different colleagues on different days of the week. If possible, vary the times you go to lunch—this is almost guaranteed to give you a varied circle of lunch partners. Mixing and mingling not only gives you a chance to practice making small talk, but helps develop your reputation as a personable, gracious individual.

You know better than to discuss controversial work-related subjects during lunch in the cafeteria—you may be overheard. Also be careful about discussing aspects of your personal life—what you did last night, what you plan to do this weekend. Keep the conversation positive. It's OK to discuss how you took your son to college, but not how you had a fight with your husband. (See Chapter Twelve, "Business Out of the Office," for Do's and Dont's of discussing your social life.)

What follows are some basic guidelines on cafeteria courtesy. Mundane as this advice may seem, we find that these sample rules can eliminate the most common complaints that we hear from clients:

- Making fun of other people's food choices is not courteous.
- If you use vending machines, report when they are broken. This not only is considerate conduct, but is in your own best interest—otherwise the next time *you* go to use it, it still might not be repaired.
- If you use a common refrigerator, don't take anyone else's food. Wipe up any spills. Don't take too much space. Remove your food before it spoils. Refill the ice cube tray.

- If you use a microwave, don't use it for extended periods during peak times. Wipe up any spills. If you don't know how to use it properly, admit it and get someone to help you.

- Clean up after yourself. No matter who you are in the organization, this shows that you are a team player and not "above" performing basic, menial tasks. Return your tray, throw away trash, push chairs back under tables.

Rules for Restrooms

It would be nice if all company bathrooms were truly private retreats, where people could perform the function for which these rooms were created in a clean, well-maintained, secluded environment. That, we must acknowledge, is why executive washrooms were invented.

But when you must share this most personal of places with others, don't make the mistake of thinking that just because it should be a private place, it is. In fact, others are watching you, whether it's how you comb your hair or whether you put the seat down. It's public space, and people notice and talk.

For example, during one of our etiquette training programs, a participant talked about an unnamed colleague who never washed her hands after going to the bathroom. Others in the class immediately identified the subject and added to the discussion. When one co-worker came to her defense, saying, "Well, maybe she just went in there to adjust her slip," the others recounted all the times she had been observed doing the same thing. (Things you really didn't want to know about your colleagues, but can't avoid finding out.)

While using the facilities, you should not only watch your behavior, but your conversation—you never know who is in the next stall. We have overheard program participants discussing our class, and, fortunately for us, their remarks were positive. If the remarks hadn't been, we would have stayed in the stall until they left, so we wouldn't embarrass them. It's best to avoid putting someone else in that position by watching what—and whom—you discuss.

Now, some nitty gritty bathroom basics that we're compelled to provide because even though they are common sense rules, we hear frequent complaints that many people don't follow them:

- Keep the bathroom clean. Flush the toilet or urinal. Put the toilet seat down. Make sure the top of the seat is left clean. Replace toilet paper.

- Turn the water off.

- Put paper towels in the trash can. Dispose of sanitary products properly.

- Promptly report any shortage of supplies or malfunction in equipment to the appropriate person.

And don't forget to wash your hands!

Conquering the Conference Room

Although the conference room is not always in use and is likely to be empty at certain times of the day, do not consider the room a hideaway, even if your purpose is as innocent as wanting to spread out your papers on a big table to organize a major project. Many companies have limits on who can use the conference room, and violating these rules could get you into trouble.

Moreover, while the conference room may be shut off from outside distractions and the immediate view of the rest of the company, it is usually not a place to avoid being observed. You never know when anyone is going to pop in, with a large group in tow.

You need to follow appropriate scheduling procedures within your company regarding use of the conference room. It's awkward, not to mention ungracious, to have to haggle with someone else while trying to start a meeting. "We were here first" doesn't hold up to "We reserved the room." (For more on scheduling and preparing for meetings, see Chapter Ten, "Must We Meet Like This? The Protocol of Meetings.")

If you booked the room and it is being used, check with the scheduler, if there is one, to confirm your reservation. If you are correct, then either you or the scheduler can open the door briefly and catch the eye of the leader before again closing the door. This is a cue for the leader to step outside for a moment to discuss the situation. It's an attempt to avoid embarrassing him or her in front of the entire group.

Give the other group a few minutes to leave. If it doesn't, enter and make an assertive statement, such as "I see you are using the room and I booked it from 10 to 11, and I need to use it now." (Of course, if it is the CEO who is conducting the meeting, you might decide to find another room.)

As one of the most public rooms in your organization—the one to which clients are brought for important presentations—it's vital to keep the conference room in good shape. When your meeting is over, make sure that you pick up papers, pull off flip-chart pages, erase blackboards, return audio-visual equipment, put back chairs, and generally straighten up. You do not want the boss to be disturbed at the state of the room, ask who was the last to use it and find out it was you!

The same rules apply wherever conference rooms may be found—in airline lounges, even on luxury trains.

ESSENTIAL ETIQUETTE IN THE MACHINE AGE

People who normally respect the need to take turns and maintain privacy sometimes have blinders on when it comes to extending that behavior to using or sharing office equipment. A colleague who would never rearrange someone's desk may routinely leave the photocopier set on legal-sized documents. Someone who would be outraged if you read her mail may think nothing of looking over the fax you received. Until someone invents the "courtesy microchip"—a silicon device that automatically programs our equipment for gracious operation—we'll have to remember that the problem lies not with the equipment but with the people who use it. Devices that enable us to do our jobs faster, across greater distances, and with less human contact increase the need for diplomatic, cordial manners.

Actually, the do's and don'ts of sharing office equipment are no different from those for any other piece of shared property. The rules are quite basic:

- Learn how to use the equipment properly. If you guess wrong, you may inconvenience others.
- If you are sharing it, take turns.
- If it's empty, fill it.
- If it breaks, fix it or get it fixed.
- If you borrow it, give it back in the same condition you received it.
- Don't take, borrow, or snoop through what isn't yours.
- When you are done, leave the area and equipment neat, clean and ready for the next user.

We'll discuss how they apply to each specific type of equipment.

The Lowdown on Downloads: Computers/Word Processing Equipment

It's your responsibility to know how to use the company computer. If you need to ask for help or instructions after your initial training period, do so at a time that's convenient for the person helping you.

Some other tips:

- Coordinate your project so everyone will know in advance when the equipment is available. Be realistic about how much time you need. Respect office guidelines and timelines, and defer to projects with higher priority.
- Fill up paper in the printer, add toner, replenish the available supply of blank disks.
- Call the appropriate person when repairs are needed.
- Do not change the programming on a computer used by several people to suit your individual needs.
- Do not use someone else's disks or sign-on password without receiving permission. Keep your own disk labels up-to-date—it is not only efficient, but could help someone else if you were away from the office for any reason.
- Keep confidential papers confidential, including computer files. Don't look over anyone's shoulders. We once discovered a co-worker guiltily signing off a computer where the boss had earlier failed to sign off after using it. The co-worker,

it seems, had been rummaging through the boss's files, snooping for confidential plans and reports. We realized he was pathetically insecure—and also just plain nosy—but either way, we lost respect for him.

If you discover a co-worker violating the confidentiality of someone's file, you'll have to weigh your response. Remember that you could be blamed for the breach of confidentiality if someone sees you at the terminal after your colleague has left. You can be assertive and say to the co-worker, "I do not think that is appropriate." (For more on handling conflict, see Chapter Six, Courtesy Challenge: The True Test of Diplomacy.")

- Keep the area clean, taking your papers with you. When you sign off, leave the area and equipment ready for the next person.

A few cautions about computer fun and games: it's courteous and smart to respect corporate rules about playing computer games on company time. Taking up memory that is needed for other projects is just plain greedy.

The Proper Form for Feeding Copiers

The person who arrives first usually gets to use the copier first. If two people arrive at the same time, the person with fewer copies goes first.

- Let others interrupt your large project if they have only one or two sheets to copy. If you arrive when a large job is in progress, you can say, "Do you mind if I interrupt? I have just two copies to make."

    However, if the person with the large job has invested a lot of time setting up the copier—to handle special paper, to make reductions or enlargements, or to place graphics on a page—it's courteous for you to return later, if possible, rather than asking the person to reset the machine.

- Check the paper supply after completing a large copy job, and refill it if necessary.

- Don't use the machine to make personal copies unless you supply your own paper and do so in off-hours, provided that's an acceptable practice in your office.

- Do any necessary maintenance—such as resupplying toner or fixing paper jams—yourself. If you don't know how to handle these situations, it's your job to make sure they are taken care of. Don't leave it for the next person.

- When you clean up after yourself, make sure you take your original with you. Many a copy user has slipped up by leaving a confidential memo where it can be discovered! One office manager was copying personal medical forms and unknowingly left a receipt on the machine. The receipt was for treatment at a drug rehabilitation clinic. A colleague returned it to her, but impolitely told other people about her short stay at the clinic.

- Always remember to reset the machine after using it—usually to one copy, $8^{1}/_{2}$-by-11-inch size.

Reasonable Facsimiles: Fax Finesse

Be creative regarding the times you send faxed materials—early morning, or lunchtime, perhaps—when others will not be inconvenienced. This can also be helpful if you are sending faxes long-distance, since you can save the company money.

In order to save paper, make up a short fax cover page that attaches to the first page or use a commercially available cover sheet. Make sure that all pertinent information (discussed in Chapter Nine, "Written Communication: Write it Right!") is listed. This includes the "to" and "from" fax and phone numbers, the recipient's and sender's names and departments, the number of pages in the fax, the time and date sent, and any messages, including whether delivery is urgent. It's gracious to make sure that your fax gets where it is going.

Respect your company's rules regarding the personal use of fax machines: in some companies, you may never use the machine for personal business, while in others you can use them to order lunch, and still others let you use them for any purpose.

When sending a fax to a machine used by more than one person, call to let the recipient know when to expect it. Don't send unsolicited faxes—they tie up the machine, use paper, and are not considerate.

If you need to send art, use black and white art, because color does not fax well. It's courteous to make sure the recipient can read the information that you send.

If you go to use the fax and find an incoming fax, put the copy in the recipient's mail box. Don't read what isn't intended for you—stop reading after the cover sheet. Let the recipient know that you put the fax in his or her box, so the person doesn't haunt the fax room, thinking that it hasn't yet arrived.

Refill the toner and paper. Fix paper jams. Follow office protocol regarding programming of automatic dial numbers. It's rude (and potentially detrimental to your career) to wipe out someone else's programming.

Let the appropriate person know if service or repairs are needed.

Perking Along With Coffee Machines

An employer impulsively decided to switch the coffee in his office coffee pots from caffeinated to decaffeinated without consulting with or informing his employees. People not only noticed the change immediately, but by noon of the first day, there was open rebellion and dissension in the ranks. He now offers both coffee choices and has taken a solemn vow never again to alter the beverage options without input from the staff.

Coffee machines don't take care of themselves—someone has to fill, empty, and clean them. If this is not part of someone's job description, the task can be rotated or randomly assigned to whoever arrives first or leaves last.

However, if you drink from the coffee pot, it's your job to help maintain it throughout the day. Keep the coffee machine filled all day. If you empty the pot, start a new one. If you don't know how to start a new pot, learn how to do so. Wipe up any spills and keep your mug clean.

Many offices provide regular and decaffeinated coffee, as well as hot water and tea bags. Cream, sugar, sugar substitute, stirrers, and napkins should also be available. If you use the last of any of these supplies, get out refills or alert the appropriate person.

If the system is pay as you go, make sure that you do.

STRATEGIES FOR SENSITIVITY ABOUT SMOKING

These days, where there's smoke, there's ire. Smokers may feel as if a right they've enjoyed for a long time is being gradually taken away from them, while non-smokers may feel that someone else's bad habit is infringing on their personal health or comfort.

Etiquette doesn't require a debate to determine the correctness of either position, but it does demand sensitivity toward each point of view. Whether a smoker feels that what he does to his own body is his own business or is struggling to break an addictive habit, he deserves to be treated with respect and courtesy. Whether a non-smoker has a serious medical reaction to smoke or just wants to avoid exposure, his or her point of view should be acknowledged with consideration.

The trick is to balance these conflicting points of view with sufficient finesse to satisfy each position.

Smokers need to examine their motives for smoking and consider the message it sends. This does not mean you need to be apologetic about your habit, just conscious of when and how you choose to exercise it. Similarly, non-smokers need to make sure they are not acting in a self-righteous or holier-than-thou fashion.

We had a colleague who daily wore a "Smoking Stinks" button. He also posted anti-smoking slogans around his desk, such as "Smoking: Stuffing Burning Leaves Where Your Food Should Go." While he had a right to his views, those actions exceeded the boundaries of polite office conduct.

Many office buildings are now smoke-free. It's good manners to adhere to company policy. If your office has non-smoking areas, honor them. Disregarding these rules shows disrespect for the organization and for others who are in the area. A good rule of thumb for smokers is, when in doubt, ask about the policy and also ask for permission from whomever you are with.

You may of course smoke in your own office if company policy permits, but it is good to have a "smoke-eater" for the comfort of non-smoking visitors. It's all too easy for someone who is accustomed to cigarette smoke to underestimate the impact it has on non-smokers.

It is not polite to ask someone not to smoke when he is in his own office, unless company policy prohibits it. What people do in their own offices is their own business. You could perhaps suggest that you meet in a non-smoking space, such as a conference room.

If the smoker asks you, "Do you mind if I smoke?" be honest. Remember, though, that you are often making a decision about whether you'd rather risk offending the person or co-exist with the smoke. If you want to say no, do so courteously, such as "I'd rather you didn't—thanks for asking," for example.

If someone starts to smoke in your non-smoking office, it's appropriate to say, "This is a non-smoking office."

A smoker is in charge of managing his or her own supplies of matches, lighters and cigarettes so that they don't delay business by going in search of materials. Pipe smoking can involve too much paraphernalia for business.

We once knew a woman who "quit" smoking ten years earlier, and then proceeded to "borrow" at least a pack of cigarettes a day from co-workers. Although she did have the manners to thank her co-workers and to periodically buy them a supply of replacements to reimburse them for the expense, her sources would have preferred her to buy her own cigarettes.

Be aware that the odor of smoke clings to your clothes and your hair. Cigars have a lingering and, to many people, an offensive smell. Other people find the odor of pipes to be nauseating. As a smoker, you need to evaluate your grooming routine and consider whether your clothing might need extra cleanings. Also consider using mouth spray.

MASTERING MUTUAL MANNERS

As simplistic as it sounds, the Golden Rule—Do Unto Others As You Would Have Them Do Unto You—applies in many office etiquette situations. We encourage you to be assertive about your feelings and rights while taking into consideration the feelings and rights of others. When people treat each other in a dignified, decent manner, it ultimately helps everyone to perform most productively.

Chapter 6

COURTESY CHALLENGE
The True Test of Diplomacy

I have never been hurt by anything I didn't say.

—CALVIN COOLIDGE

The true test of your etiquette skills comes not from dealing with people who are polite but from dealing with those who are rude. We call this the courtesy challenge. If someone calls you a name and embarrasses you in front of your colleagues, it's tempting, easy—and wrong—to reciprocate the rude behavior. When someone criticizes you unfairly, it tests your self-control and your knowledge of proper conduct to be graciously self-assertive in your response. The ability to react courteously when others treat you impolitely is a sign of strength. It's also a learned behavior, one that improves with practice.

We've identified several circumstances in which the courtesy challenge applies in business situations. In this chapter, you'll find out how to:

- handle conflict with co-workers politely.

- show appropriate respect for rank.

- provide tactful criticism as well as methods for coping courteously with criticism when you are on the receiving end.

- handle put-downs and off-color, racist, and sexist comments.

- deal with out-of-bounds behavior.

THE KEYS TO MANAGING CONFLICT

Agreement is made more precious by disagreement.

—PUBLILIUS SYRUS

Conflict can occur whenever two people don't agree on how to handle a situation. Given all the varied personalities, differing backgrounds and wide-ranging viewpoints we encounter at work, the surprise is not that there is so much conflict but that there isn't even more!

Disagreement, of course, doesn't have to escalate into bullying, back-stabbing, and bickering. When you can examine the argument as a professional dispute—rather than categorize it as a personal attack—you stand a better chance of working out your differences. However, because we are emotionally invested in our work, it's difficult to put our feelings aside when our proposal is rejected or our job description is revised. Even so, there are some techniques we have found to be effective in helping to resolve conflict.

A Polite Process for Handling Conflict

Define the conflict. This is a mental step you need to take before discussing the situation with anyone else. Take a deep breath. Be specific in determining what the disagreement is about. Don't generalize or label the person, as in "He's just lazy." Instead, describe the specific behavior or situation that causes conflict. Do two people want the same office? Does another person ignore your request to take his turn and write up the meeting notes? Is someone blocking you from accomplishing a goal?

Consider your alternatives. Because you have only so much time and energy to invest in disputes—and because you want to be considered a reasonable person—you need to pick your fights. Is this one worth pursuing? Do you have more to lose than to win? Has the boss already made up her mind? If you let the other person win, it might give you bargaining chips in the future. Is this the right time to attack the problem—or would it be better to wait and develop a long-term strategy?

Talk first to the individual involved. You need to give the person who is causing you the difficulty a chance to correct it or explain it. The sooner you do so, the better. Many people avoid this step out of fear or reluctance, going directly to the boss to solve the problem. The boss may in turn say, "If you have a problem with Jayne, discuss it with her." Accepting responsibility for dealing with issues that affect you is part of being a professional.

When you speak to your co-worker:

CHOOSE A GOOD TIME. Ideally, your discussion will be in private, at a time convenient to both of you, when both of you can be comfortable and undisturbed for as long as the discussion takes. It may help if the discussion is on neutral ground—the conference room, as opposed to your office.

BE SPECIFIC ABOUT THE BEHAVIOR YOU WISH TO DISCUSS. It's effective to be direct, as in

> "I prefer that my telephone calls not be interrupted." Focus on the action and how it affects you. Provide specific examples.

> "I need to receive the research by the deadline we discussed in order to produce the report on time." Make sure you are clear that you don't like the behavior and that you express your feelings about it.

> "When I do not receive the weekly status numbers by 3 p.m. Friday, I feel frustrated and concerned because I can't do my job."

STAY CALM. DON'T BLAME OR NAME-CALL. Assume, for the moment, that the other person is unaware of the offensive behavior and wants to stop it. You can say, "I know you may not realize this, however I have trouble concentrating when you talk loudly to yourself."

Be cautious with "you" statements. They can make people defensive and sound as if they are assigning blame. There's a big difference in tone between "You forgot to sign the contract" and "Please remember to sign contracts in the future." "You" statements also can lead to a chain reaction of aggression followed by aggression, as in "You're a jerk," "No, *you* are a jerk." Avoid them whenever possible.

Listen. Give the other person a chance to tell his or her side of the conflict completely. Relax and listen. Try to learn how the other person feels. Use SOFTEN skills (See Chapter Three, "Big Techniques for Small Talk") to show that you are listening.

Separate the issues and deal with each one separately. People will tune out if the conflict is defined in too broad terms. Notice the difference between "The bookkeeping is too sloppy" and "I have trouble reading your notations. I've also noticed that the entries were not kept up-to-date." Keeping the discussion specific and organized allows you to focus on specific, organized solutions.

Develop a mutual solution. Point out areas of agreement. Propose your solution and then listen to those suggested by the other person. It may take the form of something like, "I can provide you with the research. The deadlines we've set, though, aren't realistic."

Let each person indicate which solutions he or she would consider appropriate. Discuss each one and pick the one that both of you can live with.

State the solution in a specific way. "I will let the receptionist pick up the calls for your desk." "I will post all the week's entries in the books by 2 p.m. Friday."

Follow through. You may have to remind the person of the agreement. You may have to renegotiate. You may need to follow up in writing.

Decide whether you need to take the situation to the next level. You might have to be satisfied with some progress, even if you didn't get all you wanted. You might have to agree to disagree—in effect, to say to each other that the problem cannot be solved. You might want to continue the discussion with someone at a higher level if the matter is important enough to you, or significant enough for the organization.

STRATEGIES FOR POLITELY COPING
WITH PRICKLY PERSONALITIES

If all of our co-workers were rational, reasonable people, the steps listed above would solve most work conflicts. Alas, some people refuse to behave in a constructive fashion. We've listed several types of prickly personalities, and our ways of graciously dealing with those individuals. While we have found these to be effective and courteous strategies, remember that you can't force anyone to do anything. You can just give it your best shot.

Battling the Bully

When dealing with a bully—whether it is a boss who berates you or a co-worker who intimidates you—you might first want to avoid a confrontation if one isn't necessary. This may mean limiting your actual contact with the person and instead using memos or electronic mail for communication.

When you are attacked, though, it's important that you be assertive. If you believe in your point, don't give in. The bully may belittle you and the problem, so you need to be firm. You might need to be a "broken record" repeating the same phrase—such as, "Even so, I need your expense vouchers."

If you can avoid reacting to a temper tantrum—by keeping your tone steady and your body language neutral—it could deny the bully the satisfaction of knowing you are frightened. Even so, you may need to raise your voice so you will be heard. If you turn to face him or her and pay undivided attention, you may even surprise the bully into silence. That concentration may defuse the reason for the behavior—the need for power and attention. It can be helpful to get allies—a coalition of people who agree with you regarding a problem.

Confronting the Non-Combatant

When a co-worker refuses to discuss a problem, the appropriate response depends on your relative positions in the work hierarchy. If you are equals, you may need to take the problem to a supervisor, perhaps after warning the non-combatant that this will be your next step. Or, you can point out that even though neither of you is in charge in this situation, resolving the problem will make for a more pleasant work environment. If the person refuses to talk, you can try saying, "I assume from your silence that you agree with the proposal and unless I hear otherwise, I'll proceed." The person usually starts talking.

Co-opting the Complainer

You need to be firm with someone who whines. If the person offers excuses or states that the solution won't work, repeat how important the problem is to you and state that it's necessary to try to solve it. You can offer to re-evaluate the solution for effectiveness at a later date, but don't settle for the status quo. After the agreement is reached, you'll probably have to remind a complainer that he or she promised to try the solution. If someone complains to you about another person, suggest that you both go talk to the person who is under discussion. That usually stops the complaining if the complainer doesn't want to confront but just wants to complain.

Convincing the Conspiracy Victim

A conspiracy victim sees any criticism as the result of a plot against him rather than one with a legitimate basis in reality. This type of person may try to deflect the conversation to, "Everyone is against me. Poor me." Or, the employee may deny the validity of the complaint by attacking the source: "Who is saying that? Did you know she's never liked me?" In a paranoid manifestation, the employee might become obsessed with who else is aware of the problem—particularly if you are the employee's supervisor. The best way to deal with this personality is to point out problems early on so that they really don't generate a chorus of complaints. It's also vital that you keep the focus of the discussion on the specific issue, rather than on the motives or identity of the complainant. Emphasize that because *you* consider the issue to be a problem, you want to discuss possible solutions.

NICE GIRLS DO CONFRONT

If a supervisor or co-worker consistently asks an employee to do something that is not part of the employee's job description—such as making coffee or buying gifts—it's the employee's responsibility to point out the discrepancy and suggest that it be dealt with. Unfortunately, when the supervisor or co-worker is male and the employee is female, the woman may have particular difficulty, based on cultural conditioning, in raising the issue.

From childhood, many women learn that society expects them to be helpful, perhaps even compliant, in meeting other people's needs. They are taught subtly that a "good girl" puts her own needs last. Women also learn that it's not "nice" to pick fights, or sometimes even to disagree. They are told to "be a lady." This can handicap women in the workplace when they need to raise issues, object to a proposal, or defend their own needs. It can lead to a situation in which women silently seethe as men "take advantage" of them.

The misperception that women first need to address is that they are wrong in objecting to a situation, whatever it may be. Clearly, some expectations are not reasonable and other expectations may just not reflect your understanding of your responsibilities. In either case, it's appropriate for the woman to initiate a dialogue to clear the air.

One woman was irritated that her boss expected her to take notes during a meeting when the expectation didn't apply to any of her male peers. After she spoke to her boss, he initiated a policy in which the duty would be rotated among all team members. She was glad she had mentioned her discomfort.

Failing to stand up for yourself is being discourteous to yourself. Being quietly resentful of someone else shows disrespect for that person, because it dismisses the possibility that he or she would be willing to change. Women owe it to themselves, as well as to their co-workers, to take the first step in resolving conflicts by speaking up.

When women do bring up their concerns, it's important that they be assertive, not aggressive, in their demeanor. They need to keep a steady and calm voice, maintain eye contact, have confident body language and avoid accusatory gestures, such as finger-pointing. The words they use also are important. For instance, women should remember to use "I" statements.

HOW TO SHOW RESPECT FOR RANK

To be humble to superiors is a duty; to equals, courtesy;
to inferiors, nobility.

—BENJAMIN FRANKLIN

The United States is a relatively egalitarian society, but even so, there are circumstances in which some people's ideas and opinions are more equal than others. Everyone may be allowed to state a position during a meeting, for instance, but the view of the boss or client may have the most weight. At some level, failure to acknowledge authority or position becomes insubordination, which is grounds for dismissal in most organizations.

When you show someone deference, you are temporarily yielding to another person out of respect for his or her position, age, or role. When you come to that "yield" sign, you slow down, look around and gauge the traffic before proceeding with caution.

Too much deference is obsequiousness, a fawning flattery that may come across as insincere. Too little deference is rudeness, a failure to acknowledge or act on the respect that someone has earned.

In the United States, the best supervisors do not lord their position over their employees; they just quietly expect that their decisions will be implemented. It is not good manners (or good management) for a supervisor to treat employees as inferiors. Organizations do vary in the kinds of duties they expect subordinates to perform, but a boss should be gracious in the way those expectations are communicated. Even if the boss is rude, though, that does not relieve the employee of the responsibility to perform the task adequately.

Your actions should acknowledge your position in the hierarchy. Failure to follow the chain of command, for instance, is a faux pas that could cost you advancement. You are demonstrating respect for the position as much as for the person. Your boss is your boss—whether your boss is younger than you are, of a different gender or from a different ethnic background. Being surly or uncooperative shows bad manners.

It's reasonable for a company to expect you to show respect for elders, those of higher rank, visitors, and clients. In a meeting, lower-ranking younger executives, for example, should wait for higher-ranking older executives to sit down or wait for instructions as to where to sit. When a visitor, client, or high-ranking staff member enters an office or conference room, all should stand—male and female. When the person entering is a colleague you see daily, you certainly should look up and acknowledge that person's presence.

FINESSE WITH FEEDBACK:
Providing Tactful Criticism

Mean what you say, say what you mean, and don't say it mean.

—UNKNOWN

A client complained to the owner of a small business about the office manager's hairstyle which, she said, was too long and sexy, and distracting since she played with it when talking to clients. The owner took the office manager aside privately. Stating up front that she cared about the manager's success with the company, she added that what she was about to mention fell into the category of fine-tuning. The owner then spoke about the client's complaint, one with which she agreed now that it had been pointed out. The office manager changed the hairstyle and gained credibility.

Attacks are never good manners. Yet sometimes—if someone has made a mistake, exhibited inappropriate behavior or needs to improve his or her grooming—feedback is required.

When such feedback is unsolicited, it may not be well received. Look at your own motives before offering negative feedback. Is the situation the other person's problem—or yours? Consider whether it is "your place" to be offering what might be considered criticism.

Pay particular attention to how you provide the feedback. Try to phrase it as tactfully as you can, while still being accurate.

"This report needs additional background on the client" communicates the same general message as "You did a lousy job on this report." The first is specific, neutral, and descriptive. The latter is personal, vague, and attacking. It also uses a "you" statement, which can be considered aggressive.

Be specific about the behavior. Do not attack the person. That is not your role, although you do have a right—and sometimes a requirement—to critique performance. If you are nervous, script your statement out and practice. Pay attention to your nonverbal signals. This is one time when you especially do not want to send a mixed message. Keep a record of how you do. Remember that a bad reception does not necessarily imply that you delivered the message inappropriately—some people just can't handle criticism.

Whether it is provided to a colleague or employee, negative feedback should always be given in private.

Make sure that you are judging everyone by the same criteria—criteria that everyone is familiar with. The feedback should be constructive, clearly citing specific, relevant concerns.

During the feedback, you can soften the blow by mentioning the individual's strengths and contributions.

You also must suggest possible ways the employee can improve.

Some examples of tactful feedback:

"The work you did on the handouts demonstrated creative use of computer graphics. Please remember to use the spell-checker in the future—there were three misspelled words."

"Thank you for getting the project done on time. That was important. In addition to the time factor, the quality of the data is critical. The examples you listed were not as current as they could be. Next time, please provide up-to-date information."

COPING WITH CRITICISM:
When You're on the Receiving End

People ask you for criticism, but they only want praise.
—W. SOMERSET MAUGHAM

A lawyer had instructed his receptionist to answer the phone by saying, "Good morning. Mr. Price's office. Nancy Engle speaking." However, when she was busy, she answered instead, "Just a minute." When the lawyer explained to her the need for answering the phone professionally, she became defensive, arguing that her workload was too great and that he failed to appreciate her contributions. The lawyer remained frustrated at her inability to modify the specific behavior he mentioned, and the matter became a source of tension between them.

When you are the one who is receiving the feedback, what you should do first is to *listen*. Hear out the critique. Don't become defensive or paranoid.

While the tendency is to make excuses, admit it if you know you did something poorly. It can either stop the conversation cold, or allow it to move forward. For example, one worker told another, "You're just too sensitive." When the other person answered, "Yes, I know I am," the discussion ended quickly.

Make sure the criticism is valid. Ask for specific examples of the behavior. Consider the source, especially if the criticism is unsolicited. The person may have hidden motives.

You do not have to listen to criticism that is delivered in an antagonistic manner. If the person is yelling and name-calling, you can state, "I can see that you are upset. I will be glad to discuss the problem with you when you calm down."

You should pay special attention to any patterns in the comments you receive. Recurring remarks, particularly from several different individuals, can be a sign of genuine trouble.

Understand and accept criticism. If the feedback was given in good faith, even if you don't agree with it, don't be defensive and make the other person feel uncomfortable for having tried to help you. That's bad manners.

Particularly if the criticism comes from your supervisor, be prepared with notes or questions. State that you will work on improvement. Be enthusiastic about your ability to correct anything necessary.

Always end on a positive note. Say that you appreciate the person's comments and time. After all, if the situation were hopeless, he or she wouldn't have spoken to you!

Rebuffing Putdowns and Attacks

It is much easier to be critical than to be correct.

—BENJAMIN DISRAELI

Some people are just plain mean. Much as it might help you to understand the reasons, your priority should be focusing on how you will deal with the person's behavior. Don't automatically make assumptions about people's motives. Not all negative behavior springs from a malicious intent. One man was mortified when a woman told him she found it offensive to be called "Hon." "My grandfather always called women 'Hon,' and so did my Dad," he explained. "I meant no disrespect by it." He did, though, stop using the expression.

If you are being put down or attacked, try to keep your cool. Think about your response. Speak calmly, combining self-control with self-respect. Focus on the remark, not the person. Try to limit your emotional involvement. Take a deep breath.

A polite response can be something like, "Why are you saying that?" or "I'm offended by that." If the person is sarcastic or makes a snide remark, you can say, "That sounded like a dig. Did you mean it that way?" We provide some other examples in Chapter Seven, "What To Say When You Don't Know What to Say."

Don't try to force an apology from the person.

If someone else is being put down or attacked, calmly interject that the attack may not be fair or that the speaker may not know the whole story. You might say, "How do you know that's true?" or "That's not been my experience." If the attack persists, you can say, "I don't want to hear it" and walk away.

If the criticism is valid, mention that the criticism should be discussed directly with the person rather than behind his back.

You need to be careful in deciding whether to tell someone about remarks that have been made. Consider that person's personality: will it be hurtful or helpful for the person to know what people are saying? Is that person aware of the attacker's attitude? Does the criticism say more about the speaker than it does about the subject?

QUASHING OFF-COLOR, SEXIST, OR RACIST COMMENTS

Interested in purchasing a new car that she had seen advertised, Denise Cahill visited the showroom, asking detailed questions about the car's performance, maintenance record, and available options. She was impressed by what she heard and was thinking seriously about making the purchase when the car sales manager asked, "Is your husband here for the test drive?" The manager was unaware that one simple, sexist question cost him the sale.

What you say makes a difference. Even when the words you choose are not intended to upset or insult someone, they can cause lasting damage. Others may perceive your remarks as indications that you are ignorant, intolerant, or insensitive. It's important to think carefully whenever you speak, because casual off-hand comments can be discourteous.

Vulgarities are, by definition, rude. Comments about someone's race, gender, sexual orientation, religion, or ethnic background are rarely pertinent in a work environment. When it is pertinent to bring up these topics, they need to be handled sensitively.

Guide for "Politely Correct" Conversation

1. *Know and use the correct terms and pay attention to sensitive issues.* It is insulting to use an outmoded term—such as "girl" for a woman or "Negro" for an African-American, even if you do so out of innocence or ignorance. You also should know which current issues may raise someone's hackles, and avoid those topics. If you can't be educated about these matters, be quiet.

2. *Avoid using insulting terms.* Even if you are speaking in jest, even if you have heard a member of the designated group use the term, that does not make it permissible for you to use a slur. Jokes can be misunderstood. Minority groups often have a sort of family mentality, in which "it's OK for me to insult my sister, but it's not OK for you to do so." People will vary in their sensitivity to these sorts of remarks, but it's best to avoid using them.

3. *Ask yourself if the reference is at all appropriate.* When in doubt, don't bring it up.

   Mentioning a minority group calls attention to differences, even if the reference is as vague as Ross Perot's "you people." These labels indicate that you are conscious of these differences and that they may be affecting your behavior or perceptions.

   If a female does a poor job on a presentation, is it because her hormones are out of control? If someone who uses a wheelchair fails to return phone calls, is it because of his disability? If an African-American calls in sick on Jan. 15, is it because he is taking Martin Luther King Day off? Not necessarily.

At a manager's meeting, when a woman's upcoming wedding and vacation time for the honeymoon was mentioned, a female supervisor said, "Get used to it. Next it will be maternity leave." A pregnant female researcher was referred to by her boss as "half an employee" because he was reluctant to ask her to work the usual overtime shifts in deference to her condition. Both of these references were based on false assumptions and demonstrated a preoccupation with the employee's situation. Because the remarks were irrelevant, they were rude. When you hear someone making such a statement, dispute it politely. A simple "I don't think that's true" or "What does one thing have to do with the other?" can help keep these false assumptions from taking root.

4. *Be sensitive to all viewpoints.* Some people are not comfortable talking about sensitive topics such as race relations or providing background on personal choices, such as a strict vegetarian way of life; others welcome it. Remember that you are dealing with individuals, and that individual personalities and views vary. It's not fair or polite to make someone into a spokesperson unwillingly, just because he or she happens to be present. Acknowledge that there is diversity within all groups—there may be no "female" or "department head" or "Catholic" position on the issue, and even if there is, the individual may not subscribe to it.

If you don't want to discuss something, say so. You can say, "I'm not comfortable with having my views considered typical on this issue" or "I'd prefer to move on to another topic."

Demonstrate respect for all viewpoints, but especially those with which you disagree.

Appropriate Responses for Inappropriate Statements

Determining when a remark is offensive can be a question of judgment. However, if you are offended by something, it's appropriate to let the speaker know by saying something in a non-offensive manner.

When you hear comments that strike you as off-color, sexist or racist, you should address the remarks, not the person. Say, "I am offended by that comment and I don't want to hear it." Try to do this in private, at least initially.

You need not be shrill or strident. Just clearly state that the remarks are offensive and embarrassing and that you are asking the person to stop making them. Silence might work against you—the person might think you agree! You can communicate your displeasure through body language—shaking your head from side to side while walking away—but the behavior might not stop as long as it goes unchallenged.

You do not need to explain your feelings or apologize for them. Anyone who attempts to make you do so is acting discourteously. If something makes a reasonable person uncomfortable, that should be reason enough for anyone to stop doing it.

Be specific. Say, "I don't want you to use that term" or "I don't think those jokes are appropriate."

Get support, if you need to, from others and/or from management. Keep a record of the comments, and document the dates they were made and what you said in response.

Discrimination and harassment are illegal. Know your legal defenses.

DEALING EFFECTIVELY
WITH OUT-OF-BOUNDS BEHAVIOR

People should know what you stand for.
They also should know what you won't stand for.

—ANONYMOUS

A district manager had the habit of greeting his sales associates with a hug, which he viewed as a sign of friendliness. However, the hugs were not always welcome, and some of the sales associates considered them to be sexual harassment. As a result, they stayed away from him whenever possible.

Sometimes it's not what people say but what they do that is out-of-bounds. Someone may come back from lunch drunk every day, exorbitantly pad travel expenses or sexually harass employees.

Your ability to handle this kind of out-of-bounds behavior is part of being assertive. You should not be reluctant to call attention to this behavior and confront it: it's being polite to yourself. It's also good manners because sometimes people don't realize they are out-of-control. Sometimes when others assertively confront them, they will change their behavior. For instance, it would have been better if a sales associate had said to the district manager, "I'm not comfortable with hugging. I'd be happy to shake hands."

We know it is difficult to make this kind of statement. The alternatives are to tolerate the unwanted behavior, to avoid the person and perhaps eventually leave the organization despite the opportunities available, or to allow the tension to build to such a point that you ultimately explode. Clearly, the most difficult alternative in the short term—speaking up—is the best long-term strategy. From an etiquette standpoint, it is gracious because it is courteous to yourself and to others, who have an opportunity to continue an improved relationship with you.

When you see someone stealing company property, using drugs, or involved in some other type of illegal activity, your manners as well as your morals are tested. When reacting to rule-breakers, you need to consider not only what's proper, but what's right and what ensures your personal safety.

First, be sure of whatever it is that you are confronting the person about—you are, after all, dealing with that person's reputation. A false accusation based on a misunderstanding can irreparably damage your relationship with that co-worker, and distrust can be very divisive. Consider, of course, whether that person might use his or her power or position to instead discredit you. Before doing anything else, document instances and examples. Follow your company's guidelines.

Depending on your relationship with the person and the circumstances, you can:

- Talk to the person in private. Find out why the person is doing what he is doing. A question can be less threatening than an accusation: "Did I see you loading a computer into your car?" That gives the person the opportunity to respond, "Yes—the boss said I could use it to finish up that report on vacation."

- You can tell the person you are aware of the offending action and that this is a warning to stop. This can be effective and is often required if you are a supervisor. For your own protection, make a note of the date and content of the conversation. Regardless of your role, be specific. You can say, "I want you to stop brushing up against me in the supply room," or "I won't cover for you if you are late from lunch."

- If the action continues, report it to an appropriate person, perhaps someone in your company's legal or human resources department. Also continue to document incidents.

- If you are concerned about your safety or the impact on the company, report the situation to company security. In some cases, steps may be taken to ensure your anonymity.

Remember that it is not impolite to "snitch" on someone who is engaging in behavior that could harm others. In fact, it's actually being courteous to all those who follow the rules.

EXCEPTIONS TO THE RULE

Should you always take the high road when someone is treating you rudely or acting inappropriately? As with many etiquette dilemmas, this is a case-by-case decision, depending on the specific circumstances and your own personality.

When you face a tug-of-war between what is proper and what the situation requires, you'll have to use your best judgment about the appropriate action. Whenever possible, though, we encourage you to set a polite standard.

GRACE UNDER PRESSURE

Rising above impolite conduct has multiple advantages. You will be perceived as a person of high standards, someone who doesn't "stoop" to a discourteous level even when under fire. Your actions may raise the consciousness of others, who might even follow your example. But most important, you will have the satisfaction of knowing that, whatever the circumstances have been, you behaved appropriately and courteously—an accomplishment worth celebrating.

WHAT TO SAY WHEN YOU DON'T KNOW WHAT TO SAY

True eloquence consists in saying all that should be said,
and that only.

—FRANÇOIS DE LA ROCHEFOUCAULD

The ticking away of seconds can seem like hours when we are at a loss for words. It makes no difference why we have nothing to say: we can be equally tongue-tied if we don't know how to react when someone compliments our performance or when we've just learned that a corporate vice president has been fired. We may be stunned into silence upon learning that the boss's child has been diagnosed with a serious illness, a client is getting divorced, or our subordinate has suffered a miscarriage. At that moment, our intentions are in conflict with our reactions. We don't know what to say precisely because we want to say exactly the right thing.

Of course, silence isn't golden in such situations. Praise and compliments need to be acknowledged. In the case of bad news, while saying nothing or saying the wrong thing may not actually make matters worse, it certainly could make us—or the other person—feel that way.

Etiquette can help train your response reflexes so you know what to say and how to say it when confronted with a conversational dilemma. For instance, you may still be left with a feeling of sadness at a colleague's situation, but you can take comfort from the fact that you acted in a gracious manner.

Etiquette also can help you deal with new situations—ones in which you don't know what to say because you've never had to comment on that situation before. Perhaps a gay colleague will announce, "Today is my first anniversary with Scott!" Or, perhaps an employee will say, "My husband told me last night he wanted a divorce," or "I just found out my sister has cancer."

100

In this chapter, you'll discover

- The seven essential guidelines for listening to bad news, and the four keys for an appropriate response.
- How to weigh the pros and cons of responding verbally or in writing.
- The five categories of conversational conundrums, specific suggestions on what to say and what not to say.
- How to accept compliments and praise graciously.

Through it all, we'll provide you with ways to communicate courteously.

THE BEST WAY TO HELP SOMEONE BREAK THE NEWS

The manager noticed that the receptionist seemed unusually tense one morning. Although no one could find fault with her performance, she seemed distracted and abrupt. During a break, the manager asked what was wrong, expecting to hear about a work-related problem. Instead, the receptionist burst into tears. "Last night my car was stolen," she said. "The police still haven't found it."

When faced with unhappy circumstances, we should first acknowledge that no words can accomplish what we wish they could: to serve as a magic wand to soothe our co-worker. We will not be able to erase that person's problem or pain. The best we can hope for is to ease the listener's unhappiness by expressing understanding and support.

Our responses in the case of a co-worker's positive news are easy and automatic in part because the only negative emotion we may be experiencing is slight jealousy at the person's good fortune. A simple "Congratulations" or "That's great" rolls off the tongue. We say, "I wish you well in your new position—you deserve it" or "I'm excited for you" because we can acknowledge and state those emotions without any significant internal conflict.

But when the news is difficult, we're emotionally distracted. We may be thinking, "Could that happen to me?" or "Aha! I thought something was going on based on the number of meetings they've been holding lately," or perhaps even, "Well, the jerk finally got what was coming to him!" It would naturally be bad manners to express all our thoughts in those circumstances. But feeling the need to say *something, anything*, we might blurt out the first thing that comes to our minds—which could turn out to be hurtful or unsuitable. Or, we fall silent as we sort through what's appropriate—and what's not—to express.

In difficult circumstances, tears may be appropriate and even helpful to the person delivering the news. People sometimes break down when providing bad news because it is extremely difficult to discuss a painful situation. There's something about verbalizing a problem that makes it real. Admitting something to yourself is very different from acknowledging it to someone else. While you may ultimately be glad that you shared the news because of the help you could receive, for the moment your instinct might be to deny the truth for just a little while longer.

What to Do When You Hear Bad News

The etiquette impact, then, for someone hearing bad news is to make it as easy as possible for that person to get the words out. Here are some ways you can make it easier:

Let the person talk, and listen to what he or she says. Don't interrupt. Use SOFTEN skills (see Chapter Three, "Big Techniques for Small Talk") to communicate your attention and caring through body language.

Respond. Don't avoid or ignore the topic. Express your understanding through an appropriate phrase such as, "I'm sorry." Let the person know you comprehend how he or she feels by saying something like, "How difficult that must be for you."

Don't talk about your situation or engage in one-upmanship. The person needs to be the center of the conversation. You should never say, "I know just how you feel" unless you have confronted the very same situation in your own past. People who are distressed want and need to hear from those who have shared their circumstances, but "close" doesn't cut it. If you haven't gone through a parallel crisis, the conversation will take a comparison-contrast detour, or the person will feel more isolated as he or she thinks, "How could she possibly equate that situation with mine?" Dismissive statements such as, "Oh, well, that's nothing, I had *three* miscarriages before my son was born," are not helpful. What's more, pain is pain—it can't be objectively measured on a sliding scale. No two people are alike in the way they deal with bad circumstances. It's bad manners to tell someone how he or she *should* feel, as in "Well, just be glad this happened after you qualified for your pension."

Listen some more. Once the Pandora's box of emotions has been opened, your colleague may need to vent. Let him. Don't back off if your colleague starts to cry or otherwise expresses unhappiness, unless the colleague indicates a desire to be alone. It's a compliment if someone can feel comfortable being emotional in your presence. Give the person permission to be upset—acknowledge that it is appropriate under the circumstances.

Don't be judgmental. This is not the time to say "I told you so" or to lecture the person. We're all human, accidents happen, and placing blame doesn't make anything better. Even stating, "it may be for the best," can be insensitive. It may not be comforting, for example, for someone who has experienced a loss to hear, "It was his time." Cynical statements in times of crisis, such as "That's the breaks," also are not courteous.

Don't find solutions unless asked to do so. The person will let you know if your advice is wanted. Unsolicited suggestions—"If I were you, I'd get a lawyer and sue the pants off them"—can be emotionally confusing at best. It is not your place, unless asked, to tell anyone how to handle a crisis. In fact, people generally would prefer to hear that you think they have acted appropriately on their own.

One dentist told us he got so tired of receiving unsolicited advice from some of his patients when he was going through a difficult divorce that he asked them to keep their mouths open wide much longer than was technically necessary!

Acknowledge the importance of the situation to that person. When your life has been altered, it's difficult to carry on precisely as before. You have been changed by the event. In time, routines may resume, but you need people to understand that you will be temporarily sidetracked. The listener should handle this diplomatically, with expressions such as, "What can we do to help you out?" rather than, "Darn! I guess this means you won't be available for negotiations on the Shiemke contract." It is insensitive to focus on how a situation has inconvenienced you, rather than the impact it has had on your colleague.

It can sometimes be comforting to let a person know you have already heard the bad news, eliminating the necessity of repeating or explaining the situation to you. State it simply and directly, "I heard about your sister's car accident," and proceed from there.

How to Break Your Own Bad News

When you are the one who has bad news to share, you might want to discuss it first with a co-worker who possesses the kind of skills we've just discussed. This can help you vent some of your emotions and allow you to be more calm in subsequent retellings. To the extent possible, you'll also want to respect the chain of command and probably tell your boss yourself.

This respect for hierarchy also applies to good news. A writer and an editor who worked in different departments of a communications company decided to announce their engagement in separate simultaneous meetings with their supervisors. Each supervisor was asked not to mention it to anyone else until it could be confirmed that the other supervisor had learned the news.

THE FOUR KEYS TO MAKING THE RIGHT RESPONSE EVERY TIME

The techniques you use to respond to a difficult conversational situation can make all the difference in the way your response is received.

1. *Make your response appropriate to your relationship with the person.* What you say should always be a reflection of your relationship with the person—such as whether it's a colleague or your supervisor, a client or a vendor; how well you know that person and for how long. If you are close, it can be appropriate to comment per-

sonally, saying, for instance, on the death of a colleague's mother, "From the way you spoke so highly of her, I know what a positive influence she was on you."

However, we all have a strong sense of what is suitable in any specific situation, and a violation of that can be an intrusion, regardless of any good intentions. It's not appropriate, for instance, for a casual acquaintance to pry into the details of a medical malady. When someone oversteps the boundaries of a relationship, it doesn't matter how good the phrasing or how genuine the caring.

If the person asks that your conversation remain confidential, respect that.

2. *Don't say too much.* Many people get in trouble by going on and on, trying to fill an awkward void of silence, when a short, sincere comment would be more effective. A simple "I'm sorry" can often be enough.

For example, when Marjorie Brody's daughter was diagnosed with diabetes, many people in her office, in an attempt to make her feel better, gave examples of family members who had diabetes. However, their stories focused on the struggles and inconveniences the family members faced. Naturally, this was depressing. In most cases, "less is more."

This rule also applies in situations that you have not previously encountered. For instance, in the case of the first anniversary of the gay couple, you can always echo back what the person said, as in "Has it already been a year!" or ask a general question, such as "Are you going out to dinner to celebrate?"

3. *Say it kindly.* Your tone of voice and body language can and should be used to convey empathy. You do not want to appear dismissive or flippant. The words you choose should be tactful and gentle, not abrupt or abrasive.

4. *Go slow.* Many people want to say something quickly so they can "get it over with" and move on to the next topic. This is where those blurt-out blunders often occur. Take your time to think about what you're saying and its impact on the listener. It's OK if you appear to grapple for words, because that shows you are being sensitive. The listener probably won't remember how quickly you said it, but she will recall if it was very well—or very badly—phrased.

If you have been the recipient of a poorly-executed response during a difficult conversation, try to take the person's motives into consideration. A well-meaning blunder is still well-meaning. Undoubtedly, you are highly sensitive at this time. If it is a question of ignorance, you can gently correct the misinformation by saying, for example, "My brother contracted AIDS through a blood transfusion. His wife and four children, though, show no signs of the disease." However, it may be appropriate—and make you feel better—to tell the person courteously how such a remark hurt you. You might wince slightly, say "Ouch," or point out, "I'm not sure I want to hear that right now." This can help your co-worker to be more sensitive in the future.

WRITTEN VS. VERBAL RESPONSES:
The Pros and Cons

You may not hear bad news directly from the affected person. It could come through the office grapevine or a more official announcement. You then have two options: a verbal or a written response. Each has advantages and disadvantages.

If you respond verbally and in person, you may have to seek out the person. You might go to his office as he packs up to leave, or visit him at the hospital or at a funeral home viewing. The advantage is that the encounter is face-to-face—you can both see and communicate through body language. If you are far away and make a telephone call, the person can hear your tone of voice. In either case, the response can be rapid. You might, however, catch the individual at a bad time to talk.

A written response typically is slower. It does give you more time to provide more information about your feelings. It also can be a more permanent expression—a card or a letter may be saved and re-read when the immediacy of the crisis has passed. We have heard numerous stories of people saving and re-reading these letters to gain continual comfort. In fact, we suggest that you do send a letter whenever it is appropriate to do so. This form of communication is especially recommended for funerals and for long-distance relationships.

You can, of course, combine the two methods whenever you consider it to be appropriate.

MASTERING THE FIVE MOST COMMON CONVERSATIONAL CONUNDRUMS

While each circumstance is unique, we've found most conversational conundrums fall within five categories:

- Disappointment relating to work or employment.
- Difficult or uncomfortable family or personal situation.
- Behavior or grooming faux pas.
- Unwanted social obligations.
- Out-of-line comments.

You need to respond based on the specifics of each situation, particularly, as we've already mentioned, gearing your reaction to your relationship with the person. Nevertheless, it can be helpful to know that most situations fit these groupings. When you learn to recognize and understand the category, you will see how appropriate responses may have several common elements.

1. *Work-Related Disappointment.* Work-related disappointments include situations such as a colleague who is laid off, fired, or passed over for promotion.

What sometimes makes this category difficult is that you may understand, or even agree with, the rationale for the decision, even as you empathize with the individual involved. Or, the person may have made a mistake that justifies the action, although the last thing he'll want to hear is, "You goofed."

You may recall that the University of Michigan lost the 1993 NCAA basketball championship game to North Carolina. Some blamed the loss on U of M player Chris Webber, who called a timeout during the last minutes of the game when there weren't any left. President Bill Clinton found something appropriate to say in a special handwritten note that he sent to Webber shortly after the game. Here is what he said:

Dear Chris:

I have been thinking of you a lot since I sat glued to the TV during the championship game.

I know that there may be nothing I or anyone can say to ease the pain and disappointment of what happened.

Still, for whatever it's worth, you, and your team, were terrific.

And part of playing for high stakes under great pressure is the constant risk of mental error.

I know. I have lost two political races and made countless mistakes over the last 20 years. What matters is the intensity, integrity and courage you bring to the effort. That is certainly what you have done.

You can always regret what occurred but don't let it get you down or take away from the satisfaction of what you have accomplished.

You have a great future.

Hang in there.

Sincerely,

Bill Clinton

What that letter did, quite effectively, was:

- Acknowledge the difficulty of the circumstance and admit the inability of words to change it.
- Point out what the person did well, especially given the difficulty of the circumstances.
- Indicate to the person that he is not alone in having made a mistake.
- Remind him that others have survived, and thrived, after making serious mistakes.
- Emphasize that the way the person deals with and learns from the mistake—rather than focusing on the mistake itself—is what is significant.

- Put the mistake in context—as one incident in a long, as-yet unfinished series of events.

- Remind the person of future possibilities and opportunities, providing personal words of encouragement.

We consider all those to be great steps in a strategy for dealing with someone who has suffered a work-related disappointment.

PHRASES TO USE:

> I'm sorry that it happened to you.
>
> That's a tough break.
>
> I wish you the best.
>
> Is there anything I can do to help?

PHRASES TO AVOID:

> Things work out for the best. (That's inaccurate—they don't always.)
>
> I told you to start looking for another job. (That's judgmental.)
>
> Boy, is management stupid! (That's an unsolicited judgment, second-guessing the bosses for whom *you* still work. A ticked-off employee might just spread the word regarding what you said, and then you'd be in trouble.)

2. *Family or Personal Difficulties.* Private or family matters sometimes extend into the workplace. It could be that a colleague or a family member is diagnosed with a serious illness such as cancer, is hurt in a car accident, undergoes a divorce, suffers a miscarriage or experiences a death in the family.

Because of the personal circumstances, the appropriateness of your response will depend greatly on the nature of your relationship with the person. It could be a faux pas to comment on the divorce of a passing acquaintance, for example, just as it would be poor manners to ignore the divorce of a close friend.

PHRASES TO USE:

> I'm sorry. This must be a difficult time for you.
>
> I can identify with that. I've gone through a similar situation and know how difficult it can be. (This should be said *only* if you really have gone through an analagous situation.)
>
> Is there anything I can do?

PHRASES TO AVOID:

> Oh, she'll be fine. (Actually, the accident victim or ill person might not be, and it's not gracious to force someone to admit *that*, even to oneself.)
>
> Well, that's what happens when someone drinks too much. (That's assessing blame.)

It's about time you two split. I always thought he was a jerk anyway. (Passing judgment and insensitive.)

3. *Grooming Gaffes.* We all make minor grooming mistakes from time to time, and, usually, we can laugh about them later. Sometimes the error is minor and easily correctable—his fly is open, she has lipstick on her teeth, or her bra strap is showing. Other times, there may be an ongoing problem, such as body odor or bad breath.

You need to use good judgment about mentioning such things. Examine your motives—do you want to help or embarrass the person? Is your advice unsolicited?

It is both possible, and preferable, in some circumstances to ignore the problem. In fact, it's good manners to do so in the case of an isolated incident such as a burp or a fart. The person is secretly hoping you *didn't* notice and it's a kindness to let him or her think you haven't.

On the other hand, if it will save the person more embarrassment, it's usually best to say something tactfully. This is especially true if the person can do something about it right away—such as zipping his fly or pulling up her slip. Do it privately, kindly, and be prepared for possible hurt feelings, embarrassment, and even resentment.

Usually the best approach is to simply describe the situation. You can say, "Your fly is down" or "You might want to check your fly." The person can then figure out what to do about it. In our informal survey of participants, all the men agreed that they would want to be told.

If the problem can't be dealt with immediately—such as a run in a stocking or a button off a jacket—you might choose to let it go. Chances are that the person will discover it on his or her own.

If the problem is an ongoing one, you can also initiate a discussion about how you conquered the same problem, without ever directly mentioning the person's problem. We know a woman who casually commented over lunch one day how impressed she was with her dermatologist. You can say something like, "I have started to use XYZ dandruff shampoo. It has really helped." This allows the other person to follow up—or not—on the topic. An indirect way to handle the problem with someone's bad breath is to eat a breath mint yourself and offer the other person one at the same time.

If these gaffes are holding someone back, it is the responsibility of that person's manager to say something.

PHRASES TO USE:

Tom, your fly is open.

Sally, you have lipstick on your teeth.

PHRASES TO AVOID:

Hey, everybody, look at the hole in his shoe! (Public embarrassment, situation not immediately correctable.)

Ed, you stink! (Unkind phrasing, a personal attack.)

4. *Unwanted Social Obligations.* Sometimes we don't know what to say because we cannot tell the person what he or she wants to hear. This may be the circumstance if you need to refuse an invitation, turn down a date with a co-worker, or choose not to contribute to a departmental gift.

It's important that you not be manipulated into doing something you don't want to do—that's being rude to yourself! Don't lie. Don't make excuses, which might lead to further discussion as someone counters your arguments. Be assertive.

If someone insists after a polite refusal, that person is the one who is being rude. One man who was turned down for a date persisted by saying, "I don't give up that easily. Your mouth is saying one thing but your eyes are saying another." The woman responded, "You're wrong" and walked away.

PHRASES TO USE:

I am unable to go.

Thanks for the invitation, but I have other plans (if you do—they might ask what, or check to see whether it's true.)

Thank you, but I don't socialize with people at work.

Thank you, but I don't mix business with pleasure.

I am unable to contribute.

PHRASES TO AVOID:

That's a stupid idea. (Insulting)

I wouldn't be caught dead with you. (Insulting)

5. *Out-Of-Line Comments.* We dealt with several types of out-of-line comments in the human dynamics section of Chapter Six, "Courtesy Challenge: True Test of Diplomacy," but such situations can also leave us speechless. They shouldn't.

Sexist or racist remarks, vulgar language, off-color jokes, put-downs, and sarcasm are sometimes made specifically to provoke a reaction.

Depending on the circumstances, silence—combined with a cold stare—might be eloquent. At other times, we recommend you say something.

The best approach probably is the direct one. Focus on the behavior, not the individual. The person who issued these remarks might feel compelled to defend or escalate the statements if he or she feels under attack.

We repeat what we said in Chapter Six: it's usually best to confront the perpetrator in private, at least initially. In case of repeated verbal harassment, document your displeasure and take your complaints to the proper authorities.

We never said it didn't take courage to be courteous!

PHRASES TO USE:

I'm offended by that.

I don't think that's funny.

Why are you saying that?

She always speaks highly of *you*.

Please stop.

PHRASES TO AVOID:

You're a jerk. (Insulting, although, sigh, we've known some people who would consider that a compliment.)

That's a stupid and ignorant thing to say. (It may be stupid and ignorant, but so is attacking someone personally, as this remark does.)

Also try to avoid laughing to mask your embarrassment. It might be misunderstood as a sign of appreciation of the out-of-line comment.

THE GRACEFUL ART OF GIVING AND ACCEPTING COMPLIMENTS

To refuse praise is to seek praise twice.

—UNKNOWN

An engineer was reviewing plans for construction of new offices with his client. As they discussed issues, he took extensive notes on a legal pad, sometimes tearing off a sheet of paper to sketch how an alteration might be arranged.

When the session ended, the client thanked him for his time and input. "By the way," she added, glancing at the notes he had taken, "you have very nice handwriting." Embarrassed, the engineer answered, "Oh, no, I don't. Really, it's just my pen." Amused, the client responded, "Well, I have the same kind of pen, and it never made my writing look like that!"

Many of us have been taught from an early age not only to avoid showing pride in our accomplishments but to tune out anything that comes close to a compliment. When someone praises a suit or outfit, we may modestly say, "Oh, this old thing!" even if it is a brand new purchase. We know that jealousy and resentment may result from extra attention, so we downplay our contribution to an important project. This deprives us of enjoying the praise we have earned. It also can make people reluctant to give thanks or compliments, since the likelihood that the favorable remarks will be dismissed is very high.

Others of us make the opposite mistake: when someone praises us, we puff up and say, "Yeah, I'm really something, aren't I!" If you persist in doing this, you will develop a reputation as a conceited or arrogant individual.

It is possible to accept thanks and appreciation without false modesty, preening, or boasting. When you do so graciously, you show respect for the person giving the praise because you are not taking issue with the content of the remark or implying that you have an inflated opinion of yourself. What's more, there are times when compliments are required, and you should be prepared to give as well as receive them.

The Courtesy of Compliments

In many companies, it's taken for granted that you will do a good job. That expectation doesn't mean that a good job is easy to do. Every day, employees overcome obstacles ranging from difficult personalities to technological hassles, from constant distractions to insufficient staff, and they still manage to do quality work. For this, they receive a paycheck.

However, along with receiving a paycheck, employees need to receive appreciation for a job that's well done. How frequently this recognition is paid varies within industries as well as with the individuals involved, but some praise should be part of every work environment. When in doubt, people should err slightly on the side of excess.

Clients who hire us ask us to coach executives about how to recognize their employees and how to acknowledge employees' help and contributions. According to a study of personnel directors, 26 percent of employees leave because they do not feel they receive enough recognition.

"Keep Up the Good Work"

The number of compliments you give to coworkers will reflect your personality as well as your philosophy or management style. The way praise is delivered, though, has a great impact on how it is received.

When praise comes too late after the event, it loses some of its impact. When someone doesn't receive expected praise, he may be insulted. When someone who is lavish with praise gives a compliment, the praise loses some of its impact.

Six Ways to Give Praise

You certainly don't want a compliment to backfire and make someone feel worse than if you had never issued it. To ensure that your praise has the intended positive effect, follow these *Praise Pointers.*

Be consistent. Compliment everyone who deserves it. If you leave out one individual or one group, even inadvertently, those who are left out will be insulted. Also be equitable in your reasons for compliments. For instance, it's sexist to compliment women only on how they look and men only on what they do.

Be specific. It's nice if you say, "That report really seemed like a lot of work." However, the praise will be even more effective if you say, "Breaking out the sales figures by category helped me to see your point about market trends." Being specific can be especially helpful if you are reluctant to praise because the recipient may "get a big head" or because you want to improve the performance of a problem employee. Recognizing a particular action makes clear exactly what you approve of, without issuing a blanket endorsement.

Be direct and eliminate qualifiers. Go ahead and say you like something, assuming that you did. Qualifying a compliment detracts from it, as in "Pretty good work on the McKenzie presentation."

Don't confuse praise with feedback. You generally don't want to give a compliment with one hand and take it away with the other. If you say, "You did a fine job on the briefing for the managers. It would have been even better if you had incorporated graphics," your praise will lose some of its punch. Allow the person to enjoy your praise and then, the next time he's preparing a report, suggest in advance that he add graphics. Similarly, don't attribute motives to the person you are complimenting. It's insulting to say, "Nice suit. Do you have a funeral or a job interview after work?"

When appropriate, give praise in public or in writing. The impact of a compliment increases dramatically when it is heard by others or when it is made permanent in writing.

Be timely. There's generally no real reason to delay praise. If you delay, you might forget to give it at all. In addition, it's a basic principle of behavior modification that immediate praise helps someone understand the connection between two events and encourages a repeat performance.

The Polite Way to Accept Acclaim

Many people are so embarrassed or surprised when they receive a compliment that they become flustered in their response. If accepting compliments were an easy thing to do, Hollywood actors and actresses wouldn't need to read those little note cards when accepting an Oscar! Here are some steps to help you with your "acceptance speech."

Acknowledge the compliment. This confirms that you heard what the person said. It should be the first step you take after receiving praise. If you say nothing other than, "Thank you," you will have accomplished this goal.

Don't argue with or attempt to qualify the compliment. If someone says you did a good job on a report, don't say, "Oh, it was nothing," or "Well, it wasn't as thorough as I had hoped to make it." You're not only putting yourself down, but are insulting the person giving the compliment by implying that he or she doesn't have sufficiently high standards. Instead, you can say, "Thanks, I worked hard on it."

Even when you genuinely disagree with the reason for the compliment, don't insult the speaker. If you sincerely believe you did a lousy job on the report and are astonished to hear it praised, don't say so. Instead, you can say, "I really appreciate your words" or "Your words mean a lot to me."

Don't add to the compliment. Trying to make more of a compliment is a faux pas. If someone says, "You impressed the client," it would be rude to say, "Impressed them? I blew them away! They didn't know what hit them!" This will come across as boastful, even if it happens to be true.

When possible, anticipate praise and prepare your response. If you think you might be praised, take a cue from Oscar winners and consider in advance what you might say. Are there others whose contributions you wish to acknowledge? Lessons you learned from the experience that you wish to share? Try out your response by tape-recording it. How does it sound?

What a Nice Thing to Say

Have you ever been envious of someone who always seems to know the right thing to say, regardless of the circumstance? Well, so were we—until we stopped to consider that they weren't born that way.

Start listening closely to others in situations in which you're at a loss for words. If someone says something that seems especially appropriate to you, make a mental note. In this etiquette arena, you're not judged on originality but on effectiveness.

People learn what to say when they don't know what to say by:

- Hearing what others say.
- Trying out different expressions in different situations.
- Practicing or mentally rehearsing for spontaneous situations they may inevitably confront.

So can you.

YOUR PERSONAL CHALLENGE

Having the right thing to say at the right time is a skill that can be learned. Challenge yourself to practice a variety of techniques to see what feels comfortable for you. Being a good conversationalist has major benefits professionally and personally.

Chapter 8

THE TELEPHONE:
Your Voice to the World

If my boss calls, get his name.

—ANONYMOUS

Your business has two entrances—the front door and the telephone. Most business-es get far more telephone calls than walk-in clients. Even those companies that rely on street traffic need employees with good telephone manners, because many people call before making the trip. And just as you wouldn't blockade your public entrance, make it sloppy, or select a rude receptionist, your telephone manners shouldn't make people rethink whether they really want to do business with you.

A company representative once screamed to a caller, "What do you want!" Stunned, the client said in a cool but calm voice, "Excuse me. What did you just say?" The representative then quickly reflected and said, "Oh, did I just say that? I'm so sorry." If she hadn't realized her rudeness and apologized—and many people don't understand how badly they come across on the telephone—the client would have taken his business elsewhere.

And people do just that all the time because they were put on "hold" too long or because the person on the line was negative. Perhaps you've even done so yourself. People assume that if you aren't competent to answer the phones, how can they trust you to do other business?

It's not just what you say, but how you say it.

One otherwise amiable supervisor believed that talking on the telephone was something to accomplish as swiftly as possible. (Perhaps, as a youngster he was told telephone calls were expensive!) So, when he received a call, although he had been joking and laughing with co-workers a minute earlier, he became gruff, blunt, and unreceptive to the caller, speaking in harsh tones with short answers. Unfortunately,

114

those who dealt with him exclusively by phone had only his telephone behavior to judge him by. One client was shocked when he later met him at a convention and found out he wasn't the ogre he had expected.

In this chapter, you'll discover the keys to appropriate telephone manners. You'll find:

- tips on answering the phone, transferring calls, and handling holds.
- how to win the game of telephone tag.
- the Ten Commandments for placing calls that will favorably impress any caller.
- techniques for handling telephone troubles, including the irate caller.
- strategies for gracious use of telephone technology such as answering machines, voice mail, speakerphones, and car phones.

Equipped with these techniques, you'll be ready whenever opportunity calls.

HOW TO ANSWER THE PHONE WITH FINESSE

The telephone just might be the most convenient intrusion ever invented. It's an extremely handy tool when we're the ones doing the dialing. Through it, we get to ask our questions, coordinate our plans long-distance, and place orders for equipment and supplies. But when we're on the other end of the line, the receiving end, the telephone may be an enormous disruption. It interrupts important in-office discussions, sidetracks us from the project we were working on, and imposes the caller's priorities on top of our own.

The problem is, of course, that the caller can't know what was going on before the phone rang. It's certainly not the caller's fault that this is the seventh call you've received since arriving and that you have to prepare for a meeting that starts in five minutes!

Etiquette actually requires that callers be unaware of all these things—that you sound professional, pleased to hear from them, and ready to deal with their concerns, regardless of the reality.

You can build your business and enhance your professional reputation through polite and effective telephone answers. We know a doctor decided where to buy a beeper based on how cooperative and helpful the customer service representative was in providing information over the telephone.

What to Say

Effective telephone answers, like effective handshakes, serve to introduce you to another person through a mutually-understood protocol. Your answering technique conveys an image of both you and your company. Since you, of course, want the impression to be a positive one, it's appropriate to periodically review the way you answer your phone.

Test Your Telephone Techniques

Do you answer your phone within one to three rings?	Yes	No
Does your answer include a greeting, such as "Hello"?	Yes	No
Does it include your full name, rather than just your first name (which is too informal) or just your last name (which can sound too abrupt)?	Yes	No
Does it include a verb—as in "This *is* Debra Elliot" or "Debra Elliot *speaking*"?	Yes	No
If you share an extension, does your answer include your department's name?	Yes	No
If you regularly receive outside calls, does your answer include your company's name?	Yes	No
Is the answer fewer than 10 words long, so that the caller doesn't get worn out listening to it?	Yes	No

Score: The more "Yes" answers you can mark, the more polite your answer is.

You know that you should answer your own phone promptly and courteously. Let your phone ring once and pick it up within no more than three rings. Identify both yourself and your company.

Say, "Hello, this is Kim Stern," or "Kim Stern speaking," or "Kim Stern, Purchasing," or "ABC Company, Kim Stern speaking."

Avoid just saying "Kim Stern" or "Stern speaking"—both have an abrasive tone. Saying just "Kim speaking," on the other hand, is too informal for a business setting.

If you share an extension, say, "Sales Department, Kim Stern." It's important, too, to remember that if you answer the phone for someone else, your response will reflect on you, your company, and then the intended recipient. So if you say something unprofessional or rude such as, "She's taking another of her famous long lunch hours" or "How the heck would I know when he'll be back? He doesn't tell me what he's doing," it will cast you, and the intended recipient, in a negative light.

If your company has a long name—"ABC Company, Alphabet Soup Conglomerate"—come up with a way to shorten it. Don't combine a long identification with a long follow-up, as in "ABC Company, Alphabet Soup Conglomerate. Kim Stern speaking. How may I help you?" Keeping your telephone answer to fewer than ten words can prevent the caller from tuning out or becoming irritated.

Some phone systems have "inside rings" and "outside rings" (one ring for calls that come from inside the building and two rings for those from outside). Under these systems, you can decide by listening to the pattern whether to answer the phone by using the company identification. Otherwise, you may leave the caller wondering if he has reached the place he dialed.

If you answer the phone and it is not convenient for you to talk, explain your predicament and tell the person that you will get back to him or her. Say when you will—and make sure you keep your word!

If your phone is answered by a secretary and you are available, the secretary can say, "Who shall I say is calling?" Sometimes the secretary may ask, "Does she know what this call is in reference to?" or "Can I tell him what this is about?"

Callers, though, are not favorably impressed if they are put through the third degree before they are allowed to talk with you. You want your caller to feel valued and respected.

If you are unavailable, do not want to be disturbed or want your calls screened, it is polite for the secretary to say, "She is not available. Who can I say called? Is there anything I can help you with?"

You're either in or out, available or not. Don't blatantly base your availability to talk on the identity of your caller. It's just not gracious to obviously take only certain calls from certain people. If the caller finds out that you are unavailable only *after* he has given his name or learns that you are just not deeming *his* call worthy of your immediate attention, he'll probably feel slighted. It is, in fact, an insult to be told, if only through sub-text, "She doesn't want to speak with you" or "He doesn't have time to speak with you."

A department director we worked with told us this story: he called a company and the secretary answered. When he asked to speak to her boss, she said, "Let me see if he's here." She then thought she put the caller on "hold," but failed to do so. Turning to her boss, she said, "It's Bill. Do you want to talk to him?" The boss answered, "Not now. Tell him to call back." The secretary told the caller, "He's not in yet," although by this time the caller knew the truth. The caller was annoyed, and conveyed his displeasure when he did call back.

Remember that you always have the option of telling your secretary before the phone rings whose calls you will take.

How to Say It: The Power of Tone and Inflection

Answering the phone with a clear, pleasant voice conveys that you are both professional and personable.

When you speak on the telephone, the vocal and verbal components of your demeanor become exaggerated because the visual component of your professional presence is missing. Until visual phones come into common usage, your caller has no cues based on your clothes, eye contact, facial expression, or gestures. Through little more than saying "Hello" and your name, you may come across as preoccupied, whiny, curt, enthusiastic, or indifferent. The way you continue the conversation may give the caller the impression that you are friendly, helpful, conspiratorial, relaxed, or intense.

Try not to sound rushed, even if you are. With a little practice—and a deep breath—you can put on a convincing act.

Speak slowly and distinctly, paying attention to your diction. Smile into the telephone so that you sound enthusiastic. A mirror near the phone can serve as a reminder to put on a smiling face.

Keep your tone steady. Don't whisper, shout, or raise your voice.

If you are going to sneeze or cough, turn your head and cover your mouth or the mouthpiece. Say, "Excuse me." Don't chew gum or eat.

Avoid side conversations, including finishing a sentence before you provide your greeting. Complete the conversation with the person who is present before you pick up the phone, even if you just say, "Excuse me" before you put the phone to your ear. If you must interrupt to talk with someone who is present once you have picked up the phone, say, "Excuse me" to the caller. If you need to ask a question of someone else in the room to help the caller, ask if she minds if you put her on "hold" or say, "Let me check" to explain that you will temporarily switch your attention away.

Also be aware of background noises that might be heard over the phone and hinder conversation. If new offices are under construction nearby and a loud, high-powered drill is being used, explain the situation and apologize for the inconvenience. You may want to put the listener on "hold" while you move to a quieter location. When an editor called to discuss timeframes for one of our books, we were impolitely typing as he spoke. "Are you listening to me, or typing?" he asked. We stopped typing and apologized.

Similarly, if there is problem or interference on the telephone line, mention it and deal with it, offering even to return the call if need be. It's more polite to take the time to get rid of the sound than to go through an entire conversation irritated and distracted.

Tips on Transferring Calls and Handling Holds

In today's fast-paced business world, being put on hold is like getting stuck in gridlock: you are powerless to move ahead and uncertain when you will be on your way. Having your telephone call transferred is like being forced to take a detour: while you may eventually reach your destination, you'd prefer to take the direct route. An employee who can reduce the length of time someone spends on "hold" or who can make telephone transfers efficiently is as vital as a traffic officer at a congested intersection with a broken stoplight.

To minimize the frustrations for a caller, put people on "hold" and transfer calls only when necessary. Limit the amount of time involved in both processes whenever possible.

The first call always takes priority. If another call comes in while you are on the phone, you should put the original caller on "hold" only long enough to take a message from the second caller. Make sure that if you absolutely must terminate the original call—if, for instance, your CEO needs to speak with you—you apologize to the original caller for having to cut the call short. Also offer to call back as soon as possible, and then do so.

It's courteous to ask the person if he or she wishes to be put on "hold." To be clear, don't say, "Could I please ask you to hold?" That raises the question of whether "Yes" means "Yes, you can ask me" or "Yes, you can put me on 'hold'." It's better to say, "Could I please put you on 'hold?'" or "Would you please hold?" Then wait for the answer before actually doing it. When you return, first thank him or her.

If you have someone holding, get back every 20 to 30 seconds or so to check if the person is still there. Let the person know what is happening: "It will take me a couple of minutes to gather the data for you. I can ask you to wait or call you back in a few minutes" or "I thought he was almost through with the other call, but he's still on the line. Do you want to keep waiting or leave a message?" It's gracious to give people options—it acknowledges the importance of their preferences.

Be honest about the total length of time someone can expect to be on "hold." Don't say, "I'll be right back" unless you really will be. You also can say, "I'll be with you as soon as I handle this call."

If you can't deliver what the caller wants in a short period of time, it's better to call him back than to keep him waiting.

If you are transferring the person to the appropriate party rather than trying to handle the call yourself, give the person the extension before you make the transfer in case she gets disconnected.

Briefly explain the situation to the person you are transferring the caller to, so you can spare the client from having to do so all over again. You also want to let the next party know that this call is being transferred. It will serve as a warning that the caller's frustration level could be higher than usual and help prevent the new person from elevating it further.

Telephone Tag: The Game You Can Win

A banker with an inflated sense of self-importance had a policy regarding telephone messages: he would return calls only to those who called him three times. When he applied this policy to an important client, however, he made a serious error. It took only one call from his supervisor to get him to change his procedure.

Failure to return calls is one of the most common business complaints. In some sales companies, calls must be returned within the hour! If not, you may lose the sale.

When someone calls you, return the call within 24 hours. If the person is not there when you return the call, make sure you leave a message. Even if you don't have all the information a client or colleague may need, it's important that you demonstrate your availability and responsiveness. These are basic components of courtesy. If you can't return the call yourself, have someone do it for you.

Remember that you will be doing the caller a favor when you call back to explain that you can't help him or that you have encountered a difficulty. This allows him to move on to other alternatives. It only aggravates the situation to delay returning a "bad news" call. Someone may be holding a spot in a schedule or basing decisions on what it is hoped you will say. The sooner you let someone know the reality, the better equipped he or she will be to react.

If you promise to call someone back at a stipulated time—"next Wednesday," or "as soon as the inventory is over"—do so. You are in effect "standing up" someone if you don't call back when you said you would.

If you set a time for someone to call you back, be available when you said you would be. If something unexpected occurs and you can't be available, treat the situation as you would any other appointment that needs to be rescheduled. If you are able, you should call or ask your secretary or administrative assistant to phone the other person and explain the circumstances. Make sure to say when you plan to get in touch with the caller. When you do connect with the other person, apologize for the difficulty he had in reaching you and thank him for waiting.

When you are away from the office, make sure your co-workers have accurate information on when you will return so that repeat callers don't get several different versions of the best time to reach you. It's frustrating for a caller to hear, "He's expected in any time now," only to be told on the next call, "He'll be in this afternoon" and then on the third call, "Oh, he's on vacation all this week." Accuracy about your return is especially important in offices where your phone may be picked up by someone else before your voice mail has a chance to come on. It may be helpful to post a note on your desk near your phone indicating your expected time of return.

Messages do sometimes go astray. When that happens, it's gracious to admit it. One real estate marketing executive returned a call to a public relations copywriter a full month after the original call was made. He explained that he had just found the note buried under a pile on his desk. He apologized for the delay and asked if his assistance was still needed. That helped to erase the negative impression which had been created by his failure to return the call.

TEN COMMANDMENTS FOR PLACING CALLS THAT IMPRESS

When you are the caller, it's good manners as well as good business to try to make the conversation as convenient and efficient as possible for the person you're contacting. We've developed "ten commandments" to ease your way through the potential pitfalls:.

1. Apologize if you dialed a wrong number. Don't just hang up. It's rude, and call-tracing technology could trace the call back to you, which would reflect badly both on you and your company. When you apologize, don't argue about why the person isn't who you thought it would be. It's your mistake, not the recipient's! You may be irritated, but you should sound sincerely sorry. To avoid wasting everyone's time, a simple "I'm sorry. I must have reached the wrong number" will suffice.

However, before hanging up, ask the recipient if you reached the number you planned to dial. This keeps you from reaching the wrong party a second time. You may need to look up the number again. Remember to say goodbye.

2. Identify yourself and your company. Say, "Hello, this is Mary Jones of ABC Electronics. Is Mr. Smith available?" Identify yourself again to the client or customer if a secretary answered. It may take a few seconds for the listener to "tune in," so you might want to train yourself to speak more slowly at first than you would in a face-to-face conversation to allow the telephone listener to "catch" your name.

Don't assume that if you deal with someone regularly, you can skip identifying yourself when calling. In a business setting, that presumes an intimacy and a familiarity with your voice that just doesn't exist. It's rude to leave the person guessing for part of the conversation who you are and only ensures that she will be at least temporarily distracted during your talk.

If you identify yourself only as "John," you also may be setting yourself up for confusion (is it John in finance or John in personnel?) Even if you have an unusual name, it's best to use your full name, first and last. You can think of this as a form of personal marketing—it helps reinforce your name so that others are better able to address you and introduce you.

3. If you must leave a message or ask someone to call you back, it's polite to leave your number, even for those you call regularly, since it saves your party from having to look it up. You also should provide information on the best time to reach you, especially if you are going to be out of the office. If you are calling long-distance, good manners dictate that you call the person back yourself rather than ask the person you called to bear the expense.

4. Ask if this is a good time to talk. "Dropping in" unexpectedly by telephone can be as rude as doing so in person.

Be realistic about whether the matter in question really should be discussed over the phone. Perhaps a face-to-face encounter, when you can read the other person's expressions and have more of his attention, would be a better solution.

If you need to handle the situation by phone, take the other person's schedule into consideration. In some companies, first-thing-in-the-morning calls are best—employees have the entire rest of the day to accomplish whatever else needs to be done. Other organizations may allow more leisure for discussions at day's end, around 5 or 6 P.M., when things are winding down. If you deal with someone on a regular basis, ask if there is a day of week or time of day that is preferable. Not only is it in your best professional interest to make sure he or she has the time and mindset to devote to the discussion, it's a matter of manners. It's impolite to rush someone or to intrude when the person is actually quite busy.

Explain the purpose and probable length of your call. Be realistic and be honest. Don't say, "Do you have a few minutes?" when it will take fifteen minutes. Say something like "Tom, I need to talk about the distribution plan. It will take about fifteen minutes. Is this a good time?"

You may want to call to say you will call back later and ask when would it be convenient to do so. Of course, if the person says, "Now's as good a time as any," you need to be prepared to discuss the matter.

If you must call at an inconvenient time, apologize and explain why it is necessary.

5. Let the person know if someone else is on the line, or if someone is going to be listening to your end of the conversation, especially if one of you is on a speakerphone. You can say, "Brenda, Jason's here in the office with me to answer any questions regarding the production side."

6. Be organized. To make a call less of an intrusion, send or fax materials in advance, such as a report to be discussed that you can look at together to save time while talking. Sales personnel can send out "will call" letters, outlining the basic proposal that a prospective client can digest at his leisure, perhaps even noting where he has questions, before a follow-up call is made.

Divide your telephone message into segments and build in appropriate pauses so that the listener can respond. You don't want to make a five-minute presentation on what you want, why you want it, when you need it—only to find out that someone else deals with such requests.

Once you have reached the appropriate person, avoid squandering the listener's time by structuring the conversation, perhaps even writing an outline of key points. Start out by stating the purpose or problem, then outline the options and their ramifications, and end with some sort of a conclusion. This makes the discussion easier, more logical, and faster than a free-form, unstructured conversation.

Make sure you have all your materials ready so that you do not have to fumble for files. Cross off the main points on your outline as you address them, so that you don't get sidetracked and skip something significant.

7. Listen to what the other person is saying. Obvious as this point may sound, the impersonal nature of the telephone makes it easy to "tune out" during conversations. When the other person is speaking, it may be tempting to doodle, straighten papers on your desk, watch happenings in the office, and otherwise fail to listen. This defeats your purpose and is poor manners. You may need to force yourself to listen closely by taking notes.

8. Deal with distractions. This helps to make your call efficient, which is an important courtesy to the person you called.

Avoid side conversations with someone else in the room. As we explained earlier, this is just rude. If you must stop your conversation, let the person on the line know. Say something like: "Excuse me one moment, please."

If someone comes to your office when you are on the phone, she should leave. If she doesn't, you can pause, say, "Excuse me," to the listener, and then say politely and firmly to the visitor, "I'll be happy to talk when I'm through with this call."

If someone is in your office, don't pick up the phone unless you are expecting an important call, and then explain that to your visitor.

9. *Watch your language.* Some people become too informal on the phone; others sound stiff. Ideally, the language you use will be about the same as if you were at a meeting making a presentation. You want your diction and grammar to reflect your professionalism.

Be careful what you call the person you're speaking to. Call him or her by name with the correct title. Don't use Ms. if she prefers Mrs. Don't use "honey," "sweetie," or "dear." Don't use first names unless it's appropriate to do so. And if you are told you can use first names, don't overuse them.

Be careful about using "you" statements. "You forgot" or "You neglected" or "You must" can sound accusatory on the phone, even when said in a moderate tone. Instead, put your comments in the form of a question: "Could you get that to me by Thursday?" "Did you complete the report on that project?" Or, use "I" statements: "I need the report by Thursday."

Use verbal prompts to encourage the speaker: "Uh huh," "I understand," "I see," and "OK."

Be positive and polite when responding to and making requests: "I'd be happy to look into that" and "Please remember to ..."

10. *Close the conversation.* Talking too long is like overstaying your welcome. *You* may think the listener is fascinated but, in reality, he may be drumming his fingers and rolling his eyes, waiting for a break so he can tactfully get off the line. If you suspect this is a recurring problem for you, try placing a clock on your desk and monitoring the length of your calls. When you reach a reasonable limit, tell yourself, "Time's up. Sign off."

End your phone conversation with a conclusive statement such as, "I'll get the final figures to you by noon Friday" or "I can see we have to do more research into this before implementing the plan. Why don't we talk again? Would Tuesday be convenient?" If you leave matters hanging, it's as half-considerate as dropping someone off in the block where he lives but not at his doorstep.

Include a polite acknowledgment, such as, "It's been nice talking to you" or "Thank you for calling." You want an upbeat ending.

Finally, hang up carefully. Don't slam the phone down or drop it. And for heaven's sake, don't comment on the conversation ("What a character! I thought he'd never stop talking!") until the phone is securely in its cradle.

HANDLING TELEPHONE TROUBLE

Being polite when you are on the telephone is, of course, only half of the equation: much depends on the person at the other end of the line. You need to know how to handle telephone trouble—those situations in which something beyond your control goes wrong.

We've divided these kinds of situations into several categories, and have summarized how to handle them in the *Telephone Trouble Tipsheet*.

Telephone Trouble Tipsheet

PROBLEM	WHAT TO DO
You get disconnected.	The caller should redial.
You walk into someone's office and find he is on the phone.	Apologize quietly and leave.
Someone interrupts you when you're on the phone.	Say "Excuse me" to your caller, tell the visitor you'll get back with him later.
A co-worker doesn't return telephone calls.	Be vague but cordial to the caller. Take a message—again. Solve the caller's problem if possible.
Someone doesn't return your call.	Give the person the benefit of the doubt. Call back. Leave a message that sets a deadline.
No time to talk.	Admit the problem and offer to call back.
Callers who are difficult to listen to.	Tell the caller of your difficulty early in the conversation and ask him to correct it.
The irate caller.	Let him vent. De-escalate the emotion of the call. Restate the problem. Solve the problem if you can.
The unfocused caller.	Ask questions. Make summary statements.
The persistent caller.	Be direct. Say you will call if he or she is needed.
Overheard personal calls.	Find a private time and place to make personal calls. Pretend you aren't listening, or take a short walk when someone gets or makes a personal call.

Confusion about Connections

It's awkward when a conversation ends abruptly due to technical difficulties. No one likes to be cut off or left hanging.

If you become disconnected during a call, it's the caller's responsibility to redial. He knows where he is calling from. If you are the recipient of a disconnected call, wait a minute or two and stay off the line. The person who called you may be switching to a less problematic telephone. If you are the caller, dial your party again as soon as possible and apologize for the problem, even if it's not your fault. You can say, "I'm sorry, we somehow were disconnected. I think we were talking about the quarterly review."

It's important to complete the call by redialing, even if you were near the end of the conversation when the disconnection occurred. When you don't call back, it's as rude as walking away from someone in the middle of a conversation. What's more, even if you were almost finished, you never know if the person you called had still more to say. If the person who made the call does not call back in a reasonable amount of time, it's OK for you to call him or her back. You can say, "I'm not sure if we were through talking when the line went dead."

Disconnections often occur when someone is on "hold" or is being transferred. It can be very irritating to have to call back under these circumstances, but try not to show your frustration. Most often, the mistake occurs because of unfamiliarity with the office telephone system, not because of a deliberate attempt to "lose" your call. Of course, if you are making the transfer or putting the person on "hold," make sure that you know how to do so. If you inadvertently disconnect someone who then calls back, first apologize and then make sure you provide the number that you are transferring the call to.

Competing Communication

Talking on the telephone has enough pitfalls without having your attention diverted by someone who is physically present and wants to speak with you.

If someone is on the phone and you don't realize it when you walk into her office, apologize quietly and leave, because it's almost always impolite to loiter while someone talks on the phone. Even a brief interruption can disrupt the flow of the conversation or derail the person's train of thought.

If the call is not going to be lengthy or confidential, the person in the office may motion for you to sit and wait. Do so quietly without distracting the person.

While you may be tempted to "contribute" to the telephone conversation as you sit and wait, it's usually best not to do so. Even though you can't avoid eavesdropping, it's more polite to avoid calling attention to the fact that you're doing so. Adding to the discussion also is interrupting, and it's difficult for someone to listen to two people at once. Follow the lead of the person on the phone: if you are asked for your contribution, it's fine to give it; if the person chooses to brief you after hanging up, the topic is fair game. Otherwise, we recommend that you act as if you did not hear the conversation, since you of course weren't really meant to do so.

We mentioned earlier that if someone is in your office when you get a call or arrives shortly afterwards, she should leave. If she doesn't, you can say, "Excuse me," to the telephone listener, and then say politely and firmly to the visitor, "I'll get back with you later."

If you urgently need to speak with someone who is on the phone, don't stand by his desk. Leave a note on the desk and return to your own desk to await his return call or visit. If you have a persistent problem with someone who hovers around your desk during telephone calls, find a time to talk with him about that behavior. Explain that you find it distracting, and assure him that you will be glad to deal with him when you are off the phone.

Many Happy Returns

You can't make other people return their phone calls, much as you might like that power. You can, however, deal appropriately with other people's shortcomings in this area.

When people don't return phone calls as promptly as they should, a co-worker may be left to handle the unhappy person who had been expecting a call. No one enjoys covering for a boss or co-worker who hasn't returned calls, which is why we always recommend that you return your own calls. However, when you encounter a frustrated person who has been waiting for a call, you have three basic courses of action.

1. *Be vague but cordial.* Don't promise what you—and your co-worker—can't deliver. You don't want to say, "Jake will be in at 11" unless you know he will be. It may be preferable to say, "He's not in right now. May I take a message?" If you recognize that this is a repeat caller, you can say, "Yes, I recall speaking with you yesterday and gave him your message." This puts the burden where it should be—on Jake. Providing wrong information—such as "We shipped the materials Wednesday" when they actually didn't go out until Friday—is worse than providing no information at all.

2 *Take a message—again.* By taking a message, you are promising the other person that you will bring the matter to your co-worker's attention. This is not the result the person was looking for, but it may be all you can do. It also may soothe the caller, for instance, to vent some frustration by speaking with a live person rather than leaving yet another voice mail message. You can indicate that this is a repeat call on the message itself or say as you deliver it that the person was upset at not having heard back from your co-worker.

3. *Solve the caller's problem, if possible.* If it is within your realm of responsibility—and often even if it isn't—you can earn points for your company (and yourself) by meeting the caller's needs. This can be particularly effective when dealing with little requests, such as "Could you send me a copy of the annual report?" You can let your co-worker know that you performed this service and hope that perhaps she will some day return the favor.

If your co-worker is taking advantage of you by failing to return calls and letting you deal with his problems, you can assertively let him know that you are uncomfortable with this behavior. You can say, "This caller was upset. I'm not comfortable handling problems that are not my responsibility. Let's work out something so I don't have to handle these problems in the future."

How do you get someone to return your telephone calls? It's gracious to give people the benefit of the doubt; perhaps this is a particularly busy season for them or your message may have been lost. For this reason, it's better to call back after a reasonable amount of time has passed rather than to sit and stew. One scheduler attempting to arrange a speaker for a conference was angry that a phone call had not been returned—until she learned that the speaker had been in a car accident!

Make sure that your tone and language are non-accusatory. You can acknowledge your persistence to the person who answers the phone, "I know I just called on Tuesday, but I was hoping to finalize this order by the end of business today." You can make it clear graciously that you won't give up by asking, "Is there a good time to reach her?" or "Is there someone else who can help me?"

When someone you deal with on a regular basis fails to return calls, you can sometimes speed up the response by leaving a message that includes a deadline, such as, "Could you please let him know I need to hear from him by 3 P.M. in order to fax the materials for the meeting?" You also can leave a reverse deadline—"If I don't hear from her by noon, I'll assume the contract is in the mail." Both of these responses free you to pursue other action, and avoid pestering the person who answers the phone.

If someone complains of having had a difficult time reaching you, be sympathetic. Acknowledge her frustration, perhaps saying, "I'm sorry I didn't get back with you more quickly" or "It's been one of those weeks!" Of course, if you have a good reason for failing to return a call, provide it. You don't want to appear indifferent to the person's desire to reach you.

No Time to Talk

To help ensure that it will generally be a good time for you to talk when the phone rings, always have pen and pencil ready to take notes. To graciously speed up calls that come at inconvenient times, avoid interrupting the caller and limit your own talking. Ask questions if you are looking for information, but try not to get off on tangents to the main point under discussion. Summarize the person's request—"So you are looking for three candidates for the position of human resources director?"

If someone telephones you at an inconvenient time, you naturally have two choices: to talk, or not. Your decision on whether to take a call will be based largely on the importance of the call and on the nature of the conflict. Can the call be handled quickly? Can the other matter—such as a meeting or the completion of a report—wait? Given the circumstances, will you be able to give the call the attention it deserves?

If you decide to take the call, you have only yourself to blame: the caller probably doesn't know your quandary. It's permissible and polite to admit the conflict to the caller. You can say, "You're catching me just as I'm heading into a meeting. Would it be possible for me to call you back?" This lets the caller know that your inability to speak with him is nothing personal. It also gives him the option of stating the purpose of the call quickly, perhaps indicating if there is a crisis that needs your immediate attention.

You're being polite both to yourself and to your caller when you are pressed for time and you ask to call back someone who you know is long-winded. You will not be able to listen to the person if you are concerned about catching a train or making an appointment.

Difficult Callers

Some callers are especially difficult to handle in a calm, courteous manner. In such cases, you need to pair patience with your politeness.

Callers who are difficult to listen to: Try to let the caller know of your difficulty early in the conversation. You can interrupt a soft speaker to say, "I'm sorry, but I'm having trouble hearing you. Can you speak up?" To make sure that you understand someone who speaks with an accent or with a speech disability, repeat back what you think the caller has told you. Ask yes-no questions. If the person is speaking too loudly, you can hold the phone further away.

The irate caller: The irate caller wants attention for her concern and may scream, accuse, or threaten to get it.

Let the caller speak and vent her anger, within reason.

De-escalate the emotion of the call. Keep your tone steady. If the person screams, point that out. Say, "I'd be happy to try to help you if you could speak in a normal voice" or "There's no need to swear at me." If the caller still screams or curses, you can say, "I can hear that you are very upset about this. I really would like to help you. Please call me back to discuss it after you calm down." Then gently hang up (don't slam down the receiver).

When talking with an irate caller, restate the problem so that it is clear that you understand it—that can help reduce the caller's anger. Indicate the appropriate person to deal with that situation if you are not.

If possible, solve the problem. If you can't solve it, explain why.

The unfocused caller: An unfocused caller wastes your time. He may want to tell a long story and you might not have time to listen. You need to get him on track politely. You can interrupt when he pauses and try to sum up the situation. For instance, you can say, "So you are calling to get a price on widgets?" or "Is this about the opening in accounting?" If you regularly deal with this sort of person, it may help to fax him a list of points you need to cover during your conversation. Depending on the person's importance, you might just have to allow him to prattle on!

The persistent caller: Someone who calls back repeatedly may be doing his or her job, but that can interfere with your ability to do your job. Many sales representatives have been trained to answer every objection except, "I'm (We're) not interested." Be direct: subtlety often doesn't work with persistent callers. Tell the person you will call back when it's appropriate: "I have received your résumé, and will call you when there is an opening that matches your qualifications." Or say, "Thank you for your time. However, we've decided to use another company's services."

Overheard personal calls: Personal calls are by definition private, but many office environments are not. Even if personal calls are permitted in your company, you need to be discreet about how you make them if they can be overheard. It can undermine your professional credibility if co-workers hear you babble in baby talk to either your children or your "significant other." Using your office phone for personal purposes—such as ordering concert tickets—might be seen as stealing time or money from the company. It can be embarrassing to have to provide personal medical information as others listen.

We encourage you to find a private time and place to make personal calls. If you lack a private office, perhaps you can make the call during your break and borrow the phone in an unused office.

Courteous workers in small offices walk away when it becomes apparent that someone has received or is making a personal call. If you happen to overhear someone's personal call, it's best to pretend that you weren't listening.

USING TECHNOLOGY GRACIOUSLY

One doesn't speak unless he is sure he can improve on the silence.

—UNKNOWN

Technology has changed the nature of our telephone calls. Speakerphones have made calls more public, answering machines and voice mail have taken the personal element out of leaving messages, car and mobile phones have given us the ability to talk in transit. This has led to new rules about the gracious way to communicate.

TDD Services, Speakerphones, and Teleconferencing

To communicate effectively through technology, keep the listener's needs in mind. Some technological devices can cause confusion unless everyone focuses on making the communication clear.

If you are using *a TDD service* (telecommunications devices for the deaf), talk as though you were speaking directly to the person you are calling, although slightly more slowly. Say "Go ahead" when you are ready for a reply.

If you are using a *speakerphone*, ask the person's permission first and communicate right away who else is in the room. One man didn't do this and the caller started talking about his date the night before—who happened to be the sales associate who also was in the room. Both, of course, were embarrassed.

One of the most effective ways to use a speakerphone is to explain or ask permission when you are switching over to it. You can use a regular telephone to dial your party or receive the call, and then once the call has gone through, say, "I'm going to put you on the speakerphone now. Lisa and Paul are also here and want to participate in the discussion."

In teleconferencing, if the parties don't know each other and it's a small group, everyone can say "Hello" so the caller can become familiar with the voices. If you are the "host" of the call, you should address people by name. You can say, for instance, "I agree with the point that Samantha just made" or "I see Jared has a question." You also can set a ground rule in which you ask people to identify themselves before they speak.

To limit the times that someone is interrupted during a teleconference, build in longer than usual pauses. This will slow the pace of the conversation, but is preferable to "talking over" someone. If you are the one who is speaking, frame your remarks in parts that you announce at the beginning of your statement: "I have two questions about that idea. First, who is going to head the team. And second, is March 31 a realistic deadline?" Of course, if you do interrupt someone or talk at the same time, it's polite to say, "Sorry."

Managing Voice Mail and Answering Machine Messages

Answering machines and voice mail allow your phone to never go unanswered. They are conveniences both to the caller, who can fulfill at least part of the purpose of the call, and to the recipient, who isn't dragged into conversations when it is a bad time. These days, some people may even consider it rude not to have some sort of message-taking system! If you have a separate line for voice mail, give out the number so people can use it.

Like any other messages, those left on a machine or voice mail should be returned within 24 hours.

An answering machine shouldn't be used as a screening device in which you pick up only selected calls. People deserve to be spoken to. If you want to hear who is calling, it's better manners to listen, wait ten minutes and then call back rather than to pick up the phone and start talking right after the person leaves the message. Doing so implies that you are so self-important that you only take certain calls, and while the caller may be flattered, he may also think you're pompous. The exception: you are literally walking in the door; the caller is your most important client whom you have been trying to reach on an urgent matter; you've just heard her announce she's leaving to go out of the country for three weeks. Otherwise, call her back in a few minutes.

ESTABLISHING YOUR ANSWERING MACHINE GREETING. We've provided some sample messages for voice mail and answering machines on page 131. When establishing your greeting, keep these points in mind.

- Identify yourself with your full name.

- Keep your message *short* and to the point. Remind the caller to leave his or her affiliation, phone number, and brief message. No joking, please.

- If you insist on a "cute" message, make sure it really is. Try it out on friends and pay attention to feedback you receive. Change it weekly, because such messages grow old fast.

- Be specific about how your system works. Let people know if there is a time limit for a message. If there is more than one "beep" tell the caller to "wait for the long tone," or whatever applies. If it is possible to press a code and speak to a secretary, say so.

- Tell people when you will return or check your messages, so they know about when to expect your return call. Be as specific as possible: "I'll be back after 3" is better than "I'll be in this afternoon."

- If necessary, remember to turn on the machine when you are stepping out!

Sample Messages For Voice Mail or Answering Machines

"Thank you for calling ABC company. Please leave your name, the date and a message. We'll get back with you shortly."

"Hello. This is Sam Smith of the sales division of ABC Company. I'm either out of the office or on another line. Leave your name and number and I'll call you as soon as possible."

"Carole Rose speaking. I'll be in a training session on Monday and Tuesday and will be back in the office on Wednesday. Please leave your message so I can get back to you."

"It's Suzy Whitman, on the road again. I'll be checking for messages and will call you back when I can. If your call can't wait, please dial 0 for an operator or call my assistant, Jack Jones, at ext. 3333."

LEAVING MESSAGES BY MACHINE. If you had a reason to make a phone call, you have reason enough to leave a message. Some tips:

- Listen to make sure you have reached the person you dialed.

- Speak slowly and clearly, starting with your name and phone number.

- Make sure there is no background noise.

- Make sure the messages you leave are intended for semi-public consumption— no intimacies or confidences. Voice mail may be reviewed by someone other than the person you called. Although it's very bad manners to rummage without authorization through someone else's voice mail, it does occur.

- If someone's system seems to be malfunctioning, let him or her know that in your message.

- Repeat your name and phone number at the end. This is very important so that the recipient doesn't need to look up the number or re-listen to the message.

- Remember to exit the system, not just hang up. Follow the instructions.

Get to know your system. Many voice mail or answering machine setups offer shortcuts. In some cases, when playing back your messages, you can bypass the greeting, skip a message, or speed up a message if you know the appropriate codes. Why is this an etiquette consideration? If you miss a message, you may have insulted a client. And if you tell a client who calls you frequently about your system's shortcuts, it may save him time and win you points.

One final, significant caution: don't trust technology too much! Machines do misfunction, so leaving a message still isn't exactly fail-proof. When in doubt as to why someone hasn't returned your call, blame the machine—it's far safer than falsely accusing the person!

Consider this one actual tragi-comedy of telephone manners: a company representative, "Miss Dial," inadvertently transposed the last four digits of the number of "I.M. Waiting," the person whom she meant to call. Although she was puzzled that the voice on the machine had changed from male to female, she kept calling the same number and leaving a message, without result. "Miss Dial" also neglected to leave her full name and number so "I.M. Waiting" could call back. Finally, she did leave the number and got a call back—from a stranger. The stranger, "I.M. Perplexed," asked to speak to "I.M. Waiting," since that was the only full name left in the message. In the meantime, "I.M. Waiting" was wondering why he hadn't heard from "Miss Dial" as promised.

Getting in Gear with Car Phones

Once upon a time, the phone booth was the traveling businessperson's second office. Now we have the mobile car phone, which provides more privacy and doesn't require that we fumble for change. The tradeoff, though, is that because they are relatively new, people have not adopted the special manners that mobile phones require.

From an etiquette perspective, we recommend limiting the use of car phones whenever possible. Unless you are stopped or parked, you are, by necessity, distracted by the traffic situation and usually not giving full attention to the conversation. This is a breach of conversational courtesy.

Of course, car phones can be useful tools for polite people. Barbara Pachter was convinced of their utility one morning when she got stuck in traffic on an expressway for an hour—with no means of letting her appointment know of the delay. She got a car phone that week!

If you do use car phones, here are some tips to keep you from driving everyone crazy:

1. Inform the other party on the line that you're on your car phone. In case you get cut off or fade in and out, he'll know the reason why.

2. Pre-program the numbers you call, if possible. Dialing while driving can be dangerous. We learned of one woman whose car phone began ringing shortly after she left a presentation. She didn't know how to answer the phone—no one had ever called her before. As she struggled to drive safely, she pushed each button shouting, "Hello? Hello?" growing more impatient and frustrated with each unsuccessful attempt. She then began to wonder who could be calling—was it a work-related problem? a family emergency? She found out, when she reached her office 45 minutes later, that it was the people who had been at her presentation, calling to let her know she had left her purse behind!

3. Plan the content of your conversation ahead of time. Have an agenda so you can keep your call brief, concise, and productive.

4. Don't try to take notes while you're driving. Rather, when you see a convenient place, pull over and jot down your meeting notes, or use a dictation device. (This is a courtesy to the other drivers on the road, who want to get to their destination in one piece!)

5. Speak clearly, loudly, and try to reduce background noise as much as possible. Turn off your radio, roll up the windows, turn down the fan or the air conditioner, etc.

6. Anticipate your route. Don't begin a call a mile before you reach a tunnel, bridge, tollbooth, or any other obstacle that might interfere with reception. You'll wind up having to start over again.

7. If you must call someone on a car phone, find out first if it's OK, because the recipient of the call is charged.

NICE HEARING FROM YOU

The spoken word, alas, can evaporate as quickly as the morning mist. While telephone calls have both their place and, as you have seen, their protocol, their impact can be fleeting. When you have finished making your phone call, consider whether good manners dictate that you follow up the conversation by putting any agreements in writing. It also can be effective, from an etiquette standpoint, to send a note that says "It was good to speak with you. I look forward to our next conversation."

Chapter 9

WRITTEN COMMUNICATION
Write It Right!

Words are, of course, the most powerful drug used by mankind.

—RUDYARD KIPLING

Words have power, and written words have the kind of power that endures. You don't have to write like Shakespeare to make an impression on your reader.

While this is not a book about writing, there is a writing etiquette, and it's important to bear that in mind whenever you write. You do not want to offend people by the written word. Once you put something down on paper, you cannot take it back. Moreover, you do not want to give anyone written evidence that you are disorganized or disrespectful of the receiver's time.

You can make a positive impression on others if you communicate effectively with words. Knowing when to write, how to construct a letter or memo, when to use the all-important thank-you note and how to make a report instructive and productive are smart business survival skills.

Our language, including our written language, may have changed since you were first taught to put thoughts on paper. New words are rapidly being added to our collective vocabulary—about 2,500 words a year in the past two decades—to reflect societal and technological changes. In addition, the way we refer to groups of people, including women, changes as society re-evaluates its views.

You want your writing to be simple, clear, and conversational so that the reader can understand. It is *not* proper etiquette to use obscure words, pompous, or inflated language that is confusing. If you are polite, you will be understood.

In this chapter, you'll explore several typical business writing formats with an eye toward producing gracious and considerate written communication.

MASTERING THE WRITING PROCESS

Before you can develop an effective written communication style, you need to understand the process of writing: when to write, the essential ingredients for any written communiqué, how to get ready to write, and what to do when you actually sit down to write.

The Key to Knowing When to Write

The ease and the relatively low cost of telephone communications have made us forget just how much business used to be conducted in writing, even as recently as thirty years ago. It used to be that when you wanted to place an order, arrange an on-site visit, analyze a market or even screen potential job applicants, it was mostly done in writing.

Yet even with the advent of technology—faxes, modems, and computers—our paper-less society is still filled with paper! Clearly, there are many times when it is appropriate, even essential, to communicate through writing. Putting something on paper makes it official and permanent. It gives you a paper trail that can be helpful in tracking proposals or following those projects that need to be explored over an extended period of time.

Each company has its own internal protocol about when to write. In some workplaces, virtually nothing is done without written documentation; in others, information is rarely put in writing. If you violate these often-unwritten guidelines, you may have made a gaffe. For instance, if it has not been customary to put some performance guidelines in writing, to do so employees may consider it threatening, overly formal or even legalistic. Conversely, if you fail to put something in writing that is usually expressed that way, it may be thought that you are not taking the matter seriously enough or that you are failing to follow through.

You need to know and follow your company's criteria for written communications.

Three Essentials of Any Written Message

Whether you are sending a meeting notice, an agenda, a letter, minutes, a memo, or a thank-you note, follow these three general etiquette guidelines:

1. *Write when the situation demands it.* If something can be accomplished in person or by phone, you should probably do that. However, written communication is required in certain instances, including:

   - expressing thanks.

   - confirming a phone conversation to avoid confusion.

   - clarifying an understanding, such as a contract or an analysis of a problem.

Writing is recommended for situations in which people need time and thought to study something before coming to a decision or taking action.

2. *Aim for Clarity.* Provide correct and accurate information, a positive tone, and present the material in a visually appealing format. Short usually is best. One page for most business letters is usually plenty. One of our favorite examples is the letter a probation officer sent to the court. It said, "We tried. He didn't. Take him back."

3. *Respect your reader's time.* Meandering, unfocused writing does you more harm than good. Do the reader's organizational work for him—get rid of incidental data, structure the document in a logical fashion, occasionally underline or boldface the important points.

People today do not have time to read, and long letters or reports can be intimidating. You seldom, if ever, need a 20-page report on a meeting. However, a five-year study of proposals for expanding your business into the international market deserves a thorough, well-prepared report.

A Successful Preparation Strategy: Think Before You Write

All words are pegs to hang ideas on.

—Henry Ward Beecher

Writing is something that takes effort and some knowledge of the writing process. Like professional athletes, professional writers may make their performance look easy, but that's because they have trained their writing "muscles" so that they respond on command. With practice, your writing also can become more proficient.

Much of the actual work of writing takes place before you put pen to paper or fingers to keyboard—the stage known as "pre-writing." Many people try to avoid this step. Some don't plan what they want to write because they think it is too difficult or time-consuming; others because they are overly anxious to actually get started and see progress; still others are not sure what to include in a writing plan.

However, it is difficult to write coherently without some forethought. You can't communicate an idea you haven't fully thought through. In fact, most disorganized writing is traceable to disorganized thinking. Words can't camouflage confusion.

To get started and quickly organize your information, think first about who you are writing to and what you want to say. What do you want to happen as a result of what you're writing?

One technique that helps focus your writing is clustering, which is sometimes called "mind mapping." It also helps you get organized, find out what you know about a topic and what are the areas that need more research.

Using this method, you put your main topic in the center of a piece of paper. Then, let your thoughts flow, writing down any phrases or points you can think of, clustering them in groups around the key phrase. Don't censor your thoughts. Just put them down. It only takes a couple of minutes and it's easy. Later, you can look over what you've written and can delete out what you don't need.

The next step is to number the clusters in a logical order (a form of outlining). Or, you can create a traditional outline from your cluster.

We've included illustrations of this technique. One shows how clustering might organize a discussion of clustering. The second example shows clustering of the writing course we teach. It was done by one of our students.

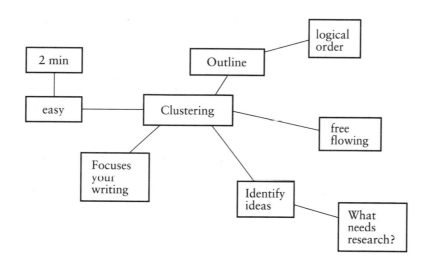

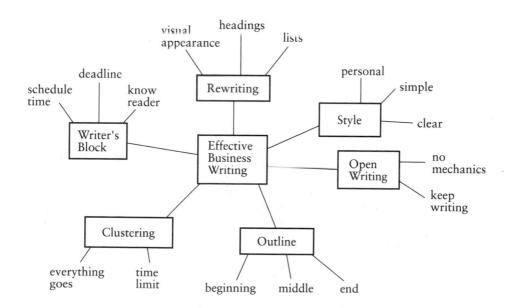

You can use our *Letter Organizer* on page 139 to outline any letter before you actually write it. By using it, you can avoid the faux pas of leaving the reader confused or uncertain ("OK, I understand the problem, but what does she want me to do about it?"). We've found it to be a useful tool to ensure that a business letter includes all the pertinent points in a logical manner.

Getting Down to Writing

Once you know what you want to say, the actual writing can begin.

Schedule a specific time to write. You want to feel clear-headed and also be relatively undisturbed. Make sure you have the materials you need on hand. If you are responding to someone else's letter or report, keep that in front of you for easy reference.

Know your reader. What kind of information and presentation is he likely to respond to? The more you know about the person you are writing to, the easier writing will be.

Create a first draft. Work from your clusters. Do not revise it as you write—just get through it once. It does not have to be perfect—yet. We call this "open writing," because you open yourself up and let the words flow. This is a very important step. Do not cross out—just write. Write the way you speak, when words flow most easily. You need to connect with the reader.

Then, it's time for rewriting. Check and correct your first draft as necessary to make sure that there is a logical flow to what you've written. Also make sure that its tone and phrasing are polite. Do you use courteous words such as "please" and "thank you"? Is the tone cordial? Are positive words (more about this later) used? Vary the length of your sentences and paragraphs. Keep your sentences short. Make sure your grammar and spelling are correct.

Set a deadline for completing the letter. We complain about deadlines, but they can be our friends. You'll be perceived as polite if you respond promptly.

A MEMORABLE MEMO

You write a memo when you have a brief bit of information to communicate. It could be a follow-up to previous discussion or an announcement of a change in a meeting schedule. This form is shorter and less formal than a business letter. It's also more likely to be used for communication within a company than for external communications. In style, it lends itself to a list format—a great way to put a lot of information in a small space.

Letter Organizer

READER:

Salutation:

BEGINNING

Purpose/Topic:
- Opening sentence . . .

MIDDLE

Explanation:

Discussion	Details	Facts	Description	Emotion

END

Action:
- You will take . . .
- You want the reader to take . . .

Complimentary closing:

©1994 Pachter & Associates • 32 Whitby Road, Cherry Hill, NJ 08003, USA • (609) 751-6141

Model Memo

TO: Bill Johnson

FROM: TONY SMITH (phone ext. 1234)

DATE: April 16, 1997

SUBJECT: MONTHLY NEWSLETTER

I recommend that we ask Thomas Printing to print our monthly newsletter.

At our request, three companies submitted estimates for printing 1,000 copies of the newsletter. Their bids, based on the specifications we discussed, were:

Thomas Printing $575

Inkwell Stationery $650

Jones Print Shop $625

Not only does Thomas Printing offer the lowest price, but the company has done some excellent work for us in the past. You may recall that they did our last annual report.

Do you agree? Please let me know by the end of this week so that we can meet our production schedule.

In keeping with its brevity, a memo can be written on paper smaller than 8 1/2 by 11 inches. Your company may have special memo letterhead. Some companies set specific guidelines for spacing and margins as well as requirements for logos. The smallest memo may be the 3 x 4-inch self-adhesive notes that are often attached to other documents. It's acceptable to use these provided that the self-adhesive note is personalized with your name and that the message is no more than a sentence or two.

It's particularly important that memos be direct, logical, and free of extraneous information. Etiquette considerations include using positive, polite phrasing and a cordial tone while maintaining its basic clarity and simplicity.

The memo is structured like a backwards joke: the punchline comes first. Information to support the main idea is then presented in logical fashion. Only essential details are discussed. It ends with the action that needs to be taken as a result. Here are some questions to ask yourself about any memo you write:

- Are my main ideas stated first?
- Does the memo flow logically?
- Are there headings or lists?
- Is it brief?
- Is the action I want taken stated clearly?

People appreciate the streamlined efficiency of a well-constructed memo.

THE EFFECTIVE FAX

The use of facsimile machines has in many instances supplanted the mail for rapid long-distance communication. When writing a fax you need to adhere to professional guidelines for brevity and simplicity.

Unlike a memo or letter, the fax has its own special protocol as a result of its proliferation and popularity. Never send an unsolicited fax! Doing so can tie up someone's machine, and shows poor manners and consideration. You may need the recipient's permission to send the fax because some machines are only turned on at stipulated times. In a large corporation, the fax may not be near the recipient, so you may need to give notice of what you're sending.

Here are some "Fax Facts" that every sender should know:

- Include a cover letter.
- It should be on company letterhead and should include the time and the date. It should also include:

The name of the recipient, his fax number, telephone number, and his department.

The name of the sender, her fax number, telephone number, and her department.

Number of pages (including the cover memo) in the fax.

The telephone number to call in case there are problems with the transmission. (This may be different from the sender's number.) Any comments relating to the fax (remarks such as "response requested by 3 P.M." or "no further information is available.")

In most instances, the formal fax cover letter should be used. Many companies have preprinted fill-in-the-blank cover sheets that are also acceptable.

Indicate if the delivery is urgent. This is especially important when faxing to a large company. Otherwise, the fax may wait until the next batch of inter-office mail is distributed.

Know your recipient's fax setup. Knowing the hours of operation, whether or not the fax is on a dedicated phone line, etc. can prevent the aggravation of having to resend a fax. Do not send lengthy or restricted-access materials without advance notice and permission.

Know when not to fax. The paper quality of a fax often is poor and sometimes the printing can be hard to read. If the recipient needs something for her files and if time permits, you may be better off sending a traditional memo or short business letter. Of course, if you require an actual signature (such as on a contract), one received through a fax will not be legally binding.

In tone and style, the fax should provide clear, courteous communication that does not waste words.

BUSINESS LETTERS THAT GET RESULTS

Business letters remain a practical, worthwhile and sometimes mandatory communications tool. From an etiquette standpoint, they are much less intrusive than a phone call.

Business letters usually are written on company letterhead. If you have input into the selection of the company's official stationery for business letters, you should recommend as high a quality as the company can afford. Use your official stationery for official business only, not for personal matters. It is unprofessional to confuse the reader as to the nature of your letter before he's even had a chance to read it.

All letters have the same basic structure: beginning, middle and end. The content will naturally vary with the type of letter, but in most letters the beginning states the topic. The middle provides the explanation, discussion, details or description and the end states the action that the writer will take or that he wants the reader to take. As we mentioned previously, our *Letter Organizer* on page 139 can be used to plan each of these parts.

The following etiquette applies to all letters.

Five Guidelines for Selecting Successful Salutations

The salutation is one of the most important areas of the business letter. If you offend the recipient in the first line, he or she may not continue to read it.

1. Use the correct name and title. This is extremely important from an etiquette standpoint. An incorrect name or title may not bother you, but it offends many people who are fussy about what you do to their names. The director of a large company, who went by either Charles or Charlie, would automatically throw away any letter addressed to "Dear Chuck" or, worse, put you on his blacklist forever. Women sometimes instruct their secretaries to throw away any letter addressed "Dear Sir."

One organization sent out two versions of a solicitation letter. The only difference was that one had "Dear Member" and the other had the individual's name. The ones with a specific name had a one percent increase in the rate of return compared with the "Dear Member" letter. For that company, the difference translated into a profit of $15,000.

Call the company to get the person's name and title. You can ask the receptionist to make sure that you spell the name correctly. Some examples: "Dear Mr. Smith," "Dear Dr. Jones" and "Dear Ms. Sullivan."

Use last names if you are in doubt about whether you should use a first name. It is always better to err on the side of formality.

You can use first names only if:

- You have a relationship with the person and know it's OK.

- You have been asked to call the person by his or her first name.

- You receive a letter that the writer signed with her or his first name only.

2. Avoid "Dear Sir/Ms." You are telling the reader that you haven't a clue as to who he—or she—is.

Not every woman likes to be called "Ms.," even though it is an acceptable legal term and usually the preferred term in business. One woman told us, "I worked long and hard to become a Mrs., and that's what I want to be called!" If you are unsure of whether to use Ms. or Mrs. and think you might offend the person if you guess wrong, just use the first and last name—"Dear Sally Jones."

Similarly, "Gentlemen" or "Sir" can sound inappropriate to some people's ears. We even heard from the director of a convent that she received many letters addressed "Dear Gentlemen." What is the writer of that letter telling her, the reader?

3. When it is impossible to know or include the recipient's name, use a non-gender-specific, non-sexist term such as "client," "customer," "participant" (in the project), "representative," etc. You can add "representative" to virtually every department name, every company name, as in "Dear Sales Representative" or "Dear ABC Company Representative." In most situations, it works quite well.

4. When in doubt about the person's gender, use both the recipient's first and last name. If you are unsure of the sex of someone, with a name such as Pat Smith, use both the first and last name and drop the Ms. or Mr., such as, "Dear Pat Smith."

5. Avoid "To Whom It May Concern." Most letters addressed this way are thrown away, sometimes by someone who says, "It doesn't concern me!" Even if the letter is saved, it could take weeks to find its way to the right office.

Eight Tips for a Successful Style

An effective business writing style creates successful written communication. Keep these points in mind as you compose the body of your letter.

1. Write from the reader's point of view. Address such issues as "Why should I care?" or "Why is that my concern?" and "What's in it for me?" Put the most important information up front—the recipient is less likely to miss it if she stops reading. Answer any objections your reader might raise to the points you make.

2. Write the way you speak. Be personal and direct. You are writing to people, not furniture. In today's world, where your fax talks to my fax, my voice-mail to yours, you must connect directly with the reader through your language and tone. Although the letter is formal in structure, it should be conversational in style. (It does, though, have to be in proper English. We're assuming you speak correctly.)

Your goal is to be understood. Write in a clear, straightforward manner so that the reader knows what you mean the first time he reads the letter.

If you feel yourself becoming too formal or flowery when writing or typing a note, try dictating it and then transcribing it.

It's OK to use "I." The personal touch actually is preferred over a formal approach. "I've enclosed the information you requested" is much better than saying "Enclosed please find."

When you read over the letter, pay particular attention to how it *sounds*. If it doesn't sound right to you, it probably won't read well. We've probably all heard about the combination restaurant/gas station with the "oops" sign that said, "Eat Here and Get Gas."

3. Use humor cautiously. If you can really pull it off, humor can be a refreshing, enlivening and personal touch to a business letter. But if there's any chance your tongue-in-cheek joshing might come across as cute or flippant, or, worst of all, insulting, avoid it altogether. The reader does not have the non-verbal humor signals that he might have in person, or even the inflection of your voice over the telephone. He may read the letter when he is rushed. He may also re-read it, and not be so amused the second or third time around. It's better to steer clear than to have the joke fall flat.

4. Eliminate extra words. One of the biggest complaints people have about other people's writing is that they use TOO MANY WORDS. Time is precious—you don't want to squander theirs or yours.

NEEDLESS WORDS: Why say, "Thanking you in advance for your kind consideration in the above matter" when "Thank you" does the trick? Some other common extraneous expressions, and their simpler substitutes, are:

ELIMINATE	USE
in the event of	when
at this point in time	now
at present	now
prior to	before
in the course of	during
at an early date	soon
at a later date	later
show a preference for	prefer
each and every one	all
due to the fact that	because
for the reason that	because
on a daily basis	daily
at all times	always
at a slow rate	slowly
with the exception of	except

ELIMINATE	USE
in reference to	about
in short supply	scarce
at the rear of	behind
despite the fact that	although
draw to a close	end
exactly alike	identical
from time to time	occasionally
in few cases	seldom
in many cases	often
in the majority of cases	usually
seldom if ever	rarely
is of the opinion that	believes
on behalf of	for
a large number of	many

REDUNDANCIES: These expressions say the same thing twice, diminishing the initial effectiveness. They also lack logic: Have you ever heard of anything being postponed until *earlier* or something that was destroyed, but not completely? Be kind to your reader. Practice economy in your vocabulary.

CHANGE	TO
unresolved problem	problem
advance warning	warning
repeat the same	repeat
fewer in number	fewer
file away	file
final conclusion	conclusion
actual experience	experience
past experience	experience
absolutely complete	complete
refer back	refer
ask a question	ask
basic fundamentals	basics
merged together	merged
mix together	mix
assembled together	assembled

(Continued on next page)

CHANGE	TO
join together	join
meet together	meet
completely destroyed	destroyed
disregard altogether	disregard
postponed until later	postponed
qualified expert	expert
brief in duration	brief
cooperate together	cooperate
filled to capacity	filled
heat up	heat
consensus of opinion	consensus
main essentials	essentials
repeat again	repeat
nominated for the position of	nominated

MODIFIERS: Ask yourself if your adverbs and adjectives ~~really~~ add anything ~~significant~~. Other examples: He is ~~currently~~ the newest partner in the firm. She read the ~~entire~~ proposal.

QUALIFIERS: Words such as "rather," "quite," and "somewhat" can sometimes be useful to soften statements. Before using them, though, make sure that's what you really want to say.

Another way to eliminate extra words is to use bullets to break out the main points in list fashion.

5. Use everyday words. The larger your vocabulary, the more precise your use of language can be. But when you stray into the type of words found only in the dictionary, college textbooks, and crossword puzzles, you lose part of your intended audience. Big words don't always impress people. They might intimidate your reader or make him think you are a snob. This is poor manners. Even if the reader knows what the word means, she might have to think about it for a minute, distracting her from your message. You want instead to use the simple words that say exactly what you want to say.

> *"I never write 'metropolis' for seven cents because I can get the same price for 'city.' I never write 'policeman' because I can get the same money for 'cop.'"*
> —MARK TWAIN

ELIMINATE JARGON. Every profession has it. You know what yours is. From an etiquette perspective, this kind of language not only can confuse, but can shut some people out.

USE SIMPLE WORDS. The quick, short, easy words generally are more effective in making your point. They also mean you will be read and will be understood.

CHANGE	TO
endeavor	try
visualize	see
solicit	ask
inform	tell
affirmative	yes
cooperate	help
indicate	show
transpire	happen
terminate	end

ELIMINATE OLD-FASHIONED WORDS. They could make *you* seem antique!

OLD-FASHIONED	CONTEMPORARY
aforementioned	previous
attached herewith	enclosed
forthwith	at once
humbly request	I ask
kindly advise	let us know

6. *Use appropriate language.* Phrasing that sounds sexist, negative, or choppy can turn off your reader.

AVOID SEXIST PHRASING. There are several specific ways to avoid gender gaffes.

- Use the correct term. Adult women are "women," not "girls," "gals," or "ladies."

- Treat both sexes equally. If you don't mention the marital status, number of offspring or the hair color of a man, don't mention those characteristics in reference to a woman. If you refer to men as "Mr.," treat women with the same respect.

- Avoid sex references in professional or job titles. Say "longshore workers" instead of "longshoremen." Use "letter carrier," not "mailman." Say "business executives," not "businessmen." Also avoid making distinctions that imply there is a "regular" sex for a profession: a female dentist is a dentist, and that's what you should call her.

- Include both sexes. Say "human beings" or "people" rather than "mankind." Use "employees" instead of "the guys." It's better to say "artificial" or "manufactured" than "man-made."

- Avoid use of masculine and feminine pronouns or adjectives when referring to a hypothetical person. Instead of saying, "The average supervisor writes 10 business letters a week to her employees and associates," you can use the plural and say: "Most supervisors write 10 letters a week." You also can vary your use of pronouns, as we have in this book, saying "he" one time and "she" another time.

USE POSITIVE WORDS: Be polite. Written words can seem far more accusatory than spoken ones because they're not accompanied by softening gestures. "Don't be delinquent with the report" will sound rude compared with "Please submit the report on time"; yet both communicate the same message. You can word most things two ways. The negative way uses words including "no" or "not" and also relies on "you" statements. An example: "You are not allowed to eat or drink in here." The positive way to say the same thing is "Please finish your food before entering the lab." Positive, polite statements are more likely to accomplish what you want and create friendly impressions.

Examples of positive words: advantage, benefit, proud, generous, success, satisfaction, pleased.

Examples of negative words: failure, regret, problem, weak, neglect, careless, deny, useless, wrong, ruin, pointless, complain.

USE TRANSITIONS JUDICIOUSLY. These word bridges can make your writing more smooth. Examples: as a result, besides, for example, however, moreover, nevertheless, and rather. Make sure that you do in fact need these words as a bridge by reading over the sentence without the transition. If they don't add to the understanding or flow of your writing, take them out.

7. *Use correct grammar, spelling, and punctuation.* People make assumptions about you if your writing includes grammar mistakes, misspellings, or typos—and the assumptions they make usually are not nice. It's incorrect (and impolite) to gauge someone's intelligence by an ability (or inability) to spell, because there's actually no correlation between the two. Smart people often can't spell! But why give people an excuse to find fault?

What's more important, having mistakes in your letter could indicate that you were in a hurry when you wrote it and so were not willing to give the recipient the time he deserved. That will raise questions about your general thoroughness as well as how high a priority you will give the client or co-worker in other arenas.

When in doubt, look it up. There are plenty of good grammar and spelling reference books. Several states also have telephone hotline grammar services you can contact with a question.

It helps to know your specific weaknesses so you can be particularly vigilant about checking for them. Computer spell-check and grammar programs can be helpful in identifying your mistakes. And if you know, for instance, that you can't spell "separate," no matter how many times you look it up, you might want to avoid using that word or resolve to *always* look it up.

Some other potential pitfalls:

- Subject-verb agreement.

  "There *are* many reasons to buy the equipment,"

  not

  "There's many reasons."

- Objects of prepositions.

  "Between you and me,"

  not

  "Between you and I."

- Wrong words.

  The "effect" of the new marketing system,

  not

  the "affect" of the system.

- "It's" vs. "its."

  It's easy to forget that "it's" is the contraction for "it is" while "its" is the possessive form.

8. Create visual appeal. Nothing turns a reader off more than masses of grey, unbroken type. Invite the reader in by using wide margins and lots of white space. Use lists and boxes. Add boldfacing or italics for special emphasis. Vary the length of paragraphs and sentences. This shows that you took the time to prepare an interesting presentation.

Closings: When It's Time to Say Goodbye

There is a hierarchy of closings that vary in formality and familiarity. They are, from the most to least formal:

"Respectfully" and "Respectfully yours." These are used when corresponding with government officials or members of the clergy.

"Very truly yours." A formal closing.

"Sincerely" and "Sincerely yours." These are frequently used for business contacts.

"Best regards," "Yours," and "Best." These are informal, but acceptable in some instances.

Don't forget to sign your letter once it has been typed or printed! Failure to do so is unprofessional. People appreciate an actual, legible signature, and some even check to make sure it's not a stamp.

The Last Step

If possible, before sending your letter, set it aside for an hour, until the next morning or after lunch, so that you can read it "cold" and see how it sounds. When you have just written a letter, you are too aware of what it is "supposed" to say and how hard you struggled with a phrase to evaluate it objectively as a reader would.

While reading, ask yourself: Is the language appropriate? Is the message clear? How would you react if you received this letter?

Print out a draft of your letter if you've composed it on the computer. Mistakes that blend in while on the computer screen can jump out at you on paper.

It's helpful to have someone else proofread your letter before it is mailed. Reading it out loud also is an excellent proofing technique. If it doesn't sound right to you, it will not sound right to the reader.

HARD-TO-WRITE LETTERS

While the previous tips apply to all business letters, we'll now focus on considerations for specific kinds of business letters—the complaint letter, the follow-up letter, and the keep-in-touch contact letter.

The Complaint Letter

Is it possible to complain and be polite? Absolutely. You do not need to be nasty or mention lawyers—yet.

When you write a complaint letter, remember these four points:

1. Identify the person to whom you are writing. Go as high as you can. The head of customer service may be a more logical recipient than the sales representative with whom you initially dealt. Letters filter down. They rarely filter up.

One woman wrote to the president of a major hotel chain to complain. He forwarded the letter to the franchise district manager, who sent a letter letting her know she would soon hear from the district manager. She did.

2. Explain the situation. Even if you have already explained the matter on the telephone, restate it for the record. Include copies of receipts or other pertinent material.

The woman who wrote to the president of the hotel chain was complaining about treatment she'd received when she had called from the airport for a hotel limousine. Told that it would be an hour wait, she asked to speak to the hotel manager, who told her there was nothing he could do. When she arrived at the hotel, management refused to pay her $28 taxi fare from the airport.

3. Define what you want to achieve and don't be afraid to ask for it. Do you seek a price adjustment or replaced parts? Do you want money back or credit toward your next purchase? Be specific and ask for what you want. The worst answer you can get is "no." Etiquette also says, however, "don't be a pig."

The woman complaining to the hotel sent a copy of the taxi receipt and asked to get her money back. She did. Note that she didn't ask for a free night's stay at the hotel, which would have been far more expensive. However, if she had just written to complain without making a specific request, it's probable she would have received a nice letter in response, but no reimbursement. In fact, when she later related her story to someone who worked for that hotel chain, she was told that it was indeed corporate policy never to give anyone money back unless it was specifically asked for.

One man told us how he and his friend each bought new thermos bottles. Soon afterwards, both the handles fell off. He sent his thermos back and asked for a new one; he got it. His friend just returned the thermos but didn't specify what he wanted. He got the handle repaired.

4. Write the letter while you are hot, but send it after you have cooled down. You'll get better results if you sound reasonable and rational. Anger is one letter short of danger. A polite tone helps put the reader on your side. Watch your wording and avoid accusatory "you" statements. Say, "I would like a refund" rather than "You owe me a refund."

We know one man who was so upset about a situation that he wrote a two-page letter. He waited a day before he mailed it, and reread it. He changed nothing, but just took out the curse words. It became a one-page letter.

If you are responding to a complaint letter:

Respond promptly. This will help the writer feel that you are taking his concern—and thus him—seriously.

Word your response carefully. Don't aggravate the writer further. And don't make any promises you can't keep, which will only add insult to injury.

End on a positive note. Tell the writer if his complaint has led to any internal changes, but especially address what you will do to resolve her own situation.

The Follow-Up Letter

The follow-up letter can be a useful way to keep a project moving forward. For example, you can send one to report on steps you have taken to prepare for a conference. From an etiquette standpoint, it's a way to connect again with the customer and continue to build the relationship.

These letters need not be long; they're following up on a problem or situation, as opposed to initiating a discussion. In most cases, a page will do it.

It's important to use an appropriately encouraging tone. You want to prod politely or to remind gently, but not nag. Be careful about using phrases such as "Since I have not heard from you yet."

Some additional tips:

State that the purpose of your note is to follow up. You can say, "I'm writing to see how that marketing study we discussed is proceeding" or "I thought I would follow up on our conversation regarding the production schedule."

Include key phrases or points from your conversation or previous letter to help jog the reader's memory. "As we discussed, it's important to have the results in hand by Oct. 1" or "As you know, the main issue regarding the schedule has been the difficulty in arranging consecutive days off for workers."

Remind the reader of what you are willing to do. "I'd be glad to forward you the data I've accumulated" or "If you'd like to arrange a meeting to discuss the status of the project, please give me a call."

End on a positive note. "I'm looking forward to working with you on this project," or "Our company specializes in handling these kinds of situations."

The Keep-in-Touch Letter

A matter of both good manners and good business, the keep-in-touch letter is a way of nurturing and sustaining the relationship with a client, customer, or business contact. It's basically a way of saying, "How are you doing?" as well as "I'm still here." From a marketing standpoint, it can be good to "schedule" these letters at regular intervals throughout the year.

Keep this letter short. If it goes on too long, it can seem like one of those multi-page formatted holiday letters you sometimes receive from people who long ago dropped out of your life. The reader asks, "Why is he telling me all this?" and says, "Why should I care?"

The tone should be friendly, upbeat, and professional.

Some additional tips:

Find an excuse to justify the letter. It could be "I bumped into our mutual friend Cathy Bishop" or "I saw a reference to Amalgamated Textiles in the paper and thought about you." You often can use the sending of newspaper or magazine clippings as the excuse. The topic of the article could be your reader, you, or something in the industry that might be of interest.

Express interest in how the reader is doing. This "How are you doing?" part of the letter should come before any update on your situation. It's always nice to say, "I hope you're doing well."

Briefly mention anything new regarding you and your operations. "Since we last spoke, we've added a computer system with improved graphics capabilities."

Make at least a vague reference to the possibility of another business-related contact. This is the "I'm still here" part of the letter. "It looks like I'll be heading out your way next spring—perhaps I'll see you then." While you, of course, have a business motive in writing, it can be more effective if the implied request for additional business is subtle.

THANK-YOU NOTES:
The Payback Power of Gratitude

People think of the ability to write thank-you notes as a social rather than a business skill, but thank-you's are both practical and polite in business settings. They can help personalize the business relationship, demonstrate attention to detail and assist in providing good public relations. Putting praise or gratitude into writing takes a little effort, but that effort is in turn appreciated by the recipient.

When do you send a thank-you note?

- When you receive a gift—from Christmas gifts to wedding gifts to condolence flowers.

- When you go to lunch with someone such as a new supplier or when you go to someone's home. (Never send one to people you lunch with every day.)

- When you want to praise an employee or even vendors in writing. It can be your own employees or others who have done work for you. You can also send a thank-you note to someone's boss.

- After a job interview or a sales call. In a job search situation, you may want to type the thank-you, because it may come off as more professional.

Timing is crucial with thank-you notes, because they lose their effectiveness rapidly. Ideally, the note should be sent within 24 hours of the event that prompted it.

Four Keys to Gracious Thank-You's

1. If you have legible handwriting, it should be handwritten. A handwritten note is more personal than a typed one. However, if no one can decipher your scrawl, type it so that the message can get across.

2. Keep it short. Many people drag out a thank-you, and that's a mistake. There is no need to go on and on about the decor, food, ambiance, conversation, etc. at lunch. It is, after all, a note. Three to five sentences should do it.

3. Thank everyone who deserves it. Since word about the receipt of thank-you notes has a way of leaking out, be democratic in your distribution. Leaving someone out of the loop can cause more harm than not thanking anyone. If more than one person needs to be thanked, you can ask the receiver to convey your thanks to others, such as, "Please tell your secretary that I appreciate her hard work." If everyone has equal status, send separate notes.

4. Use good quality note paper. The type of paper on which the note is written is important. It should be good quality, 5- by 7-inch size, or folded note paper. It should have your name and company on it, but should not look too official. Neither should it be "cute"—save those cards for relatives or friends.

Sample Thank You Notes

Dear Ms. Jones,

Our lunch at Peter's Restaurant was outstanding. I don't know what was better—the food, the setting, or the conversation.

Thank you for an enjoyable meeting.

Sincerely,

Dear Charles,

What a wonderful thing to do! The crystal bowl is beautiful. Ed and I both love it and will use it often when guests come to dinner.

Thank you.

Sincerely,

Dear Mr. Owens,

Thank you for meeting with me. I appreciate the opportunity to speak with you about our services. If you decide to expand your business, please call me. I will be happy to work with you.

Sincerely,

Dear Ms. Parillo,

Thank you for taking the time to interview me for your upcoming opening in data processing. I enjoyed meeting you and learning more about the firm. Based on our discussion, I'm sure I can provide the qualifications you seek.

Sincerely,

Dear Ms. Parker,

Thank you for letting me know that the data processing position has been filled. I hope you will keep my résumé and consider me for future openings.

Sincerely,

Dear Marjorie,

A special thanks to you for a thoroughly enjoyable two-day program on "Powerful Presentations." The program was high energy, fast, and extremely informative. You are a *dynamo* of a presenter.

I had a wonderful experience and believe everyone else did also.

Many thanks again.

Best regards,

   You do not have to send a thank-you for a thank-you. However, if you wish, you can verbally thank the sender.

REPORTS THAT IMPRESS

The written report provides a chance to explore an issue or situation in depth, providing a narrative on background, options, and recommendations. In many ways, it is an expanded version of the business letter that is divided into sections instead of paragraphs.

Each report should be sent with a letter or memo explaining why the reader has received it. Is it just for the person's information? For his review? Because she asked to read it even though she was not on the committee? By sending the report, you are intruding into your reader's time, desk, and filing space, so it's courteous to explain why she's on the receiving end.

Writing a report involves striking a delicate balance. You want to give plenty of relevant background information without veering into boring detail and present the material in an approachable style without a patronizing tone. You have to provide appropriate graphs and statistics to communicate your message and organize it in an easy-to-follow, logical format. This, naturally, is not an easy task! From an etiquette standpoint, the more that you can do to make the information convenient, pertinent, and easy-to-follow, the better it will be. Summaries, headings, tables, checklists, and occasional boldfacing are all appropriate, because they meet the reader's needs.

The length of a report requires you to make sure you have assembled all the needed materials when you set out to write. Consider the following as you plan your presentation:

- Purpose.
- Reader.
- Format.
- Existing information.
- Information needed.
- People to contact.
- Visuals.
- Progress reports required.
- Deadline.

Taking the time in the early stages to think through each aspect will speed the actual writing.

As you prepare your report, ask yourself these questions:

- What should the reader *know* after reading my report?
- What do I want the reader *to do* after reading my report?
- Do I want the reader *to feel* something about the information?

To organize your research, you can cluster the entire report, and then do smaller clusters from your originals.

Expect to gather more information than you will include in the final document. Stifle the impulse to pad the report to impress colleagues with the volume of material you have gathered. It is better to impress them with the fact that the information included was relevant to the discussion and well-organized. Ask yourself what you will accomplish by including each part of the material. Does it provide additional background, support an argument—or just distract the reader from the main points?

Structuring the Report

Once you've determined what to include, make sure the report is organized in a logical fashion. For example, don't draw conclusions until you have outlined the pros and cons of possible solutions. Are the key ideas clearly identified as such, both by their typeface and/or placement in the report?

The short report consists of a statement of purpose, supporting evidence and discussion, the conclusion and recommendations.

The structure of a long report includes a title, summary, table of contents, introduction, main body, conclusion, recommendations, bibliography, and appendix.

The title should explain the purpose or topic, such as "Effectiveness of the Supervisory Training Program." The summary is a short version of the report, and should be written last. An example:

"Engineering conducted a year-long study on the training of new supervisors. While the program is effective in helping newly promoted employees make the transition to supervisor, more instruction is needed in problem-solving, decision-making, and presentation skills. Given the small Engineering and Human Resources staffs and the need to improve supervisory performance in these areas, it is recommended that all supervisors take the five-day supervisory skills workshop taught by 'Bosses R Us.'"

The introduction gives background information, a description of the problem or situation, the main factors to consider and how the study was conducted. The main body presents that information in detail.

Conclusions interpret the data without introducing new information. Recommendations explain how to put those conclusions into action.

The bibliography and appendices list the sources used, as well as presenting tables and graphs that support your ideas. Appendices may contain additional information not needed for an understanding of the discussion.

While your report may not contain all of these elements, good manners require that it be easily understood. Ask yourself the following questions to determine whether your report fulfills that objective:

- Is the report's purpose clear?
- Do I address the reader's needs?
- Is the summary stated at the beginning?
- Are the main points readily identifiable?
- Does the background information answer all possible questions?

- Are there extra words or sections that should be eliminated or condensed?
- Is the report technically accurate?
- Do the conclusions and recommendations follow from the information as presented?
- Do the visuals effectively illustrate and enhance the information presented?

EFFECTIVE RESPONSES TO WRITTEN COMMUNICATION

We all have a little grade-school student inside of us who can't wait to see what the teacher says about our book report, even as we partially dread the day that the graded reports are handed back.

When someone communicates with you in writing in a business setting, you should keep that grade-schooler in mind. The letter writer or the report preparer will be interested in feedback from you, and failure to provide it would be rude. With all that's involved in preparing a document, it would be ungracious to fail to acknowledge the time and effort someone invested.

When you receive written communication, handle it professionally. Read it immediately to determine what action may be required.

Good etiquette says to answer important mail within 48 hours, unimportant mail within two weeks.

If you are backlogged, it can be appropriate to let someone know you will be getting back to him when you can. In such situations, a postcard or memo stating, "I've received your information and hope to reply soon," is better than dead silence or no response at all.

When you do respond, try to include some favorable comments. To a follow-up letter, for instance, you can say, "It was good to hear from you. We might need your help on a project in March, and I'll be calling to let you know."

A WAY WITH WORDS

We started this chapter by noting that words have power, that written communication affects both people's perceptions and actions. The guidelines we've provided here will enable you to tap into that power, to use words in a way that positively affects a reader's perception of you. Even when people don't agree with your message or recommendations, they value your ability to communicate clearly and politely. Choose your words carefully, and your reputation will benefit.

Chapter 10

MUST WE MEET LIKE THIS?
The Protocol of Meetings

*Those who are unable to learn from past meetings
are condemned to repeat them*

—MCKERNAN'S MAXIM

Meetings are a way of life in corporate America. Statistics show workers spend an average of four hours per week in meetings. In fact, one whole year of an average person's lifetime is spent in meetings! Middle management spends about 35 percent of the work week in meetings, upper management over 50 percent.

Meetings are also expensive. More than 13 million dollars a day is spent on meetings in the United States. While they are going on, phone messages pile up, work backlogs, and, afterwards, if the meeting is not productive, time is spent complaining about the meeting instead of working. If the attendee's annual salary is $50,000, a three-hour meeting involving ten people costs about $1,500. And that's just salary—not heating, electricity, overhead, preparation time, or food.

Yet meetings are, of course, necessary to accomplish business, and, if properly planned, can be effective and efficient. Good business manners, in fact, require that you plan your meetings well in order to show courtesy to others and respect for their time. As both a meeting leader and as a meeting participant, you can do specific things—in planning, participating, and following up—that will make meetings less frustrating and more productive.

Naturally, not all business meetings are official or structured. Someone might unexpectedly stop by your office to discuss an issue, or a spontaneous gathering of managers may lead to a debate about company practices. However, there are also steps you can take to make these informal, impromptu sessions into more cordially efficient situations.

In this chapter, you'll find:

- tips on transforming meetings of all sorts into gracious encounters.
- keys to effective presentations and the protocol of special meeting situations, including conferences and trade shows.
- ways to make sales calls graciously, as well as how to handle yourself during job interviews and when meeting with the media.

The thing to keep in mind throughout these discussions is how efficiency enhances civility. When situations from sales calls to budget sessions are handled correctly, everyone feels more comfortable and more gets done.

MASTERING MEETING PLANNING AND PREPARATION

Many meeting foul-ups come from poor or no planning. It's poor manners if you fail to consider adequately who should attend, what the agenda should be or what the objectives are. Good planning helps prevent poor performance.

Informal meetings particularly have a tendency to waste time. Without forethought, they have no defined purpose; people aren't prepared for the discussion or presentation; and there are no time parameters to make everyone comfortable.

There are seven steps according to the 3M Meeting Management Institute that should be followed when planning a formal meeting or preparing for an informal one:

1. *Define Objectives*—make sure they can be accomplished in the allotted time.
2. *Select Participants*—based on the goal of meeting the established objectives.
3. *Arrange Facilities*—keep interaction in mind and make sure you have the proper equipment.
4. *Prepare Agenda*—in a logical order, with names and times on each item.
5. *Develop Ground Rules*—to maintain standards of behavior.
6. *Invite Participants*—giving them time to prepare.
7. *Touch Base With Non-Participants*—so they are informed.

Defining Objectives: Is this Meeting Necessary?

Your first task is to determine if a meeting is necessary.

If you are meeting "because it's Wednesday and we always meet on Wednesdays" or because "I have to talk to Barbara about something so we might as well go ahead and have a departmental meeting," those are not good reasons. The decision to hold a meeting should be carefully considered and planned, rather than an assumed ritual or routine of business. A meeting should be your last alternative.

Clearly understanding the meeting's objectives can help you determine if a meeting is needed. What is the result desired from this meeting and is a meeting the only way to get it?

Even casual or informal meetings should have a purpose. It is rude to waste people's time if there is no reason to meet. Keep a running list, for instance, of things you need to discuss with a particular co-worker before making a visit to his office, or keep the list on hand so it's available when he stops by.

To determine if a structured meeting *is* necessary, the meeting leader needs to ask himself if the task can be accomplished without it. Time and cost should be considered when making the decision. Meetings should not be held out of habit.

Would a phone call, a memo, a message on voice mail, a notice on the bulletin board, a one-on-one meeting—or just making a decision on your own to proceed on a project—be more effective? If only 5 percent of your meetings are eliminated, that's time and money saved.

As a meeting leader, what kind are you considering? The main categories include problem-solving meetings, problem identification meetings, team meetings, training meetings, a review or presentation, and motivational meetings. Nevertheless, you may be able to find other ways to identify problems, present material, review options, or even train and motivate employees.

Meetings are necessary for problem-solving and decision-making, although these sessions often can be shortened if participants receive the necessary information in advance.

We will discuss more about conveying the objectives of a meeting in the section on establishing an agenda, but do make sure the meeting's objectives are realistic and that you can reasonably meet them in the time allotted for the meeting. Don't over-do it. Ask people presenting at the meeting how much time they will require. Limit what you hope to accomplish. If you expect a lot of discussion, limit your objectives. Meetings are usually more productive when they are short: try to keep them under an hour.

Note: If you are invited to what you consider an unnecessary meeting and have not received an agenda, ask the meeting leader politely what the objectives of the meeting are, noting that you'd like to come prepared. Other questions you can ask include: "Why was I asked to come?" "What part do I play?" "What do I need to have prepared?" "Where is the agenda? I need to plan my time." If the meeting leader can't answer these questions, you might say, "I have other things that require my attention at that time." If company politics require you to attend, be as prepared as possible.

Selecting Participants: Let the Objective Guide You

In meetings, "more" is not always "the merrier." The more people who attend a meeting, the more complex it gets. The more complex, the more time. The more time, the greater cost.

This is true of both structured and informal meetings. By definition, casual meetings already lack formal agendas, perhaps a designated leader, or even agreement on rules of conduct—all of which can help keep discussions and decisions on track. When more people are added to this mix, the likelihood of utter chaos increases. When you have an informal meeting, limit its size to make sure that you aren't taking up the time of people who do—and don't—need to be there.

A structured meeting called just to disseminate information can stay simple even with many people involved. But as soon as there is interaction, the number of people involved becomes important. With interaction, the number of people you invite is directly proportional to the length of the meeting.

Studies have shown that when you add a fifth person to a four-person meeting, the complexity level increases by 127 percent. Does that mean you should keep the fifth person out? Not if you need that person. It does show, though, how quickly the complexity of a meeting and its consequent cost increase. It also illustrates that you often are acting politely to all when you limit the number of people who are invited to a meeting.

The 3M Meeting Management Institute, which conducts studies at the University of Pennsylvania's Wharton School of Business and at the University of Minnesota, suggests the following is the ideal number of attendees for various types of meetings:

Problem-solving	Fewer than five
Problem identification	Fewer than ten
Review or presentation	Fewer than 30
Motivational	The more the better

There are significant differences between informational and decision-making meetings, in leadership and communication styles, in the meeting's emphasis, and in the keys to its success—all of which affect the optimum number of people. Once you've determined your objectives, you can then plan to invite the appropriate number of people.

Informational meetings can accommodate almost any number of people, because the information is generally conveyed in a one-way presentation, perhaps followed by a question-and-answer period. The emphasis is on content and the key to the meeting's success is in the planning, preparation, and clear presentation of the information.

Decision-making meetings are best limited to fewer than seven people, because, to be successful, there should be interaction and lots of participation by attendees. The emphasis is on interaction and problem-solving, and the key to the meeting's success is a climate that supports open and free expression.

There are four types of participants in a decision-making meeting:

1. *Information givers*: Those who provide data.
2. *Decision makers*: Those who will analyze the information and/or make decisions.

3. *Decision implementors:* Those who will be responsible for putting into effect whatever is decided.

4. *Benefiters:* Those who will gain from the results. If a group of people will benefit, the person who manages those people generally participates in the meeting. In turn, this person may hold a meeting to inform the others of this meeting's results.

Are all these types necessary to meet the objectives in a decision-making meeting? Yes!

You can't function without information, so information givers are required. If the person who is going to make the decisions can't come, you do have polite alternatives. You can put a proposal together and present it to him afterwards for his decision. You can make the decision yourself if appropriate or ask the decision-maker to send a representative who can decide. You can call the person ahead of time and move the meeting to fit her schedule or cancel the meeting.

If you don't include implementors, who are often forgotten, you may not have enthusiastic follow-through on the decision. They also may have ideas on the best way to do it. Benefiters need to understand *why* what is being done is being done so they can better appreciate it.

If all these people cannot attend, you should strongly consider changing the agenda or moving the meeting. Occasionally, in the case of a long meeting, not everyone has to be present for the whole session. The courteous solution may be to arrange the agenda around their schedules so they can attend the portion that is relevant to them.

There may be people who feel they should attend the meeting, even if they have nothing to contribute or gain. In some situations, company policy or a person's position may be a factor in who gets invited. Ideally, only those who can directly affect the meeting objectives should be present. Therefore, the more specific your objective, the more it cuts down on the number of participants.

Arranging the Facilities: Creating a Positive Environment

One thing that few people think about is the meeting environment and how important it is to the meeting's effectiveness. The lighting, seating arrangements, layout, etc. all affect how people feel. You can walk out of a meeting wondering why it didn't go well when, in fact, it was the room.

SELECTING THE ROOM: Part of what can make an unstructured meeting casual is its setting. The same discussion will not feel the same if it is held in the company cafeteria instead of the boardroom. Let the purpose of your meeting determine the setting. For instance, to discuss any important matter, you'll probably find it more productive to pull up a chair in someone's office than to chat while eating a snack in the breakroom.

Of course, there are times that you have no control over where a meeting is held. But for those times when you do, consider the *Meeting Room Selection Checklist* on page 163, which covers the basic responsibilities.

Meeting Room Selection Checklist

YES NO

1. Is the room large enough for all the participants and the necessary equipment?

2. Is there adequate ventilation and lights?

3. Is the room isolated from outside interruptions and activities?

4. Are the furnishings functional and comfortable for your purpose and meeting length?

5. Is the room convenient for all?

6. Is the cost of the room manageable?

7. Is the room available when you need it?

What happens when the meeting room is too small? The participants will probably get claustrophobic and want to get out quickly. You have to compensate by keeping the meeting short, whether you want to or not, or schedule more frequent breaks. If the room is too big, people will spread out too much, distancing themselves from the business under consideration. In that case, your solution is to cordon off part of the room.

If a room is dark or poorly ventilated, energy levels drop and creativity wanes. Keep a meeting room bright, and cooler than you normally might, particularly if it is going to be filled up with a lot of people.

A room should not be too comfortable in its furnishings or people will get lazy. However, if the seating is uncomfortable, they will get irritable.

Also consider how people will get to the meeting. What is most convenient for them? Have you taken into account the needs of any person with disabilities?

Cost is a factor when meetings are off-site. You don't want an otherwise successful meeting to be remembered as the one that cost an "arm and a leg."

It is amazing how often people don't check on the availability of the meeting room. Think of all the times you have been in a meeting and someone pokes their head in and says, "Oh, somebody is already in here." Then, off that person goes, wasting time searching for a room. Meanwhile, late arrivals who don't know where their group went interrupt your group again, burning up even more time and money.

Every time a meeting is interrupted, the participants have to repeat themselves. The group wastes time getting back on course. Put up a sign on the door that says "Meeting in progress." And then shut the door! If the meeting is in someone's office, make sure that the administrative assistants know that calls should be held.

Remember that it is the constant in-and-out of people that is distracting during meetings, not the person who must leave for a specific purpose. It's perfectly acceptable to leave an emergency phone number with your office that allows you to be called out of a meeting.

Avoid technological disruptions as well. We have attended meetings where cellular phones were ringing throughout the session. The most distracting was when the speaker got a call—mid-speech—and took it while the audience waited for him to finish his presentation.

SETTING UP THE ROOM: Once the meeting site is selected, you need to prepare. Depending on the meeting, you will have to:

1. Make certain the room is set up with tables and chairs arranged according to the type of meeting scheduled.

2. Make sure materials such as paper, pens, and handouts are on hand.

3. Place name cards on the tables if attendees are not well acquainted with one another.

4. Supply audio/visual equipment and check to make sure it is working. This includes flipcharts (with marker), chalkboards (with chalk), overhead projector and screen, VCR and monitor (with tape), slide projector (with slides), audio/video recorders (with tape or film).

5. Arrange for snacks and refreshments, and sometimes meals and hotel accommodations.

You need to go through all these steps in advance to avoid wasting meeting time. The steps also apply, on a modified basis, to setting up sites for informal meetings.

Table and chair arrangement: Proper table and chair arrangement is very significant, both psychologically to the participants and for the efficient and courteous functioning of the meeting. You may recall that it took three months to negotiate the table shape and size for the Vietnam peace talks before they ultimately settled on a round table.

If any participant has a disability, his needs take precedence. Consider where you can fit a wheelchair, where you can place a blind person so she is able to hear clearly and where a hearing-impaired person is able to see both presenter and interpreter. Factoring in those concerns, the person also should be placed as close as possible to his colleagues.

Arrangement for Productivity, on page 165, shows several seating arrangements. Each option has benefits and drawbacks.

The rectangular table is fine for a meeting, but it can cut down on interaction. If the leader sits at the head of the table, the power position, interaction will be reduced. A leader who is signaling "we are all in this together" will sit on the side in the middle. This arrangement, though, can interfere with use of visual aids, since some people will have to get out of the way and others might not have a good line of vision.

The round table helps to promote interaction. It cuts down on the positioning for power since there is no head. However, arranging visual aids also can be a problem with this shape.

ROOM ARRANGEMENTS

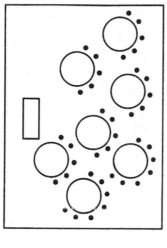

Restaurant Style

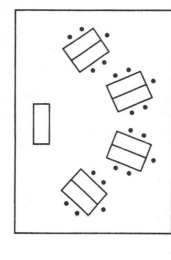

Modified Herring Bone

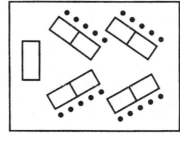

Sample Room Arrangement
For Information Meeting

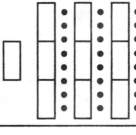

Sample Room Arrangement
For Information Meeting

Sample Room Arrangement For
Either Information Meeting or
Decision Making Meeting

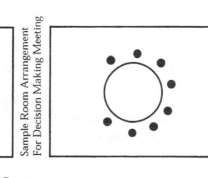

Sample Room Arrangement
For Decision Making Meeting

Sample Room Arrangement
For Decision Making Meeting

The U-shape (sometimes an arrangement of three rectangular tables) is good for meetings that include presentations. It works well for visual aids. It should not be used for groups larger than twenty, though, when it becomes too cavernous.

The herringbone (in which tables are arranged, herringbone fashion, at angles to the speaker or leader) and the classroom (rows of tables facing the speaker) are good for disseminating information. They are not at all good, however, for interaction—they remind people of their school days and put them into a passive, receiving mode.

A good way to handle a large group but to encourage interaction is to use a modified herringbone that has people sitting across from each other. It allows the leader to stay in control but still makes it possible to encourage discussion. A restaurant-style setup, in which round tables are arranged so that people sit halfway around them, works well too.

Even small, informal meetings need to be comfortable for attendees. Think of using a small conference room rather than an office—power is equalized outside an office. If the meeting is in an office, make sure there is room for everyone.

Equipment to be used in the meeting: Any equipment used in a meeting should enhance its effectiveness. If it doesn't, eliminate it as excess clutter.

Name cards: Particularly if your participants are not well acquainted, name cards can be a valuable and gracious addition. They help participants get to know each other and they keep the names right in front of you so you can politely call each other by name. Whether you are the leader or a participant, if you are not using name cards, consider writing the names of meeting participants on the top of your pad in a rough diagram of where they are seated.

Work materials: Pens, pencils, notepads, etc. should be provided. It's a good idea to make a list in advance of all the things you think you will need. If you are attending, make sure you bring at least a notebook and pen in case the leader neglects to provide them.

Audio-visual equipment: As the meeting leader, it is your responsibility to ask your presenters what they need and to make sure that the equipment is there and working. However, if you are a presenter, not a leader, don't wait to be asked; tell the leader what you will need.

If you are the leader and someone else is going to set up the room, give him a list of the equipment needed and a diagram of how you want it set up. Then, arrive early for the meeting to make sure it is all in place and working. Make sure you bring the name and phone number of the audio-visual person in case of an emergency.

Refreshments: Be careful about what you provide to eat and drink. Sugary things like doughnuts are routinely provided at meetings, but they're not a good idea. Sugar gives you a quick energy high, and then a crash. You don't want that happening to your meeting members. Complex carbohydrates, such as bagels, are much more appropriate.

Food can be a good bribe if you are concerned about attendance. But consider sending a meeting notice message such as, "Refreshments 8 to 8:15 A.M., meeting starts promptly at 8:15 a.m." Otherwise, the meeting will start late because the participants come exactly when it was scheduled, and use valuable meeting time to get their refreshments and socialize.

Keep the food easy to eat to avoid noise or a mess. You may want to consider keeping the food outside the meeting room so it doesn't become a distraction.

Another etiquette consideration to take into account is the variety of people's dietary needs. Not everyone, for instance, drinks caffeinated beverages. Snacks should include options for diabetics or vegetarians. You don't want to offend an attendee because his or her tastes or needs were ignored.

Safe foods for morning meetings include: bagels with cream cheese and butter; muffins; cut-up fruit; orange juice and cranberry juice; coffee—both regular and decaffeinated; tea—both regular and decaffeinated, and water.

Safe snacks for afternoon meetings include: popcorn; pretzels; cheese; cut-up fruit; a variety of juices; regular and diet sodas and water.

If you offer a variety of foods, you will most likely meet the needs of everyone. People with special dietary needs can bring food with them.

Preparing the Agenda: Plot the Direction

A divisional vice-president at a Bell Company sent a memo to all his employees stating that if they didn't receive a meeting agenda ahead of time, they did not have to attend.

Why do we need an agenda? An agenda is a map. We get farther when we have a direction, when we know where we are going. It says, "Here is where we are going, and here is how we are going to get there." It also provides a way to determine if we got there at all. It's right in front of everyone, so that the meeting can stay focused.

Your meeting map, or agenda, should be relatively detailed. You will rarely, if ever, hear someone complain that an agenda provides too much information. A complete agenda also shows that we value everyone's time enough to plan an efficient schedule.

For informal meetings, the agenda may consist of a list of questions or points you'd like to resolve. Even placing materials you'd like to discuss in a folder marked "Janice" can serve to focus your discussions with her. Thinking about the meeting in advance can help you to determine how much time to allow and when it would be best to hold it.

PRE-AGENDA PLANNING: Before setting the agenda for a structured meeting, ask the committee members what matters they might like to see covered. This will ensure that the agenda is planned with them in mind. It also is a good way to force hidden agendas to the surface.

It's especially helpful in the case of regularly scheduled meetings to circulate a request for input before the agenda is set. If you are the leader, you can send it out a few days ahead of time, with a deadline for getting back to you.

Ask the participants:

- What topics would you like to present at our meeting?
- How much time will you need to present your topics?
- What issues or concerns would you like discussed?

Based on the feedback you receive, you might find that the meeting can be canceled or that it can be shortened from one hour to ten minutes. Or you might decide you can take care of what is needed by visiting everyone individually. You also might determine that it would make more sense to break up the meeting into two smaller ones.

Discovering hidden agendas—those unstated ulterior motives and secret plans that people often have—can be essential to keeping your meeting on course. You can then manage the concern by dealing directly with each person, or by asking that they all hold their topics for a separate meeting.

When someone says he will need ten minutes for a topic, give it to him—no less, and definitely no more. After all, he established the time. If he was not realistic about how much time would be needed, giving him exactly what he asked for will help him learn to be more accurate in the future. Don't solve his problem (lack of time) by turning it into yours or a problem for the rest of the group.

DETERMINING THE LENGTH OF THE MEETING: Once you know what items are to be covered, you can determine how much time to allocate to the meeting.

Outside of requests for presentations, how do you know how much time to allow? There are several methods.

If the meeting is going to be a straight talk (no discussion), the 75 percent rule applies. Plan and practice a presentation that takes up 75 percent of the allotted time for the meeting. For a one-hour meeting, plan to present for 45 minutes. Allow the extra time because presentations often take longer than expected and because time should be set aside for questions. This rule applies to anyone who will be presenting at the meeting.

If there is going to be discussion, plan to speak for no more than 50 percent of the time, maybe as little as 20 percent. Interaction burns up a lot of time. Meeting leaders often assume they can cover much more than can actually be addressed in a given amount of time.

Unless you are engaged in contract bargaining talks, it's no solution to say the meeting will last "as long as necessary." If participants do not know exactly how long a meeting will be, they will be thinking of things like, "When I get out of here, I have to make that phone call" or "When am I going to find time to finish that report?" You will not have their full attention.

Even with casual meetings, it's best to establish time limits up front. Otherwise, the free-floating talk could burn up a considerable part of your available time. You can say, "Let's set aside fifteen minutes to discuss the personnel review schedule" or "Why don't we try to resolve the publication schedule before lunch?"

SETTING BREAKS: People can sit for up to 90 minutes, maximum. Smokers have a hard time even with that length.

If your meeting is going to be more than 90 minutes, schedule a short—approximately 5-7 minute—break, close to midway through the meeting. That's long enough for one call or a restroom visit. If you provide more time, people tend to get involved with other things and you'll have trouble getting them reassembled. It's better to have two seven-minute breaks than one 15-minute break.

If you are going to provide a break, make sure it is included on the agenda. Give it an exact time, and stick to it, so participants can inform their secretaries or customers that they will be calling then.

SCHEDULING THE MEETING: When selecting the date and time for the meeting, it's polite and wise to consider other people's schedules. How long will the meeting take? What time of day is best? Which day of the week is best? What impact will rush hour have?

Generally speaking, Friday afternoons and Monday mornings are bad times for meetings. On Monday mornings, people want to come in and get their bearings. If you must have a Monday morning meeting, at least set the starting time a half-hour after people normally arrive. Late-day meetings can cause problems. People want out. They have trains to catch, day-care deadlines, evening plans. Friday afternoon meetings are a waste. If people are present physically but not mentally, they are not going to give you their best.

Also consider the meeting's proximity to lunch time. A meeting before lunch should be no more than two hours long. If you want a short meeting, schedule it an hour before lunch—everybody wants to eat.

If you want a real short meeting, consider a standing meeting. It should be planned to last no more than fifteen minutes.

It might be helpful to set the starting time at an unusual time not precisely on the hour or half-hour, 1:55 instead of 2 P.M., for example. People may remember the time better.

Advance notice is courteous for informal meetings. Even if you don't set a precise time, it's better to tell someone that you plan to stop by her office tomorrow morning to talk about the computer upgrade than to visit her office unannounced and without giving her time to mentally prepare.

Our *Meeting Planner,* on page 170, can help you prepare for a meeting. You should be able to fill one out in about ten minutes, and doing so will save considerably more time during the meeting.

Meeting Planner

Objective: What is (are) the desired result(s) of this meeting?

Time: How long will it be? When is the best time to schedule it?

Attendees: Who should attend? Are the decision-makers, information-presenters, and information-gatherers invited?

Agenda: What is the schedule of events? Who is involved in preparing and distributing the agenda?

Physical Arrangements: What kind of facilities and equipment are needed? What are the specific arrangements?

Evaluations: How will the meeting be evaluated?

PREPARING THE AGENDA: *The Agenda Planner,* on page 171, can be completed for each meeting you arrange. You will notice that it does not follow the traditional outline format, but instead is both more detailed and compact. Use it every time you call a meeting. Familiarity with it will streamline your meeting preparation task, and will help those who attend, particularly as people learn how to read it and know what to look for. (If an item does not apply to your situation, omit it from your form.) The Agenda Planner is not meant to be a rigid planning document, but a helpful guide. Each section of the planner has a specific purpose:

A place is designated for the group name because when you give a meeting group a name, it helps focus the members and give them a team feeling. Also, when the name is established ahead of time and used in a meeting notice, it can discourage attendance by those people who have no role to play but still insist on coming to meetings.

State the meeting objective in behavioral language. Some examples: "To select a team representative to make a presentation at the conference," "to plan the training schedule for the rest of the year," or "to explain the methodology that will be used to collect data for production reports." People need to know what the point of the meeting is.

The section "Called by" should have not only a name, but a phone number or some other way that an invitee can easily reach the planner. You want to make it easy for invitees to pose questions or concerns that could make the meeting go more smoothly.

"Meeting Type" refers to such designations as "information-gathering," "problem-solving" or "decision-making." Be honest. If a decision has already been made and the purpose is to explain the decision, don't call it a "decision-making meeting." Employees aren't stupid or naive, and to treat them as such is insulting.

"Background Materials" and "Please Bring" tells participants how to prepare for the meeting. You can attach these materials to the agenda when it is distributed. For instance, attach a budget to a "budget approval" meeting so it can be reviewed in advance and meeting time will not be used up.

P.O. Box 8868
Elkins Park, PA 19027

BRODY COMMUNICATION**S**

Phone: 215-886-1688
1-800-726-7936
Fax: 215-886-1699

AGENDA PLANNER

Group Name:_____   Date: _____

Meeting Objectives: _____   Starting Time: _____

Called by: _____   Ending Time: _____

Meeting Type: _____   Breaks: _____

Background Materials:_____   Place: _____

Please Bring: _____

_____   Decision-Making Method: _____

_____   _____

Leader: _____   Final Decision Maker: _____

_____   _____

Recorder: _____   Special Notes: _____

Facilitator: _____   _____

Participants: _____   _____

_____   _____

_____   _____

AGENDA	PERSON RESPONSIBLE	TIME ALLOTTED

What happens if you send something out and a meeting participant announces that he or she did not read it? Don't go over it for that person's benefit—if you do, more people will not look at your advance materials in the future. This may seem rude, but it actually is courteous to the majority. Make it clear that you assume that all participants have read the distributed materials and are prepared to discuss them.

With "Date," include the day of the week along with the calendar date to avoid mistakes. For people who are habitually late, you might want to consider highlighting the "Starting Time" on their agenda.

Consider padding your "Ending Time." Say noon when your goal is really 11:30. Even if you miss your goal by fifteen minutes, you'll still be a hero.

Avoid wasting time by being specific about "Place." Send maps if necessary.

"Decision-Making Method" lets people know if there will be a vote. If you have already made a decision, say whether you will reconsider it based on input from the meeting. Let people know who the final decision-maker is.

In the "Special Notes" section, you can list ground rules (more about these later).

Specify in advance who will be filling the various meeting roles—leader, facilitator, recorder, time-keeper—so the participants can come prepared. It's a good idea to spread around the role of leader so people gain experience.

Even if you have a secretary take formal notes or minutes, don't use a secretary as the recorder. Rotate the function among the participants and have them take notes on a flipchart rather than a notepad on the table. This gives participants the opportunity to refer to what they have decided and even to say "wait a minute, that's not what we agreed to." Agree that spelling and grammar don't count.

The facilitator is the person who helps the leader keep on track, who makes sure that all the ground rules are followed. This role is becoming increasingly more important as U.S. corporations move into a team approach. The facilitator is not concerned with the specific task to be accomplished but rather with the process of getting everyone involved.

It's not gracious to just stick people with these jobs. Get volunteers or work out an agreement ahead of time. Establish a strategy for assigning who is going to be given what job.

Filling out the "Participants" section could allow someone to notice that a key person has been overlooked. Or, as a participant, you might say, "Hey, what am I doing on this list?" and call the leader to say you don't feel your participation is appropriate.

Give plenty of forethought before completing the section marked "agenda." Begin each meeting with an opening that takes up 10 to 15 percent of the time allotted for the entire meeting. In a one-hour meeting, for example, that would be between 6 and 10 minutes. In this period, issue the welcome, make the introductions, provide a statement of purpose, allow the participants to "buy in" to the objectives, establish ground rules, make role assignments, deal with housekeeping matters, and review the agenda.

In structuring the agenda, put the items requiring the most amount of creativity first, because energy tends to wane.

If you want people to participate, state agenda items in a neutral way. If you put down "vote *for* the new budget," for instance, it automatically removes any notion that this will be a fair discussion—you've signaled the decision you want. It's better to say, "vote *on* the new budget." Of course, you can choose to deliberately use the agenda to telegraph your desires. It's just best not to do so inadvertently.

List the agenda items in the order in which they will be covered. In doing so, take into consideration when people can and will be arriving and departing.

Always list who is responsible for a particular agenda item. You need to have accountability.

Setting time parameters is a crucial part of the courteous overall management of the meeting. You may even go so far as to let everyone know that the facilitator is going to signal people when they have two minutes to wrap up. Too often, when agenda items are not given time parameters, the first items get most of the time and the last items get either cheated or dropped altogether. The person responsible for that item may feel neglected or may think you feel the topic is unimportant and decide not to prepare the next time around.

If you have to stop someone, explain that the subject will be brought up again at the next meeting. Or, the group can agree that it is so important that some other part of the meeting should be postponed. That should, however, be negotiated and agreed on.

Here's a sample meeting agenda; it may be more formal than what you will use, but it is a starting point (*comments not printed in the actual agenda are in italics*):

2:05-2:10 1. Opening. *(Welcome, introductions, group objectives, announcement of ground rules)*

2:10-2:25 2. Current sales figures. Elizabeth Stratton will provide a month-end update and discuss year-to-date figures.

2:25-3:00 3. Marketing budget. We have been asked to review the proposed marketing budget and recommend possible changes. *(Send out a copy of the budget with the agenda and do your background and political work before the meeting.)*

3:00-3:25 4. Management training program. Personnel has asked us to select two senior staff members to describe our marketing program to the trainees. *(If you are a participant and want this job, this will be your signal to round up support before the meeting.)*

3:25-3:30 5. Closing. *(Discuss objectives that were accomplished, review assignment, thank participants for input.)*

This agenda makes it clear: what to expect, how to prepare, what the objectives are.

Even informal meetings do better with an agenda. It might not be as specific as this example, but the parties involved need to know why they are meeting and have a list of the topics to be discussed. We even used agendas when we met to discuss this book: it kept us on track, and gave us a sense of accomplishment when we were finished.

Developing Ground Rules: Establish a Smooth Flow

Ground rules are the rules of the game. They are set so that the meeting will go smoothly.

Think about your last meeting. What kind of things did people do that interrupted the flow of the meeting or irritated the participants? Your ground rules should discourage this sort of behavior.

Poor Meeting Manners

FOR THE LEADER

Not maintaining control of the group
  or the discussion.

Not starting or ending on time.

Not introducing self or participants.

Not including younger, newest attendees.

Not scheduling breaks.

Not sticking to the agenda.

FOR ALL PARTICIPANTS

Being late, leaving early or intermittently.

Exceeding the time allotment as a presenter.

Not introducing yourself or others.

Not doing advance work or coming
  prepared.

Not including all those in attendance.

Slouching, sprawling.

Doodling, playing with things, drumming
  fingers, yawning.

Interrupting or cutting people off.

Being sarcastic, attacking people rather
  than ideas, unfairly criticizing.

Not participating, not listening.

Going off on tangents or filibustering.

Engaging in side conversations.

Reading, smoking, eating, slurping, burping.

Making messes.

Falling asleep.

Not doing follow-up work.

The ground rules can be sent out as part of the agenda, or they can be established at the meeting.

Sample Ground Rules

Keep an open mind.

Look for ways to use the information.

No personal attacks or put-downs, including body language put-downs.

Limit your war stories.

Be back from breaks on time. If you need to leave the room to go to the restroom or to get coffee, go ahead.

The information mentioned here is confidential and stays here. We don't want our discussion to be inhibited because you are afraid someone is going to repeat what you said to co-workers or supervisors.

Questions can be asked at any time.

Participate.

Leave your ego at the door.

All of these sample ground rules may not apply to your situation, and some of them may sound too basic to be explicitly stated within your company's environment. However, we're often told how important it is to have courteous concepts like these as the foundation for a meeting. It's a good idea not only to set ground rules, but to have the group negotiate them, so people feel included. Many meetings fall apart because people consider the ground rules to be "implied" or "given." Although you may think that "keep an open mind" and "participate" are universally understood standards of conduct for meetings, they aren't.

For the rules to function, you have to announce them. You can say something like, "We want to make sure we hear all the information that everyone has about this new production schedule, so please participate in the discussion" or "It's OK to disagree; we want to get as much information and as many opinions as possible from all of you."

If you have the same group of people meeting over and over, you can establish the ground rules the first time and post them in the room. You don't have to bring them up again unless people start breaking them.

If you meet only periodically, you can remind everybody by saying something like, "Let's just agree on a few things."

Deal with ground rules in the beginning of the meeting. You may just take a moment to point them out before getting into the business.

When you discuss ground rules, your tone of voice is extremely important. It's even more significant than what you say. If you come across as tough, you will offend people. If you sound patronizing, people will act like the children you are treating them as, and possibly rebel. Present the rules in a friendly, diplomatic way, and people will be much more willing to go along.

People sometimes mistakenly define informal meetings as ones in which ground rules don't apply. Even though your meeting is not formally structured, you need to behave civilly toward each other, and ground rules can ensure that that occurs.

Inviting Participants: Plan Ahead

Distribute the specific agenda two to three days in advance. If it goes out any sooner, it could get buried at the bottom of an in-basket. If it goes out later, the participants may not have enough time to prepare. Of course, the date and time of the meeting already need to have been established.

With informal meetings, which may arise on the spur of the moment, it's important to try not to leave anyone out. You can say, "Lou really should be in on this discussion. Let me go see if he's available."

Touching Base with Non-Participants

Some people come to meetings only because they feel it is politically correct to do so. If you are concerned about this, you can send them an agenda with a note saying, "You don't have to attend, but I did want you to know what we would be covering." Your note can go on to say, "I'll send you a follow-up report on what took place."

People, understandably, get concerned about being left out. But if you tell them what is going to happen and promise a report, it can often be enough to keep them from attending.

Although it is playing rough, you also can use this technique to deal with people who *should* show up, but are habitual no-shows (talk about rude behavior!). You can send an agenda to their boss, with a promised follow-up report that lists attendees. When it is clear that you have done this, chances are your no-show will attend.

If someone was not able to attend an informal meeting—perhaps because it occurred spontaneously—it is important to brief that co-worker on what occurred. It's best if you can say, in all honesty, "We checked to see if you were available, but you were tied up with the Antosh project."

TEN STEPS TO CONDUCTING A WELL-RUN MEETING

Meetings can be like a dramatic production—people all have a role to play, with the agenda serving as the script and discussion creating the need for improvisation. *Meeting Roles*, on page 177, lists the responsibilities for the meeting leader and the participants. It is important to know your role and perform it appropriately if the meeting is to be a success. It begins with determining who gets which seat.

Meeting Roles

LEADER

Before the Meeting

Define the objectives.

Select participants.

Make preliminary contact with participants to confirm availability.

Schedule meeting room and arrange for equipment and refreshments.

Prepare agenda.

Make role assignments.

Develop ground rules.

Invite participants, distribute agenda and any supporting materials.

Touch base with non-participants.

Make final check of meeting room.

During the Meeting

Start promptly.

State objectives.

Follow the agenda.

Manage time.

Facilitate discussion.

Deal with difficult participants.

Help resolve conflict.

Allow for questions.

Clarify action to be taken.

Summarize.

After the Meeting

Restore room and return equipment.

Evaluate the meeting, including the effectiveness of the leader.

Send out minutes.

Follow up on action items.

Start planning the next meeting.

PARTICIPANT

Block time on schedule.

Confirm attendance.

Define your role.

Determine what your leader needs from you.

Suggest other participants.

Know the objective.

Know when and where to meet.

Do any required homework.

Listen and participate.

Be open-minded and receptive.

Stay on the agenda and subject.

Limit or avoid side conversations and distractions.

Ask questions to assure understanding.

Take notes on your action items.

Evaluate the meeting.

Review meeting minutes.

Brief others.

Follow up on action items.

Selecting Seats

If you are a junior person or a guest and arrive first, wait to be assigned a seat or ask where to sit.

The leader usually sits in the power chair, farthest from the door. The seat to the immediate right of the leader is for the guest of honor or senior management.

To equalize power and encourage participation among attendees, the leader can sit in the center. This demonstrates she doesn't need to prove her power.

If two people of equal status attend the meeting, the leaders sit in the center of the table, flanked by their officers, across the table from each other. However, if the two leaders are known to be in confrontation, it would be best to place them next to each other. Don't seat known antagonists across from each other. Don't seat trouble-makers together—they can gang up on you.

When you settle in your seat, sit up straight, yet be comfortable. Keep your feet flat on the floor and your back flat against the back of the chair. Lean slightly forward at times to show interest. Keep your hands on the table. Don't fidget or play with things. Use hand gestures appropriately.

Take only a reasonable amount of table space. Try to give the person next to you some room to breathe, and don't move your chair from the position in which it has been placed. Ask before using others' pens, paper, etc. Avoid looking for too long or too often at someone else's papers. Be aware of floor space as well: keep your brief-case and/or purse close to your chair and feet, and keep your feet under your own chair (no playing "footsie" or sprawling out).

As a leader, make sure there are enough handouts so people don't have to share or lean in.

These guidelines apply at informal meetings as well. While you may be more likely to select your own seat at an informal meeting, for instance, you should be aware when you do so how your choice reflects your position in the hierarchy of the meeting.

Of course, much of the effectiveness of a meeting is determined by how strong the meeting leader's performance is. Using the information in *"Meeting Roles,"* we will discuss each of the leader's responsibilities, with comments, where appropriate, about the participant's role.

Step 1: Start Promptly

You have set a specific starting time that is stated on the agenda. Remind people a day in advance, through memos, telephone calls or voice mail.

If someone is habitually late, ask another meeting attendee to pick up the offender. Or slot the person's presentation early on the agenda, so if he's late, he'll miss out on presenting his material.

Make showing up on time a ground rule. Offer an incentive for getting there on time; also offer disincentives for being late: shut the door, don't repeat what was missed, cover the "best stuff" first, charge a fine.

Start within five minutes (this is the typical differential on people's watches) whether everyone is there or not. Do not backtrack for latecomers; this is rude to those people who were on time.

If you are a participant and find out you will not be able to attend or will be late, notify the leader as soon as you know.

Informal meetings may not have a stated, precise starting time. For example, a colleague may say, "Why don't you stop by my office this afternoon before 3 to go over the outline for the year-end report?" This gives you some flexibility, but not total freedom to show up whenever you please. If you don't come until after 3, you'll be late. To avoid this kind of uncertainty, it's best to set a specific time for an informal meeting, even if it needs to be changed as the day's events evolve.

Step 2: State Objectives

Get participants to agree upon the meeting's objectives. Then, state them verbally at the start of the meeting or post them on a flip chart. Explain why they are relevant and re-emphasize them, as needed, to stop discussion from drifting away from them.

Using a flipchart also relieves you from having to repeat information for late arrivals. All the information they need is right up on the chart to be read. The meeting does not have to be set back, and late arrivals can get right up to speed. When the meeting is over, the minutes are easy to type up, and you don't have to waste time at the next meeting reviewing the minutes and sorting out who agrees and who doesn't agree with what they say.

This step may not be necessary at informal meetings that are held to discuss only one topic. However, whenever two or more issues will be handled, you should review the objectives even during informal meetings. If only two or three people attend, you can use a list written on a legal pad that is placed where everyone can see it instead of a flip chart. Cross off each item as it is resolved.

Step 3: Follow the Agenda

The leader should bring extra copies of the agenda, or post one for all to see. Refer to it repeatedly. Note any changes at the beginning of the meeting. Limit the length of time allotted to each item to what is stated on the agenda.

Keep a separate sheet for any newly-raised items, with an agreement that they will be addressed later.

Don't return to any finished items. If more discussion is needed on a topic, put it on the list for the next meeting.

As a meeting participant, it's courteous to respect the agenda. Don't bring up something related to the first topic when you are on item four. Don't try to leapfrog to something of special interest if you have to leave early. Pay attention to the item under discussion.

Informal meetings may lack printed agendas, which is one of the ways they can careen out of control. You might have to allow the list of objectives to substitute for an agenda, but don't let discussion become free-form, which will waste people's time. Instead, keep the dialogue focused on the business topic or, better yet, develop a simple agenda.

Step 4: Manage Time

The leader should use both a recorder and a facilitator to keep the meeting on target. This is not a sign of weakness, but rather an acknowledgment that you recognize it's important to focus on your job of leading the meeting.

Distribute materials ahead of time, leaving them in front of where people will sit. This is also a good way to enforce a seating plan, especially if you leave the materials in a packet with each individual's name on it.

Keep a clock in view. Assign a timekeeper. You can set an egg-timer for each speaker, or use the "hourglass" silent variety.

Discourage irrelevant interruptions (see the section on handling difficult people on page 181).

Limit breaks. Start again on time, whether everyone is back or not.

Participants should limit or avoid side conversations or distractions.

At informal meetings, remind people of time limits through repeated references to time. You can say, "We could go into the background on that issue, but it would take an hour to explain it," or "I wish we had time to revise the mockup, but right now, we need to focus on how to get the prototype off the ground." A leader can set the tone by saying, "I could talk all day about the importance of a logical copy flow, but here's my five-minute synopsis."

Step 5: Facilitate Discussion

Managing discussion can be one of the meeting leader's most difficult roles. By its very nature, dialogue is free-form and random, while as a leader, you need it to be controlled and, if not logical, at least focused.

If people don't know each other, be sure to do a round of introductions. This alerts all participants to each other's expertise. Using names helps people to feel comfortable. Name tents—standup cardboard index cards with people's names—provide easy identification.

State "come prepared to discuss" on the meeting notice or agenda. Announce that all ideas are welcome. Compliment an individual for "bringing up that point," especially if it is a sensitive concern that others may share but fear to voice.

Include all the participants. Break up into smaller groups. This can free people to say things they might not in large open forums.

Schedule a question-and-answer period (more about this later). Ask for clarification, examples, additional information and feelings. ("So far, there seems to be a lot of agreement on this issue. Does anyone have a different viewpoint?")

Use open-ended questions that require something more than a "yes" or "no" answer. ("Please describe the problems you've encountered from that change" instead of "Did you have any problems with the switch?")

Call on the participants. Go around the table, with an option to pass. Give everyone time to answer.

Turn off the equipment if the meeting is being recorded or if the hum of the overhead projector makes it difficult to hear what people have to say.

Remind participants of courteous ground rules: no put-downs or negative non-verbal signals allowed; the discussion will remain confidential; there will be no side discussion, which excludes people.

During the discussion, it's crucial that the leader engages in active listening (see Chapter Three, "Big Techniques for Small Talk"), responding to the body language, facial expression and tone of voice, not just the literal words spoken. ("You seem a bit hesitant. I'd be very interested in hearing more about your findings.")

The leader states his or her opinion last, which encourages others to participate.

At informal meetings, the same techniques apply. However, the nature of the session may create an environment in which some behaviors that would disrupt more structured meetings—such as side discussions—may have to be tolerated. You can allow discussion at informal meetings to meander slightly, as long as you keep steering it toward its eventual destination.

Step 6: Deal with Difficult Participants

The best way to handle difficult participants is to not invite them, if that's possible. Barring that, you also can use peer pressure. Stretch the boundaries of the courteous ground rule about no negative put-downs, to allow people to drum their fingers in restlessness or shake their heads at a point they disagree with. Difficult people are that way partly because they tune out the subtle signals that others heed, so sometimes it takes a stronger measure to alert them that their behavior is unacceptable.

Distract difficult people by keeping them busy. Give them responsibilities, or involve them in planning a meeting. Let one run a meeting about something he or she wishes to accomplish; make the difficult person the recorder. Assure a complainer that the matter will be discussed later. Or discreetly put her on the spot: "Why do you feel that way? Does anyone else feel that way?"

There are several categories of difficult participants. While the methods of dealing with each type vary, these suggestions apply equally to formal and informal meetings:

Dominators: Credit the speaker's knowledge of the subject and the person's constructive contributions. Intervene in any personal attacks by partially paraphrasing the information contained in the remark. Ask the group or another individual for views/reactions to what the dominator has said. State the need to get opinions from other participants.

Ramblers: Find a natural break or pause and interrupt. In this case, interrupting is polite to the group, even if it seems rude to the individual. Confirm your understanding of the point of the story. Restate the urgency of the objectives and the time constraints. Direct a question to another participant or to the entire group. Ask the rambler to summarize. Cut in when the rambler breathes. Limit the response. ("In order to hear from everyone, let's limit our responses to our main concern.")

Side Conversers: Pause and look directly at the conversers. Move toward them and ask if they have any questions. Restate the importance of the meeting objectives and state that the group will accomplish more if one person speaks at a time. Make it a ground rule to have one conversation at a time.

Non-contributors: Find out why they are quiet. Get them involved through small group interaction. Talk to them during the break to get their opinions. Ask them if they have any questions, but be careful about putting shy people on the spot.

Naysayers: Find out how widespread the negative feeling is. Put the antagonist to work—ask him/her to act as recorder. Talk with the person at break.

Step 7: Help Resolve Conflict

When disputes occur during discussion or during a problem-solving meeting, it is the leader's responsibility in both formal and informal meetings to help resolve them.

The leader acts as a mediator, encouraging opponents to work it out themselves. Stay neutral. Listen impartially and objectively to all sides. Acknowledge each position. Emphasize what is rational and indisputable. Assign the combatants a place on the agenda, but insist on adherence to its time frames.

Look for common ground. Invite opponents to restate satisfactorily each other's positions. Make sure the point of conflict is clearly defined. Remind the antagonists that the goal is to work toward understanding. Pull in the rest of the group, if appropriate.

Create alternatives. Compromise. Offer both parties an opportunity to discuss the matter later. Refer the question to a subcommittee. Get them to agree to disagree.

Table the issue. If it cannot be resolved, move on. If tempers are flaring, call a break.

Invoke humor, if possible. Laughter dissolves anger.

Step 8: Allow for Questions

Question-and-answer periods give you more time and opportunity to advance and clarify your ideas. To get the best results:

- Let the participants know early on when you will answer questions.

- When asking for questions, pay attention to your nonverbal signals. You don't want to seem defensive or dismissive.

- Anticipate questions in advance so that you can have the answers.

- If you are the leader or speaker, come prepared with some of your own questions, in case there are none from the others.

- Understand the motivation of the questioners. Are they interested in information? In showing off what they know? In advancing their own perspectives?

- Restate or rephrase the question. This helps everyone hear it and gives you the chance to put it in your own terms. When repeating, look at the questioner. When answering, look at the entire group.

- Listen for the substance of the question. Sometimes people make windy pre-question statements that have little to do with what they really want to find out.

- Answer briefly.

- Always be positive.

- Conclude the question-and-answer session with a closing statement.

There are five ways to handle questions, depending on the situation:

When you know the answer, answer briefly and to the point.

When you don't know the answer, admit it—don't lie. Tell the questioner you will get back with him, or tell him where to find the answer. If you promise to get back with someone, be sure to do so. Unfulfilled promises are rude.

When you have an expert in the group, first say the expert's name to alert him that you will be directing the question to him. Re-phrase the question for the expert, and let him answer. Regain control of the session (for instance, don't allow others to ask the expert questions directly) immediately afterwards.

When you have a stage hog in the group, try to curb her in advance if you know she's there. Say you would like to hear her thoughts after the meeting. Maintain control.

When you are asked a hostile question, determine the questioner's motivation. Paraphrase the question to your advantage.

(For information on handling questions in a small group setting, see "The ABCs of Questions" in Chapter Three, "Big Techniques for Small Talk.")

Step 9: Clarify Action

Confusion is an uninvited participant at many meetings. People sometimes hear what they want to hear, even if it is not quite what the speaker is saying. Afterwards, when participants at the same meeting compare notes, their perceptions may be in direct conflict.

That's why it is important as well as polite for the meeting leader to clarify what has been stated, what form of action will be pursued and what issues need to be addressed at the next meeting. This applies at both formal and informal meetings.

The leader should review and restate the action items for final agreement. ("So these are the problems we've encountered with the new plant. Are there any more?")

Include an accountable person with each action item listed. Ask the accountable people to state verbally what they are responsible for. Have the accountable parties leave the meeting with an action item list. Send that list to their managers. Set deadlines with interim checkpoints.

As a participant, it is your job to clarify any point on which you have not been clear during the meeting and to make sure you understand any action items that you have been assigned.

Step 10: Summarize

The leader needs to provide time at the end of the meeting for summarization. Graciously give advance warning when the time is almost up. In an informal meeting, this may be as simple as stating, "I'm going to have to leave in five minutes. What do we need to resolve before I go?"

Check the outcomes or action items against the original objectives.

Review the flipchart list of decisions made. Ask if there are any questions, or if anyone is confused about anything.

Discuss the meeting's effectiveness. Ask participants what areas of the meeting could be improved.

Summarize the conclusions by stating:

- How the meeting was useful.
- The objectives that were achieved.
- The steps to be taken.
- Who will be responsible.

Thank the group for everyone's participation and give credit to particular individuals. It's courteous to make people feel valued.

Schedule the next meeting, if one will be necessary.

EFFECTIVE AFTER-THE-MEETING FOLLOW-UP

The meeting leader's responsibilities don't end when the meeting does. The leader needs to restore the room and see that the equipment is returned. At least informally, the leader must evaluate the meeting, including his or her own effectiveness. In addition, the minutes need to be sent out, and action items followed up. The process begins all over again as the leader starts planning the next meeting.

For major meetings, you can send out a questionnaire or a prepared evaluation form. These may rate the session's effectiveness, on a scale from 1 (low) to 8 (high), on such aspects as clear goals, task completion, teamwork, listening, use of different ideas, and use of time. The evaluation also can ask for comments on areas that need improvement.

Another way to assess a meeting is to have an outside party observe and evaluate it. The observer can rate the leader from 1 (very ineffective) to 5 (very effective) in such areas as:

seeking cooperation and participation from all members,

enhancing the communication flow,

handling conflict,

keeping the conversation on course,

actively listening to others' concerns,

summarizing and making assignments,

initiating a follow-up plan of action.

Even if you don't do a formal evaluation, you should note if the meeting ran over the set time limit and if so, determine why. You also need to track progress toward the stated goals and objectives.

The meeting isn't finished until the minutes are out. The minutes should go out within 48 hours. They need not be a copious, detailed narrative, but can instead be a synopsis (see *Sample Meeting Summary* on page 186). List the objectives achieved, actions to be taken, assignments, comments, and the date of the next meeting. This form is quick and easy to put together, and provides all the needed information.

The final step is communicating the meeting's outcomes to the appropriate people. Leaders can brief their bosses, and participants can inform others, as appropriate.

THE KEYS TO POWERFUL PRESENTATIONS

The ability to handle presentations effectively is a valuable business skill, whether you are the person making the presentation or the one making the arrangements for it. Many people balk at giving speeches or reports, but with the proper preparation, these situations need be no more wrenching than a one-on-one conversation. We'll provide the protocol of speaker arrangements and introductions, followed by tips for the speaker in the house.

What to Do When You're Hosting Someone Else's Presentation

At conferences, association meetings, and in some corporate settings, you may hire speakers or ask someone from outside your department to make a presentation. If that is your responsibility, it's courteous to handle as many of the details as possible for the speaker, so that she can concentrate on her presentation.

Talk directly to the speaker so that there are no mistakes. Get background information, discuss the audience, the nature and length of the presentation, etc.

This is a good time to explain what the audience wants to hear. "We're interested in ways to access data from CD-ROM sources" or "There's been a lot of turmoil about the proposed move to the third floor." If you can, suggest possible strategies for the presenter, such as "This client really likes presentations that make liberal use of statistics."

Make sure you can pronounce the speaker's name correctly. Ask what title he or she prefers: Dr., Ms., Mr.

SAMPLE MEETING SUMMARY

Follow-Up Memo Checklist

Date: _____

To: _____

From: _____

MEETING SUMMARY

Date/Time: _____

Who Attended: _____

_____

_____

Objectives
Achieved: _____

_____

_____

Action to
Be Taken: _____

_____

_____

Assignments: _____

_____

_____

Other
Comments: _____

_____

_____

Next Meeting : _____

_____

_____

Get details on what is needed for the presentation: an overhead projector? a flipchart? a projector and screen? a microphone? Also find out if any rehearsals will be necessary.

If the speaker or presenter is coming from out of town, make any necessary reservations for accommodations, and send directions. Ask if there will be any special guests attending, and if so, designate someone to assist them.

Discuss any photo opportunities, press time, or time for book signings. Keep the schedule light right before the speech, providing a time and place for the speaker to rest about an hour beforehand.

Put the contract, including the fee and any expenses that will be reimbursed, in writing. Determine whether the speech can be taped or videotaped.

Write a thank-you note, or at least be sure to verbally thank your colleague, as soon as possible after the presentation.

Pay the speaker promptly. Pay colleagues by immediately telling them about the impact of their presentation: "We'll use CD-ROM data for the annual report" or "People still don't want to move to the third floor, but they feel better for having aired their concerns."

How to Make a Polished Presentation

Most professional business speakers make presentations on a regular basis. They may not be making "formal presentations," but they will present informally at staff meetings, team meetings, etc.

If you have been asked to make a presentation or give a speech, congratulations! The request indicates that someone believes you have valuable information and an effective communications style. While it is understandable that you may be nervous, remember that a request for a presentation is a compliment.

KNOW YOUR TOPIC. The general topic may be provided to you by whoever asked for the presentation, but it's up to you to hone and define it. Write a one-sentence description of your central theme—the main thing you wish to communicate. Organize and develop the information in a way that supports that statement. Keep in mind what's current, relevant, accurate, and acceptable to your audience. People think in pictures, so tell stories and use figures of speech along with statistics and other logical support.

KNOW YOUR PAL—PURPOSE, AUDIENCE, AND LOGISTICS. Do you want to inform your audience about a new product? Motivate a sales group? Who is in your audience? What are their attitudes toward you, your company, and your ideas? How much time do you have? Will you be the only speaker? These are all questions that need to be answered so you can target your presentation.

PRACTICE. Say your presentation out loud three to six times, perhaps in front of some chairs you have set up. Tape yourself after the third practice, and as you listen, ask yourself "Would *you* like to sit in this audience?" If possible, practice it in front of someone else, someone who is like your audience.

THINK ABOUT WHAT YOUR BODY IS SAYING. Some gestures can turn an audience off to your message, while others help relax you, warm an audience to you, and help you emphasize key points of your presentation.

DONT'S: Folding your arms in front on your chest makes you look defensive and uncommunicative. Putting your hands in your pockets and playing nervously with the pocket's contents distracts listeners from your message and can be risky, since some people have trouble getting their hands back out of their pockets. It's a waste of time to gesture behind a podium, where it can't be seen. Fidgeting with your hands on the podium distracts from what you are saying, as does using your fist to gesture or pointing your finger at the audience.

DO'S: Use open palms and send the gestures up and out, where they will be visible. Move the arm and hand as a single unit; this will eliminate any suggestion of weak, floppy wrists or elbows. Keep your arms between your waist and shoulders. Drop your arms to your sides when not using them. Hold gestures longer than you would in normal conversation so that you don't appear to be nervous.

Use gestures sparingly, to emphasize major points, and vary them so they look like a natural extension of yourself rather than a rehearsed series of movements. Switch from hand to hand; at other times use both hands or no hands.

Maintain proper eye contact. This does not mean looking over the tops of your listeners' heads (which will leave you looking at no one) or continually scanning the room (which distracts you and won't allow you to pull in your audience). Instead, focus on one person among a small group of listeners. Once you have made a connection, move on to someone else, in random zig-zag fashion. In a large audience, hone in on one area of the room at a time, starting with people in the back corners. Hold your eye contact for approximately three to five seconds, longer (10 to 25 seconds) for larger audiences. Finish a brief thought, phrase, or idea before moving on. "Catch their eye"— and don't stare. If someone avoids your glance, move on. Nod periodically and watch to see if they nod back. If they do, it means they are buying your message.

BE PHYSICALLY PREPARED. An effective speaker protects and prepares his or her voice, the instrument that will be used for the presentation.

The best beverage for a nervous speaker with a dry throat is room-temperature water with a touch of lemon. Ice water constricts your throat. Room temperature or warm water will help your voice sound rich, and the lemon will clear any mucus buildup.

Avoid:

- Milk—It coats your throat and causes phlegm. Also avoid eating ice cream and yogurt before a speech.
- Soda. The carbonation can make you burp.
- Coffee and tea. The caffeine will make you jumpy and dries the throat.
- Alcohol. It will relax you when you want to be sharp.

If your throat is dry, as a last resort you can *gently* bite your tongue, which will cause your glands to produce saliva that will moisten your mouth.

Use petroleum jelly on your teeth to keep your lips from sticking to them.

Proper etiquette requires speakers to be ready for their presentation. That means having information that is well organized and developed with the audience in mind. It also means practicing so that the delivery is comfortable and enjoyable for the audience to hear. It means ending on time. Speakers should be available to their audience for more questions following the presentation.

Occasionally, you might be asked to speak at the last minute. Although you have had no preparation time, your job is to be as clear and succinct as possible. Don't apologize or put yourself down. Pause, then start with an opening. You could begin by restating a question or the topic you've been asked to address. Make your points using clear, simple language. Then, add a closing statement.

If there is a chance that you might be asked to speak—for instance, to give an update on a project or to go over the budget—come prepared. Think about the points you want to make, and rehearse mentally.

STRATEGIES FOR SUCCESSFUL SALES CALLS

Making sales calls graciously may seem to be a contradiction in terms, but that's only because sales calls are too often handled in an unprofessional manner. It is possible to be courteous and persuasive at the same time.

When you call on the telephone, be fresh and upbeat. Always ask if your contact person has time to talk before you start your spiel. Give your contact person a benefit or a reason to see you—"we're having end-of-season specials" or "we offer lower costs without compromising quality."

Make an appointment that accommodates your contact's time schedule. Be on time, look neat and professional. Smile and shake hands. Don't immediately hand out your business card. Wait until you are seated, and then begin.

Get to the point. Be organized. You do not need to be brusque, but do be respectful of time.

Don't be apologetic about asking him to buy your product. It will reflect badly both on your company and on your product.

Be polite, helpful, and sincere. At the beginning, thank the person for agreeing to see you. At the end, express gratitude for his time and attention.

Before leaving, establish a call-back time or another meeting. Don't leave without stipulating the next step.

Write a note thanking your contact for his time, whether or not you get the sale. Send any promised information right away.

Update your record of calls, and analyze both your progress and the potential this client represents.

Learn to handle rejection gracefully.

WORKING THE CROWD:
Conferences and Trade Shows

Conferences and trade shows are a specialized form of meetings, in which the objectives are to network with others, present your product and acquire current information relating to your business. Although the setting may seem relaxed and informal, and you may not be under the scrutiny of others from your company, you should still be on your best behavior. Word about your misdeeds or a faux pas could easily follow you home!

Remember that you are there to mingle. In this situation, it is rude, as well as counterproductive, to keep to yourself or talk only to your friends. Work the room, making your way around it so that you cover the territory. Introduce yourself to others, and demonstrate genuine interest in their products or specialties.

Wear your nametag on the upper right shoulder—it is easier for the other person to read when shaking your hand. Always use professional titles on nametags, such as "Bill Smith, managing director," not "Mr. Smith."

If the attendees are from different companies and cities, include the company name and home city beneath your name. For spouses, you can use both names, such as "Mary Smith, Mrs. John Smith." That can be a springboard for conversation.

The conference coordinator should make provisions for the spouse if the conference lasts more than three days. Make sure your spouse understands the nature of the business at the conference and can talk intelligently about it. Spouses should not remain aloof from the group. If your spouse does not enjoy the environment, he or she should stay home.

"Significant others" —lovers, live-in companions—must act like a spouse. They should be discreet in demonstrating physical affection toward you, polite toward business associates, and patient regarding the demands on your time. A convention or trade show is not a vacation, and should not be viewed as such.

TECHNIQUES FOR IMPRESSIVE INTERVIEWS

Job interviews are pressure-cooker situations: you are being evaluated while you are nervous; you are competing with others; you are an outsider. If ever there were a situation that called for grace under pressure, this is it!

Fortunately, there are plenty of rules about behavior for job interviews. Following these rules not only enhances your chances of success in getting the job, but gives you the comfort of knowing that even if you aren't hired, you performed properly.

These rules, of course, apply to many interview situations, not just job interviews. You could consider your first meeting with the division head to be a sort of interview, for instance, along with any one-on-one meeting with a client.

Dress appropriately, according to the business climate and the position you are interviewing for: suits, if possible, and shined shoes and a nice briefcase or handbag. Double-check your grooming.

Be early by ten minutes for the interview, just in case of problems with the elevator, parking, or the wrong room. Do not be late. Go to the restroom first to check your appearance.

Wait to be seated in the office. If no seat is offered, ask where you should sit.

Always shake hands, both at the beginning and the end of the interview.

Bring a résumé with you, and have names and numbers of references ready. Know what the résumé says—you might want to read it over as you wait to be called into the office. If the interviewer asks you what year you served at a particular company, or the exact title of your last position, you should be able to answer.

Be confident in your abilities and goals. Emphasize your strengths, your flexibility, willingness to learn, communication skills, understanding of the organization, and honesty.

Ask for the job. Consider this a self-sales interview. State, directly, "I am very interested in this position because..."

Be aware of your posture and facial expressions at all times. Gesture naturally. Use SOFTEN, the skills we discussed in Chapter Three, "Big Techniques for Small Talk."

Mind your manners. Don't put anything on the desk. Don't take candy unless offered. No gum chewing or smoking. Do not fidget or play with things. Maintain eye contact.

Answer and ask questions pleasantly and briefly. Smile and use the person's name once or twice while answering.

Focus on the questions asked. Do not go off on tangents. Try to anticipate what questions might come up, such as:

"What are you looking for?"

"What are your strengths and weaknesses?"

"Tell me about a difficult situation you handled."

"Where do you plan to be five years from now?"

"Why did you leave your last job?"

Use silence wisely. Don't feel you have to fill in every pause. If you need time to figure out an answer, say, "I haven't considered that before" or some similar phrase while you stall for time. It's better to take your time and provide a good answer than to blurt out a bad one.

In case of personal and/or offensive questions regarding race, religion, age, home life, or credit rating, you always have a choice. You can:

- Ignore the nature of the question and answer it anyway.

- Ask, "Why do you need to know this information? How does it relate to the job?" If you are uncomfortable with the interviewer's answer, you can say that you would be happy to discuss business information that would help determine your qualifications and interest in the position.

- Use humor. "Oh, my great-grandmother, who lived to be 102, taught me a lady never reveals her age to anyone but her mother."

Do your homework in advance to learn about the company. Know the corporate culture, current developments in the field, the company history, and main officers. Bring a good pen and some paper in a nice small leather portfolio. Have questions prepared in advance, and think of others as you go through the interview.

If you have questions after the interview, wait until you are contacted unless you were informed that it was OK to call for additional information.

Establish the "next step" at the end of the interview. When does the company expect to make a decision? Is any more information needed from you? When might you expect to hear?

Send a thank-you note. In a job search situation, you may want to type the thank-you because it may appear more professional. Say, "Dear Mr. Bartash, Thank you for taking the time to interview me for the account executive position at the ABC Group. Based on our meeting, I'm sure I can fulfill the requirements you seek. Sincerely,...." (Thank-you notes were discussed in detail in Chapter Nine, "Written Communication: Write it Right!")

Make sure the thank-you note arrives before you call back to follow up. If you are being interviewed by several companies and recruiters, send thank-you notes to each one, even if you are not interested in that particular position.

MANAGING THE MEDIA

Contrary to popular belief, reporters are people too! Like you, they have a job to do, one with its own specialized set of rules. The nature of their business often requires them to act quickly, to focus on the dramatic nature of events under way, and to eliminate all but the most essential information in their reports. However, if you treat a professional journalist with respect and courtesy, you might be pleasantly surprised by the response you receive.

Important functions may require press coverage. Handle them through your public relations firm or communications department. Listen to their suggestions on ways to make the best media presentation, since it is their business to know what's involved.

When dealing with reporters, appear open and courteous at all times. Don't be hostile or defensive.

Give the facts. Return calls promptly. If you are slow to respond, reporters will go to other sources to meet their deadlines. You want them to get *your* version from you.

Nurture the press relationship. Maintain a press mailing list. Know who covers your industry. Do not offer bribes to get your story printed.

Press releases should be written with an angle or hook. What is of interest to the reader? Don't submit releases for every little thing, because when something big happens, it will not stand out. Your materials should include good photos, a grabby lead or headline, and error-proof copy. Be prepared for the reporter to follow up on the information, using the press release only as a starting point.

Give appropriate lead time.

It is not accepted practice to see an article before it goes to print. Make clear ahead of time what is on or off the record. If you want something to stay off the record, don't say it. If you want to say it but not have it be attributed to you, explain that first. "You can quote 'a senior company official'—but not me by name—on what I'm about to tell you. Agreed?"

Be precise in your language. Don't call someone your business partner if she actually is not. Be especially careful when taping a radio or television interview. They may not edit out your slang, ums and ahs, even an oath. And in the meantime, many people will have witnessed the poor impression you made.

If you are on television, don't glance off stage. It makes you look unprofessional and shifty-eyed. Get coaching in media relations or speaking before your interview.

MEANINGFUL MEETINGS

When you strip meetings, of any type, of the business that forms their substance, what you're left with is human interaction with all its promise and pitfalls. If you apply the essential principles of business manners to meetings—basic courtesy to others, polite and cordial communication, respect for other people's time—the agendas and other arrangements will become tools you can use rather than obstacles to overcome. We may have to meet on a regular basis, but we don't have to meet in an unproductive, frustrating fashion! Meetings, like encounters of any kind, can be opportunities to present yourself as a professional while making others feel respected.

Chapter 11

DINING FOR FUN AND PROFIT
The Business Lunch

The world was my oyster, but I used the wrong fork.

—OSCAR WILDE

The business lunch is much more than a meal because food isn't the only item on the "menu." A business lunch can serve many purposes including helping you to get to know a customer better, encouraging new business, or keeping a present client happy. It also can be used to interview prospective employees, to reward employees for a job well done and to provide an opportunity for an in-depth discussion away from office distractions. In each case, the setting and the situation should serve to enhance the business at hand. The meal may be the centerpiece, but the main course actually is the work-related discussion that is going on around it! There is, of course, an etiquette involved with all this.

Do not make the mistake of thinking that just because you are out of the office for a business lunch, how you behave is not important. *It is.* The social appearance of the business lunch is deceiving. This is not an appropriate time to kick back or relax. Jobs, even careers, have terminated because people were not aware what their lunch manners were saying about them.

Suppose your boss took you to lunch expecting to offer you a complex but prestigious task with a tight deadline, only to discover that you demonstrated indecisiveness by interrogating the waiter for twenty minutes about the ingredients of each item on the menu? Or imagine that you took a client who you wished to impress to a restaurant at which the service was indifferent and the food unappealing? One American industrialist would not hire anyone who salted his food before tasting it. To him, this demonstrated making an assumption without full information.

How you act creates an impression. You want it to work for you.

You also want to be comfortable. Unless you and your guests are at ease, you can miss out on the positive aspects of the lunch: its special significance, the chance to take more time to eat than you otherwise might, the enjoyment of well-prepared and well-presented food, the opportunity to get to know someone a little better outside of the office environment. If you spend all your effort worrying about which utensil to use or how to eat, you will not concentrate on that main course of business.

This chapter will take you through a typical business lunch from start to finish—from selecting the restaurant to retrieving the coats. We'll cover food, utensils, conversation, and payment procedures.

We've focused on the business lunch because that is the most common setting for business meals. Although the place setting for dinner is usually more elaborate, the general guidelines are the same. After our discussion of lunch, we'll explore briefly dinner and some other eating occasions.

An effective business lunch has two main components: proper planning and perfect performance.

THE KEYS TO PROPER PLANNING

Good business lunches don't just happen. They take the same kind of planning that any other business encounter—a meeting, a sales campaign kickoff, a project update—would take. *If you are the host you need to:*

Select the restaurant.

Issue invitations.

Make reservations.

Decide and confirm where and when to meet your guests.

Plan seating arrangements.

These procedures must be followed each time you arrange for a business lunch.

Choosing the Right Restaurant

A business lunch can be ruined if the restaurant selected is not suitable. In most situations, the business lunch is not the time to try out a new restaurant.

Keep a file of good restaurants, and, when in doubt, stick to the "safe" ones. The adventure in your business lunch doesn't come from the restaurant, but from the human dynamics. Avoid the ultra-exotic in terms of cuisine, decor, and atmosphere—although you may find them stimulating, your guest may be uncomfortable. A wide-selection menu is preferable to accommodate all tastes. Stay away from places that emphasize fast service because they will not want you to linger and talk. You'll probably want to avoid your own company's "business hangouts" where your conversation may be inhibited or where you or your guest might feel on display.

When inviting a guest, consider how convenient the location will be for him.

If, for some reason, the restaurant is new to you, check it out ahead of time, even if you've heard from reliable sources that it is suitable. Introduce yourself to the host or hostess. Look at the menu. Try the food. Observe the lunchtime clientele, which can be different from the crowd that congregates on weekends or evenings.

If it has been a while (six months or more) since you've visited the restaurant, check it out as if it were new. A change in management or chefs can alter the appropriateness.

Become a regular customer, so the staff knows the importance of your patronage.

If you are from out of town, ask your hotel's concierge to suggest suitable locations for business lunches. You also can do some research before you arrive, asking other people in your company who have been to that town where they would recommend dining. It is acceptable to ask the guest if she has any favorites. Naturally, you want to make sure that you can afford the most expensive items on the menu—there is no point feeling uncomfortable with the prices once you have arrived.

Issuing Invitations Graciously

Each company has its own standards of what constitutes an appropriate occasion for a business lunch. Besides those we've already mentioned, a business lunch may center around a holiday observance, the celebration of an employment anniversary, or a co-worker's retirement. In some professions, such as sales, "working lunches" are commonly used to cultivate clients or to seal deals. In some industries, such as the entertainment field, lunches substitute for the in-office meetings that prevail in other businesses. Having lunch with others from similar companies to discuss common concerns may be considered part of your networking responsibilities.

It's important to know your company's attitude about the appropriate frequency and purpose of business lunches. It can be a faux pas either to exceed or fall short of your co-worker's or client's expectations. For example, we know of one insurance company salesperson who used the business lunch to entertain clients *before* they had purchased a policy. He was reprimanded. Company policy was that lunches were appropriate only *after* the purchase.

In another instance, the client invited himself out to lunch with the salesperson. Since she had not issued the invitation, the salesperson recommended that they split the check. The client was angry. The salesperson was later told by her boss, "We always pick up the check!" The moral: Always know your company's protocol. When you don't know, you should, of course, ask.

When arranging a lunch, good etiquette requires that you call the other party to arrange the date. Call a week to two weeks in advance and offer a few choices. It's both prudent and polite to be sensitive to the other person's business rhythm. That means not insisting on a Wednesday if that is her most hectic day, and perhaps delaying your regular 11:30 lunch for an hour if that is more convenient for her. After the date has been set, it's your responsibility to reconfirm with the client, co-worker, or his secretary on the morning of the luncheon.

If you do the asking, you are the host. The host chooses the restaurant, often with input from the guest. Again, give choices. Be sensitive to your guest's dietary requirements and food preferences. Ask if she likes seafood, for instance, before taking her to the restaurant on the wharf. If you are the guest, be as open and flexible as you reasonably can be, but etiquette does not require that you agree to something that would make you uncomfortable.

The host also pays the bill. To avoid any awkwardness, the purpose of the lunch as well as your plans to pay should be clear when the invitation is issued. You can say something like, "I'd like to take you to lunch to celebrate the end of the tax season. Would Wednesday the 26th be convenient?" Avoid any ambiguity in this area. One woman who met periodically for lunch with a business associate panicked when the other person said, "Oh, I'm so glad you invited *me* to lunch." The woman had forgotten that she was the one who issued this particular invitation, and had neglected to bring enough money. Fortunately, they were well enough acquainted that she could explain the situation. They agreed to "go dutch."

Going dutch—paying for your own lunch—is an acceptable practice between people who know each other well or who lunch frequently. To issue an invitation for this sort of lunch, rather than saying, "Please join me for lunch" or "Will you be my guest?" consider saying, "Shall we have lunch together?" or "Let's split lunch." It's best to avoid surprises. If you are unsure whether you are splitting lunch with someone, you can say, "Allow me to split this" or "How much is my half?" or "This one is mine. The next time we go out, you can treat."

As a guest, don't abuse your invitation. We know of one woman who was astonished when the client invited himself to dinner with her—and then expected her, the vendor, to pay. What's worse is that he brought along, unannounced, a friend. She was terribly put off by the expectation that she would pay the total bill, even though she did so to maintain client-customer relations.

Lunch invitations are generally safer than dinner invitations because they don't put people into awkward situations regarding their marital status, children, and outside-of-work obligations.

One female lawyer asked a number of times for her client to go to dinner with her after his lawsuit was successfully concluded, only to be put off repeatedly. She persisted, because celebratory dinners were considered customary by her firm. Finally, she asked him directly why he wasn't interested in accepting her offer. He blurted out, in a frustrated fashion, "I'm an old man. I don't make love any more!" It was a humiliating admission for him to make and for her to hear.

Whether you are male or female, make it clear, both by your wording and your tone of voice, that you view your business invitation strictly as a business proposition. Then, be professional and act accordingly.

When you make the invitation, it's a good idea to let the invitee know if anyone else is invited, if there is a specific business topic you'd like to discuss, and if there are any materials you would like him or her to bring along.

Making the Required Reservations

Many routine business lunches take place at large establishments, known for prompt, reliable service and quality food, that do not require reservations. But if a lunch is important enough to involve an invitation, it is significant enough to need a reservation. You can always cancel the reservation if necessary, or inform the restaurant of any changes in the number of people attending or the time of arrival. It would be an etiquette gaffe to keep your guest or guests waiting during a busy lunch hour for the next available table.

In order to make reservations, you need to have some additional information beyond the time and the date. You should know the precise number of people attending. When in doubt, err in excess: it is easier to remove places than to add them. In some locations, it's important to stipulate whether you want the smoking or non-smoking section. If your dining partner has a physical disability, mention that as well. Someone who is in a wheelchair may prefer a table to a booth. Add any special requests that are specific to the restaurant, such as "in the garden room, please" or "overlooking the waterfront." You may even wish to request a specific waiter or waitress.

An Impressive Start: Meeting Your Guests

Confirm directions to the restaurant in advance. Provide them to your guest, along with information on parking availability. Determine whether you should allow extra travel time for lunchtime traffic.

If you are the host, arrive early and schedule plenty of time for lunch. You don't want to have to excuse yourself early.

If you are the guest, you should arrive on time. If you need to leave by a certain time, say so up front so the host can plan the meal and discussion accordingly.

If this is the first time you will meet your guest, describe the color of your coat, your height, or hair color.

Check in at the reservation desk upon your arrival.

If there is more than one entrance, make sure the guest knows where to meet you. The host should wait in the lobby. If the guest is more than fifteen minutes late, call her office (remember to bring the phone number with you). If you are the guest and are delayed, call the restaurant.

Check your coat after your guest arrives.

In the case of a large party, don't ask to be seated until everyone has arrived. However, if only one or two in a large group are more than ten minutes late, the host can escort the rest to the table, arrange for them to get seated, and order drinks while leaving word at the reservation desk of his location.

When the maitre d' or hostess leads the way to the table, the host brings up the rear; otherwise she leads the way for the guest.

How to Plan Polite Seating Arrangements

Think out the seating plan ahead of time.

The best seat, the one that looks out, always goes to your guest. The seat to the right of the host is the place of honor. You may ask for another table if it is too close to the kitchen, underneath an air duct or stereo speaker, or otherwise doesn't meet your needs.

If your guest is blind, guide his hands to the back of the chair and let him pull it out and settle in himself. Explain if the chair is a captain's chair or any other unusual design. Do not say, "Your chair is there"—it's too vague, and thus dangerous. He will also arrange a cane in a matter that suits him.

If you discover an "atmosphere" problem after you sit down, try to resolve it without moving. If the sun is in your eyes, you might ask that the shades be adjusted, or similarly request that the music be turned down or the temperature raised.

THE KEYS TO CONDUCTING A PERFECTLY ORCHESTRATED BUSINESS LUNCH

Once you've settled in your seats, the true "performance" part of the meal begins. This is the area in which most people feel uncomfortable—probably because there are so many choices and so many things that can go wrong. We will review each part of the meal in sequence—ordering food and wine, the proper use of utensils, handling food problems, excusing yourself to use the restroom, paying the bill, and saying goodbye.

First, though, a few words about the importance of perspective. Proper etiquette for eating is significant, and we have been deliberately detailed in our description in order to leave you with as little ambiguity as possible. It's equally important, though, that you not become overwhelmed by the numerous details. If you can't remember what to do at some point during the meal, relax! Consider what is logical, or practical, as well as what seems most gracious—and then proceed to do it. (Later, you can check yourself against our recommendations and do the correct thing the next time.) It is more likely that you will ruin a meal by becoming tense and awkward than by failing to leave your utensils in the appropriate position or stirring your parfait. Do your best to behave properly, but also enjoy your meal.

Ordering with Flair

WAITERS AND WAITRESSES: Soon after you are seated, you'll receive menus. The person who provides these usually, but not always, will be your waiter. If it is the hostess or maitre d', she'll usually say, "Jacqueline will be back to take your order in just a few minutes."

Notice your waitperson's name. Also pay attention to what he or she looks like so you can make a connection later if there is a problem or request.

Address the waiter as "waiter" or "waitress" and do NOT use "Honey," "Boy," "Dear," "Sweetie," "Garcon," etc. You may use your waitperson's name if asked to do so. Do not snap your fingers to call a waiter or waitress—catch his eye or use a discreet wave of the fingers. In extreme circumstances, a gently called-out "Waiter" or "Waitress" can be used.

If you have a problem that needs immediate attention (something is spilled, for instance), ask for help from any available staff member.

ORDERING DRINKS: Drinks (soft or otherwise) are usually offered shortly after you are seated.

The three-martini lunch is no longer customary in today's business environment. In fact, alcohol is usually not part of the business lunch. If, however, a drink or wine is served, it is important that you feel comfortable and know the etiquette involved.

If your guest declines a drink, you should too. If your guest orders a drink, you should too. If you don't want alcohol, choose something else; you do not want your guest to drink alone.

If you are drinking alcohol, limit yourself to one. As a guest, it is recommended that you abstain.

HOW TO ORDER WINE: Even if you aren't a connoisseur, you should know how to order wine. The basic guidelines are simple: generally white wine goes with fish or fowl, and red with meat, although this is not a rigid rule.

Because this is a highly specialized field, don't pretend to know a lot about wine if you don't—it will show. You can defer to the recommendation of the sommelier (wine steward) or waitperson: "Do you have a nice white?" Some restaurants have "house" wines; others don't. House wines are generally a safe selection at a reasonable cost.

Although it is increasingly common to order wine by the glass, it is gracious to offer to order a bottle you can share with your guests. The sommelier or waitperson will open and serve the wine.

The procedure will be as follows: The bottle will be brought to you, unopened, so that you can look at the label and indicate whether it is indeed what you ordered. Then the wine is uncorked and the cork is handed to the host. Squeeze the cork to see if it is moist. If it is dry, the wine probably will not be good.

If the cork is OK, nod approval. The steward then pours a small amount into your glass. This ensures that any piece of cork will be in your glass, not the guest's. Raise the glass and discreetly sniff it to see if it smells the way it should. Take a sip, and nod approval if the wine is acceptable. You are tasting the wine to determine whether it is spoiled, not whether you like it. On rare occasions, you may need to send the wine back. Do not be pretentious and send the wine back just to impress someone. After all, you ordered it.

The wine is poured into your guests' glasses first. Your glass is the last to be filled. The waiter will refill the glass, although hosts can assume this responsibility if the waiter does not. Guests should never have to refill their own wine glasses.

ORDERING THE MEAL: If your guest orders a second round of drinks, switch to a non-alcoholic drink, ask for menus, and order.

If you are the host, make some suggestions to the guest about the restaurant's specialties, if you can. It's also polite while reviewing the menu to discuss what entree "sounds good." It gives a clue as to what you are ordering, helping the guest feel more comfortable about the price range and type of item you are selecting. Ask the waitperson about the day's specials if he or she does not volunteer the information.

See that your guest's order is taken first. Tell the waitperson, "Let my guest order first." This also signals that you are to receive the bill.

If the guest orders a first course—soup or salad—so should you.

As a guest, you should ask what the host recommends. If there is no recommendation, order something in the mid-price range.

If you have allergies or specific dietary restrictions, ask the server how the food is prepared. It is acceptable, within reason, to make requests ("Please omit the anchovies from the Greek salad, and put the dressing on the side.") If you feel the need to redefine the dish ("Could I have that baked instead of fried, with no breading, and substitute lemon juice for the butter?"), order something else. Keep in mind the business meal puts business first. You can always eat again later.

Don't order foods you don't know how to eat or that are too messy. If you want to learn how to eat something, do it at a non-business lunch where you can practice. (Take someone with you who does know how to eat it!)

We recommend you don't order a whole lobster, French onion soup or, in most instances, pasta, because they are messy to eat.

An engineer in one of our classes was indignant at this advice, saying, "If I want a big, juicy hamburger, that's what I'll order." We tried to convince him that a business lunch is business and the food is not the priority item. The rest of the class proceeded to paint the unappealing picture of him with his mouth around a fat hamburger, as the juices from the meat and tomato dripped down his chin. This was not the corporate image he wanted to convey, and, with this bit of humor, he was converted.

Be realistic about how much you can eat. It is a mistake to over-order and waste food. Overeating can diminish your effectiveness in responding to conversation. As a host, don't press guests to consume more than they want to eat or drink.

Sharing food is not recommended at business meals. If you want a taste of something, order it.

ORDERING DESSERT: If time permits, encourage your guest to order dessert. If the guest orders one, so should you. If you are watching your weight, order fruit.

ORDERING COFFEE: Coffee typically is ordered after the meal, although in some parts of the country it will be served with it. When the coffee is served and the entree cleared away, ask for the check.

Handling Problems

When problems arise, you want to handle them as graciously as possible so that everyone is comfortable. Avoid exclamations of disgust or other intense emotions. Do not berate the staff, over-apologize, or otherwise overreact. Your guest will not hold you accountable for the restaurant's mistake, but she will hold you accountable for your own behavior!

IF THE ORDER IS INCORRECT, point it out to the waiter immediately so that it can be corrected.

IF THE TIMING IS OFF so that your guest's food arrives before yours does, encourage her to eat before it gets cold. Ideally, both of you should be eating at the same time, and each of you should adapt to any delays. However, if yours needs to be sent back, encourage your guest to eat. If his needs to be sent back, stall in eating yours, or ask the waiter to hold yours.

IF THE FOOD IS NOT GOOD, as long as it is basically edible, eat it anyway. It's better not to make a big deal about sending an item back—it makes people uncomfortable and interrupts the flow of the meal. We recommend that you eat what you can, even when you don't like the meal, assuming that it has been well-prepared. At a restaurant with a fixed menu, eat what you can or quietly ask for substitutions so that you don't embarrass the others at your table. You may be able to get along by focusing on the part of the meal that is to your liking—bread, or vegetables, or rice, for instance.

Of course, if there is a problem with the guest's food, it should be addressed. However, if you are the guest, you should attempt to smooth over any minor complaint about the food as long as it is not health-threatening.

Remember that the food is not the sole purpose of the meal. You don't want to embarrass your guest or host by making a big fuss.

Dishes, Glasses and Utensils:
Solving the Perplexities of Placement

Use the time after your order has been taken to briefly inspect the silverware, glasses, and dishes. If you are missing a piece or something's not clean, point it out politely before the food arrives, rather than delay the start of the meal.

What's what and what's yours? Your food dishes, including the bread-and-butter plate, are to the left, while all drink containers are to the right. One way to remember this is that both "food" and "left" have four letters.

If they are on the table when you arrive, your coffee cup and saucer are to the right of the dinner plate. They may, however, be brought when you order coffee.

Sometimes, there will be a service plate on the table when you arrive. The appetizer and soup are usually placed on it; the waiter will remove it before the main course is served.

Different drinks have different glasses. Know the distinctions in wine glasses. There is a white wine glass and a red wine glass. White wine has a smaller bowl than the red wine glass. There is usually one wine glass with lunch. The water glass is the largest. It often will be filled shortly after you arrive, leaving little doubt as to its purpose!

Utensil placement can be extremely tricky. American restaurants don't always follow the proper place setting, so you will see lots of variations. This, naturally, creates dining dilemmas. Sometimes you will use utensils from the outside in, other times from left to right. The more courses, the more utensils. The best advice we can give you is to take your cue from the table setting.

We have illustrated several sample lunch place settings that you might encounter on pages 204–207.

The *Outside-In* place setting (see illustration on page 204) is the most correct although it is not the most commonly used in the United States. In this setting, the idea is that you work your way through the utensils, from both sides, from the outermost one to the innermost one. You will find forks to the left and knives and spoons to the right, but even so, the order can be confusing.

On the left, the salad fork will be outside the entree fork, since you will use that first at lunch. At dinner, salad can be served after the main course, which would then place the salad fork in a different position. Now are you beginning to get confused?

On the right, the soup spoon will be on the outside, then the entree knife and finally a teaspoon for dessert or coffee. Of course, if you use the teaspoon to stir sugar in your coffee during the meal, the philosophy doesn't support the setting, but that's the exception to the rule. The cup and saucer, the salad and bread-and-butter plate may or may not be on the table when you arrive.

Another frequently used setting is the *Left-to-Right* place setting (see illustration on page 205). Generally, on the left should be the salad fork, then the entree fork. There may be only one fork.

What you should find at the right of the plate are, the soup spoon, the entree knife and the dessert spoon. This setting may be simplified to include only a knife and a teaspoon on the right side of the plate.

Another common setting you will often find is *"User's Choice."* This is what we call a mixed setting (see illustration on page 206). It isn't exactly left-to-right or outside-in, but often a combination of the two. The key to navigating through this setting

OUTSIDE-IN
PLACE SETTING

Wine Glass

Water Glass

Bread & Butter Plate
& Butter Knife

Salad Plate

Soup Spoon

Entree Knife

Teaspoon

Service Plate

Entree Fork

Salad Fork

LEFT-TO-RIGHT PLACE SETTING

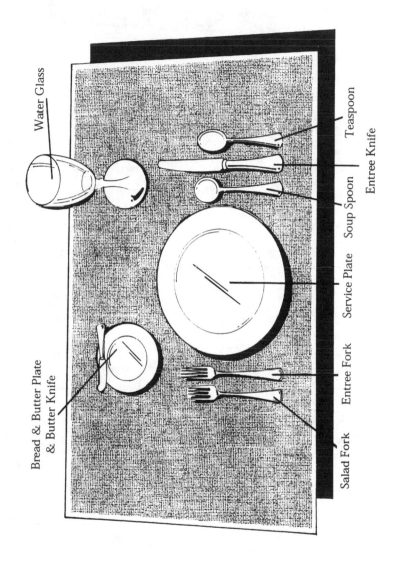

Water Glass

Teaspoon

Entree Knife

Soup Spoon

Service Plate

Entree Fork

Bread & Butter Plate
& Butter Knife

Salad Fork

USER'S CHOICE
PLACE SETTING

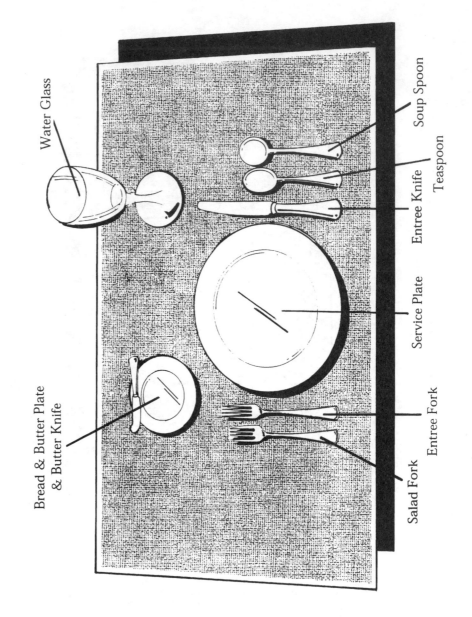

Water Glass

Soup Spoon

Teaspoon

Entree Knife

Service Plate

Bread & Butter Plate
& Butter Knife

Salad Fork

Entree Fork

FORMAL
PLACE SETTING

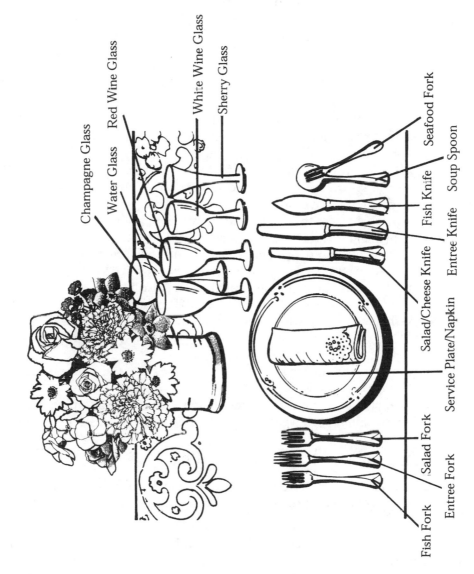

Champagne Glass
Water Glass
Red Wine Glass
White Wine Glass
Sherry Glass

Seafood Fork
Fish Knife
Soup Spoon
Entree Knife
Salad/Cheese Knife
Service Plate/Napkin

Fish Fork
Salad Fork
Entree Fork

successfully is to recognize the utensils by their shape. (The soup spoon, which is oval-shaped, has a bigger bowl than the teaspoon; the salad fork is smaller than the entree fork.)

There are many "User's Choice" settings out there. We recently attended a wedding, where we found three teaspoons to the right of the knife. This was a new one for us! Again, take your cue from the utensil or follow the lead of the host.

The *Formal Place Setting* (see illustration on page 207) differs from the others because it includes more utensils and some have highly specialized uses. Chances are that you will not encounter this setting at lunch (it's more common at dinner) but if you do, you will be prepared.

The formal setting is set up to be used from the outside in. On the left side, from the outside, you may find a fish fork, an entree fork, and then a salad fork. On the right, from the outside, will be the seafood fork, resting in the bowl of the soup spoon. It will be followed by the fish knife, the meat knife, and then the salad/cheese knife, because this setting assumes salad will be served after the meal. The dessert spoon and fork are usually brought in with the dessert.

In a restaurant where this formal setting is found, a sorbet course may be served between the fish and meat course. This sherbert-like food is intended to refresh the palate and is not the dessert—as one woman thought the first time it was served to her as a teenager in Europe. The small sorbet spoon is served with the sorbet.

Each of the many glasses in this formal setting also has a specific role. The sherry glass is above the soup spoon, because sherry is consumed during that course. It is the small, V-shaped glass. A white wine glass is at the front center, with the red wine glass to the left. The water goblet is behind the wine glasses, and to the right of it, a champagne glass, for use with dessert.

When in doubt about how to proceed, observe others. If you stay just one step behind them, you can sometimes bluff your way through.

If you happen to use the wrong utensil, don't panic or make a big deal out of it. You can often substitute with what you should have used or just ask for a replacement.

Now That I Know What They Are, What Do I Do With Them?

Proper use of dishes, glasses, and utensils requires proper handling. This is the area in which many people have problems that are noticeable and potentially damaging to their image.

WINE GLASSES: If the wine is cold, hold the glass by the stem. Sip from the glass and never wave it. If you are drinking red wine, it is acceptable to hold the glass by the bowl and stem, since the heat from your hand will not affect the taste of the wine. Left-handed people should remember to use the right hand to drink wine or water because they might then incorrectly place the glass back on the left side.

COFFEE CUP: Always hold the coffee cup by the handle, not the bowl.

SOUP BOWL: If the soup bowl has two handles, you may pick it up by the handles and sip from the bowl. If not, use the soup spoon.

KNIVES, FORKS, AND SPOONS: The butter knife may be on top of the bread plate, which is on your left. If no butter knife is on the bread plate, use the entree knife to butter the bread. Leave the knife on the bread plate until the main course is served, at which point you move it to the entree plate.

Use the soup spoon to skim the surface of the liquid starting near you and going away from you. Sip from the side of the soup spoon, silently.

The soup spoon is held between the thumb and the first two fingers. It should rest on the middle finger and be held gently in place by the thumb and index fingers. When you finish, leave the soup spoon on the soup plate, or if the soup was served in a cup, on the saucer underneath.

A seafood fork is used to eat shrimp, clams, and oysters. If the shrimp cocktail is on a pedestal dish, never use a knife to cut the shrimp. Eat by taking several little bites.

You can eat dessert with either the dessert spoon, or fork, or both. The spoon is kept in the right hand.

There are two acceptable styles in the United States for holding the knife and fork during the meal. These are called the American and Continental styles, and we've included illustrations of each on page 210.

Both styles start with the fork in the left hand and the knife in the right. Both utensils are controlled by the thumb and index finger. The cutting motion also is the same—slice, but don't saw your meat.

In the American style, which is most commonly used, you transfer the fork to the right hand after you cut something, putting the knife down on the plate. Do not have it rest on the table. You bring the fork, tines up, to the mouth. You do not use the knife to push food onto the fork. If you can't eat something with just the fork once the food has been cut, don't eat it. In other words, leave the extra vegetables on your plate!

With the Continental style, you keep the fork in the left hand, tines down, to spear the food. The knife remains in the right hand. Some people find this method to be more convenient, efficient, and logical than switching back and forth. In the Continental style, the knife also can be used to help with placement of a small amount of potatoes or vegetables on the fork.

The key is to be consistent in using whichever style you select.

Cut no more than two or three pieces at a time if you are eating American style. The Continental style automatically lends itself to cutting one piece at a time.

If the entree and the salad are served together, you may use the entree fork for both. The fork is held between the thumb and first two fingers. It should rest on the middle finger and be held gently in place by the thumb and index finger. Avoid the "pitchfork approach" of making a fist around the fork when cutting or eating.

If a salad, such as a chef's salad, is your main course, use the entree fork.

If you order iced tea, you may be brought a long-handled spoon which is to be used only to stir sugar or sweetener in the tea. Afterwards, place it on the small plate on which the iced tea glass rests. If no other plate is provided, use the dinner plate.

When pausing for bites or conversation breaks, put the utensils back on the entree plate. Never rest them half-on, half-off the plate. We've included an illustration of the proper rest and finished positions of utensils on page 211.

HOLDING
UTENSILS

CONTINENTAL/AMERICAN

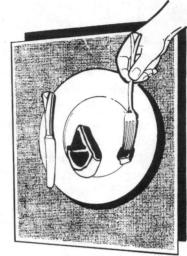

AMERICAN EATING

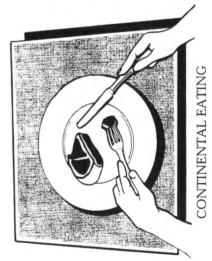

CONTINENTAL EATING

210

UTENSILS
FINISHED POSITION

AMERICAN/CONTINENTAL

UTENSILS
RESTING POSITION

AMERICAN

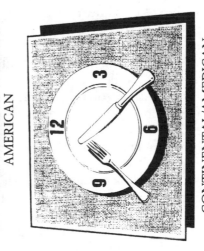

CONTINENTAL/AMERICAN

The rest position can be an inverted V-shape. If you are eating American style, the fork tines are up. If you are eating Continental style, the tines are down. Another rest position you will see occasionally is to place the knife across the top and the fork at 10 and 4 o'clock. A well-trained waiter should know these mean you have not yet completed your meal.

The finish position is so that the utensils are parallel to one another diagonally at approximately where the hour hand on a clock would be at 10- and at 4- o'clock.

NAPKIN: You will usually find the napkin either atop the dinner plate or next to the forks. Sometimes, a waiter will unfurl the napkin for you after you have been seated. This is especially likely if the napkin happens to be placed in a goblet.

The napkin goes in your lap when everyone has been seated. Etiquette dictates that you wait for the host to do so first. Do not put it in your shirt or belt. If it is a very large napkin, keep it folded in half with the crease toward you.

When leaving the table temporarily during the meal, place the napkin on your chair. When leaving following the meal, place the napkin to the left of your plate.

If your napkin falls to the floor, ask for another one; it can be retrieved later.

Rules for Better Eating

You do not have to clean your plate. Leave parsley, carrot curls, and other garnishes.

Do not salt and pepper your food before tasting it.

If you don't know how to eat something that comes with what you've ordered, leave it or watch to see how others eat it, and imitate them.

Do not turn your wine glass upside down if you do not want wine. Say "no thank you" or, if that will interfere with the conversation, gently shake your head to indicate "no more" while you put your fingertips over the rim of the glass. These are polite gestures, because you do not want to waste good wine.

Never cut bread or rolls. Break off one piece at a time and butter the piece as you are ready to eat it.

When in doubt, eat with a utensil rather than with your fingers, even those foods that you may eat by hand at home. If something is served on a plate, you should use utensils! Use a fork to cut french fries into bite-sized pieces. Eat bacon with a fork. Chicken, or any other meat with a bone, is not a finger food; you should use the knife and fork.

Use the edge of the plate to twirl pasta, not a spoon, because using a spoon can result in messy hanging strands.

If you spill coffee into your saucer, ask for another saucer. Do not dunk cookies into coffee. Do not blow on your coffee—give it time to cool.

Tuck paper trash—the empty sugar packets, the plastic cup from the creamer, the wrapper for crackers, the wrapper for the straw—under the rim of your plate, or on the edge of the saucer or butter plate.

We also recommend that you don't ask for a "doggy bag."

How to Eat Difficult Foods

The best way to handle difficult foods is to not order them, but sometimes you have no choice.

Use a knife and fork to cut a cherry tomato into pieces.

Be cautious with crackers. Do not break crackers into the soup. Do not hold a cracker in one hand and a soup spoon in the other. Take a bite of the cracker, put it down, and then pick up the soup spoon.

Cup a lemon in your hand before squeezing it over tea or seafood to avoid squirting anyone.

Use a knife and fork to eat watermelon.

If you find a fishbone or other bone in your mouth, remove it unobtrusively with your thumb and forefinger and place it on the rim of your plate.

When eating a parfait, start at the top. Do not stir.

Power Table Manners

Table manners are designed to ensure that we don't offend anyone. You do not want the way you eat to be an eyesore or to interfere with someone else's enjoyment of his or her food. We've listed some key points below:

Dining Do's and Don'ts

Do	Don't
Say "please" and "thank you" when food is passed to you.	Discuss business until after the meal is ordered.
Eat slowly and chew your food with your mouth closed. Swallow before speaking.	Talk with your mouth full.
Eat your food once you have put it on your utensil. If you drop a utensil, ask the waiter for a replacement	Wave utensils with food on them.
Pass salt and pepper together.	Eat before everyone has been served. Wait for the host. The host may say, "Please start eating, it will get cold."
Hold the water glass with all fingers touching the glass.	Slouch in chair.
	Push away plate and say, "I'm stuffed."
	Complain or criticize the service or the food. It can be an insult to the host.
	Reach across the table or pick up dropped utensils.

(Continued on next page)

Do	Don't
Keep handbag/briefcase off the table. Put it on your lap or the floor. For security purposes, wrap the strap around the chair leg	Put elbows on table while eating.

GROOMING. Grooming (including combing your hair, picking your teeth, or applying fresh lipstick) should not be done at the table. You can excuse yourself for this purpose by saying, "Excuse me"; you don't need to say where you're going, people will figure it out! If you must leave the table during the meal, you can indicate whether you are finished eating through proper placement of your utensils in case the waiter stops by the table during your absence. Remember, the "finished position" is placing your fork and knife parallel to each other, with the handles at 4 o'clock and the heads at 10 o'clock. This prevents the utensils from falling off when the server picks up the plate.

SMOKING. If you expect to smoke after the meal, ask to be seated in the restaurant's smoking section. Ask your guest's preference before being seated.

Don't smoke unless the guest does. As the host, don't even ask permission.

As a guest, you should ask permission to smoke. However, refrain from lighting up until after everyone has finished or almost finished dessert, and coffee has been served. Cigars and pipes are unacceptable in restaurants.

CONVERSATION AND CONDUCTING BUSINESS. Dining conversation follows the guidelines we gave in Chapter Three for small talk. General conversation should take place until the meal has been ordered. Use that time to build your relationship with your host or your guest. Keep all comments pleasant and tasteful.

Once the order has been placed, you can discuss business topics. Remember to keep your voice soft enough so that the conversation isn't overheard at other tables or by the servers. If possible, wrap up the discussion before the food arrives. It makes the experience more pleasant.

Once the food arrives, the guest should not criticize the food or the service—it can be an insult to the host.

Do not keep a notebook on the table unless it has been approved by your dining companion. You can use a small leather notebook in which to scrawl quick notes, but put it away as soon as possible. We also recommend that you keep papers off the table until after the entree plates have been cleared. This is not only more gracious, it helps keep food off the paper.

If you must refer to papers and discuss business during the meal, ask for a booth if the restaurant has one. Place the papers on the seat next to you rather than on the table.

The Right Way to Pay the Bill

You'll recall that the person who issued the invitation is the host and he or she pays the bill. Try to arrange ahead of time how the bill will be paid. Use a credit card; it makes paying quick, easy, and discreet (the guest, theoretically anyway, should not know the grand total).

Don't pull out a calculator to verify numbers. Go to the head waiter's station to resolve any problems with the bill.

Don't argue about who pays the bill. If a woman is the host and the male guest is uncomfortable when she pays the bill, the woman can say something like, "The ABC Company would really like you to be our guest."

If paying cash, it is acceptable to ask the waiter or cashier for a receipt for business purposes.

Practical Tips on Tipping

Remember to add the tip. First check the bill to make sure it isn't already included. (Sometimes the restaurant does so automatically, particularly in the case of large parties).

Although calculating the tip involves some mental gymnastics, try to avoid being obvious. Don't count on your fingers, or roll your eyes, for instance. Instead, come up with a shortcut way to determine the amount—typically 15 to 20 percent. In states with sales tax, for instance, you sometimes can use a multiple of that amount for an approximate tip. Another suggestion is to figure 10 percent, a more simple calculation, and then add half or double that amount, depending on the restaurant and the quality of the service.

Restaurant Tipping Guidelines

POSITION	TIP
Waitperson	15% to 20% plus 5% of the bill to captain (the one who took the order) if there is one.
Sommelier (Wine Steward)	$3 to $5 per bottle or 15% of the cost of the wine.
Coatroom Attendant	$1 per coat
Garage Attendant	$1 to $2

You can leave the tip for the waiter in cash on the table, if you prefer, or include it in the credit card total. You also can indicate the amount for the sommelier on a credit card. The money should be handed directly to the coatroom attendant, unless there is a tray that has been left out for that purpose. Also pay the garage attendant directly. Some people are more comfortable folding up the dollar bills for the tip so that the amount is not so noticeable. Say "Thank you" as you give them the money.

A Grand Finale: Saying Goodbye

The meal isn't over until you are out of the restaurant. A side trip to the restroom is permissible, but the parties should then meet and leave the building together.

The host thanks the guest for coming, shakes hands and perhaps discusses the next meeting.

The guest should thank the host and send a handwritten note within two days.

WHEN LUNCH IS TOO MUCH OR NOT ENOUGH

You may eat with a colleague or client at a setting other than lunch. Regardless of the option or the location, good dining rules apply.

Other Options

BUSINESS DINNERS: As we mentioned earlier, all the guidelines for lunch apply for a business dinner. You may also have to contend with more silverware, more courses, more elaborate food, or more wine.

Business dinners can be more social in nature, which of course means you should limit or eliminate "hard core" business discussions. The business dinner may include spouses or "significant others." If that is the case, the conversation is general.

Wine and liquor often are consumed at business dinners. Under all circumstances, limit your intake. You don't want to make business decisions while under the influence, nor do you want to embarrass yourself.

BUSINESS BREAKFASTS: Another dining option—breakfast—usually takes less time and is increasingly popular with organizations because it doesn't cut as much into the business day.

EATING "IN": You might invite a client or guest to eat in your company cafeteria, but be cautious about doing this with international visitors, who might consider it an insult.

You may invite a client to lunch in your office when a long day of work is involved. Try to use real silverware. Hold all telephone calls, and for the duration of the meal, suspend the work discussion.

AFTERNOON TEA: Afternoon tea is usually served at a hotel from 3:30 to 5:30 P.M. Teas, pastries, and light sandwiches can be served. People enjoy it because it's different. Liquor is not part of the meal. Tea can be brief—45 minutes to an hour. People can return to work afterwards if they want to.

COCKTAILS: Cocktail parties are generally a form of networking and entertaining. Don't think of them as a place to eat heartily. Take foods in limited portions. Try to hold the plate and glass in your left hand, leaving the right hand to eat the food, and to shake hands. Take small bites.

BUFFET: A business buffet should be approached delicately. Don't use the opportunity to pile up your plate. Take several trips to the buffet table.

Ensuring an Enjoyable Experience

Meals are meant to be enjoyed, and applying appropriate business etiquette should not interfere with that experience. Familiarity with the rules, in fact, can make the actual eating more automatic and less troublesome, freeing both the host and the guest to focus on the conversation and on the food. Properly completed, a business lunch can leave you with a comfortably satisfied feeling, both physically and psychologically. We hope that proves to be your experience. Bon appétit!

Chapter 12

BUSINESS OUT
OF THE OFFICE

If you say a bad thing,
you may soon hear a worse thing said about you.

—HESIOD

The new hire who was on the fast track was invited to the boss's house for a Christmas Eve party. She accepted gladly since she and her husband, as newcomers to the area, had no special holiday plans until the following day—a Christmas brunch at her uncle's house in a neighboring state. She and her husband mingled at the party over cocktails, and then, to prepare for an early morning two-hour drive the next day, began to say their farewells. Unfortunately, that was just when the boss's wife brought out the hot food she had been preparing in the kitchen. The employee and her husband tried to explain and then made a hasty, but guilt-ridden, retreat. After that, despite continued excellent work, the woman's fast track slowed down. If she had sent flowers, or even a nice note, to the boss's home after her quick exit, the damage might have been neutralized. However, because she failed to do so, the negative impression lingered.

The boundaries of business extend well beyond the walls of your office building. You may find yourself mixing socially with your co-workers or clients in environments ranging from a company picnic to sporting events. Clearly, formal workplace etiquette rules don't apply unilaterally in such scenarios, but guidelines for suitable conduct nonetheless exist.

We want to help you to feel comfortable—but not too comfortable—in combined business and social situations. You know better than to confuse these events with a family gathering at Aunt Dorothy's: the two situations may look the same, but the subtext is entirely different. After all, your family is pretty much stuck with you for good, no matter how badly you behave. Your co-workers, on the other hand, can and will carry over judgments about your off-duty performance into the office arena. When clients are part of the equation, your behavior at social functions reflects both on you and your organization. So, whenever you mix business with leisure, you want your actions to enhance your professional reputation.

In this chapter, you'll find out:

- The do's and don'ts when discussing your social life.

- Ten tips for appropriate out-of-the office etiquette.

- What to do in social situations—from cocktail parties to baseball games, from a round of golf to dinner at the boss's house.

- How to handle chance encounters of the social kind with clients and co-workers.

TALK ABOUT YOUR SOCIAL LIFE?
Six Essential Do's and Don'ts

What you choose to do on your own time is, for the most part, your own business. However, the minute you bring your social life into the office—perhaps through a casual comment about evening or weekend plans—it becomes part of your work persona. As is the case with any part of your professional presence, you want these impressions to work for you.

Like it or not, you're judged by your hobbies, interests, and lifestyle. Regardless of your professionalism at work, people will react to you one way if they know you are a stamp collector and gardener and another way if they know you enjoy pick-up basketball games and drag races. Alas, people looking for the "key" to your personality may seek shortcuts in stereotypes about "the kind of people" who engage in those pursuits.

Your corporate culture also may affect what are considered "acceptable" off-duty activities. Conservative organizations may frown on employees who bar-hop, while at other companies, you may be seen as unusual for singing in a church choir.

The solution is not necessarily to adjust your interests to fit in with the office environment. Although many an employee has developed a sudden interest in tennis to find favor with the new boss, you are allowed, even encouraged, to have your own life. What we recommend, though, is a selective sharing of your "secret" side. We consider this a social survival skill rather than dishonesty. Your co-workers do not have a right to examine and judge your life—to do so would be rude—and you are graciously helping them resist that temptation by limiting their vantage point.

Genuine friends, of course, will accept you for who you are, even when they don't share your leisure-time pursuits. It is nice when co-workers can develop that kind of accepting relationship, and if you're lucky, you'll find some people who will fall into that category. However, for casual office contacts, we've developed a few Do's and Don'ts.

1. Don't tell everything. It's OK to be slightly mysterious. As long as you aren't aloof, you can pick and choose what you want to tell. "A quiet weekend at home" could include the post-party hangover of the century, a new chapter completed in the romantic novel you're writing or a Monopoly marathon with your kids. You're probably safe mentioning the Monopoly marathon, but we'd save the details on the hangover or your novel for a trusted friend.

2. Don't say anything that could reflect negatively on you professionally or personally. You may have spent the weekend serving part of your probationary community service sentence for a reckless driving charge. We suggest you say something like "I had a lot of things to catch up on."

3. Do tell anything that could reflect positively on you professionally or personally. If you attended an intensive computer-training course over the weekend or a seminar for professionals in your field, do tell. Ditto if you worked on remodeling your home, baked a soufflé, visited your mother, or hiked through a state park—all indications that you are a competent and well-rounded person.

4. Do limit discussion of your romantic escapades. "I went skiing with a friend" is far better than "I had a torrid time in a ski lodge with Babbette (or Brent). We never made it to the slopes, but we wore a hole in the rug in front of the fireplace." Yes, we'll listen with great interest if you do tell us, but no, it doesn't help us to relate to you as a professional. And at some point, discussion of sexual exploits verges on verbal sexual harassment. It detracts from our ability to take you seriously.

In today's social climate, discussion of a gay or lesbian relationship—however bland the reference may be ("Jeff and I went camping")—may stretch the boundaries of your co-workers' tolerance. You'll have to gauge the wisdom of such discussion based on your knowledge of your colleagues and their built-in biases.

5. Don't criticize others based on their leisure activities. It's a compliment when someone chooses to share a part of his life with you, so accept that compliment graciously. Of course you'll form your own opinions about the co-worker who spends every Saturday practicing the accordion or the colleague who journeys each weekend to a cabin without running water and electricity. Even so, we encourage you to keep an open mind during these discussions. It's amazing what you can learn from people with lifestyles very different from your own. Understanding someone else's choices can provide valuable perspective on your own decisions.

And while to judge is human, to announce negative judgments can be impolite and dangerous. You may be bored as your office mate recounts his quest to find the region's best barbecue. Nevertheless, stating "Barbecue isn't food—it's overspiced leftovers" could be an insult, especially when said in an unfriendly tone. If you can't say something nice, it's better to change the subject. Or ask appropriate questions, such as "How did you become interested in the accordion?" or "How much wood do you need for heating and cooking all weekend?"

6. *Do pay attention to how people respond to discussion of your social life.* We admit that we've sometimes been disappointed at the way others have reacted to our reports about the activities we find so fascinating. How could anyone not be interested in the demise of the downtown department store? Doesn't everyone want to restore a Victorian mansion? When people not only fail to share our interests but their eyes glaze over or their comments take on a cutting edge, we take the prudent course and drop the discussion. It's not courteous to repeatedly bring up something others don't want to discuss.

TEN TIPS FOR OUT-OF-OFFICE ETIQUETTE

Taking a client to a symphony concert or a baseball game is an unofficial business meeting with a hidden agenda. The purpose of the event is to get to know each other a little better outside the formal office environment, not only to discuss business. You do of course want the impression you make to be favorable, so that the next time you sit down to negotiate a contract or to place an order, the positive impact of your social time together may provide business dividends.

When it comes to socializing with colleagues or clients after work, some essential etiquette considerations apply regardless of the specific circumstances.

1. *It's still business.* It's always good to get to know someone in a less formal environment than an office, but don't forget who you are and whom you're with. If you suddenly start calling the boss by his first name, or bad-mouth the work someone did on a project, or use inappropriate language, it will still count against you.

2. *Attend.* Participating in business social events marks you as a team player. People take attendance at these events, and your absence will be noted. If an important conflict prevents you from attending, make sure the host knows about it in advance. You can say, "I was really looking forward to the cocktail party, but that's the night of my daughter's high school graduation."

You don't necessarily have to make the regular Friday "week in review session" at the local bar, but you should plan to join in occasionally. Even joining your colleagues when they go out to lunch makes good business sense.

One woman who put herself through college working at a restaurant found that she was the only student employed there. All the other waiters and waitresses were full-time employees. She usually couldn't join the nightly after-work drinking sessions because she had classes the following day. However, she made it a point to join in on Fridays, and that made all the difference—she was perceived as being part of the team. As a result, she always received help from her co-workers when she needed it.

The reverse is also true. One executive we were asked to coach had a reputation for unfriendliness among his colleagues. When we asked why others thought that, we were told, "He eats lunch in his office and never joins the afterwork group." After receiving this feedback and our coaching, he now makes it a point to have lunch with his colleagues at least twice a week.

We encourage you to be a team member. For instance, join in company sports. You get to know other people and develop a relationship. Business is usually not discussed.

Mark your personal calendar to include major office social events, such as the holiday party, which shouldn't be missed.

Also remember to RSVP. It's just poor manners not to—it leaves the host buying more food or drink than is necessary, or not enough.

3. *Dress appropriately.* Appropriate attire for a symphony concert with a client is naturally different from that for a football game. Dress for the event. "Business Dress"—the acceptable wardrobe for formal events such as a trip to the ballet or a cocktail party—may be more "feminine" for women and more formal (perhaps a tuxedo) for men than usual office garb. Sporting events require more casual attire, although torn T-shirts are not appropriate for "business casual." (See Chapter Four, "Professional Presence: How to Make Your Appearance Work For You.")

Whatever you wear, though, should be tasteful, clean, and fit well. At a Christmas party held by a health care facility, the administrative assistant to the vice president wore an outfit with a plunging neckline. Now people at work see her differently. They're still talking about it, as they wonder what she'll wear to the next event.

If you happen to arrive at an event and find that you are not dressed appropriately, gently acknowledge your gaffe. Doing so can make you feel more comfortable and smooth over the situation. You can say, "I didn't realize this was a jacket-and-tie event." This indicates that if you had known, you would have dressed appropriately. Once that is out of the way, concentrate on being a charming guest. Sulking in the corner will only draw more negative attention to yourself. Next time, check in advance what the appropriate dress will be!

4. *Network—meet and greet.* The purpose of the event is to socialize, so do so. Sticking to your usual crowd won't allow you to meet others, and actually shuts them out. Engage in appropriate conversation with spouses. We've attended parties at which employees and their spouses or dates were assigned to sit with different people to encourage networking.

Time yourself so that you don't spend too much time with any one individual or group. A ballpark number is four to seven minutes. Seek out those who are unfamiliar to you. Although this may feel uncomfortable, force yourself to do it. If you see someone is hanging back, draw him into a conversation. Leave the group when you have finished saying something rather than when someone else has stopped talking. This provides for a smoother exit. (For conversation openers, see Chapter Three, "Big Techniques for Small Talk.")

5. *Limit business discussions.* This is not the time to press your point about the importance of expanding the clerical staff. A brief mention of business is appropriate—that, of course, is what unites you—but concentrate on discussion of other topics. Especially avoid controversial topics and office gossip. If someone else won't dis-

cuss anything but business, or brings up gossip or controversy, change the subject. You also can use that situation as an excuse to go network with others.

6. *Limit alcohol.* Remember company guidelines on alcohol consumption, if there are any. As long as you can handle alcohol, it's OK to drink socially, but don't become inebriated. Alcohol loosens tongues, lowers guards, and reduces inhibitions, sometimes bringing out the worst in people. It's also OK if you don't drink alcohol at a business party, but don't draw attention to that. If pressed, which is rude of the other person, you can simply say, "I am not drinking tonight" or "I don't drink," or "I'm the designated driver." Order something else to drink, like seltzer or soda. When you drink beer, drink from a glass, not a bottle.

If a colleague whom you know fairly well becomes inebriated, offer to get a cab or drive him home. This is really a safety concern, rather than an etiquette issue, and in terms of safety, do what needs to be done. You might be able to say, "I'm switching to coffee. Shall I get you some?" or "I'm going to order some food. Want to join me?" If he presses you to keep drinking with him, you can say, "I've had enough" or "I've reached my limit." Using "I" statements is more courteous, and safer, than asking, "Haven't *you* had enough?"

7. *Maintain a positive attitude.* No one likes a "party pooper." You might as well try to enjoy yourself, whatever the event may be. Enjoy the nice day and the exercise, even if you aren't the world's greatest golfer. Have fun listening to the music at the concert. Unless you're a total grump, there should be something about the event that appeals to you.

Even if there isn't, you should *act* as if you're having fun. To do otherwise would be discourteous. People's perceptions of whether you are having a good time are based on your body language more than your words. Conduct a body check. If you are standing with arms crossed, or are slouching and scowling, you are sending a negative message. Tell your body to look happy.

One woman at a party wasn't aware how much she was communicating her unhappiness until someone asked her what was wrong. Although she still was not pleased to be at the event, she changed her demeanor so that she would not give others the satisfaction of knowing how miserable she was.

8. *Remember, family and "significant others" represent you.* If spouses are invited and you have a "significant other" but no spouse, ask if you can bring your friend. Don't, though, bring anyone whose behavior will reflect poorly on you. If you're dressed appropriately and your spouse is not, guess who looks bad from the corporate perspective? Any improper behavior from your family—too much to drink, failure to mix and mingle—will reflect on you. Coach your relatives to act accordingly.

9. *Send thank-you notes.* Business social events often are special occasions, and therefore deserve a special, written acknowledgment of appreciation. If you choose not to write a note, it's good manners to compliment verbally those who organized or coordinated the event.

10. *It's still business.* We can't emphasize this enough. You can't go wrong by remembering that from beginning to end, in business-social situations, the emphasis is on a professional performance.

SAVVY SOLUTIONS FOR SOCIAL SITUATIONS

Each social setting has its own guidelines for gracious behavior. We'll explore several situations that you might encounter to provide tips on appropriate conduct. While you may be familiar with much of this advice, we've found through our seminars and coaching that many people benefit from a review of polite practices.

Cocktail Parties

Whether they are at a colleague's home or organized after-work gatherings at a nearby watering hole, cocktail parties have become one of the most frequently used venues for combining business with leisure. Despite their popularity, many people forget how to behave at these events.

For instance, remember to RSVP; don't assume it's understood you will or won't be there. Hosts and hostesses need to be able to plan the appropriate amount of food and drink.

When hosting a party, offer a variety of drinks (alcoholic and non-alcoholic) and a variety of foods. If the group will be large, hire help or ask a colleague to help tend bar. You may want to bring out hot food half-way through a party, both to generate a diversion and to allow for late arrivals. Make sure your setting allows for movement—group chairs into conversation clusters, place drinks away from the food.

As a host, you also should make sure that introductions are made. Provide names and information about the person you're introducing to other guests. Depending on the group, name tags may be helpful and can be prepared ahead of time. Hosts and hostesses should make sure to speak with all their guests and also help bring people into conversations. These steps are part of creating a gracious environment. Don't spend too much time with any one person or group.

A host's other responsibilities include making sure that the party area is continually cleared, that platters are filled, and that ice remains available.

If the cocktail party is an evening, at-home event, guests dress basically as they would for the office. Women can wear dresses rather than suits. You can always ask the host what type of dress would be appropriate. As the host, you should determine the dress and make sure the guests are informed.

Once a guest arrives at the party, she should work the room. Introduce people as they join your conversation. Everyone must mingle and meet new people. Don't leave spouses out of the conversation. Cocktail parties often are stand-up events, making it easy to be mobile, but even if there are chairs, don't let inertia trap you in your seat. Replenish your drink, stretch your legs, visit the bathroom, examine the artwork—whatever it takes to get around.

Carry drinks in your left hand so your right hand is available for handshakes. Limit the number of drinks or the amount of alcohol. Sip and talk. Let the ice cubes melt.

Cocktail party food is finger food. Use the napkin or small plate and toothpicks or a small fork to handle food. If you are hungry, eat a snack beforehand. Do not hover over the hors d'oeuvres.

Avoid smoking; you must carry an ashtray with you or go outside. Remember that some people do not allow smoking in their homes.

Behave yourself basically as you would in the office, although the party might allow you more time for a relaxed, friendly conversation. Save your flirting for a real date. People, including spouses, pay attention to who is talking to whom at parties, so the sexual signals you think are subtle could instead be broadcast all over the room.

Don't be the last to leave. An hour or two probably is appropriate, but not too much more. If you notice the people who came right after you are leaving, that may be a clue to get ready to depart. Follow, don't break, the curve. A host can signal the winding down of the party by not replenishing the food and by abandoning the bar. If people linger, the host can give them hints about their expected departure by saying, "Can I give you coffee to help with your drive?" or "Thanks for coming. It's been nice having you here."

Write a thank-you note to the hosts, including both your business associate and spouse.

Dear Steve and Joan,

All of us, Tom, Samantha, and I, had a wonderful time at your cocktail party.

Thank you for your hospitality and the opportunity to meet so many of your colleagues.

Sincerely,

Vivian

Today's Tea Parties

Tea parties are acceptable work-day substitutes for cocktail parties, part of a new entertaining trend. They're usually from 3:30 to 5 or 5:30 P.M., but no later.

You don't have to drink tea to attend, any more than you have to drink alcohol to attend a cocktail party. Coffee or other beverages also may be served, along with light snacks. The point of the event, as with any business social situation, is to see and be seen.

If you are planning a tea party, the event should be held in a room with a "warm" atmosphere—a library, near a garden, or a room with a fireplace. You will need tea service, linen napkins, and china. The server should be trained to serve tea. Some caterers specialize in this service.

The tea and the food can either be laid out or served individually.

As is the case at cocktail parties, guests drink, mingle, and talk.

The Office Party

The office party is more than a party—it's usually an annual event that works its way into office legend by the following morning. This is not the time for someone to stand out for his outlandish attire, her distinctive dancing style, or a record-setting number of trips to the buffet. Attendance is not really optional—you should attend. Think of it as a good opportunity to increase your network.

Arrive on time. Whether the event is at your office building or elsewhere, the planners will have arranged a schedule for food and entertainment, and interrupting the sequence is rude.

Network. Meet other people. Get to know colleagues outside your area. Don't just hang around with your friends, but don't ignore them either.

Treat your bosses with respect: don't suddenly resort to first names, for instance. Do say hello, though, and engage them in small talk.

Look like you are having fun, but also be on your best behavior. You know what this means: do not flirt or make passes at anyone. Do not tell off-color jokes and stories. Don't air grievances or office gossip. Don't only discuss business.

Women can ask male co-workers—peers, employees, or bosses—to dance at a party if others are dancing. Don't dance exclusively with one person, except your spouse.

Stay an appropriate length of time, even if the party is dull.

Send a thank-you note to the person or persons who organized the party.

Dear Michele,

Your efforts and time paid off! The office party was a huge success. Thank you for a job well done.

Sincerely,

Alan

Company Picnic

The company picnic is a family-friendly event, a chance for co-workers to mingle in an informal setting. Even so, it's still business, and needs to be approached from that perspective.

You can volunteer to help with organizing and with the cleanup. This is gracious. It also gives you another way to get better acquainted with your co-workers.

Participate in the activities. Don't be a pool potato. Be a good sport about joining in the three-legged race, etc.

Mingle. Introduce your family. Speak to the people at your picnic table.

Keep your children under control. Try to help them find playmates of about the same age or join activities that are geared to them. Emphasize to them that their behavior is important.

Box Office Basics

Whether you are going to a play, opera, ballet, or sporting event, try to become familiar with what you are seeing before you go. Get coaching, if you need it, so that you don't ask inappropriate questions.

Food and drink may make you sleepy during a "dark room" performance. If you must eat at all, eat lightly before you go. Avoid alcohol at the event.

If the client is invited by the host company, he does not pay. If the client asks for tickets from the host company, the client pays for them.

If you are the host, order tickets well in advance. Go for the best seats you (or your company) can afford. Be aware of any disabilities your guests may have that could affect seating arrangements. If you or they might be paged during a performance, ask for aisle seats.

If your tickets are at the "will call" window, make sure to confirm the pick-up time and the payment procedures.

Arrive at the event early to park, pick up tickets, get seated and settled before the event starts.

Have the client or your guest follow the usher to the seats. Ushers do not receive tips. If there is no usher, the host leads.

Make sure all guests receive a program.

Behaviors that are inappropriate in a theater include:

- talking,
- whispering or humming,
- tapping your feet or fingers,
- chewing gum,
- opening anything wrapped in cellophane,
- sighing loudly,
- falling asleep,
- reading anything except the program,
- arriving late or leaving early. If possible, limit your trips to the restroom to intermission or after the performance.

You can chuckle (as opposed to laughing loudly) and applaud as appropriate. Appropriate applause is especially important at an orchestra performance. If you don't know when to react, take your cue from others. Be prepared to discuss the performance at intermission or afterwards. It's insulting to a host when a guest is overly critical, so be careful with your comments.

Behaviors that are inappropriate at sporting events include:

- booing,
- hissing,

- "coaching" from the stands
- failing to watch the action.

Applaud and cheer in accordance with what is occurring. If you are not in a private box, limit trips to the snack bar and restroom, which could leave your guest alone.

Games People Play

In participatory sports, if you are the host, consider the interests and abilities of your guests. If you are the guest, understand that the way you handle yourself here—your competitiveness, your graciousness—reflects how you handle yourself in business situations.

If the sport is new to you, get coaching and practice in advance. Know the rules.

Of course, exercise good sportsmanship. Specifically, that means: Be on time. Don't hold up others. Know the rules. Never cheat. Don't complain or brag. Watch temper flare-ups and foul language.

Shake hands at the end of the game or match, and thank everyone for including you.

We have developed a few pointers for private clubs.

- *As a host:* Do not invite guests to clubs if they will be treated as "less than equal"—such as women to men's clubs.
- *As a guest:* Adhere to the club dress code.
- Explore the club only when accompanied by your host.
- Bring appropriate equipment. Tennis players, for instance, should bring one can of unopened balls.

Since golf is one of the most popular forms of corporate entertainment, we've developed these golf-specific guidelines:

- Host should arrive early to greet the guest.
- Guest should bring his own balls and clubs. Wear a collared shirt.
- Guest tees off on the starting hole, men before women. On other holes, men tee off before women because their starting tees are farther back. If all the players are the same gender, the person with lowest score tees off first. In a foursome in which three are guests and of the same gender, the tee-off can be by handicap or mutual agreement.
- Host drives the cart and keeps the score. Clubs go on the cart behind each player.
- Mark your balls if you are in the path of someone else's ball on the green. If you are playing in a foursome and a fast twosome is behind you, let them play through if no one is in front of you.

- The person who is farthest from the hole hits first. If you swing and don't hit the ball, it counts as a stroke.

- If you are using summer rules, you should not touch your ball. In winter rules, you can pick up your ball to clean it and to improve your position only if you are on the fairway.

- Golf protocol requires you to always replace your divot—the chunk of earth that may be displaced when you swing. It also means: Don't talk while someone else is hitting. Don't cheat. Don't hold up the game. Keep your temper—be a good sport if you win or lose.

- The host pays greens fees and tips caddies, although the guest can offer to pay for a caddie. At the club, the host pays for everything.

In all types of games, good sportsmanship is critical. Share sporting equipment. It's courteous to curb your competitiveness. Take your turn at horseshoes, for example, but don't overdo it. Lose graciously.

A Wedding

An office wedding is the ultimate hybrid—a personal milestone that you are attending by virtue of a work connection. As a guest, you need to be at your most gracious, mingling amiably with the bride's and groom's family and friends, as well as with your co-workers. You should of course bring or send a gift (see Chapter Thirteen, "Gifts That Package You Well.") You also should compliment the bride and groom, participate (if you're single) in bouquet- or garter-tossings, and exhibit appropriate dining manners.

If it's your wedding (congratulations or best wishes!), the guest list need not read like your office roster. You can select only one or two persons from your department, provided you limit it to those individuals. Depending on your office environment, you might want to "include" the rest of the office by bringing in the wedding photo album for interested individuals to examine, or invite co-workers to your home for a separate celebration. However, if you are going to invite most of the department, go ahead and invite the rest—no point risking hurt feelings. If you are the boss, remember that people may think you are signaling who are your favorites if you invite only some of those you supervise.

Although we have heard of situations in which the bride and groom invite co-workers to the ceremony but not the reception, we do not see this as an acceptable practice. It is, though, appropriate to invite co-workers only to the reception or to have a separate reception just for co-workers.

Should you invite your boss to the wedding? Not necessarily. It depends on your relationship. Be aware that even if invited, the boss may decline for reasons of office diplomacy that have nothing directly to do with you.

When arranging seating at the reception, try to make people feel comfortable. This could include seating co-workers together or placing them with people of similar age, background, interest, or profession.

It's gracious to be clear so that people know in advance what to expect in terms of food and drinks, since "reception" can have many meanings. If you invite people to a reception at 6 P.M. on a Saturday, they will expect food. We and many other guests were surprised to be served cookies and punch at one wedding reception; we had anticipated more food since the event occurred at the dinner hour, and we had to make last minute dinner arrangements. If everyone had known of the food arrangements in advance, the confusion and disappointment could have been eliminated.

Dinner Out in a Restaurant

A senior partner in an accounting firm took the owner of a small business out to dinner in hopes of pursuing a merger between the two companies. The spouses also were included. During the dinner, as talk turned to the logistics of the merger, the small business owner asked what would happen to his employees. "Oh, screw the employees," the accountant said. The business owner's wife quietly gasped, and he decided right then not to merge businesses. He felt the accountant could not be trusted.

Dinner at a restaurant with co-workers or clients can have a significant impact on business, just as a business lunch can. You want your courteous conduct to be a positive reflection on your professionalism.

Most of the etiquette guidelines for dinner out are the same as those for lunch. The main difference is that business dinners often include spouses.

Remember that your spouse's behavior reflects on you. Whether you are the host or the guest, help your spouse to know the cast of characters as well as a few basics about the business. You can provide your spouse with a list of who's who, as well as the names of other people's spouses, to help in sorting out the players. You can also prepare your spouse by suggesting safe topics, for instance indicating if someone has an interesting hobby. Introduce your mate to at least one of the other spouses. Include him or her in the conversation.

You may dress up a little more than normal business attire, depending on the restaurant. Women may wear dresses or fancy suits, provided they are not too sexy, tight, or low-cut. Men usually wear suits.

Allow your host to establish the seating. The host will often separate couples to encourage conversation. The guest of honor is placed to the right of the host.

You are more likely to have wine at dinner than during a business lunch. Limit the amount you drink. As the host, make sure all the guests arrive at their cars safely.

Dinner at the Boss's House

This ritual of American business has been satirized in film and comedy routines because it can be a career-making or -breaking event. It's important not only that the boss get along with you, but that your spouse represents you well. It's OK to approach the event with some nervousness, but try not to let it show.

If you are the host of a home business dinner, first make sure that all introductions are made. Allow time for cocktails, but not too long—don't let your guests drink too much.

Plan the seating to encourage conversation. Our preference is to separate spouses. A female guest of honor sits to the right of the male host. A male guest of honor sits to the right of the female host.

Dress tastefully. Men should wear suits and women, a suit, dress, or skirt with blouse. Make sure your shoes are shined. Pay attention to your grooming.

As a guest, arrive promptly—not too early or late. If the timing will be tight, you might want to do a trial run to double check directions in advance, so you have a good sense of how long it will take. Allow for traffic and for getting lost.

Bring a gift or send one ahead of time. Stay away from wine or gifts of food that must be served unless you have checked their suitability with your host ahead of time. Safe gifts are flowers sent ahead of time, chocolates or candies, cocktail napkins, and unusual boxes of tea.

Address the boss and his or her spouse formally unless they ask you to do otherwise, or your relationship is already less formal. Shake hands upon greeting them.

Compliment the host on the home at least once. Do not wander into rooms alone or ask for "a tour," although you can accept one if it is offered. It's OK to be impressed, but don't act like a hick from the sticks. This is a good chance to discover and talk about the boss's hobbies and interests.

Don't discuss business unless the boss brings it up. Include everyone in all dinner conversations. Avoid controversial topics.

Compliment the host on the dinner at least once. Remember your dining etiquette. If someone other than the boss is serving the meal, thank that person as the portion is put on your plate or as your plate is delivered. If you are unsure of how to eat something, observe your host or hostess. Have the dessert that is offered.

Eat what is served to you unless you have an allergy to it or a medical problem. In that case, try to nibble around the edges (eat the vegetables but not the main course) or inconspicuously rearrange the food on the plate to make it look as if you've eaten it. If you must decline, do so graciously, expressing regrets at not being able to eat what "looks good."

Don't smoke unless your host does, and only after the meal.

Remember that you and your companion are "being observed," so be conscious of all courtesies. Remain cordial and friendly. If the atmosphere is informal, you may offer to help clean up.

Don't rush away as soon as the plates are cleared. Stay and talk over coffee or while taking a brief walk around the grounds. Don't, however, overstay your welcome.

Send a thank-you note to the boss's home that includes both the boss and the spouse.

FINESSING CHANCE ENCOUNTERS
OF THE SOCIAL KIND

A colleague of ours was coming home from a business trip looking tired and bedraggled. Much to her embarrassment, on the plane she sat next to a meeting planner whom she had been trying to woo. Unfortunately, her topic was professional presence. She didn't look like she walked her talk!

Many business social encounters take place when we least expect them—at the supermarket, at the doctor's office or hairdresser's, even on vacation—when we meet clients, potential clients, or co-workers as we're "off duty."

As long as you are dressed appropriately for the situation, don't be embarrassed about your attire. The possibility of this occurrence, however, is adequate incentive for you to always look your best. You never know whom you will meet and where they will be. You want to represent yourself as best you can. One speaker stopped wearing jeans when she did her errands on weekends—she bumped into too many customers!

When you do see someone from work in an unexpected locale, greet the person and shake hands. Introduce whoever may be with you, including your children.

Say a few pleasantries. Don't discuss business. You may discuss the location, or the unexpectedness of your encounter.

After a few minutes, terminate the conversation graciously. Say, "nice seeing you" and continue on your way.

A GOOD TIME CAN BE HAD BY ALL

Office social events often feel stiff and awkward not just because of what is occurring at the event itself but because of what may have come before and what may take place afterwards. It's impossible for people to forget, for instance, that the person chatting cheerfully with your spouse is your direct competition for your next promotion, or that the person sitting next to you at the theater holds the key to the most important contract you've ever negotiated. Under such circumstances, it may even be fitting that you feel somewhat torn between the desire to relax and enjoy yourself and the need to keep your guard up.

Proper business etiquette, though, lets you function on both levels. It temporarily suspends both the past and future, allowing you to focus only on the present. If you behave suitably for the specific social situation in which you find yourself, you can build on a positive past for a bright future. You *can* have a good time when you act appropriately in business social settings. In fact, we hope that you do.

Chapter 13

GIFTS THAT PACKAGE YOU WELL

The manner of giving is worth more than the gift.

—Pierre Corneille

The new employee was delighted when, one morning at work during her first holiday season, she received a box with two dozen shiny golden apples from her employer. The unexpected goodwill offering made her feel cheerful. Soon, however, as she spoke with other employees, her attitude altered. It seems that in years past, the company had provided a 20-lb. turkey. The apples were part of a cost-cutting move. Workers grumbled and worried at the omen: would their jobs be next? The new employee wondered, as the person with the least seniority, whether she would then be the first to go.

In the corporate culture, gift-giving can be a double-edged sword. As a gesture of friendship or human kindness, it can slice through all the bureaucracy of a business to make an individual feel valued. However, when gift-giving is badly handled, it can cause pain and problems, even generating the type of negative feelings that the donor may have been trying to eliminate. That's true whether the gift is presented from a boss to an employee, a company representative to a client, or between fellow employees.

Yet being savvy about gift-giving can influence any businessperson's career. Knowing what gifts are appropriate, when to give a gift as well as how to accept or *not* accept one are all important pieces of information.

This chapter will focus on the protocol of presents. You'll learn:

- the things you should think about *before* giving a gift.
- when sending a card is more appropriate than a gift.

- the four things to consider when giving gifts, with detailed discussions on gift-giving occasions, relationships, financial guidelines, and types of gifts.

You'll find out how to present a gift, how to refuse one and how to accept one graciously. (For a discussion of international gift-giving, see Chapter Twenty, "A Global Guide to Gift-Giving.")

MASTERING MOTIVATIONS AND MEANINGS

To give or not to give is not the question. At some point, you will need and/or want to give a business gift.

A business gift can convey many meanings: thank-you for a job well done, congratulations on your promotion, sorry to hear about your sister's death, happy holidays, best wishes for your retirement.

When you give or receive a business gift, you are dealing with both etiquette and expectations. It's not just a question of what's correct but what's customary. Gift-giving protocol is part of the corporate culture. One department may be known for its generosity, another for its rare acknowledgment of significant events in the lives of employees. Some companies, in an attempt to avoid the appearance of bribery, have strict rules limiting the exchange of any gifts.

Before giving a gift, think about:

- company and/or department policy regarding gift-giving.
- company and/or department traditions regarding gift-giving.
- circumstances surrounding the gift.
- likes/dislikes of the recipient.
- cost of the gift.
- nature of the gift.

COMPANY AND/OR DEPARTMENT POLICY REGARDING GIFT-GIVING: If your company or department has rules about gift-giving, obey them. As you know, failure to do so demonstrates disrespect for the organization. If you don't know what the rules are, it's a good idea to ask. Ignorance could put you—and the recipient of a gift—in an awkward position. A management consultant sent a corporate meeting planner tickets for a Broadway show as a thank-you for her work. The planner was very embarrassed—company policy did not allow her to accept gifts that cost more than $25—so she had to return the tickets (to a show she wanted to see!)

COMPANY AND/OR DEPARTMENT TRADITIONS REGARDING GIFT-GIVING: Traditions are different from rules—they are not mandatory, although it is always a good idea to follow them. Like any other aspect of corporate culture, traditions can be company-specific, or even department-specific. Traditions may also influence the nature of a gift. Since your gift will be judged in comparison with others, it's helpful to know those expectations in advance.

CIRCUMSTANCES SURROUNDING THE GIFT: It may be perfectly within your company's policy and traditions to give holiday gifts to clients, but if you are also in the midst of contract negotiations, be careful that your gift isn't construed as a bribe. The circumstances need to be examined whenever there is inequality in the relationship between the donor and the recipient. Whether a gift is appropriate depends not just on what it is or how much it costs, but if there is an obligation implied by giving it. It's bad manners and bad business to present a gift with strings attached.

LIKES/DISLIKES OF THE RECIPIENT: The more you know about the recipient—his or her taste, hobbies, interests, the holidays he or she celebrates—the better you can tailor the gift to that person.

COST OF THE GIFT: The amount that a gift costs can influence its appropriateness. It might be OK to give a small, inexpensive gift in circumstances where a larger gift would be out of line. We discuss this in more detail later in this chapter, but you should consider carefully the amount you spend on any present.

When the boss of a department was getting married, most employees gave to the pool for a gift, while the rest purchased presents that cost $10 to $20. One new employee, however, bought the boss a set of dishes, which, of course was worth considerably more money. She was teased repeatedly by her co-workers who accused her humorously of trying to butter up the boss.

NATURE OF THE GIFT: Even if you are able to satisfy all of the other considerations, a gift can still be inappropriate if it is tacky, sexually suggestive, or otherwise unprofessional. For instance, we can't imagine an occasion in which a garish plastic flower centerpiece would be an appropriate gift.

WHEN A CARD MAKES BETTER SENSE THAN A GIFT

For many business purposes, a card can be a very appropriate acknowledgment, a gracious way to maintain contact over the years and to express that you are thinking of the person. We often receive wonderful notes from people who have attended our presentations. Marjorie Brody even gets notes from clients thanking her for her newsletter and asking that she make sure they are kept on the mailing list.

It's almost always appropriate to send a card, even when a gift would not be suitable. When sending a card, ask yourself these questions:

- Is it appropriate for the person?
- Is it appropriate for the situation?
- Is it timely?
- If it is a congratulations card, a thank-you or a condolence card, does it have a handwritten note?

- If it includes the family, can it be sent to the person's home?
- Is it appropriately addressed?

The card should be appropriate for the person and for the situation. It's helpful to know the person's sense of humor, for instance. You need to be very cautious with funny cards. While many people think of selecting a card as self-expression, it is also a matter of matching the sentiment to the recipient. A card that confuses or insults the recipient is worse than no card at all.

During December, make sure the card is for the appropriate holiday. You can't err with a card that says "Happy Holidays" but you might with one specifically for Christmas or Hanukkah. A holiday family photo card is usually not appropriate for business. Some people purchase two separate sets of cards—one for personal friends and relatives, and one "universal" card for business associates.

Also stay away from sending religious cards to express bereavement condolences or wedding congratulations.

The card should be timely. A card that arrives too long after an event, whether it is the holidays or a wedding, will lose some of its impact. However, if you are away, perhaps on vacation, and learn of a situation that occurred in your absence, such as a death, it's still timely to send a card as soon as you find out.

A card offering congratulations, a thank-you, or condolences should include a handwritten note. The note need only be a few sentences, but it's important to personalize your response.

If you or your company has holiday business cards printed with your name or your company's name, you need to sign them individually. A personal note ("It's been a great year. I'm looking forward to working with you again next year.") is always appreciated. In a bereavement card, you can write, "I'm so sorry to hear of your loss. You are in my thoughts."

If there is a personal relationship and you know the home address, you may address the card to the person's home, especially if you are including the family in your greeting. For the most part, though, the business relationship should be handled at business, and that's where cards should be sent.

Make sure it is appropriately addressed. If a woman uses her maiden name professionally or someone has a medical degree, you should use that name or title on the envelope. If the card is a thank-you, for example, for a dinner at the person's home, address it to both your colleague and your colleague's spouse.

FIVE SIGNIFICANT GIFT-GIVING CONSIDERATIONS

There are no hard and fast business etiquette rules about gifts in the United States. Gift-giving rules and customs vary greatly within companies, and expectations play a powerful role. It's important that whatever you do fits in with your corporate climate.

When giving a gift, though, you should consider:

The Occasion: Familial, personal, company occasion, Secretary's Day, thank-you, holiday.

The Relationship: Boss to employee, employee to boss, colleague to colleague, company representative to vendor/client/customer, vendor/client/customer to company representative.

Financial Issues: company policy, your salary, number of donors, number of times gift is given.

Type of Gift: Temporary vs. enduring, personal vs. professional.

Although they are highly interrelated, we'll discuss each of these separately. In order for a gift to be truly appropriate, each of these factors must be weighed and balanced. For instance, a holiday gift from a boss to an employee is appropriate only if it is of suitable type and cost.

One additional consideration—probably the overriding gift-giving consideration—is your own personal relationship with the person. It could be that in a small office, you are unusually close to your boss, for instance, which can make a holiday gift appropriate. Or, you may be barely on speaking terms with someone, in which case a birthday card or gift would border on hypocrisy.

When it comes to group gifts, your relationship with the recipient also should be your guide. It's perfectly proper to refuse to donate to a departmental gift; you may not know the person well, and it can get expensive! You should, though, be gracious in your refusal. You can say that you intend to do something on your own, if you do, or just say that you are unable to give at this time.

If your workplace has a "Pollyanna" holiday tradition—in which each employee pulls a co-worker's name from a hat and gives that person a present—it's generally gracious to participate, even though there is no guarantee you will like the person whose name you pull. Usually, there are reasonable financial limits for such gifts, and failure to join in could "cost" you far more in good will than the actual expense. If, however, you decide against participating in a Pollyanna, you must make sure to keep your name out of the drawing so that you are not left in the awkward position of receiving and not giving.

When to Give

In a business setting, there are basically six gift-giving occasions: familial, personal, company occasions, Secretary's Day, thank you, and holiday. Each has its own guidelines. Remember that while you are required, from the standpoint of good manners, to recognize most of these events, it's your choice as to how to do so. Sending a card or contributing to a charity or group gift can also be appropriate and acceptable recognition. It's up to you.

FAMILIAL EVENTS: Familial occasions include births, weddings, showers, and funerals involving employees and their families. These are the few times during which there is an opening in the invisible wall between work and home life. Although the events themselves have no official relationship to work, they can be major milestones in an employee's life.

Accordingly, to ignore them or not to send an appropriate gift would be discourteous. It may create an irreparable rift, for instance, if you fail to acknowledge the birth of an employee's child, regardless of whether the employee is male or female. If both spouses work, there may even be some unstated comparisons made between the acknowledgments received from the two work places.

In one instance, a female boss's failure to acknowledge the birth of a male co-worker's son had a negative and long-lasting impact on his wife's attitude toward her. This affront stung, and affected the spouse's subsequent dealings with the boss.

What's more, an appropriate gift can take on highly symbolic significance during a situation in which emotions already are heightened. Even a small gesture can mean a lot to someone. It's not unusual for employees to take personally—and long remember—the way co-workers and bosses treated them during these memorable times. You may clearly recall the gift you received for your wedding from a co-worker years after you have shifted jobs.

So do you generally need to send a gift to mark a familial occasion? Let's look at each situation.

Births—You can send a gift to acknowledge the birth of a child to an employee, client, customer, and colleague. Popular presents include baby clothing (check to make sure the size and color are appropriate), stuffed animals, toys, books, picture frames, and receiving blankets. Cups, silverware, and rattles can be engraved with the child's initials. To acknowledge the birth of a child to a boss, you can send a group gift from the entire department. Of course, if you have a special relationship, an individual gift may be appropriate.

Wedding—Send a gift if you go to the wedding. If you do not go, it's optional but thoughtful. If you are not invited, the department as a group could send a present. Check the bridal registry for an appropriate item.

Showers—If you are invited to a wedding or baby shower, provide an individual gift or contribute to a group gift.

Funerals—Sending flowers or fruit with a card is appropriate in cases of the death of a close relative (parent, sibling, spouse, child) of an employee, boss, colleague, vendor, client, or customer. You also can make a donation to the deceased person's favorite charity or to a related medical organization, such as the American Cancer Society. Newspaper obituaries often indicate the family's wishes for donations vs. flowers.

Personal Events. Personal events are those directly affecting the employee, including a birthday or a serious illness.

Cards are always appropriate, in any direction, although it is not required to send cards to clients or customers in these circumstances.

You may observe a colleague's "special" birthday—such as the 40th—even if you have ignored the day in other years.

It is acceptable for a boss to give an employee a gift, such as flowers, or, in the case of a birthday, a lunch or dinner certificate. It is generally not acceptable, however, for an employee to mark a boss's birthday with a gift, since this can come across as brown-nosing.

In many cases, though, these decisions boil down to a personal judgment call. We once counseled the office manager in a two-person office not to give her boss a holiday present. She followed our advice, although she felt awful since she couldn't reciprocate when the boss gave her a holiday present. The following month, when the boss's birthday rolled around, she ignored our advice and bought a present. It just made her feel more comfortable. The boss, who hadn't been expecting anything for her birthday, was surprised by the gift, but was most gracious in accepting it.

Plants that need little care are good for hospital patients, although you should check before sending any flowers or plants, since some hospital departments may not allow them. You can send cut flowers when the person goes home.

COMPANY OCCASIONS: Company occasions include promotion, retirement, and special employment anniversaries.

In these circumstances, official gifts often are department or company-provided and are standardized: a pen-and-pencil set for five years of employment, a mantle clock for retirees.

Individual cards are appropriate, and a good selection of "business" cards with suitable sayings can be found in a card shop. Sometimes, depending on the relationship, a gift is appropriate.

At one midwestern company, a woman's fondness for cats was well known. Her retirement was announced as "the all-cat retirement party" and co-workers brought small gifts that were cat-themed.

SECRETARY'S DAY: Secretary's Day has become a holiday unto itself, with traditions and observances varying widely among corporate offices. It is recommended that if you have a secretary, you participate in what's appropriate for your corporate culture: provide flowers, a special lunch out, or a small gift such as a picture frame. If you work with a secretarial pool, coordinate with others who work with the same secretaries, possibly sending a floral arrangement from all of you to each secretary. As a customer, vendor, or client, you may choose to recognize the work of a client's secretary if she has been especially helpful.

THANK YOU: A thank-you gift is relatively rare in American business, making it thoughtful but not required. The exception is a host/hostess gift, which is required, regardless of the relationship, every time you are treated to dinner at someone's home. Gifts of boxed chocolates or flowers sent ahead of time are usually appropriate as hostess gifts.

A business thank-you gift can be appropriate if someone has done something above and beyond his usual duties. It's OK, for instance, for a boss to acknowledge an employee's extra effort to make a deadline, or for an employee to thank a client or customer for patience during production problems, or for a number of years of loyal patronage. A division vice-president for an international pharmaceutical company decided to use an Olympic theme to thank volunteers who worked extra jobs, presenting them with "gold medals" as a thank-you.

These gifts sometimes can be small gestures that help to build morale—ordering pizza when employees work through dinner or distributing T-shirts that commemorate the annual inventory weekend.

Thank-you gifts often are most effective when the relationship has been well-established, when the gift is unexpected, and when the gifts are awarded on an infrequent basis. In the United States, if a thank-you gift is made to a client when business is first being established, it could appear to be a bribe. If the gift is made for what may be considered routine actions on a regular basis, it could raise expectations falsely that gifts will be forthcoming every time the situation occurs.

HOLIDAY: Holiday gifts are seasonal year-end remembrances. It is important to remember that not all people celebrate Christmas, so you want to make it clear that your gift is for the season rather than a specific holiday. It is appropriate to give these gifts any time between Thanksgiving and New Year's Day.

Holiday cards are always appropriate, but if you send a card, be careful about the message. Make sure it says something like "Happy Holiday Season" or "Season's Greetings." Handwritten notes personalize cards and make them more special.

You can send a holiday gift if it is appropriate for the relationship. Holidays offer convenient occasions to maintain a business relationship, and often are acceptable annual times to connect with those whom you may not see on a regular basis.

Who Gives to Whom?

To determine when it is appropriate to give a gift, we've divided gift-giving relationships into five categories (see *The Gift-Giving Grid* on page 241). While this chart can serve as a general outline for suitable behavior, we repeat our statement that whether a gift is ultimately appropriate will be influenced by the *personal* relationship and by the *company's rules and traditions*.

BOSS TO EMPLOYEE: Bosses may give gifts to employees on every gift-giving occasion. This is based in part on a presumption of greater income and in part on the boss's role as leader and as an official company representative.

Bosses need to be aware of precedents regarding presents. All employees of an equal level should be treated equally, so if you honor one employee's birthday, do the same for all others. Executives, for instance, may make it a policy not to attend weddings of anyone who is not on their personal staff, because they obviously won't go to every employee's wedding. They should send a note, but they do not have to send a gift, although it is gracious to do so.

While all department heads are not strictly bound to treat their subordinates in exactly the same way other department heads do, workers will be aware of any glaring inequities. At one company, the personnel department always was taken out for

The Gift-Giving Grid: Is It Appropriate?

Remember, many factors affect the appropriateness of giving a gift, but especially your relationship with the recipient. This chart is meant to offer general, but by no means inflexible, guidelines.

OCCASION	BOSS TO EMPLOYEE	EMPLOYEE TO BOSS	COLLEAGUE TO COLLEAGUE	COMPANY REPRESENTATIVE TO VENDOR, CLIENT, OR CUSTOMER	VENDOR, CLIENT, OR CUSTOMER TO COMPANY REPRESENTATIVE
FAMILIAL Birth, Wedding, Shower, Funeral	Yes If attending a wedding or shower, it's required.	*Yes	Yes	*Yes	**Yes
PERSONAL Birthday	*Yes	No, but cards & flowers OK for illness	*Yes	No, but cards & flowers OK for illness	No, but cards & flowers OK for illness
Illness	Yes		Yes		
COMPANY Promotion Retirement Special anniversary	Yes	*Yes	*Yes	*Yes	**Yes
SEC.'S DAY	Yes	N/A	N/A	Sometimes If secretary has helped you	Sometimes
THANK YOU Special projects	Yes	No	No	*Yes	**Yes
Hostess Gift	Yes	Yes	Yes	Yes	Yes
HOLIDAY	Yes	Usually Not	*Yes	*Yes (for client, customer)	**Yes

*Yes means it's appropriate, but not required. Remember that a card is always a gracious touch.
**Yes means it's appropriate, but not required and may depend upon company policy.

241

lunch at the holidays, while the administrative staff only had doughnuts brought in one morning. The situation created resentment that reduced the holiday spirit.

A company party can be the gift provided by a boss to workers. One manager invited his staff to his home for a Sunday holiday brunch. They were impressed to see him chipping in at home—making omelets—the same way he chipped in at work.

Company-provided bonuses are not "gifts" because they are income that is awarded based on corporate criteria rather than the occasion.

EMPLOYEE TO BOSS: Because of the inequality in the relationship, an employee generally has far fewer occasions to provide the boss with a gift. Giving a gift to your boss when it is not appropriate to do so may be seen as currying favor, or just gauche. The boss generally does not expect presents from those who report directly to him or her.

Presents are usually not given by employees to bosses for personal occasions, although a hostess gift is always appropriate. Employees also don't generally give holiday presents; sometimes, however, depending on the company, employees might band together for a group gift. A holiday gift also may be suitable if the employee has been with the boss for a while and has developed a personal relationship. Some employees give bosses their homemade holiday cookies. If the boss has an extended illness or is hospitalized, you can send cards or flowers.

Gifts can be made by employees to bosses for familial occasions and for company occasions. One secretary gave her boss a money clip when he left the company. It was engraved "Thanks a million."

COLLEAGUE TO COLLEAGUE: Employees can give co-workers gifts for all occasions except Secretary's Day.

COMPANY REPRESENTATIVE TO VENDOR, CLIENT, OR CUSTOMER: The company representative-to-vendor relationship is, by definition, somewhat less personal and less permanent than relationships between co-workers. The same is true for relationships between company representatives and clients or customers. This puts gift-giving into a different arena. Company representatives generally do not give vendors presents, although gifts can be appropriate depending on the specific relationship.

VENDOR, CLIENT, OR CUSTOMER TO COMPANY REPRESENTATIVE: The vendor, client, or customer can provide a gift to thank the company representative. One speaker thanks the meeting planner who books her appearances with both a thank-you note and a small bag of jelly beans, which has become her signature gift.

We should caution you, though, not to put the company representative in an uncomfortable position because of the cost or appropriateness of the gift. When in doubt, don't do it.

American companies have grown increasingly sensitive to giving or receiving any gift that could be considered a bribe or an inducement to do business. In fact, many companies will not let their employees accept any gift, going so far as to define lunch as a gift. Some companies will send letters to employees right before the holiday season requiring them to advise their vendors of their gift policy. Even if you consider such guidelines to be rigid or petty, adhere to them. It's gracious to show respect for company rules.

Small gifts with corporate logos (pens, calendars, clocks, coffee mugs) can often be accepted without appearing as a way to influence business. Large expensive logo gifts—such as a duffle bag or suitcase—may send the wrong message.

Financial Considerations: Dollars and Sense

Figuring out how much is reasonable to spend on a gift can be a thorny decision. No one wants to appear cheap, but it can be just as inappropriate to overspend. We know one small business owner, for instance, who purchased a video camera for the birth of an employee's child—an extremely generous or an excessively impressive present, depending on your point of view.

You do want to give something of quality, but it doesn't have to be expensive. Cost, after all, is not always correlated with taste or with quality. It is probably just as important that the item show thought as that it fit within a stipulated price category. Savvy shoppers might find great bargains (that are not recognizable as such) while traveling to different cities, in museum gift-shops, or through artists' cooperatives.

Having said all that, and depending on the region of the country in which you live, we suggest that $10 to $100 is generally a good range for business gifts. There are, though, four considerations:

COMPANY POLICY: Follow your firm's guidelines. They have been established for a reason, and usually with considerable forethought. If you don't have any official guidelines, you can choose to institute some. There also may be "unofficial" guidelines. Especially if you are a new employee, it's appropriate to ask what people usually spend, or how much the typical contribution is.

YOUR SALARY: People in your workplace may not know the specific amount you make, but they have a pretty good idea where you fit into the overall salary picture. Spending too much on a gift may be either viewed as generosity or extravagance. Spending too little may be viewed as stinginess. Rather than trying to keep up with those who are paid more than you are, spend what is comfortable for you.

NUMBER OF DONORS: You can contribute less to a group gift than you would spend if you had to buy something worth giving as an individual. This is the beauty of office collections—the honoree gets a nice present, and donors obtain good value for their dollars.

To avoid the implication of coercion, it's best if someone other than the boss is in charge of collecting money for the gift. Otherwise, people may feel pressured to contribute. This duty can be rotated.

The collector also is honor-bound to keep the amount of the contributions confidential. One worker decided deliberately to give a larger than usual amount to the group collection for a wedding gift—a $20 donation—because she wanted to ensure that the recipient received a generous present. She was upset that the collector told the recipient the amount of her donation, even though the collector thought she was being helpful. The revelation made it awkward for the donor, who had hoped to pass as one of the crowd.

NUMBER OF GIFTS: Assuming that you are going to spend the same total amount of money on office gifts during a year, you will naturally be able to spend more per gift if the final tally is low. This is where you might want to establish a personal policy to cover those few gift-giving occasions over which you have some control. If you work in an office with many young couples, for instance, the chances are greater that you will have to buy more baby gifts. You might then decide to always contribute to the office gift rather than to buy individual presents, except for close friends or those who are part of your immediate team.

The Right Gift

The element of surprise is vastly overrated in business gift-giving situations. People often make major mistakes in the quest to find something "different" or "unusual" or "unique"; you're better safe, and staid, than sorry.

It's acceptable to ask a co-worker's secretary or a spouse for gift suggestions. Don't expect to be able to automatically pick something the recipient will like just because you work with him or her every day. The nature of business often keeps people from revealing such personal information as tastes and interests.

We've divided our gift suggestions into two categories: temporary vs. enduring and personal vs. professional.

TEMPORARY VS. ENDURING: Gifts differ in the length of time that they will last. A temporary gift can be appropriate for a short-lived situation, such as an illness, or even for situations in which someone might not want a permanent reminder of the event, such as a death. This is a judgment call, although retirement gifts, in particular, often fall into the long-lasting memento category.

Among temporary gifts, the most popular are flowers and food.

Flowers: Flowers are symbols of greeting, celebration, condolence, and thanks. They are available in a wide price range, and sometimes come combined with a permanent present, such as a coffee mug or special vase. Accompanying cards can be tailored to the situation.

With the exception of long-stemmed roses, which generally imply a romantic connection, flowers can be sent by anyone to anyone. Women may send flowers to men in business.

For a hostess gift, send cut flowers to the home ahead of time or the next day. Don't arrive with them, because it is work for the recipient to find a spot to put them.

Send an arrangement or a plant to the office. Funeral flowers can be sent to the funeral home. Frequently, though, the family requests that in lieu of flowers, contributions be made to a favorite charity. Good etiquette requires that you honor this request.

Food: Food is a generally appreciated gift that can be personalized to the recipient's taste. Like flowers, it comes in a wide assortment of price ranges and sometimes is packaged with a gift, such as a basket. An advantage is that it can be shared with co-workers or with family.

Food gifts appropriate for business are tins of baked goods, fresh fruit baskets, candy, nuts, and baskets of cheese and crackers.

Wine and liquor are often appropriate host/hostess gifts or holiday gifts, but you need to be careful. If you bring wine as a host/hostess gift, tell the host it is for another occasion. That way, you don't put the person on the spot to serve it with the meal. Don't assume the recipient drinks. If the hosts do, what is their preference? Wine? Scotch? Brandy? If you don't know much about wines or liquor, consult with a spirit shop employee.

You might be invited to a co-worker's home for a cookout or a holiday party in which everyone is asked to bring "a dish to pass." This is technically not a gift, but participating is required. Consult with the host or hostess for suggestions, and stick to the category—salad vs. dessert, appetizer vs. vegetables—that you promised to bring. If the person hosting the event says no food contributions are needed, bring a host/hostess gift instead.

PERSONAL VS. PROFESSIONAL: The gift you select could be intended for personal use, perhaps reflecting the person's hobbies or interests, or it could be a practical present geared toward the recipient's professional side.

To select an appropriate personal gift, you need to know something about the person's taste (contemporary vs. modern), lifestyle (casual or formal), hobbies and interests. You could give golf balls or kitchen gadgets, for instance. Be as specific as possible within the category, since someone who likes antiques may prefer a certain period or style, and someone who likes books may favor biographies over novels.

It's also important that you not overstep the bounds of your actual relationship with the individual, since giving a gift that is *too* personal—such as clothing—would be a faux pas. Some accessories may be acceptable—such as a scarf or pin for a woman, or cufflinks for a man. However, the secretary who received a flannel nightgown from her boss was embarrassed by the implied intimacy, and it created awkwardness in their relationship.

A professionally-oriented present can be used in the work environment. Examples include: a pocket calendar; a card case; a pen-and-pencil set; a desk caddy (for paper clips, rubber bands, tape, etc.); a letter opener; a picture frame; a bookmark; bookends; a candy jar; a dictionary-thesaurus set; a subscription to a business magazine or newspaper; a business book.

Those who travel for business might enjoy an address book for foreign addresses; an international travel alarm clock (which shows time at home and in the location); a diary for trip notes, or a wallet-passport case.

We caution that if you give someone a professional present, it is up to the recipient to determine how and whether to use it. It's not gracious to ask someone where the letter opener you gave her is—that puts pressure on her to keep it on display, whether she wants to or not.

Whatever you choose, we encourage you to pause briefly before buying it to consider what, if any, symbolic significance the gift could have. If it could send any unintended message, buy something else. An accountant gave a co-worker a nice paperweight, and neglected to notice the etching on it which depicted a couple in a suggestive pose.

PLAN AHEAD: Selecting an appropriate gift can take time as well as knowledge of the recipient. Given the significance of office gifts, it's best not to rush out and purchase the first thing you see. You can often plan ahead, particularly for holiday presents, baby presents, work anniversaries, and retirements.

Become familiar with the stores in your area that stock quality business gifts and become a regular patron. Department store gift departments often have a good selection, particularly around the holidays. Some people we know hit after-holiday sales, stock up on these items, and then present them year-round.

Other possible sources include bookstores, mail-order catalogs, museum gift shops, gourmet food shops, antique shops, and stationery stores.

PRESENTATION PROTOCOL

In the United States, business gifts are generally presented informally. This is not the same thing, though, as being too casual. When giving a gift, remember to:

- Wrap the gift with appropriate paper.
- Personalize and sign the card.
- Present the gift in person if possible.

Wrap the gift with appropriate paper. Tasteful all-occasion paper, plain paper, or paper with the suitable sentiment, such as "congratulations," are recommended. Even using tin foil or the comics section of the newspaper is better than nothing! However, we suggest that if you are unable to make a package attractive, ask that it be gift-wrapped at the store where it was purchased. Make sure the price tag is removed before the wrapping begins!

Personalize and sign the card. You also can use good quality notepaper. The card or note should always be enclosed in an envelope.

Present the gift in person, if possible. There may be a stipulated time for the exchange, such as during the annual holiday party. You can say, "Enjoy the holidays. I hope you like your present," "I was thinking of you at this time," or "Happy Birthday! Enjoy!"

Refusing a Gift with Grace

Sometimes it is necessary to refuse a gift. It might exceed the monetary limit set by company policy or just be something that is inappropriate for you to accept. When refusing a gift, follow these steps:

1. Act promptly, within 24 hours.

2. If the donor had good intentions, explain why the gift is being returned (such as company policy) and thank the giver.

3. If the donor had bad intentions (sexual overtones, implied obligation with acceptance), say only that the gift was not appropriate. Keep a copy of the note explaining the return, noting the date and the way you returned it, in your files for your personal protection.

Why do we distinguish between two types of senders—those who are well-intentioned and those who are not?

Well-intentioned senders may be unaware of company prohibitions on gifts. They may have genuinely tried to select something you would like, unaware, for instance, that you are highly allergic to nuts. You do not want your refusal to embarrass them.

It might be possible to accept the gift courteously, such as the can of nuts, and then discreetly dispose of it. Or you can indicate for future reference, "How kind of you! I'm allergic to nuts, but my family will love them." (Otherwise, you might receive the same present each year. We know one man who has an annual New Year's Day ritual of pouring down the drain the after-shave he receives each Christmas from a relative.)

If you need to return the gift, an appropriate written response to a well-intentioned donor might be, "What a nice thought! However, since company policy prohibits my acceptance of this gift, I am returning it to you."

Accepting a gift from someone who lacks good intentions would convey acceptance of the underlying message. You want your refusal to communicate graciously your displeasure at the situation. You can make your dissatisfaction clear without lengthy explanations. Your note might state simply, "I don't consider this gift appropriate. I am returning it to you." Or "This gift is really not appropriate. Please don't send me any more presents."

If the person telephones for an explanation, you can just repeat what you said in your note, or be more specific, explaining, "It's too intimate (or personal). Our relationship doesn't warrant such a present." If the person persists, he's being rude, and you need only say, "I've given you my reason" or "I still don't want any more presents."

Make sure to keep in your files a copy of the note to the donor explaining the return, as well as a copy of a note that informs your boss of your refusal of the gift.

That note to your boss can say, "I just wanted to let you know this present exceeded our financial guidelines."

The gift should be returned quickly and efficiently—within 24 hours.

Accepting a Gift with Aplomb

Most of us are fortunate enough to have had plenty of practice in accepting gifts, but that doesn't mean we always do so in an appropriate manner.

Say thank you. Amazingly, many people forget this simple and essential step. They may comment favorably on the gift, even seem to be thrilled by the item, but the actual words "thank you" never cross their lips. This is a necessary acknowledgment of gratitude, one that addresses the act of giving rather than the reaction to the item itself.

Appear pleased. You really can find something positive—or at least pleasantly noncommittal—to say. You can acknowledge the effort made by the donor: "How nice of you to think of me!" or "Where did you find it?" You can recognize the attempt that was made to find something suitable, such as "You remembered that I collect antique maps!" Of course, if you genuinely like it, say so!

Handle the gift with respect. Do not make jokes or wisecracks about the gift, unless it is a gag gift. Don't stick it in a corner—take it home if you must, and stick it in a corner there. Carry it out of the office in a respectful fashion.

Write a thank-you note. This applies even if you remembered to say thank you in person. It shows that you took a bit of time—just as the buyer took time selecting the present. You can acknowledge the circumstances surrounding the present as well as the gift itself: "Dear Sharon: You certainly fooled me! I never expected the wonderful surprise 40th birthday party you organized in the office on Friday. Your thoughtfulness, and the bookends you selected, are much appreciated! Sincerely, Don."

In the case of a group gift, or if a large number of people from your office attend a relative's memorial service, you can post a thank-you on the bulletin board.

You do not have to send a thank-you for a thank-you.

A TOKEN OF APPRECIATION

It's a reality of corporate life today that business gifts may not be as elaborate or as common as they once were. When all is said and done, gift-giving is an optional expense. Much as we mourn the passing of a time when civility and courtesy were more common, we acknowledge the practicality of such a position.

That should, however, make us appreciate all the more the gifts we do receive and all the more inclined to select presents for others that suitably express our friendship and respect. It's good manners to communicate "I care."

Chapter 14

BUSINESS TRAVEL
Skillful Manners in Motion

The world is a book,
and those who do not travel read only a page.

—Saint Augustine

It's ironic, but the importance of good manners really hits home when you go away from home. The courtesy often demonstrated by strangers—their friendliness as they greet you, their graciousness in providing directions, their helpfulness in suggesting places to visit—all affect your impression of a location. A smile here, a welcoming word there, can make all the difference.

When you are on a business trip, you're more an ambassador than a tourist. Although, like a tourist, you are forced to rely at least partially on the kindness of strangers, you're also representing your company, and, in some cases, your country. As a business traveler, you are technically "on duty" for the entire duration of your trip. You want to conduct yourself in a professional manner no matter where you are and no matter what the circumstances may be.

Alas, business travel—with all its inherent stresses and hassles—can test your diplomatic resources severely. Without an understanding of business travel manners, it can be difficult to perform properly when you are tired and harried and miles from the comforts of home. Knowing what to do can help you arrive at your destination relaxed and confident, so that you can be at your best for business.

This chapter shows you what you need to know as you go, from planning your itinerary to dealing with the hotel concierge. You'll discover how to:

- maximize the business opportunities that take place during your trip.

- ensure your safety during the journey and at your destination.

249

- find out the best role for your spouse.

- host international travelers in the United States.

- prepare for the international assignment.

Knowing and using proper etiquette during your business travels will cut your stress level, making you a more pleasant traveling companion and guest.

PLANNING YOUR TRIP

There are plenty of reasons for a business trip: sales calls; contract negotiations; visits by district managers; presentations to another division; researching company expansion; attending a convention. Your job may involve travel regularly if you give seminars, cover a large territory, or are a trouble-shooter. Whatever the reason may be, though, you need to chart your voyage before you set sail to keep the trip from drifting off course.

Before leaving, you should be able to answer these four questions:

1. *Why are you going?* You need to be clear about the purpose of your trip, and so do those who will greet you. Making these expectations understood will make everyone feel more comfortable and also will focus the preparations so that everyone's time can be well spent.

2. *Who do you need to see or call?* It's rude to "drop in" on someone without advance notice (unless, of course, it's your job to assess performance during an unannounced visit). It's also inefficient to go through all the effort to make a trip, only to find out that the key person you need to see is out of the office for the entire week. Good manners require that you announce your plans for a trip and that you schedule it at a time that is as convenient as possible for your hosts.

3. *What do you need to take with you?* The value of a face-to-face meeting can be diminished if you lack the appropriate documents or equipment. Considering this question in advance can ensure not only that you remember to bring what you need, but also that it is ready to go with you.

4. *After the trip, what's the next step?* Your trip may be only one leg of a longer corporate journey toward a goal. If you are aware of the ultimate destination, you can avoid detours.

Plan Your Itinerary

Plan your itinerary in advance. Type it up with the dates and phone numbers of where you will be. Include the meeting schedule. Make three copies. One is for your family and one is for your secretary or someone back in the office; both of these need to be adjusted for local time at your home base. The other one is for you, with the times listed as they will be at your destination.

Factor any time zone changes into your planning. If it is a short trip, you might be able to use the change to your advantage without adjusting your own body clock. You might, for instance, work in a breakfast meeting at the time you would normally be at the office or squeeze an extra hour of business in and still get home in time for a late dinner. On longer trips, arrive a day or two ahead so that you can adapt. When we travel to the Middle East, we build an entire day into the schedule for jet lag.

Check with those in your company who may have made a similar trip in the past, and get their recommendations. Ask what they can tell you about their experiences: Is it a long way between gates at the airport? Is there anything in particular you should know about the city? What should you expect regarding the physical environment of the business you are visiting? What tips would they give on dealing with your contact person? What is the appropriate dress?

Make Reservations

Make confirmed hotel reservations, and consider making advance restaurant reservations for any important business dinners during your stay. Pick a hotel close to the places you are visiting, not the airport.

There are several things to ask a hotel when you make reservations: Does it have a corporate rate? What kind of amenities does it offer: suites? concierge services? dry cleaning? airport limo? quiet rooms? exercise facilities? doctors? fax machines? business centers? no-smoking rooms? rooms for those with disabilities?

If you plan to use the hotel as a base of business operations, check to see if it has a suite available. This is especially important if you need to meet with clients at the hotel. Otherwise, you may be forced to use the bar, coffee shop, or lobby as your surrogate office, which can be less effective. Ask if the hotel has a small conference room available. Don't plan to meet in a hotel bedroom—at best, it could create discomfort, and at worst, it could lead to charges of sexual harassment.

Confirmed reservations can ease anxiety. Using a credit card can guarantee that your room will be available no matter what time you arrive, although you will have to cancel to avoid a charge if your plans change.

Be Professionally Prepared

Make sure that you have all the work materials you need during your trip. Write out a list, or designate a separate pile, file, or briefcase as the location to stash all the materials for your trip as you accumulate them.

Arrange for work at the office to be handled during your absence. Giving plenty of notice not only is gracious, but can help others juggle their schedules.

Discuss your plans to check in with the home office with your secretary or coworkers. Arrange specific times when you will call them. Include that on your daily schedule (converted to the local time). Allow time in your schedule before you leave to deal with any loose ends that need your attention and set aside "catchup" time upon your return. You might want to make a checklist before you leave of the follow-up that might be needed when you get back: necessary calls, reports, thank-you notes, and action items.

Determine How to Use Your Time Productively

Think before you leave about how to get the most out of your time away. While traveling, are there papers you could review, reading you could catch up on? Does your route take you near other business contacts that you could meet for dinner? Can you have materials faxed that weren't available until after you left?

View the experience as a learning opportunity about the city and the business. You might mention to your hosts, "When I'm in town, I'd like to sit in on your marketing meeting." This is your chance to see how others come up with different solutions to some of the same problems you face. Read the local newspapers to see what different insights they might offer into your business. Plan to keep a file of basic information on people you meet who can assist you in future contacts.

LUGGAGE AND PACKING TO EASE YOUR JOURNEY

Seasoned travelers know that the purchase of sensible luggage is an investment worth making. Your luggage needs to be durable enough to withstand rough handling, lightweight enough to lift, and functional enough to allow for easy, compartmentalized packing.

Consider how you will move the luggage through an airport or hotel, since baggage handlers are not always available. A combination of wheels and a pull strap can be effective when the suitcase is balanced; otherwise, it will topple over and slow you down. Fold-up cart-style carriers can be good choices when you have to move several items, such as a suitcase, carry-on bag, and briefcase.

Your luggage should have sturdy locks. Carry your keys separately; don't stuff them in the suitcase's side pockets.

Luggage with side pockets is practical as a carry-on. You can have your tickets and passport readily available when needed. Women might consider carrying an over-the-shoulder briefcase that eliminates the need for a separate purse.

Use identification tags, but don't put your home address on them; some thieves scout airports to see who will be out of town. You could use your business card. Include a separate identification label on the inside of the luggage, in case the outside tag becomes separated. Some people also recommend placing an itinerary inside so that the luggage can find its way to you at your next stop.

You want to pack as lightly as possible. To know what to include, you need the answers to two questions:

What will the weather be like? To find out, you can check the all-weather channel or city temperature listings in the newspaper. Investigate the weather not just for your destination, but the stops en route, in case you happen to get stuck there.

What will you be doing or attending? The more specific your schedule, the better prepared you can be. Is a dinner out planned? Will you be doing a lot of walking? Will you relax by playing racquetball at the hotel?

If you travel frequently, it can help to keep your suitcase "ready" with an alarm clock, laundry bag, travel iron, and cosmetic bag or shaving kit always stocked with grooming supplies. That way, you need only add the clothes that are required for each trip. It also can be helpful to develop a standard checklist that you use while packing—two long-sleeved shirts, three pair underwear, etc. Our *Packing Checklist* gives the basics. Taking along a list of the specific clothing and jewelry you brought can be helpful if your bag is stolen or lost.

Packing Checklist

SUITCASE	CARRY-ON
Lightweight, non-wrinkle business clothing	Necessary documents: passport, visa, names and phone numbers of contacts, itinerary, tickets
Evening clothes for dinner out	Money, traveler's checks, and charge cards
Socks, underwear, and pajamas	Work materials: contracts, reports, master copy of handouts, business cards
Two pairs comfortable shoes	Presentation materials: slides, photos, overhead transparencies
*Alarm clock	Medication
Limited jewelry that goes with several outfits	Valuables
Spare pair of glasses	Cosmetic and/or shaving supplies, including contact lens solutions and equipment
*Plastic bag for dirty clothes	Sunglasses
Laundry detergent	Extra socks, stockings, and underwear
*Hairdryer	
*Travel iron	
Outlet adapter and/or converter	

*Can sometimes be obtained from hotel

Always put all your important items, including medication and valuables, in a carry-on. Women should include a cosmetic bag and men should take a shaving kit. This is also good protection in case your luggage is delayed.

Be sure to keep the names and phone numbers of your contacts with you in the carry-on tote, so you can call them upon your arrival and if there are any delays. Also keep with you any papers for your meeting, as well as presentation materials, such as slides or photos, and one master copy of your handouts. Both of us have had to have our seminar materials re-copied on the morning of the seminar because our luggage didn't arrive.

Plan for emergencies. In your carry-on bag, take an extra pair of underwear and socks or stockings, so you can wear them if your trip is unexpectedly extended. Make sure you have a full supply of any prescription medications. Keep them in the pharmacy container to avoid problems with custom inspectors. You'll also need contact lens supplies and perhaps an extra pair of glasses.

Know how to pack. Use plastic dry cleaner bags or tissue paper between clothes to help limit wrinkles. Packing loosely can cause wrinkles, as well as waste space. Consider "interweaving" your clothes—draping long garments across the suitcase, folding shorter items inside, so they cushion each other. Stuff shoes with socks or underwear to save space and to help the shoes retain their shape. Balance your load—put heavy items, such as shoes, near the hinge so that they will be on the bottom when the suitcase is upright. Put the clothes most sensitive to wrinkling on the top, so they won't get as crushed. Pack related items (shirt and pants) for an outfit together so they are easy to find. Make sure your pajamas and underwear are accessible without disturbing the entire suitcase.

Invest in a travel iron and in an alarm clock. Carry a small package of laundry detergent or cold water washing liquid. Regular travelers can scout luggage stores or specialty catalogs for compact versions of travel necessities.

Double-bag anything—such as shampoo bottles—that might leak or explode from rough handling or changes in air pressure and spoil your clothes. Use unbreakable containers whenever possible, and don't fill them to the top if you are flying because the air pressure may cause the contents to expand.

Bringing Along Business Gifts

Business gifts are usually not necessary in the United States, but often serve an important role in the protocol of international business. (See Chapter Twenty, "A Global Guide to Gift-Giving.")

However, even in the United States, a business gift can be a friendly gesture and there are times when it can be appropriate to present one. One Indiana man learned that his Southern counterpart was particularly interested in Hoosier high school basketball, so he gave his host a book on that topic as a goodwill gesture. It helped to establish a personal connection with the host.

As we mentioned in Chapter Thirteen, "Gifts That Package You Well," it is important that you adhere to any company rules regarding gift-giving, especially if you are dealing with clients or vendors.

Of course, if you will be invited to someone's home during your visit, a hostess gift is mandatory. Your hotel doorman can help you find a suitable location to purchase one if you didn't bring one along.

In the United States, a business gift can be presented at the start of a visit—to say thank you in advance—or at the end, to indicate your appreciation for the hospitality you received. Taking your hosts out to dinner, to a sporting event or to a live performance may be another form of a thank-you, provided it is an acceptable practice within your company.

Regional food gifts—salt water taffy from a coastal community, cheese or sausage from Wisconsin—can be suitable presents, particularly if you have traveled a long way and the item is exotic in the locale you are visiting. It may also be appropriate to send a fruit basket to the office as a thank-you upon your departure.

The guidelines we listed in Chapter Thirteen apply, including wrapping the gift in appropriate paper and signing the card.

MOBILE CLOTHING:
Taking Your Professional Image Along for the Ride

When you travel for business, you want to be comfortable, but you should dress to reflect your professional status. Depending on your corporate policy and the nature and purpose of the trip, you should take either a regular business wardrobe or a business casual wardrobe (see Chapter Four, "Professional Presence: How to Make Your Appearance Work for You"). It's always best to err on the side of professionalism.

Even while you are in transit and even if you don't expect to be met by a company representative, you should not dress down and wear, for instance, jeans and a T-shirt. You never know what might happen: you may need to call for someone to pick you up, or your luggage may be lost. It happens even to celebrities: we once saw Liza Minnelli perform an entire concert in black jeans and a black turtleneck because her luggage didn't arrive. "I thought you'd rather see me like this than not at all," she explained. Could you make a presentation in what you are wearing?

You also never know whom you might meet on the way—a potential new client, perhaps, or a member of the board of directors. We have both met new clients on planes.

Take clothing that travels well: items that are lightweight, relatively wrinkle-resistant, and that do not show soil. Focus on practical, versatile attire—mix and match clothing that maximizes your wardrobe.

Think about evening events: Do you need anything dressy? If your business trip is to a convention at a resort, be prepared for the activities; bring ski or golf clothes. If you plan to use workout facilities or the swimming pool, bring something you can wear as you travel from your room to the facilities or pool. As you pack each outfit, remember to include all the parts of the ensemble—the belt, the tie, the appropriate socks. Limit your jewelry to basic items that go with several outfits. Take two pairs of comfortable shoes. Women should pack extra stockings.

If you are making presentations in several cities—perhaps five cities in five days—remember that the people in one location don't know what you wore the day before. You might be able to build your travel wardrobe around one or two outfits.

EFFECTIVE EN ROUTE ETIQUETTE

When strangers are thrown together in relatively small spaces for extended periods of time, good manners become a survival skill. Following the travel protocol described here will ease your journey.

Don't invade a fellow traveler's space. Travel conditions often are crowded, so it becomes especially important to respect your fellow traveler's territorial boundaries. Don't stick your feet in the aisle or sprawl out into someone else's seat, either physically or with your belongings. Stay seated while the plane, bus, or train is moving. If you bump into someone, excuse yourself.

Be cautious about conversing or creating distracting noise. Make sure the person who is next to you wants to talk, or, for that matter, listen. If he or she doesn't respond or responds only briefly to your initial statement, take the hint. The best location for two people traveling together who wish to talk with each other is adjacent aisle seats. This allows you to turn your body to face the person without rubbing noses. Naturally, you need to respect the needs of flight attendants or ticket-takers to use the aisle.

Barbara Pachter once was sitting in a train's dining car when a man placed a cassette player, with portable speakers, on his table. He started the tape and then asked all those around him if the music was acceptable. Barbara appreciated both the music and the man's courtesy in inquiring.

Wait your turn. While boarding, exiting, or seeking to be served, follow the announced order or the established line. Of course, if you have special needs, such as a disability that makes it difficult for you to move quickly, you can use early boarding or other special assistance. Also wait your turn for your luggage and in taxi lines. Pushing is not polite.

Keep your requests reasonable. Travel is a fast-paced business, geared toward handling people quickly and, for the most part, treating them less as individuals than as interchangeable members of a group. It's not reasonable in most circumstances to expect individualized, specialized services. You can order a special vegetarian meal on an airline flight, for instance, but it is your responsibility to remind the ticket agent and alert the flight attendant. Even then, the meal may not have been loaded as requested, and you'll have to decide whether to eat what's provided or go hungry. If you are traveling coach, know that you can't be and won't be catered to in the same way as if you were in the first class section. It's best to be as flexible as you can.

Soaring Through Air Travel

Airline travel has its own particular set of courtesy rules. Business travelers who heed them can enhance their travel experience.

When traveling on business, select the most direct flight possible. The more legs your journey has and the more layovers, the more opportunities there will be for delays or mixups that inconvenience you and your hosts.

Select your seat when booking the flight. Make arrangements for the trip to the airport and back, determining whether you need to call a taxi service or rely on a friend or a relative. It's rude to call, unexpectedly, from the airport to ask someone to come and get you. Give the person enough notice to build the pick-up or dropoff times into his or her schedule. You should also verbally thank whoever picks you up for his or her assistance.

Confirm international flights and other travel arrangements 48 hours before leaving. This gives you the chance to make alternate arrangements if need be. If you don't get the flight you want, continue checking with the airline. Openings do occur. We have often been able to get the flight we wanted at the last moment.

Monitor the weather. It could be that your flight will be delayed because it is coming from a location that is fogged in or at which there is a backlog of planes taking off. In winter or during peak travel times, such as holidays, it can make sense to call before leaving your home or office for the airport to make sure your flight is on time.

Arrive at the airport early. This allows for delays at the security gate, time to process your luggage, and time to make your way to the appropriate gate. Use the extra time to make phone calls. If you are a member of an airline club, local calls are usually free. The clubs also provide a comfortable setting for phone calls and meetings. For example, Marjorie Brody has taken advantage of extended layover time in a city to coach clients from the region, using the airline client meeting room as her away-from-home office. That process saved the client time and money by avoiding the need to schedule a separate trip.

Avoid bumping other passengers when you enter, exit, or walk through the aisles of the plane. When stowing luggage, make sure yours fits in the overhead compartment or under your seat. If it doesn't, your steward or stewardess can check it. It is rude to other passengers when you take up too much space.

Know ahead of time what, if any, meals will be served during the flight and plan accordingly. Special meals, such as vegetarian, kosher, or low-salt, can be ordered, but that must be done in advance. You might want to include a non-perishable snack in your carry-on.

Don't overeat. Internal organs expand during flight and you may become uncomfortable.

Avoid too much alcohol. The effect in the air is four times greater than on the ground. Alcohol also causes dehydration and worsens jet lag.

Be considerate to the people around you: don't kick the back of the seat of the person in front of you or rest your legs on it. Don't let your materials intrude into someone's space. When adjusting the air, the light, and the window shade, make sure it does not make a neighbor uncomfortable. If possible, wait to go to the bathroom until your neighbor's drinks and food tray have been cleared.

Check your appearance before landing to avoid the sleepy look. If you are using the plane's bathroom to spruce up (wash your face, apply fresh makeup, or shave), don't take too long.

Upon arrival at your destination, check to see what taxis or other services might be available to drop you off in time for your return flight.

Attend to your luggage, and stay calm if the luggage is lost. Remember that airports differ in the speed with which they handle baggage—it may be on its way. When it doesn't appear, report it to the appropriate person—the employee at the rental car booth won't be able to help you!

Traveling by Taxi: Getting Around with Grace

A California day traveler to Tijuana once thought he was quite well prepared as he stepped off the trolley from San Diego. Picking up his briefcase, he crossed the border, hailed a cab and announced his destination. The cabbie assisted him inside, and then drove away as his passenger settled back for the ride. The journey took them through highway overpasses, around cloverleafs and winding ramps until, at last, they arrived. The traveler paid the cabbie, thanked him, and as the driver left, the newcomer took a moment to survey the scene. Looking around, he could see that he had just paid, handsomely, for what could have been a brief walk from where the trolley had dropped him off. He had been, both literally and figuratively, taken for a ride.

Traveling by taxi isn't as straightforward as it often seems it should be. While many cities consider it part of good public relations to regulate the cab industry, in many instances the passenger is on his or her own. You can be charged a flat rate, a metered fee, or on a per-passenger basis. Moreover, taxi etiquette varies from location to location. In cities such as Washington, DC and in some foreign countries, people may share a cab if they are going to different destinations and split the costs.

We were pleasantly surprised recently by the friendly, accommodating service we received from a Texas cab driver. He knew the shortest route to the airport, assured us we would make our flight in time, and refrained from extraneous conversation. At the end of our journey, he gave us a business card with his phone number, encouraging us to call him the next time we were in town. We will!

Some tips about taxis:

- Know if you must call ahead or if you can hail a cab on the street. If you need to hail one, lean toward the street, but do not step into it—that's dangerous—and raise your hand. In most circumstances, you don't need to gesture wildly or whistle loudly.

- Know how to tell "official" cabs from "gypsy" or unofficial cabs. There may be a medallion or license posted to indicate the cabbie is registered with local officials. If you are, for any reason, uncomfortable with the cab or driver, wave it on and get another cab.

- Know exactly where you want to go. You can check in advance (with someone other than your cabbie) as to how long the trip should take. Also check approximately how much the ride should cost.

- Carry enough cash for all surprises. One woman set up a meeting with a prospective client while she was attending a conference. She took a taxi to the location, and was astounded when she was told the fare was $72—checks and credit cards not accepted.

- If you are unsure about how the fare is calculated, ask in advance. Keep the door open until you are satisfied with the situation.

- Have the tip ready, so that you can exit quickly.

What to Do When Problems Arise

Missed connections. Unexpected delays. Illness far from home. Damaged equipment. Lost luggage. It's probably not mere coincidence that *travel* and *travail* are almost homonyms, because travel can, indeed, be hard work.

Each travel hassle is unique, but what stays constant is the need for courtesy. You need to remember that the new people you meet could be potential new clients, customers, or employees. Good etiquette should travel with you. Here are some tips that will help you navigate travel problems.

1. *Be polite.* Always use "Hello," "Thank you," and "Please," no matter whom you are dealing with or how upset you are. These can be magical phrases: they not only treat the listener with respect, but can help lower your own blood pressure if said in a gracious tone.

   Barbara Pachter once inadvertently dripped ink from her fountain pen on the skirt of a fellow traveler. She apologized and gave the woman her business card, adding "Send me the cleaning bill." The woman responded, "That's very kind of you" and took the card. That led to a conversation about the work she did, turning the accident into a marketing opportunity.

2. *Don't lose your temper.* It is natural and even appropriate to get angry when travel problems arise, but it's rude to show it. People know you are upset if you missed a plane or if your suitcase has been stolen, so there's no need to berate them while explaining the situation. You never know who is witnessing your tantrum, which, even if it does get results, will not enhance your professional reputation. The reality is that you may not get better service by demanding it—you may be the tenth person that day to scream at the customer service representative, who may be on the verge of losing her own inclination to help you.

3. *Look for alternatives.* Explain calmly your problem and how you hope to have it resolved. Ask what solutions are available and be flexible about accepting them. Emphasize what has the highest priority to you: is it arriving in the city on time, even if your luggage comes later? The answer may not be the most direct route or the most convenient departure time, but it may get you there when you need to be there. Know what you can subsist on: Can you manage with an airline-provided necessities kit and use your credit card to buy the clothes you need? Most people will empathize with your predicament—isolated and frustrated—and will try to help. Be aware, too, that special assistance may

be available, at the American embassy, perhaps, or through a Traveler's Aid Society.

4. *Keep focused on your goal.* How you get there really doesn't matter, and neither, to a certain extent, does when you get there. What is significant is your ability to accomplish the business purpose of your trip. Deem any trip that meets that goal to be a success, regardless of what was required to accomplish it.

5. *Learn from your experience.* You can't "mistake-proof" your business travel, but you can reduce the possible problems you face by planning ahead. Inside almost every travel disaster is a lesson that can be applied to a subsequent trip.

MAKING THE MOST OF HOTEL HOSPITALITY

For a business traveler, a hotel can be a home away from home. If you travel regularly, try to get familiar with a certain hotel and its staff. This will make your stay more comfortable; you will feel more at ease and so be able to better concentrate on business. Some national chains may give you discounts or special offers as a frequent customer. Your employer may allow you to keep these points for your personal use.

Once you've settled in at your hotel, call your local contact to let him or her know you've arrived. Confirm your plans to meet. As a host, you can leave a welcoming note with a home phone number in case of problems. A gift of flowers or fruit in a guest's room is always appreciated, but often is not necessary for American business travelers in the United States. If the guest is coming to your city as a special favor, though, this extra touch is very welcoming.

Deciphering the Hotel Who's Who

Many people don't know who's who at a hotel, much less who to ask for a particular service. While the front desk can always direct you to the appropriate person, it's good to know each staff member's role and responsibilities.

THE DOORMAN: The doorman's domain is everything on the outside of the hotel. It is his job to make sure the front entrance is presentable and that everything at the entrance flows in an orderly fashion. (And since most doormen are still men, we don't have a gender-neutral term for this position.)

He handles the greeting and departure of guests, and often is your first contact with the hotel. He also directs the traffic flow and the handling of cars and taxis. Although duties vary with the hotel, the doorman usually just coordinates the loading and unloading of luggage with the bell staff. He may sometimes carry your luggage to the door. If you need information regarding matters outside the hotel—city sights, restaurants, etc.—he often can provide it.

THE BELLMAN: The term, bellman, comes from the use of an actual bell that was once rung at the front desk to summon these employees (generally still men), although bells generally are no longer in use.

The bellman usually takes luggage from your cab or car to the front desk and handles all the inside hotel needs of the guest. He may pick up and drop off dry cleaning, arrange transportation, or deliver messages and packages. His work on the outside of the hotel is coordinated through the doorman, and on the inside, by the concierge—if these positions exist.

This staff member should never be called a "bell hop" or a "bell boy," since these terms are demeaning. The preferred title is "bell man" or "bell staff."

THE CONCIERGE: The concierge is both an information source and a resource who responds as needed to guest requests. He or she may help you get tickets to a sporting event, arrange for flowers to be delivered to your host, or track down a new battery for your laptop computer. His or her role is to make your stay as pleasant as possible.

THE PORTER: Porters are at apartments, airports, and on trains, but not at hotels. Their role is to handle luggage.

Travel-Tested Safety Suggestions

"Trust in Allah, but tie your camel."

—ARAB PROVERB

Crime is ungracious, but it's also a modern-day reality. A traveler unfamiliar with an area can be especially vulnerable, and a business traveler—because he or she is well-dressed and sometimes encumbered with equipment—may be a particularly attractive target. We consider it important to practice what we call "defensive etiquette"—to courteously employ street savvy that enables you to avoid becoming a victim.

We have three guiding principles for safe sojourns:

Be cordial, but alert. When someone engages you in conversation, be aware that he or she may have ulterior motives. You should respond, but it's best to be cautious and vague, especially at first. Naturally, you should say you're "in sales" as opposed to "a diamond courier." Also be aware of what is going on around you—could this person be trying to distract you while someone else "accidentally" bumps you and steals your wallet? Be aware of credit card scams—retrieve your carbons, or watch as they are destroyed. When using a telephone company calling card, cover the numbers or, better yet, memorize them. Thieves at airports and bus stations have been known to use binoculars to get the number and then have massive phone bills charged to your account.

Minimize your potential losses. Take only what you really need and never what you can't replace. There's no need, for instance, to carry your local department store credit card or your library card to a far-flung location. Use traveler's checks. Carry only the credit cards that you plan to use. Do an inventory of your wallet's contents so you know exactly what it contains in case you need to replace it. In a safe place at home, keep a listing of all credit card account numbers along with the number to call in case of theft.

While traveling, carry any valuable items you brought with you whenever possible. Don't leave money or valuables in your room. Put any jewelry, cameras, documents, etc. in the hotel safe.

Take charge of your personal safety. If the hotel front desk announces your room number when calling the bellman, ask for another room and stipulate that it not be announced. This can be especially important for female travelers.

Ask for a room near the elevators so you don't have to walk down a long corridor.

Upon arriving in your hotel room, always check first to see that the windows and the pass-through door are locked. It's been our experience that approximately 50 percent of the time, they are not. If the hotel staff can't get the doors to lock, ask for another room.

When you exit the room, you can leave the TV on, for security's sake. While staying in the room, close the door securely and use all locks.

Don't open the door unless you are expecting someone. Check the peephole. If a person claims to be an employee, or if you have any other concern, call the front desk.

Keep your key in the same place in every room where you stay so that it is easy to find. We suggest you leave it on top of the television. If you need to leave quickly, you can grab it. Plus, you don't need to search.

Don't display your room key in public or leave it on a restaurant table, in the exercise room, or other places where it can be easily stolen.

Consider packing a plug-in nightlight or sleeping with the bathroom light on. Know where the fire exits are. Know where to seek help.

ETIQUETTE FOR EXPENSES:
Who Pays for What, How to Tip

Your company naturally has rules on which business travel expenses it will cover. To avoid awkwardness and embarrassment upon your return, check on the rules before you leave. You might want to find out whether a reasonable dinner is considered one that costs $20 or $50, for instance, as well as whether room service is considered reimbursable. It also will be helpful to know how detailed your receipts need to be, along with what sort of accounting is expected for any cash advances. Perhaps most significantly, you'll need to review your company policy and practices on treating your hosts, clients, or vendors.

If the person picking you up at the airport is from your company or from your host's company, it's not required that you pay for airport parking, buy gas, or pay bridge and highway tolls. However, you should always verbally thank the person for his or her help.

It's courteous to treat your hosts to a dinner or a lunch during your visit. If you attend a sporting event or live performance, the host generally pays. The guest, though, can offer to pay for refreshments.

At conventions, colleagues usually treat one another to drinks. Make sure that you take a turn "buying a round." Remember, though, that you should limit consumption of alcohol at conventions and sales meetings—it's still business.

The easiest way for either a host or visitor to handle these transactions is to use a corporate credit card if one is available. The next choice would be to use a private credit card; it keeps you from having to carry a lot of cash, and provides an automatic receipt for reimbursement purposes.

Practical Tips on Travel Tipping

The well-prepared traveler keeps a ready supply of change and small bills for use in tipping. Many Americans are uncomfortable with this aspect of payment for service, finding it to be an undemocratic holdover from the days of nobility when servants gratefully accepted tokens of appreciation. However, wages for the hospitality industry are structured with the assumption that employee income will be supplemented by tips. The people who work in restaurants and hotels not only rely on the additional funds, but are aware they have an incentive to provide better service to increase the amount of the tips they receive. They are, in effect, working on commission, even if it is provided through direct payment from the customer.

Tips on Travel Tipping provides general guidelines, and should be considered a starting point for tipping. (For information on restaurant tipping, see Chapter Eleven, "Dining for Fun and Profit: The Business Lunch.") The amount you give the doorman, though, varies with the extent and quality of the service. If he escorts you from the lobby and holds an umbrella over you during a drenching storm, hails a cab, oversees the loading of multiple pieces of luggage, all while giving you directions and recommendations on tourist attractions, be generous. Carry a number of dollar bills and keep them accessible. You don't want to fumble through purses or wallets.

Tips on Travel Tipping

Cab Driver	10 to 15 percent of your fare.
Shuttle driver for car rental agency	$1 or 15 percent of what the taxi fare would have been if you took one.
Doorman	$1 to $3, depending on the extent of the service.
Bellman/Porter	$1 per bag, or $3 to $5 if there are a lot of bags.
Concierge	No tip for small services, $5 to $10 for making reservations or getting tickets.
Chambermaid	$1 to $2 per day, more for special tasks.
Bathroom attendant	50 cents to $1.

(Continued on next page)

Parking attendant	$1 to $2.
Hair stylist and manicurist	15 to 20 percent of cost of service.
Shoeshiner	$1.
Room service	15 to 20 percent of items delivered, if not already included in bill. Do not confuse service charge with tip.
Desk clerks, elevator operators	Do not tip.

You should be aware that tips may be pooled, or that the individual you are tipping may split his or her tip with a colleague.

If you receive bad service, do not withhold a tip in protest. The recipient may not get the message but think instead that you merely forgot or were cheap. It is more effective to leave a small tip after graciously communicating your reason for dissatisfaction.

Tips to porters, cabbies, bellmen, parking attendants, bathroom attendants, shoeshiners, and hair and nail attendants are provided on the spot, immediately following the delivery of the service. You can tip chambermaids and doormen at the end of your stay, although because people work shifts that don't necessarily coincide with your visit, it's acceptable to tip them as you go.

WHEN YOU TRAVEL WITH YOUR SPOUSE

When your spouse or "significant other" accompanies you on a business trip, the risks may outweigh the rewards. While everyone appreciates a change in environment, being accompanied on a business trip can create role conflict. Yes, it would be nice to enjoy an exotic locale with someone close to you, but that is not why you are there in the first place. Your traveling partner needs to understand that his or her "job" while accompanying you on the trip is, first, not to interfere with your work! Some people find it best to have the spouse join them at the end of the work period so that they can spend time together that actually is a vacation.

If your partner is going to be with you, have him or her plan to do something while you are working, and schedule your time together just as you would at home— meeting for dinner or the weekend, for instance. If it is a business trip as opposed to a conference, the spouse should not accompany you to the working session. Also check with your hosts whether it is appropriate to bring your spouse for evenings and social times. A truly gracious host may even provide an itinerary or another spouse to escort yours.

Your partner needs to act professionally, polite toward business associates, and patient regarding the demands on your time. It is not appropriate for a spouse to sit around the pool and complain about the unreasonable work schedule or the boorish behavior of a boss. He or she could be speaking to the boss's spouse!

When attending conferences, spouses should not only understand the nature of the business at the conference, but be able to talk intelligently about it and interact with the group. If the spouse does not enjoy the environment, he or she should stay home.

At some functions, such as a company-sponsored visit to a resort as a reward for reaching a sales quota, the spouse's presence may be considered mandatory. When in doubt, check to see what others are doing. If such is the case, the spouse should mingle with the other spouses, dress appropriately, and behave professionally.

You, too, should be on your best behavior, even if no other colleagues are on the trip. Word about misdeeds and faux pas from either you or your spouse could easily follow you home.

HOW TO SUCCESSFULLY HOST INTERNATIONAL VISITORS

We now do more business internationally than ever before. In subsequent chapters, we'll discuss in depth etiquette considerations for international business. Most of our advice in those chapters applies in reverse to overseas travelers coming to the United States. For instance, while looking someone in the eye may be the "American way," it's not realistic to expect a visitor from a country where an averted gaze is a sign of respect to automatically change his behavior during his stay here. The key, as always, is respect for the other person's cultural norms.

We've come up with eight basic tips on ways to make an international visitor feel less like a stranger in a strange land.

1. *Learn about the visitor's culture.* You need to know, in the literal sense, where the person is coming from. Imagine, for instance, being asked about living among the cowboys if you come from Maine, and you can imagine how important it is to understand the visitor's home country. You want to be able to discuss any neutral, newsworthy events.

2. *Always have someone meet the visitor at the airport.* While a greeter at the airport is an optional practice for American business travelers, it's a vital courtesy for international visitors. Again, consider how much more comfortable you would feel while visiting a foreign land if you knew you would have someone to greet you.

3. *Understand and use the appropriate greetings and titles.* This simple gesture can get you off on the right foot. It shows respect both for the visitor and his culture.

4. *Have foods or flowers delivered to the visitor's room.* This is a gracious, welcoming touch. If you can provide something to his or her taste, that's even better. Remember that some flowers have symbolic significance in other countries, so make sure that the arrangement is appropriate.

5. *Arrange for a driver and transportation during the visitor's stay.* This allows for safe exploration without your presence.

6. *Respect the visitor's dining customs.* If the visitor expresses an interest in trying local cuisine, that's fine, but don't force unfamiliar foods on him or her. You'll also want to show sensitivity—don't feed a Muslim person a pork roll sandwich for lunch.

7. *Plan interesting things for the visitor to do at night.* The visitor will want to enjoy as much as possible of the local culture. Remember that what may seem routine to you—such as a dinner cruise—may be enjoyable to a stranger. If a visitor brings family members, arrange for appropriate activities.

8. *Show the visitor how Americans live.* Invite the visitor to your house. Provide materials about your city. Conduct a tour of your city if it is a first trip. You're being gracious and helping the visitor understand Americans, including you.

PREPARING FOR THE INTERNATIONAL TRIP

When it comes time for you to travel overseas, practical preparations can help you arrive in a courteous frame of mind.

Keep your passport and visas up-to-date. If you plan to travel repeatedly to several countries, you may want to apply for a 48-page passport which provides additional space for visas. Make two photocopies of your passport; pack one separately from your passport and leave the other copy in the United States with a trusted friend. Check about any immunizations that may be required, and allow sufficient time to recover from any side effects before embarking on your trip. Also consider whether you will need an international driver's license.

When packing, avoid any tags or luggage labels that scream "United States." These may attract the attention of thieves or terrorists. Know the voltage used to determine whether you need to bring an adapter and/or a converter for appliances such as a hairdryer. Know if there are differences in the type of clothing you should bring.

You will need some local currency for taxis and any emergencies (about $25 to $50), but for most of your needs, do plan to use traveler's checks and credit cards, which sometimes can get better exchange rates. Metropolitan banks and major airports may be convenient locations to make currency exchanges. Don't travel without any local currency: you do not want to arrive late at night, find the airport banks closed, and be stranded with no way to get funds.

It is especially important to have culture awareness and to do your cultural homework regarding Do's and Don'ts before you leave for your visit. This is one area in which "learning by doing" is not recommended—by winging it, you could commit a serious faux pas from which you could not socially recover, and your business could suffer as a result.

You should study guides, attend an intercultural training seminar or speak to citizens of the country you are visiting. You can get additional information about the country from its embassy or consulate. The U.S. Department of State's Bureau of Public Affairs can be a valuable source of resource material through its series of background notes. These brochures can provide you with up-to-date information on a country's geography, government, economy, and history, as well as the languages spoken there and the names of principal American officials, such as the ambassador.

Make sure that your trip is not planned during a religious holiday or a civic holiday.

As you plan for the trip, stay current on events—political situations can change overnight. It will also be helpful for you to know ongoing controversies, particularly those involving the United States, so that you can avoid sensitive subjects.

The process of traveling may, of course, be different outside of the United States. Major European cities often have train systems from the airport that will take you to the center of the city, where you can get a cab. If you plan to make part of your journey by train, know that some trains require advance reservations. Be cautious if you don't use an "official" taxi when you are in a foreign country. Some private citizens may attempt to offer you this service, and it can be unreliable and unsafe.

MAKING YOUR TRIP WORK FOR YOU

Whether you are in the United States or abroad, it's important that you make the most of your time during your business trip. You can use informal dinners to become better acquainted with business associates, read the local paper to understand issues of concern to area residents, taste local specialties to get the true flavor of the area. Part of the success of your trip will come from its lasting effects on your outlook— what you learned as much as what you did. If you approach the trip as a sort of intensive educational seminar, you may benefit more from it.

But all journeys come to an end. Before separating from your host, thank him for seeing you; visitors, are, after all, a disruption. Determine the next step business-wise: a reciprocal visit? further negotiations? a report?

When you arrive home, send thank-you notes and any follow-up material promptly. You can send copies of business photos that you took during your trip and any articles you come across that are pertinent to the discussions you had.

To thank someone for the plant tour, you can write:

Dear Joe,

Thank you so much for your time during my recent plant tour.

The information I gathered will help our industrial engineers create better implementation plans for our own expansion.

Please also thank your secretary, Sally, for all her help.

Sincerely,

Tom

After a conference, you can write:

Dear Elizabeth,

Wasn't the conference great!

The special attention that you gave both Tom and me made it even more special.

You certainly represent your company well and I look forward to doing business with you.

Sincerely,

Jessica

And although the last thing you may want to contemplate upon your return is another business trip, you should take the time to assess your trip. What would you do differently if you had it to do over again? What worked well? Use that information when, inevitably, your next trip looms on the horizon.

A Fantastic Voyage

Business travel can be an effective way to achieve corporate goals, and gracious conduct during your journey and at your destination will enhance the productivity of your trip. When good manners travel with you, you demonstrate that you are able to handle new situations courteously. By behaving in a polite fashion, you spread good will for yourself and for your company.

Part 2

BUSINESS
AROUND
THE WORLD

Chapter 15

GAINING INTERNATIONAL PERSPECTIVE

There are truths on this side of the Pyrenees,
which are falsehoods on the other.

—BLAISE PASCAL

There is an old story:

> An American visiting a local cemetery was on his way to his mother's grave when he noticed a Chinese man who was honoring his ancestors by putting food on one of the nearby graves. "Why are you doing that?" the American asked. "When do you think your ancestors will get up and eat the food?"
>
> The Chinese man answered, without missing a beat, "When *your* loved ones get up and smell the flowers."

Culture undeniably determines perspective. Notions about what conduct is correct are rooted in each country's environment. While there are a few universal standards (most societies have taboos against cold-blooded murder, for example) there are many more areas of disagreement about appropriate behavior.

Not so long ago, sociologists began changing the metaphor of America as a melting pot—in which many cultures converged and merged, melting away their distinctions—to one of a salad bowl, in which the ingredients remained intact even as they were mixed. That's also a useful image for the global marketplace, in which many cultures are tossed together. Each ingredient makes its own contribution, and the result is more than the sum of the parts: a blending of tastes and textures that play off each other and make the whole much more interesting.

Americans, though, are at somewhat of a disadvantage in appreciating and understanding other cultures, a failing that can be attributed in part to geography.

Because we are so physically isolated from most other countries, we often grow up without much international sensitivity training. Most of the blunders Americans make while doing business internationally can be attributed to ignorance rather than malice.

Consider, for a moment, the American manager from southern California who was sent to Japan by his company to negotiate a contract. He was not an uneducated man, but he didn't know the enormous impact of what he considered to be an innocuous joke.

The man had been invited to the home of the president of the Japanese company for dinner—a rare honor. A car had been sent for him at his hotel. On the way to the home, they passed a McDonald's restaurant.

To make conversation, the manager joked, "I have a difficult time with Japanese food—why don't we stop at the McDonalds?"

His Japanese host did not find that comment funny. In fact, it wasn't funny, but it was costly. The company lost the contract and the president of the American company had to go to Japan to smooth things over.

Even so, that company was lucky. Its officials realized how damaging and expensive bad manners can be, and, as a result of that incident, set up an international awareness program to prevent employees from making similar mistakes in the future.

Whether you are visiting another country where different rules of conduct apply or are hosting a foreign representative in the United States, you want to act in a courteous, gracious fashion that will make everyone feel comfortable.

MAKING AN IMPACT IN A WHOLE NEW WORLD
The merchant has no country.

—THOMAS JEFFERSON

Business today is increasingly international, in areas from drug research to computers. A small company in Michigan may find itself expanding its operations to Mexico or Japan. An American conglomerate may find that many of its suppliers have overseas addresses.

The world is indeed far smaller now than ever before, and ignorance of the rules is no longer any excuse, if indeed it ever was. Blunders carry a high cost. Your host probably will not dismiss your actions as the inept misdeeds of a well-meaning but uninformed American, especially when your competitor might demonstrate international savvy. As citizens of the world and as knowledgeable, well-versed employees, it is important to understand and appreciate the importance of international protocol.

Cross-cultural training makes a difference. The Business Council for International Understanding Institute, which is located at American University in Washington, D.C., estimates that international personnel who go abroad without cross-cultural preparation have a failure rate ranging from 33 to 66 percent. In contrast, those who have the benefit of such training have a less than 2 percent failure rate. It costs an organization from $145,000 to $500,000 to move an executive and his or her family overseas. The costs include subsidized housing, transportation, and living expenses. If they return early, this money is wasted.

Dr. John Bing, President of ITAP International, an international training firm based in Princeton, N.J., estimates that an even more prevalent problem with overseas transfers is "brown-out," or loss of the transferee's productivity in the overseas workplace. Without training, employees transferred overseas learn about subtle management differences that influence their success only through their on-the-job experience. With the fast pace of business today and the accompanying emphasis on the bottom line, your company might not be able to afford this slow system. When employees learn by doing overseas, productivity usually suffers. A little prevention costs much less than a lot of cure!

What's more, when you work in the international arena and know appropriate protocol, you'll be more comfortable. You can concentrate on business and not worry about committing blunders or inadvertently making mistakes that will negatively affect your bottom line.

MASTERING THE DISTINCTIONS THAT MAKE A DIFFERENCE

Language. Geography. Social systems. Religion. Economics. History. There are many phenomena that make a country what it is, defining the differences that distinguish it from all other lands.

This story also helps to explain the importance of perspective:

An Arab sheik was proud of his young son and wanted to show him off to his friends, so he brought them with him as he went to the classroom to see his son and his tutor. "Son," the father asked, "What is 1 plus 1?" The son didn't answer. "Son, what is 1 plus 1?" Still, the son didn't answer. The sheik nervously asked, "Son, what's the difficulty?" "Father," the son answered, "Are you buying or selling?"

For the international business traveler, these distinctions have a significant impact on the way business is conducted. To operate successfully, you need, first, to be aware of the differences and then to understand the impact the differences have on a country's etiquette.

Just because something is different doesn't mean it is wrong. Business is conducted in vastly varied ways in different countries. Ask Americans what side of the street the British drive on, and chances are, many will say "The wrong side." In fact, it's just "the other side" or "the left side." When you notice differences, it's possible—and preferable—not to make judgments about the correctness of the difference. Whether something is proper depends on your perspective. There is no global ctiquette code.

Naturally, this makes international business etiquette much more complicated. Instead of learning one set of semi-permanent rules, you now are confronted with hundreds of evolving guidelines. In each country, you may encounter differences in formality and in the pace of business. There's a protocol to getting acquainted, from knowing the greetings of the country you are visiting to understanding how to make a toast so you don't offend.

We can, however, give you three general guidelines of international etiquette:

1. *It is the visitor who must adapt—not the host.* Just as we expect visitors to our country to adopt our customs, you are expected to figure out how to function properly in the host country. You are the one who is doing the selling or representing your company; the focus is on you. A very gracious host will help make the visitor comfortable and perhaps meet him or her "half way." That's what you hope your foreign host will do for you and what you should do when you host international visitors in the United States. However, even Dorothy knew she had to behave differently when she was not in Kansas any more.

2. *Don't embarrass someone else.* Why is it that we are able to recall clearly our most embarrassing moments long after they occur? Possibly because embarrassment can conjure up a mix of such powerful emotions as guilt, shame, and the uncomfortable sensation of having done something stupid. If you embarrass your host or guest, even inadvertently, it could cost you or others business.

3. *Don't criticize someone's bad manners.* It's poor manners under any circumstances to criticize someone else's behavior, but it's especially rude to do so when conducting business internationally. What you think are "poor" manners actually may be, by local standards, exemplary conduct. After all, you can exhibit your best American behavior and still offend people. There is relatively little that could be considered universally rude. Also take this admonition into account before judging negatively the behavior of an international visitor in the United States.

There are, of course, many reasons why people behave the way they do. Culture is just one of them. Others include personality style, gender, individual differences, environment, religion, education, and the organizational climate in which the person works.

When we were negotiating with an overseas client, an intermediary created a lot of difficulty that we wished to resolve. The client was very frustrated. We were frustrated. Before taking action, though, we paused to consider the possible reasons for the intermediary's behavior. We ran through a mental checklist of possible causes, including culture-based beliefs. Only after having done that did we feel comfortable in asking, "Is this typical behavior for people of his country, or is it just him?" As it turns out, we would have been wrong in assuming his behavior was acceptable in his culture, because there, too, he had a reputation for being a difficult person!

What it boils down to is that there are absolutely no absolutes. We can give you general guidelines about international behavior, but for every rule there is an exception. It will be up to you to learn how to apply what we tell you in the specific situation you encounter. We can hope, at best, to raise your consciousness about the kinds of considerations that you will confront country-by-country.

Will what we talk about always matter? No.

Will it sometimes make a difference? Yes.

Will it occasionally make THE difference in whether you get the sale or establish the needed relationship? Absolutely!

Therefore, is it worth doing? Yes!

INTERNATIONAL AWARENESS QUIZ

How much do you really know about the wide world? Do you consider yourself suave when it comes to savoir-faire? Take this true-false quiz to find out.

1. True or False? The circle sign with three fingers raised is the universal sign for OK.

2. True or False? In Germany, the proper toast is "Prosit."

3. True or False? In Brazil, it is offensive to send purple flowers as a thank-you.

4. True or False? If you are in an uncomfortable situation, try some humor to lighten the tension.

5. True or False? In Sweden, it is offensive to toast your host before he toasts you.

6. True or False? The United Kingdom of Great Britain and Northern Ireland is comprised of England, Scotland, the Republic of Ireland, and Northern Ireland.

7. True or False? In Thailand, the proper greeting is the wai.

8. True or False? It is always recommended that a woman wear a suit when conducting business internationally.

9. True or False? The universally accepted distance between two people when they are discussing business is three feet.

10. True or False? In Europe, a man should wait for a woman to extend her hand in handshaking situations.

11. True or False? In Japan, it is impolite to pass out your business card when first meeting someone.

12. True or False? The French often invite business guests into their homes.

13. True or False? Pasta is usually served as a main course in Italy.

14. True or False? Most Greek food is served lukewarm.

15. True or False? White suits are acceptable for men in Hong Kong because of the high humidity and the temperature.

16. True or False? In Scotland, the people are called Scots.

17. True or False? Portuguese is the language of Brazil.

18. True or False? The concept of the "designated driver" began in Chile.

And now the answers:

1. False. The OK sign is not universal; in fact, it's obscene or rude in Brazil, southern Italy, Greece, Germany, and parts of the former Soviet Union.

2. True. The proper toast in Germany is "Prosit."

3. True. In Brazil, purple flowers signify death and so are inappropriate as a thank-you.

4. False. Humor in the global arena can backfire badly, and so should be avoided.

5. True. Your Swedish host should toast you first.

6. False. Wales is included in the United Kingdom, but not the Republic of Ireland. Britain consists of England, Scotland, and Wales.

7. True. The wai is the proper greeting in Thailand.

8. False. If surrounded by saris, as in India, a woman in a suit would be out of place.

9. False. The appropriate distance between two people who are discussing business varies with the culture.

10. True. A man in Europe should usually wait for a woman to extend her hand in handshaking situations.

11. False. Passing out your business card is part of the ritual greeting in Japan.

12. False. The French rarely invite business guests to their homes.

13. False. Pasta is an appetizer in Italy.

14. True. Greek food is at the proper temperature when Americans would consider it lukewarm.

15. False. White suits symbolize mourning in Hong Kong. They are acceptable only when worn by Peter Lorre in old American movies.

16. True. The people of Scotland are Scots; Scotch is what you might drink.

17. True. Portuguese, not Spanish, is the language of Brazil.

18. False. The concept of the "designated driver" originated in Norway.

ZEROING IN ON YOUR CULTURAL FOCUS

You start learning your culture as soon as you are born. Bit by bit, you learn the language, how to get along with others, how men and women act, what is considered important, the meaning of time, the significance of distance, the expectations you must meet. Without anyone sitting down and telling you "This is how we feel about being prompt" or "Here's the appropriate way to act toward a woman," you gradually acquire the values and attitudes of your society.

In due time, you will see things according to your cultural background. It is as if you put on cultural glasses. The way you view things through your glasses may be very different from the glasses of someone else, but the general focus probably is similar to that of others from your culture.

Every culture has a different set of glasses, which affects its vision of reality. What are Americans like? To Mexicans, Americans are unemotional and serious, likely to work as a team but rather time-conscious. The Taiwanese see Americans as emotional and fun-loving, easy-going although inclined to be independent. To the French, Americans are friendly but aggressive, competitive, and entrepreneurial. They're all correct in their assessments, because they are measuring Americans against their own society. Comparatively speaking, Americans are all of those things.

How we view ourselves depends in large part on how we have been taught to think of ourselves. Indeed, much of our educational process is designed to mold that view. When you grow up hearing that "America is the land of opportunity," for instance, it shows that the society values those who make something of themselves. Historically, we have downplayed the differences between the "haves" and the "have-nots." While other countries might see the class into which you are born as the key determinant of your life, our focus instead is on what you can achieve.

This has two implications—one internal and one external. It means that while in the United States, we are considered responsible for whatever we make of ourselves. And it means that when traveling to foreign countries, we must remember that the lower priority we give to class or status distinctions will not be universally shared.

Culture shock is what occurs when you encounter a setting that varies dramatically from your home environment. The unusual sights, sounds, and smells may all contribute to a feeling of sensory overload, as you find yourself to be, literally, a stranger in a strange land. You may become physically and psychologically disoriented as you struggle to find your way without knowing any of the local landmarks. Your basic beliefs may be called into question as they clash with an entirely opposite set of principles.

However, you can emerge from that experience with a stronger appreciation for the pervasive and powerful impact of culture in shaping human behavior. By recognizing the role your culture has had in shaping you, it's possible to see more clearly its equally significant influence on your international counterpart.

BENEFITING FROM CULTURE COMPARISONS

Through his research, American cultural anthropologist Edward Hall, author of *Beyond Culture*, has provided two key ways to help us understand how cultures differ from each other: Context and Organization of time.

CONTEXT is how information is conveyed and how much should be conveyed.

A Cultural Continuum

HIGH CONTEXT: The social circumstances are significant.

↑

Chinese

Korean

Japanese

Vietnamese

Arab

Greek

Spanish

Italian

French

English

North American

Scandinavian

Swiss

↓ German

LOW CONTEXT: Documents must be explicit.

In low context cultures, messages are explicit and direct. Words carry most of the information. The social circumstances of the conversation or agreement are not all-important. What is important are the written agreements, which tend to be detailed and meticulous. In such cultures, a contract you draw up will be explicit in defining the terms of the agreement and usually followed to the letter. *A Cultural Continuum* shows several cultures from high-context to low-context.

Conversely, in high context cultures the exact phrasing and verbal part of the message are less significant than your relationship with that person and the context, or circumstances, in which it occurs. What is not said is as important as what is said.

We were told by someone from a high context culture, "I look forward to establishing a joint business relationship with you based on confidence and good will." What that statement meant is that the relationship between us was more important than any contract we would write.

You need to take these distinctions into account in order to be successful in international business. What matters is not just where your host country falls on the overall scale, but how it compares to the country you come from. In Arab culture, which is higher context than the United States, you can expect to talk around and around on a point until agreement is reached. High context cultures such as Mexico, which follows the Spanish model, function largely around who you know and your relationship with that person.

ORGANIZATION OF TIME concerns the importance of schedules and deadlines.

If your society organizes time monochronically, it usually prefers to do one thing at a time. This requires some kind of scheduling. Promptness and deadlines are stressed. Monochronic cultures include the United States and Northern Europe.

Under polychronic time, many things happen at once. Interruptions are routine. If you value people, you must hear them out and cannot cut them off simply because of a schedule. For example, deadlines are "targets" in Mexico.

High context cultures tend to be polychronic. Some examples include Latin America, the Mediterranean, the Middle East, Greece, and Turkey.

Implications in terms of business etiquette come in the way appointments are handled, the kinds of relationships that businesses establish with their customers and how meetings are arranged.

Under polychronic time, appointments can be broken and meetings may be held with many people at the same time, although Americans think this rude. By contrast, in monochronic cultures, you must leave when the time allocated for your appointment is up, whether the work is finished or not.

In the upcoming chapters we'll explore some additional differences that spring from these views as we discuss several specific impacts of culture on business etiquette.

ACHIEVING A GLOBAL OUTLOOK
Six Strategies for International Success

The key to being successful in international business revolves around knowing where you've come from as well as where you're headed. Keep these differences in mind as you visit other countries or host international visitors.

1. *Be respectful and non-judgmental about the differences you encounter.* This requires that you take the broad view, maybe even temporarily removing your own cultural glasses and trying on someone else's. It can be helpful to see yourself as a student learning about new and different behavior as opposed to a teacher who imparts acquired wisdom. Your role is not to convert your contact to the "superior" American way.

   As a traveler, don't compare cultures unless asked to do so, and then be careful to make the comparisons complimentary to your host country. Many of us make negative comparisons and don't even realize it. For instance, an American overseas might ask, "Don't you have any decent coffee here?" While sitting at an outdoor cafe in Paris, a consultant heard a group of Americans ask for a pastrami sandwich and then become very indignant and much louder when the waiter didn't understand the request. You are required to show respect for the mores of the country you are visiting or those of your international guest.

2. *Understand your own viewpoint.* Remember that your perceptions are relative, not absolute. One of the most invigorating aspects of travel can be the way it allows you to examine your own beliefs and habits, taking them off of "automatic" if you so choose.

3. *Be empathic—try to place yourself in another's shoes.* When someone does something in a way that frustrates or baffles you, try to consider motivations and perspectives. Intention counts for a lot: someone who did not look at you didn't mean to insult you but instead was showing you deference, and you should take that into account. Women, for instance, may not be treated as equals in the country you visit. In the Middle East, this may include eating at tables in public places that are marked "for women and children only." While this will be uncomfortable for most American women, it helps to understand that it is not directed at you, but is part of the culture. As a business traveler, you are not there to change the culture, but to work within it.

4. *Be flexible and patient.* A rigid person who is set in his or her ways will have difficulty on international assignments, where the rules change the minute you step off the plane or greet a visitor. One North American businessman in Mexico admitted to his host, "We North Americans tend to be a bit impatient." In new environments, try new foods, new ways of behaving. At first you might feel "silly," partly because the new behaviors are unfamiliar. But even if you miss the mark somewhat, your hosts will appreciate the positive attitude demonstrated by your attempt.

5. *Practice good listening skills.* A host's role typically includes explaining the way things are done, and sometimes even why they are done that way. If you are the guest, you can learn much by listening and asking appropriate questions. If you are the host, help "interpret" for your guest.

6. *Be ready for the unusual.* Each trip is an adventure, so it's vital that you be adaptable and even ready to accept a degree of frustration. "Adventure," said Amelia Earhart, "is worthwhile in itself." Try to react positively to unusual encounters. The fewer rigid expectations you have, the less time you'll waste contrasting how you thought things would be with how they actually are.

We also offer these three not-so-serious survival tips for international travel:

1. Eat when food is offered.
2. Go to the bathroom when there is one!
3. Avoid humor, but be able to laugh at yourself.

Four Ways to Minimize Culture Shock

You can lessen culture shock by preparing well for the journey.

1. *Read and study before you go.* Many culture-specific guidebooks are available to tell you about the particular customs of the country you are visiting. General international knowledge also helps. Barbara Pachter's contact in Colombia stressed the importance of knowing about soccer and the World Cup before visiting South America. She went so far as to mention Colombian newspapers that could be purchased in the United States.

Start by learning geography. It's all too easy to make mistakes. During the 1992 American baseball World Series, CBS said that Toronto is on Lake Erie. It's on Lake Ontario. That drives Canadians crazy! Some other examples:

New Zealand is not part of Australia. The island of Tasmania is part of Australia, however.

An Arab is someone whose first language is Arabic. Not all Arabs are Muslims (some are Christians). Not all Muslims are Arabs (they are also Russian, Chinese, and Iranian).

Mexico is officially the United Mexican States.

The greater the depth and breadth of your knowledge, the better able you will be to function in the international environment.

International Savvy: What You Need to Know Before You Go

Greeting rituals.

As much knowledge of the language as is possible.

The dress code.

Basic geography, including main cities.

Religious beliefs and customs.

Cultural heritage: art, music, museums, universities, landmarks, theater.

Key personalities: prominent politicians, the U.S. ambassador, celebrities who are citizens.

Brief country history.

Attitudes toward Americans, stereotypes.

Currency system.

Social structure: role of women, class divisions, role of family.

Gift-giving etiquette.

Popular sports and newspapers.

Customs regarding punctuality.

Typical weather.

2. *Observe.* Be sensitive to your surroundings as you watch for clues on how to behave. Try not to stick out like a sore thumb.

3. *Ask questions.* When you are overseas, if you don't know, ask. People know that by asking, you are demonstrating respect. "We appreciate your thoughtfulness and understanding to our local culture" was the response Barbara Pachter received when she asked about appropriate dress for a seminar in the United Arab Emirates.

4. *Find a mentor on site.* When in unfamiliar territory, a guide can be helpful and also can keep you out of danger zones.

READY TO TAKE ON THE WORLD

In the following chapters, you will discover several specific differences in what constitutes proper behavior internationally:

- initial greeting.
- how to use an interpreter.
- ways to make presentations.
- giving gifts.
- eating foreign food.

This information is a tool that facilitates effective cross-cultural communication. You will find out more about yourself as you find out about other cultures. You'll also come to see your life differently as you pay attention to the little details that differentiate you from other people and other cultures. Doing business internationally can expand your horizons—in every sense of the expression.

Chapter 16

GREETINGS WITH A FOREIGN FLAIR

You cannot shake hands with a clenched fist.

—Golda Meir

Representatives of two companies—one American and one Japanese—agreed to meet in Hawaii to discuss a project. Both groups wanted to demonstrate sensitivity to the other group's customs and culture.

The American company president told his team that the Japanese dress more formally than Americans often do and explained that a bow is the traditional greeting. The Americans were instructed to wear three-piece suits and to bow.

The Japanese company president told his team to be sensitive to American informality. "We will dress casually," he said, "and we will shake hands."

At the first meeting, the Japanese delegation wore Hawaiian shirts and extended their hands just as the suit-clad Americans were preparing to bow! Each side had a good laugh about the situation. They all recognized that despite the different styles, each team had communicated its willingness to work with the other side. The relationship was well launched.

Perhaps nowhere is it more important to get off on the right foot than when you are on foreign soil or dealing with people from other cultures. In the global marketplace, greetings take on a significance not unlike the raising of a theater curtain. While much may occur in the acts that follow, many of the audience's ideas about the personalities and motives of the characters will be formed by their initial introduction.

If you are originally cast as a "good" player, you can build on that reputation. If you create a negative impression, you may have to spend the rest of the performance trying to overcome it. Because your stay is, by definition, limited, you will not have abundant opportunities for your hosts to get to know the "real" you. Moreover, the significance of your role is exaggerated because you are to your host "audience" the only "new" part of the drama that is unfolding. They are already familiar with their home setting and its customs, leaving them free to focus their attention on your presentation. If all the world's a stage, you want to be a performer with an appropriate entrance.

The old expression, "When in Rome, do as the Romans do," applies to global greetings and introductions. By showing, right from the start, that you are aware of your hosts' customs and willing to conform to them, you can establish yourself as willing to meet them, literally, on their own ground. A strong initial connection can ease subsequent interaction.

This applies equally to the way you greet international visitors in the United States. You want to come across as gracious and make them feel comfortable. This will enhance the business relationship.

In this chapter, you'll discover:

- how to make effective use of the four main types of greetings used around the world (the handshake, kisses and hugs, the bow, and the wai/namaste).

- a practical guide to international introductions and helpful suggestions on the use of names.

- how to exchange business cards with suitable style.

- smart strategies for international small talk.

THE EFFECTIVE INTERNATIONAL HANDSHAKE

In countries other than the United States, handshakes can have a different set of rituals and rules than those to which you are most accustomed. Your host will help establish the tone, but it's important that you first be aware that the standard American handshake is not the universal greeting.

The differences in handshakes worldwide include who extends whose hand first, how many hands you shake, and whether you shake hands with women. The firmness and duration of the handshake also change, depending on the location. The standard American shake—a firm, solid grip with two or three pumps—doesn't apply in Europe, for instance, where generally one small pump will do. The significance of handshakes also varies internationally.

When visiting other countries, you will usually want to use their appropriate greeting. When hosting foreign visitors, using a greeting with which the visitors are familiar can be a welcoming and courteous gesture.

How to Shake Hands Around the World

When greeting someone, it's important to be able to think on your feet about how you shake hands. If you let your host be your guide and then apply his or her handshaking technique to subsequent handshakes with others, you will probably act appropriately.

Do not make assumptions about people based on their handshakes, whether you are the visitor or the host. The variations indicate cultural differences rather than, as some Americans believe, a person's personality. For instance, a limp grip in Japan is the accepted behavior, not a sign of weakness. A Japanese visitor to the United States may not change his typical shake until he has become accustomed to the American method.

To be safe, always extend your right hand. Be cautious with the left hand. In parts of Africa, Asia, or the Middle East, there are taboos against using the left hand. It is considered "the dirty hand"—the one used for bathroom functions.

Also be careful about assigning too much significance to a handshake, particularly as a symbol of commitment at the end of business negotiations. In Italy, the handshake is an important gesture of trust, but, in general, doing business on a handshake is dying out in Europe. While it remains a highly valued indication of agreement and obligation, legal documents are becoming a more common and standard way of sealing an understanding.

It is always a good idea to check before you go with someone familiar with the customs of your host country, so you know just what others will assume that you mean to communicate when you shake hands.

When to Shake Hands Around the World

In the United States, we encourage people to shake hands at the beginning and end of each gathering, but it doesn't always happen. Outside of the United States, you should generally plan to shake hands with everyone in the group and to do it regularly upon arrival and departure. In addition, it's important internationally to observe differences in status—whether based on position, class, or age—and not to slight anyone by failing to shake his hand.

Handshakes Around the World

USA	Firm, solid grip—two to three pumps.
Germany	Firm grip, one pump.
France	Light grip and a quick shake.
Japan	Limp grip.
Australia	Firm grip.
Latin America	Light to moderate grasp, repeated frequently.
Middle East	Gentle and limp, light shaking throughout the greeting.
Asia	Delicate grip and brief shaking.
Sweden	Firm grip, eyes meet.
Belgium	Quick, light pressure.
Russia	Firm grip.

In Sweden, Russia, Germany, France, Belgium, and most of the rest of Europe including Eastern Europe, you must shake hands with everyone on arriving and leaving. Don't stop halfway. Start with the highest-ranking person or the oldest. The highest-ranking person usually extends his hand first. When you part, do not simply "wave" goodbye to people. Shake hands.

In Asia, be cautious. You do not want to force a handshake on anyone. In Japan, take your cue about whether to shake hands, bow, or do both, from your Japanese host. In South Korea, you will probably shake hands.

In Arab countries, men may find themselves shaking hands several times a day, whenever you go apart and then remeet. Shake hands with the most important person first. Shake hands with all and maintain eye contact throughout.

A gracious American host will help international visitors in the United States feel comfortable in handshaking situations. For instance, you might want to make sure you shake hands with *all* the members of an arriving foreign delegation, even at moments that are not typical "handshake moments" in the United States.

KEY DIFFERENCES FOR MEN AND WOMEN IN INTERNATIONAL HANDSHAKES. In the United States, there are no longer established differences between men and women in shaking hands. See Chapter Two, "Powerful First Impressions: How to Meet and Greet"). Outside of America, however, practices vary widely.

In Europe, including Romania, the Czech Republic, the Slovak Republic, and Hungary, a man should usually not extend a hand until the woman does so first. Women should make sure that they do extend the hand; they will lose credibility if they don't. In some countries in Europe, such as Holland, many of the old formal rules are loosening, especially among younger people of equal status. This means you will have to gauge the appropriate action by the specific situation.

In Asia, a man should usually wait for the woman to act before he extends his hand. If she doesn't extend her hand, don't extend yours. Women should be sensitive to this; it's not polite to force it. In China and Korea, however, a woman can extend her hand first. In Japan, you need to judge by the situation. You can accomplish a lot by bowing.

Arab men and women do not shake hands with each other. A woman should be cautious about extending her hand to an Arab, though many Arabs now are familiar with American customs and will shake hands with women. However, when shaking hands with a woman, some men will withdraw the hand into the clothing and then extend the covered hand. This is done to avoid skin-to-skin contact, and the woman should shake hands with the dangling sleeve.

Handshakes between men and women also are unusual in India. Hasidic Jewish men worldwide will not shake hands with women because a man is not allowed to touch any woman other than his wife.

American men and women doing business internationally should always check with their host as to local customs and abide by them. When hosting international visitors in the United States, be gracious and don't make anyone feel uneasy if that person will not shake hands.

KISSES AND HUGS THAT COMMUNICATE COMPETENCE

Kissing and hugging can be part of the official greeting in other countries, in contrast with the United States where such actions take place only in certain industries, between good friends, and rarely between two men.

The Meaning of this Embrace

There are two major psychological barriers that typically prevent Americans from accepting such a welcome graciously. One barrier comes in the form of confusion about its meaning, since, in the United States, such gestures imply closeness.

Keep in mind that especially in other countries, these actions do not have romantic connotations, but rather are part of a polite and friendly protocol. What a kiss or hug from your international counterpart generally means is that you are being officially welcomed—no less, and no more. To the greeter, a kiss-and-hug "hello" has no more significance than a handshake would to you.

However, Americans, particularly men, are often tempted to issue a sort of disclaimer, along the lines of "Gee, um, good to meet you too," to the greeting. Calling attention to differences, of course, is not courteous; therefore, good manners require that you quietly accept and return the greeting in the same courteous spirit in which it was offered.

The other barrier involving kiss-and-hug greetings is the element of surprise: If you extend your hand, only to be pulled in and kissed and hugged, you may be too stunned to have time to react appropriately. The way around this obstacle is to be mentally prepared for such a greeting, knowing before you go that it is part of the country's customs.

Visitors from countries with kiss-and-hug greetings may use them reflexively when meeting people in the United States. When a Brazilian in the United States met her new American neighbor for the first time, she kissed her new acquaintance good-bye after the visit ended. The American was surprised, but fortunately not rude. The relationship developed into a good friendship.

If a foreign visitor kisses or hugs you in the United States, it's appropriate to accept those gestures in the spirit in which they are offered.

Getting Accustomed to the Abrazo

In Latin America, you may encounter "the abrazo"—a full embrace with pats on the back. Men greet each other with this gesture in Mexico, and you may experience it after a couple of meetings with your international counterpart. There is usually less hugging and kissing in Colombia and Argentina.

In Greece and Italy, you may also experience this custom. In Spain, you may encounter the abrazo, although handshaking is most common in business, but by the second visit, your arm may be grabbed.

Becoming Comfortable with a Kiss

You may be kissed and hugged in Russia. In the United Arab Emirates, men will kiss other men three to four times on the cheeks. In Saudi Arabia, a male guest may be kissed on both cheeks after shaking hands.

In France, handshaking is common, although you might see people kissing alternate cheeks (actually, rubbing cheeks and kissing the air). Generally in Europe, kissing occurs only after the relationship has become somewhat more personal. As the foreigner, when you are unsure it is a safe bet not to initiate the practice but let the other person start.

The number of kisses may vary within a country. In Holland, people in the southern part often kiss three times, while in the northern section it is only two. In Northern France, it's two kisses and in Southern France, it's two to three kisses.

Your role as a gracious visitor to another country is to accept the greeting that is offered. In time, you may become more comfortable with the gesture and even return it.

Mastering Other "Physical" Greetings

You'll find out about global gesture gaffes in Chapter Seventeen, "Communicating Across Borders: Verbal and Nonverbal Communication." However, since some forms of physical contact often occur around greetings, we'll explore some of these now.

Arab businessmen sometimes hold hands as they walk. Men, don't be alarmed if your Arab counterpart takes your hand—it's friendship! In Russia, physical contact, including walking arm-in-arm, is also common.

Americans, both in the United States and in Latin America, often pat children on the head or touch them as part of the greeting. However, in some countries, including Japan and India, that gesture is too familiar. In parts of Southeast Asia, including Thailand and Malaysia, and in some Islamic countries, the head is sacred—the source of one's intellectual and spiritual powers—so it can be insulting to pat it. A pat on the back also is considered overly familiar.

Don't embrace, hug, kiss, or pat a Chinese person. Chinese do not like body contact with strangers, particularly with the opposite sex. Barbara Pachter still waits for a close female Chinese friend to initiate any hugs, even though she has known the woman for five years.

Also don't be surprised by what you see others do, and especially, don't misinterpret what it means. A Lebanese man who relocated to the United States always hugged and kissed both his mother and father, and couldn't understand why his American wife didn't kiss *her* father as much. She had to explain to him, "Just because I don't kiss my father as much doesn't mean I love him any less."

BENEFITS OF THE BOW

While most Americans associate "taking a bow" with receiving the applause one deserves, to bow as part of a greeting is an act of humbling oneself before another, of showing respect. The bow often is one part of the greeting, which also may include the exchange of business cards.

The bow is part of the ritual greeting in Japan. The Chinese may nod or use a slight bow. A slight bow also is used in South Korea, Singapore, Indonesia, and Malaysia. While handshakes are done in most of these locations, adopting the local custom of making a bow shows respect for the individual and the culture.

Bowing is just a gracious way to say "hello," to acknowledge the person. There is, in fact, an expression sometimes used by visitors in Japan, which states, "You know you have been in Japan a long time when you start bowing into the telephone!"

Men bow with their hands at their side, palms down on their thighs. Women bow with their hands folded in front.

There are three etiquette guidelines for this ritual:

1. *You must return a bow!* Failure to return a bow is rude. After all, the gesture implies not just greeting, but humility. Failure to humble yourself in turn could be interpreted to mean you consider yourself superior, or as a refusal to accept the other person's gracious gesture. Either way, you're insulting the person who bowed to you.

2. *The person lower in status bows first.*

3. *The person lower in status bows lower.* Some Americans, who typically hate to acknowledge any difference in status among people, may have difficulty initiating this gesture or in "lowering themselves" to others. Again, the cultural context needs to be taken into account.

When we say to a prestigious person, "I'm pleased to meet you, it's an honor," we are, in fact, communicating the same thing that a bow communicates. And much as we Americans don't like to publicly acknowledge differences in class or position, we privately admit they exist each time we call the boss "Mr. Boss." To make these differences explicit may feel unnatural, but the truth is, we do so at home all the time in our own subtle way. The key is to "Just Do It."

As part of a training program for a Japanese family who had just relocated to the United States, Barbara Pachter bowed and said "good morning" in Japanese when they entered. She found that it made a big difference in her acceptance and in the way they perceived her—as a gracious and knowledgeable person. In this instance, she did not shake hands.

Proficiency in the Wai and the Namaste

The wai, pronounced "why," combines a bow with a sort of salute.

In Thailand, the wai is done with the palms together, fingers up (not folded or clasped) and a slight bow. The hands are usually at chest level. When performing this gesture, you say, "wai." The younger person does the wai first. In addition to signifying "hello," it can be used to say, "goodbye," "thank you," and "I'm sorry." The higher the hands, the more respect you show, although eye level is the highest anyone goes.

In India, a similar greeting is called the "namaste." It's done with palms together and with fingers up and together, usually at the chin level. It's combined with a nod. You say "namaste," (pronounced "nah-mast-tay") which means, "I bow to you." It's a sign of appreciation. The host usually does it first, and it's polite to return it. Do this for "good morning," "good afternoon," or "good evening."

An Air India newspaper advertisement overseas said, "When two hands come together in the form of our traditional greeting, you'll know you're being welcomed by a friend."

MORE WAYS TO SAY HELLO

There are, of course, many other greetings that you may encounter in your travels. In Fiji, people can greet each other with a smile and an upward flick of the eyebrows. Filipinos may greet each other by making eye contact and then raising and lowering their eyebrows if they know the person well.

MAKING IMPRESSIVE INTERNATIONAL INTRODUCTIONS

People in other countries tend to be more formal than Americans when it comes to making introductions. While much of what we said in Chapter Two, "Powerful first Impressions: How to Meet and Greet," about American introductions applies in a general sense on a global scale, we would like to point out some adaptations of those guidelines.

1. *Mention the name of the person of authority or importance first.* When you don't know who that person is, mention older people and women first. You can say, "Mr. Host, I'd like you to meet my colleague. He's just arrived from the United States."

In most situations you will encounter in other countries, the person you usually want to flatter is the host. However, you will usually be the one who is being introduced and your role instead is to respond. In fact, it is usually best to wait to be introduced. Don't be an aggressive American and jump right in.

If you are making introductions, your host's name generally is said first.

In many countries, you use the more formal way that used to be applied in the United States before the work environment stressed gender-equal relationships:

- Older people should be mentioned and greeted first.

- Women should be mentioned and greeted before men.

2. *Repeat the person's name.* Although in the United States one mention is sufficient, you usually repeat the name or names in other countries. This helps everyone catch both the name and the pronunciation.

3. *Use the appropriate response for that country, if you can.* If you are the person being introduced in the United States, you say, "I am pleased to meet you." In Mexico, it's "I am enchanted to meet you." If you can learn the appropriate response in the language of your host country, you'll win points. We have included a guide to international greetings in the next chapter on verbal and nonverbal communication.

You may also encounter another style of introductions. This more formal approach, which is sometimes used in the United States, is the norm in Britain, the Netherlands, and Germany. We call it the "To" approach, because the focus is on who is introduced *to* others.

Using this method, you mention the name of the person of lower rank or the younger person first, and introduce that person TO others.

You always introduce the junior person *TO* the more senior person. "Mr. Junior Person, I would like to introduce you to Ms. Senior Person."

A gentleman is always introduced *TO* the lady, regardless of rank. "Mr. Lichtenberg, I would like to introduce you to Mrs. Habkirk."

However, in less formal situations in Europe, you can say, as in the United States, "Mr. Greater Importance, this is Mr. Lesser Importance," and then "Mr. Lesser Importance, this is Mr. Greater Importance."

ACQUIRING A KNACK
FOR THE NUANCES OF NAMES

Americans are fond of nicknames and the use of first names, and many people almost automatically shorten "David" to "Dave" or "Susan" to "Sue." This informality can sometimes get you into trouble even in the United States, but in the international arena, names are highly personal commodities that require treatment with respect.

In this arena, there are four key considerations:

1. *Always be formal until told otherwise.* Don't call the person by his/her first name, unless asked to do so. Use the person's honorary title and last name. In the United States and English-speaking countries, use Mr., Mrs., Miss, or Ms. In French-speaking countries, it's "Monsieur" (Mr.), "Madame" (Mrs.), or "Mademoiselle" (Miss.) In Spanish-speaking countries, it's "Señor" (Mr.), "Señora" (Mrs.), and

Señorita (Miss). In Germany, use "Herr" (Mr.), "Frau" (Mrs.), and Fraulein (Miss). In Lithuania, it's "Ponas" (Mr.), "Ponia" (Mrs.) or "Panele" (Miss).

The British generally don't use first names until both parties know each other well. The French won't use first names unless invited to do so. It takes a long time before it's acceptable to use first names in the Netherlands and Germany. The Dutch are getting less formal, but for a foreigner it is very difficult to figure out what is acceptable when. The safest bet, then, is to not use first names until invited to do so.

In Bulgaria and Hungary, first names are reserved for close friends and family members.

In China, first names are rarely used except among close friends or members of the family circle. Titles are used.

Africans use "Sir" or "Madam" in business dealings.

There are, of course, exceptions. In Iceland, they use first names because they have no last name that is passed from generation to generation. Instead, your "last" name is the possessive form of your father's first name, combined with "dottir" (daughter) or "son." In Thailand, they use Mr., Mrs., and Miss along with the first name, or the title with the first name, such as "Doctor Mike." They started using surnames only about sixty years ago.

2. *Use the correct name sequence.* There are many variations around the globe in how a name is structured.

In Latin America, the names are a combination of the mother's and the father's. In Spanish-speaking countries, the father's name comes first; for example, in Mr. Dejo Suarez's name, Dejo is the name of his father and Suarez that of his mother. In conversation, he will often go by "Mr. Dejo," but in writing, use "Mr. Dejo Suarez." On the other hand, in Brazil, where Portuguese is spoken, it's the reverse: the mother's name is first.

The family name (what Americans call the "last name") appears first in such countries as China or South Korea. Tan Hong Bo would be Ms. Tan. You need to be careful—many Chinese people in the United States have switched the order of their names to fit the American sequence.

Women in the United States are not the only ones to keep their maiden names professionally. In Belgium, women generally keep their name. Women in South Korea and China also do not take their husband's family name.

3. *Respect the importance of titles.* In Europe, professional titles, such as "engineer," are more prestigious than work titles, such as "manager," because titles that are earned through academic degrees have more honor than those that are given to you by the company because of your position.

Listen closely when people are introduced. A business card can also give you a clue as to what to call someone.

In Germany, the equivalent of "Mr." or "Mrs." comes before the title, and both are used: "Herr Doktor Jon Schmidt" (a male physician) and his wife, "Frau Doktor Ingrid Schmidt" (a female physician). An engineer would be "Herr Ingenieur."

In Italy, if you earn a bachelor's degree, you are entitled to use "Dr" or "Dottore," or, if you are a woman, "Dottoressa," in front of your name.

People in the Philippines also address business superiors by their title (engineer, attorney) plus the last name. One advertisement in an Arab newspaper by a German dentist listed the name as "Professor Dr. Mrs. Brandt."

If you are unsure what to call someone, ask them. Say, "What would you like me to call you?"

In Japan, you can add "san" to a name as a sign of respect, such as Ishikawa-san. That "san" is the closest equivalent to Mr. or Mrs., but it is an honorific. Never add it after your own name. In South Korea, the honorific term is "songsaengnim," pronounced "song-sang-nim," which means "respected person."

Also remember that corporate titles may mean different things in different countries. The position of managing director in Britain is equivalent to the president of the company in the United States.

4. *Check your pronunciation.* It may seem embarrassing initially to ask someone how his or her name is pronounced, but in most cases, it will be considered a compliment. After all, you know how you wince internally every time someone mispronounces your own name. It can discredit the speaker to make a mispronunciation.

When speaking to foreign visitors in the United States, the same general guidelines apply. Especially remember to be more formal, such as using "Mr." and "Mrs." with the last name.

EXCHANGING BUSINESS CARDS WITH SAVOIR-FAIRE

Presenting business cards can be an important part of international protocol, especially in Japan. Unlike the optional and informal exchange that occurs almost randomly in the United States, the presentation and acceptance of business cards is part of Japan's formal greeting ritual. When doing business internationally, you should be prepared to exchange your card in the locally appropriate manner. In some countries, it's a big deal, while in others, it's not.

The four key points to remember when exchanging business cards internationally are:

1. *Use bilingual cards.* Have your cards printed in both languages—English on one side, the host country's language on the other. You often can make arrangements for the double-side printing of your card at a hotel in Asia.

The need for bilingual cards applies to such locations as the Middle East, Asia, and Eastern Europe. You may even use a bilingual card in places like Germany, where many people speak at least some English, because the card will then be appropriate for doing business in smaller cities where English might be less common.

On the card, list your position and title, such as Dr. John Bing, President of ITAP International. Your title allows the person to know your rank and how to treat you, which can be significant particularly in Asia. Don't exaggerate your title; they will find out, and this destroys trust.

In Europe, it's impressive to put your advanced degrees on your card; it establishes credibility. In dealing with Germans, the Dutch, and the Swiss, you also can put the company's founding date on the card, provided it is an old one.

Be cautious about using your company slogan ("The experts in business etiquette") on your card. It may be seen as American aggressiveness.

Make sure you print the cards with the correct language for the region you will be visiting—either Flemish or French for Belgium, Portuguese for Brazil.

2. *Have cards readily available* in your pocket or briefcase. As we said regarding American business cards, the cards should be in good shape and in a good case. You also should have plenty available—overseas, you often give them to everyone you meet, perhaps distributing 50 to 100 cards a week.

3. *Know when to hand out cards.* In the United States, the exchange of business cards is an informal activity and sometimes it's not done. That's also true in Australia.

However, other places have a more formal ritual:

In Japan, the exchange of business cards, known as the *meishi,* takes place after the person has introduced himself and bowed. The visiting party should be the first to give his cards.

If you are being introduced in Japan, hand out your business card only after your boss or superior has introduced you.

In China, business cards may be exchanged between head people.

In Arab countries, present your card Arabic side up. It is usually presented at the end of the meeting, but often may be exchanged while shaking hands.

The card is exchanged in Portugal upon meeting people in meetings. In Denmark, it's usually done at the beginning of the meeting. However, in Italy and Holland, cards are usually not presented until after the first meeting is completed.

As always, it pays to research the card exchange etiquette in the country you will be visiting.

4. *Know how to hand out cards.* Particularly overseas, where American informality can lead to serious gaffes, you need to exchange cards with respect.

Present your card with the native language side up.

Use the right hand in the Middle East, Southeast Asia, and Africa.

Use both hands in Japan, China, Singapore, and Hong Kong. This shows respect.

When you receive a card, say "Thank You" or nod, and study it. Don't play with business cards. Put them away with respect, perhaps in your own business card case or attached to a document, but not shoved haphazardly into your pocket.

You can do as the Japanese do and put the cards out on the table opposite the person and pick them up when the meeting is over. Years ago, before Barbara learned this trick, she sat next to a visitor from Japan at a Chamber of Commerce dinner. After the greeting and before dinner, they exchanged cards. Barbara put hers in her purse. The Japanese man put his next to his dinner plate. He remembered Barbara's name all evening, but Barbara didn't remember his!

THE KEYS TO CULTURALLY CORRECT CONVERSATION

Overseas, small talk isn't something that precedes the negotiation; it's *part* of the negotiating process. What you say during this time will be used to establish a sense of who you are and how others will deal with you. It will be a sort of personality test, and since you want to pass with flying colors, you need to be aware of the cultural differences in small talk around the world. You'll also want to provide a level of small talk that makes international visitors in the United States comfortable.

Control your volume—Americans typically speak too loudly when interacting in other cultures. Also monitor your gestures.

Listen attentively—this can give you clues about the personalities you will be dealing with. While it may seem natural for you, as the visitor, to be the focus of attention, it's smart and gracious to get the host talking about his own country. Similarly, you should listen attentively to your international guests.

Small talk often occurs over coffee, so it is usually best to accept it when it is offered.

There are several things to remember about casual conversations:

1. *Be prepared to discuss the country you are visiting or the homeland of your visitor.* Read about the country in advance. When you are there, pick up any newspaper and learn what is happening. Showing an interest in their country and their culture will help to build the relationship. To know what's going on in the world, read the International Herald Tribune, the Financial Times, or a major metropolitan newspaper with significant international coverage.

As a visitor, plan in advance what you will say to the inevitable question, "So, what do you think of our country?" Find something positive to remark upon that does not directly compare the country to the United States, such as "I'm fascinated by your architecture," or "The scenery is breathtaking."

2. *Understand that the amount of small talk varies among countries.* In the United States, we pride ourselves on "cutting the small talk," and getting down to business. Overseas, however, more small talk will occur than most Americans are accustomed to. Relax, participate, and do not appear impatient.

In Mexico, people tend to place a special value on small talk and so will spend much time in personal conversation before getting into business matters.

In the Middle East, plan to use your first meeting with your counterparts just for social acquaintance and trust-building, not to conduct business. This is changing and business can be discussed in some circumstances at the first meeting, but you should be prepared to follow your host's lead either way.

Understand also that the need for small talk extends into goodbyes. It may be considered abrupt to just get up and leave at the conclusion of business. Your international counterparts may take a lot of time to end the conversation. One Mexican woman we know says it takes her husband "twenty minutes at the door just to say goodbye."

3. *Avoid discussing religion and politics and asking highly personal questions.* We also repeat our American small talk admonitions against foul language, cursing, and humor.

The Problems with Discussions of Politics and Religion

Unless you are a missionary, it's usually a bad idea to discuss religion while on an international assignment. If you do exhibit a natural curiosity about someone's beliefs, don't pass judgment on them.

Avoiding a discussion of politics may be more difficult to accomplish but is just as worthwhile. One good reason to steer clear of this topic is that you will unavoidably be seen as a "typical" American, and your views, however unorthodox in reality, may be seen as representative of the country at large. There's also built-in potential for conflict, because you generally can expect your hosts to back their country's position over that of the United States. However, just as we cautioned about American small talk, you never know what side of an issue someone is likely to take.

When discussing the politics of other countries, it's quite difficult to speak intelligently and diplomatically about long-simmering conflicts with which you have little personal familiarity. Moreover, your hosts may be just as uncomfortable discussing the Arab-Israeli conflict, for instance, as you would be trying to explain the status of race relations or gay rights in the United States. You may inadvertently upset someone with a remark meant to be innocent. Noble as your intentions may be to have an enlightened dialogue, it's just bad manners to bring up a controversial topic, especially during a time in which you are attempting to lay the groundwork for a long-term connection.

We should note that some Europeans love to talk politics and religion, and you may have to feel your way about what is appropriate in any given setting. Take your cue from the host. In Holland and Italy, for example, it's OK to discuss politics, but not American politics. The French generally enjoy a spirited debate.

Also be careful about making comparisons between countries, and not just with the United States. A case in point: it's considered rude to compare the Dutch to the Germans. It's also impolite to consider all Europeans the same!

If American politics are mentioned, perhaps as a test of your own diplomacy, you can always make a nodding reference to the subject and then quickly move on. When we conducted a training program in the Middle East, people paused with anticipation to see how we would react when the U.S. president's name was brought up. We handled it by saying, "We're not here to discuss politics—that's another class." Everyone laughed, and discussion moved on.

The "How Are You?" Dilemma

The third area to avoid—highly personal questions—is subject to many different definitions around the world.

Americans often ask questions as part of small talk without really being interested in the answers: "How are you today?" or "How's business?" or "How's your family?" The only type of answers you would expect in the U.S. are "OK," "Fine, thanks," or "Could be better." In fact, a question such as "How are you?" doesn't even have to be answered. You can very well respond with another "How are *you*?"

Europeans are not used to this! When you ask a question like that, they will interpret it as a serious question and start giving you a detailed answer—or they may think that it is none of your business. In Russia, they will answer you in great detail, and asking the question without waiting for a response is rude.

This explains why asking what, to Americans, are innocent questions—such as "How's business?"—can be shockingly indiscreet in Europe. Asking a British person, who is usually very private, "What do you do?" can be too forward and impolite. Asking a French person, "What do you do for a living?" also is too personal a question. In Arab countries, you don't inquire about a man's family even if he asks about yours. Instead, you can talk about sports, local industry, travel, or sites.

In reverse, you may find that you receive what you consider to be highly personal questions in Japan, China, India, Pakistan, Thailand, and the Philippines. They may want to know how much money you make. In Luxembourg, they may inquire, in all seriousness, about your health, and in Greece, you may be asked about your income level and about what your family members do for a living.

The key is to not become insulted or indignant, since these questions are not meant to be prying. You do not need to "expose" yourself or respond in a way that would make you uncomfortable. Instead, you can be general and say, "People in the United States in my position would make in the range of ...." Or, "I make enough to live on."

Try to keep these differences in mind during your discussions with international visitors to the United States. While on our home ground, it may seem natural to ask a visitor a question about a topic that others are discussing—such as family—but if it will make your guest uncomfortable, change the topic.

BECOMING WORLDLY WISE

International business travelers sometimes suffer from sensory overload: there seems to be so much going on—new sights, sounds, food, and customs—that it's difficult to take it all in, much less focus on the business at hand. That's why knowing before you go—investigating appropriate behavior in the particular country you are visiting—can make a significant difference in both your comfort level and your ability to function. If you greet someone appropriately so that you get off to a good start, it can increase both your confidence and your competence.

COMMUNICATING ACROSS BORDERS
Verbal and Nonverbal Communication

Words are the root of all evil.

—JAPANESE PROVERB

When we say someone "speaks our language," we usually mean far more than that the words are comprehensible. We mean that we are able to communicate easily with that person, that we can share our thoughts without interference from obstacles to understanding. In some way, we have made a mental connection with that person. We may even be able to talk with each other through a shorthand of key phrases or selected gestures.

When communicating across borders, the language barriers are quite real. So, too, may be the barriers created by body language—the cues and signals that we send through the *way* we talk with people. Our method of expression may not translate well in another culture. We can even "say" something wrong without ever opening our mouths! Yet it is possible to learn to "speak someone's language" without ever becoming fully fluent in a foreign tongue.

In this chapter, we'll focus on helping you to be understood—both verbally and nonverbally—when communicating across borders. You'll discover:

- how to avoid misunderstandings.
- tips on communicating effectively when English is the first language and when it is the second language.
- four keys for effectively using interpreters.
- the importance of keeping your distance in space, touch, and posture.

298

- the varied international interpretations of facial expressions, eye contact, and gestures.

We'll conclude with a section on a world-conscious wardrobe.

IMPRESSIVE VERBAL COMMUNICATION

The written word offers many clues to the values and mindset of a culture. The way things are expressed indicates the culture's attitude about something's significance as well as the country's own particular perspective. Consider the subtle differences, for example, between the Japanese proverb, "The nail that sticks up gets hammered down" and the American version, "The squeaky wheel gets the grease." The Japanese emphasize the group, while for Americans, it's individualism that is important. Or contrast the attitudes about time demonstrated in the British expression, "Better late than never," and the German one, "A little too late is much too late."

The etiquette implication for those doing business internationally, then, is to respect the language of your host's country or the language of your international visitor. Knowing even a little bit about the language can help provide you with better understanding of your international counterpart. In some places, such as France, where the purity of the language sometimes is a political issue, you may be expected to demonstrate respect by speaking the language well or by conducting your business in it with the assistance of a translator.

THE KEYS TO AVOIDING MISUNDERSTANDING AND CONFUSION

When doing business internationally, there are plenty of natural opportunities for confusion and misunderstanding. What you don't want to do is add more. Instead, your goal should be to keep your communications as clear and as direct as possible.

Here are five guidelines that will help you limit misunderstandings:

1. *Do not use jargon, buzz words, or regional expressions.* Many expressions and metaphors do not translate well across languages. One Swedish man, attempting to use American slang in one of our classes, said he needed a break to "reload my batteries so to say." What he meant to say was "re*charge* my batteries, so to *speak*."

When people attempt literal translations of local expressions, the result can be humorous, confusing, even unintentionally insulting. It's best to avoid these possibilities.

When doing business internationally, try not to use such American expressions as:

- "I'm all ears"
- "Let's put on a dog-and-pony show"
- "raining cats and dogs"
- "Don't make waves"
- "Y'all come back for another visit"
- "run that by me"
- "ball park figure"
- "run a tight ship"
- "down time"
- "beef it up"
- "off line."

Barbara Pachter once used "carved in stone" during a class overseas, and was greeted with puzzled expressions.

2. *Avoid humor—but have a sense of humor.* We have learned to appreciate the saying, "If there is one thing that isn't funny in a foreign country, it's humor."

It takes time to understand what people think is funny. Children, for instance, have to be taught how to tell a joke—*after* they've had the humor explained to them! When this learning process attempts to cross international boundaries, the explanations can become highly complex. We asked a Chinese research scientist who worked in the United States if she understood American humor. "I'm just beginning to," she answered, adding, "I've only lived here eight years."

Cultures vary greatly in the extent to which they take themselves seriously, and so in the extent to which they are able to laugh at themselves. There also are vast differences in the appreciation of different varieties of humor, such as slapstick or witticisms.

It will not enhance trust if your jokes are misunderstood or, far worse, considered insulting. Something that you consider to be fair game for humor may actually be a cultural icon. You should not, for instance, joke about the Queen in England or the late Chairman Mao in China.

Even joking about the United States can be a bad idea. Without knowing much about our culture, your international counterpart may not understand that you are (mostly) kidding when you joke about "our crooked politicians."

Related to this is the need to avoid sarcasm when doing business internationally. Asking "Are you alive?" or "Is anyone there?" may perplex your listeners.

3. *Use standard grammar and terminology.* American English breaks many grammar rules. We split infinitives—"to better communicate" instead of "to communicate better." Our verbs are complex enough—"he goes," "they went"—without such technically wrong adaptations as "they're gonna" instead of "they will." When speaking or writing to those who speak English as a second language, we often confuse words, which only confuses the other party. We sometimes rely on negative questions, such as: "Don't you agree?"

When doing business overseas, try to communicate as if your fifth grade grammar teacher were still grading you.

4. *Use current, correct, and clear terms.* You also need to avoid using out-of-date terms, such as "Soviets," "comrades" or Leningrad—which has been renamed St. Petersburg. The preferred terms now are "Asia" and "Asian," not "Orient" and "Oriental." Keeping up with these changes can be a challenge in a rapidly moving world, but you could offend someone if you fail to do so.

When doing business abroad, always specify which country you are referring to. If, when you say "president" you mean the president of the United States, make that clear.

Is your phraseology precise? In Scotland, the only scotch is what you drink. The people are "Scots." Coffee in Greece is Greek coffee, not Turkish coffee.

Does your language take into account political sensitivities? Canadians do not like to be called Americans. Britons do not like to be referred to as Europeans. Taiwan is "The Republic (or Province) of China," not "The People's Republic of China," which is Mainland China. (However, don't call it "Mainland China," or "Red China" or "Communist China.")

People also are sensitive to the possible connotations of the words you choose. It's not gracious to refer to guests from abroad as "foreign." Use "overseas guests." In Africa, do not use "hut"; it's a home.

5. *Understand the role of silence.* Americans generally are uncomfortable with silence, but in other countries, it can be part of the "language." It also can be a powerful negotiating tool. When doing business internationally, you should be prepared to add silence to your speaking style.

Silence often is employed deliberately in Japan to indicate thoughtfulness and quiet appreciation. A "wise" person in Japan is supposed to speak slowly, quietly, and with many pauses.

There also may be long periods of silence in the Arab world. They are just "digesting" what has been said. To "fill up" that silence would be rude.

In fact, people from other countries sometimes say Americans will just keep on talking, and will talk themselves out of the best price!

WHAT TO DO WHEN ENGLISH IS THE FIRST LANGUAGE

England and America are divided by a common language.

—GEORGE BERNARD SHAW

Just because the residents of a country speak English doesn't mean you won't have any trouble communicating. British, Australian, and Canadian English (to name a few) all differ from American English, in both pronunciation and word usage.

Someone doing business internationally needs to take these variations into account—or risk being misunderstood.

In Canada, for example, there is jargon that may be unfamiliar to many Americans. The expression "Hollywood stop" refers to rolling through a stop sign and a "winter mole" is a person who lives in a high-rise that is connected to other buildings by underground tunnels.

The two key points that you need to be aware of for international business is that even in countries where English is the first language, some words have different meanings and that some words have different spellings. Good manners require that you modify your Americanisms to suit the situation, whether you are the visitor or the host.

Different Meanings

In the United States, "table the motion" means to put aside. In London, "table the motion" means the opposite—to "put on the table" for discussion.

In the United States, "My presentation bombed" means it was a failure. In London, "bomb" means a great success.

A British student once mentioned that a fellow student was "pissed" when the group of students went out after one of our classes. We were concerned: what was the matter with the class? How had we made him angry ("pissed")? As it turns out, what he meant, however, was that the guy was a little drunk.

We've compiled a list of common American vs. British expressions, to show you some additional examples:

AMERICAN ENGLISH	BRITISH ENGLISH
bathroom (toilet)	water closet (W.C.) or loo
policeman	bobby
two weeks	fortnight
hood of a car	bonnet
subway	underground
undershirt	vest or singlet
wake you up	knock you up
elevator	lift
cookie	biscuit

Different Spellings

When corresponding with English-speaking countries outside of the United States, you might want to reprogram your American-based computer spellcheckers to reflect some of these common variations:

AMERICAN ENGLISH	BRITISH ENGLISH
bank check	bank cheque
catalog	catalogue
program	programme
color	colour
jewelry	jewellery

WHAT TO DO WHEN ENGLISH IS THE SECOND LANGUAGE

Americans working in countries where English is the second language are often astounded at the seeming ease with which other people speak English and with the excellence of their speaking skills. Actually, what's more astounding in this increasingly interdependent world is that more Americans don't speak more languages. Unlike American schools, educational institutions in other countries encourage fluency in other languages. We have a French friend, Yves, who considers himself a late bloomer because he didn't learn his fifth language until he was 22!

However, just because someone is skilled in speaking English as a second language doesn't let visiting Americans or American hosts completely off the hook when it comes to making themselves understood. In fact, there still will be adjustments. Four key ones are:

1. *Speak slower, not louder.* Americans as a rule speak quite quickly. When a language is someone's second language, it may take time for that person to mentally translate what is being said—a synapse gap as the brain catches up with the ears. The more rapidly you speak, the more difficult it can be for your international counterpart to keep up with you.

Remember that you are speaking your language, not theirs. Speak clearly and build in frequent pauses.

This also is true when speaking American English in England. Marjorie Brody was told by her British contact before she went to England that she needed to slow down her speech. She did!

Face the person to whom you are speaking, so he or she can see your lips. Avoid loud background noise, as in a bar.

Also be aware that the person who is speaking English may not be the person who will make the decisions. Especially in Japan, it's often the young and inexperienced who speak the language.

Speaking more loudly will not help you be understood. Actually, just the opposite may occur. It is more difficult to understand someone speaking in a foreign tongue when that person seems to be shouting. It's a human reflex to want to back away or "tone down" the loud volume.

In fact, Americans who are just speaking in their normal tone of voice may already sound excessively loud to people from some other countries. In Asia, where people tend to be soft-spoken, loudness is considered a sign of lack of education or refinement.

Of course, acceptable voice volume is culturally relative, since people in Latin America, Greece, and Italy tend to speak more loudly than Americans do. Remember that when the normal volume of a culture is loud, it should not be interpreted as a sign of anger.

2. *Learn a few key phrases in the language of the country you will be visiting.* Speaking even a few words of a language can be a sign of mutual respect. Pope John Paul II delivers part of his sermon in the language of the country he is visiting, knowing this brings him closer to the worshippers.

We suggest that you learn the basic greetings including "hello," courtesy comments such as "please," "thank you," and "you're welcome," as well as the numbers. The doorman or concierge at the hotel often can be helpful in refining your pronunciation.

Useful Words and Phrases Around the World

JAPANESE	GOOD MORNING	GOOD AFTERNOON
	Ohayo gozaimasu *(Oh-high-oh goh-sigh-mahss)*	Kon-nichiwa *(Kohn-nee-chee-wah)*
	PLEASE	THANK YOU
	Dozo *(Do-zo)*	Arigato gozaimasu *(Ah-reeng-ah-toh-goh-sigh-mahss)*
FRENCH	GOOD DAY	GOOD EVENING
	Bonjour *(Bawn-JOOR)*	Bonsoir *(Bawn-SWAR)*
	PLEASE	THANK YOU
	S'il vous plait *(SEEL voo PLAY)*	Merci *(mayr-SEE)*
SPANISH	GOOD MORNING	GOOD EVENING
	Buenos dias *(BWAY-nus DEE-us)*	Buenos noches *(BWAY-us NOCH-ez)*
	PLEASE	THANK YOU
	Por favor *(Por fa-VOR)*	Muchas gracias *(MOO-chas GRA-see-us)*

(Continued on next page)

GERMAN	GOOD MORNING Guten Morgen *(GOO-ten MOR-gen)*	GOOD EVENING Guten Abend *(GOO-ten AH-bend)*
	PLEASE Bitte *(BIT-uh)*	THANK YOU Vielen Dank *(FEEL-en dahnk)*
ARABIC	GOOD MORNING Sabah el-khair *(SA-bah-al-CARE)*	GOOD AFTERNOON Masa-el khair *(MAH-SAH-AL-CARE)*
	PLEASE Min fadhlak *(min FAHD-lock*	THANK YOU Shukran *SHOCK-rahn)*
CANTONESE	GOOD MORNING Jou Sahn *(Joe-sun)*	GOOD EVENING Jou Tau *(Joe-'tow' as in 'cow')*
	PLEASE Ching Neih *(Ching-nay)*	THANK YOU Do Jeh *(Doh-jeh)*
ITALIAN	GOOD MORNING Buon giorno *(Bwahn Jawr No)*	GOOD EVENING Buona sera *(Bwahn-ah Say-rah)*
	PLEASE Per favore *(Purr Fah-voh-Ray)*	THANK YOU Grazie *(Grah-zee)*
RUSSIAN	GOOD MORNING Dobroyeh oot-ro *(Doh-bruh-yuh oo-truh)*	GOOD EVENING Dobriy vy eh chyeer *(Doh-bri-ee vy eh-chihr)*
	PLEASE Pozhaloosta *(Pah-zhah-li-stuh)*	THANK YOU Spaseeba *(Spah-sy-ee-buh)*

Knowing the language also can be appropriate because even if your host speaks English, the spouse may not. It could be helpful to communicate with the spouse, when appropriate, because he or she may have a lot of influence.

Regional identities can be as important as territorial boundaries, influencing the language that is spoken. In Flanders, which is in northern Belgium, residents speak Flemish (a dialect of Dutch), while Walloon, which is southern Belgium, is French-speaking. Make sure that the few phrases you know are in the appropriate language.

Some languages are especially difficult for Americans to pronounce. There's an old joke that Dutch is a throat disease, not a language. In Chinese, a tonal language, one word can have many meanings, depending on the pronunciation.

If you are speaking a second language and do not know how to say something, ask for help.

3. *Understand the concept of saving face.* Saving face involves much more than preserving someone's pride. It includes preventing embarrassment—sometimes not only that of the person directly involved, but of another party as well.

We use this story to illustrate the concept:

A Japanese man visited his neighbors. The door was open. He overheard a lot of screaming and the throwing of pots and pans. Aware that they were in the midst of a fight, he decided to leave, but they saw him first. "Sorry," he said, "to disturb you during your housecleaning."

When doing business internationally, you do not want anything you do or say to cause someone to be embarrassed. This is just bad manners. If you say to someone in Japan, for instance, "Your English isn't clear," that can cause the person to lose face. Ask him instead to repeat what he has said.

The concept of saving face may affect how people respond to you, particularly whether they say a direct "no."

In Japan, because saying "no" may cause someone to lose face, they might instead use "Hai" which means "Yes, I understand"; not necessarily a sign of agreement. The Japanese society puts a high value on surface harmony, so your counterpart might only be frank when socializing. Only "drunkenness" provides someone with an excuse for being direct.

Other ways that the Japanese might say "no" include:

- "I'll check on it and do whatever I can."
- "I'll think about it."
- "It is difficult."
- "I'm not sure."

The Filipinos rarely say "no" as we do. They resist confrontation and may instead say "yes" verbally while putting down their heads to indicate "no."

In Arab countries, it's possible to say "no" by saying "maybe" or "perhaps." Our Middle East agent uses "inshaalah," which means "If God is willing," many times during the conversation when we are negotiating a deal.

4. *Do not assume that English, or any other language, is not understood.* Speaking another language specifically to exclude people is bad manners, and sometimes it can backfire badly.

A CPA in the United States once was in an elevator at his company when two Polish men got on. Assuming him to be a typical American, the two men discussed, in their native tongue, how they had just "pulled the big one" over on the accounting firm. The CPA, as it turns out, was born in Poland and speaks Polish, although he has lived in the United States for thirty years. He didn't say anything or seem to react at all, even though he understood perfectly. But the minute the two left, management was informed and changes took place.

We know an older woman who confided to us that sometimes, she deliberately "couldn't hear" what people were saying to her—both when it was something she didn't want to hear, such as a request to move from a chair, or something she did want to hear, such as a confidential discussion. The strategy often worked well.

In either case, the principle is the same: if you say something in someone's presence, it just might be understood, even if you don't think so at the time. Conduct your conversations accordingly.

EFFECTIVE TRANSLATIONS THROUGH INTERNATIONAL INTERPRETERS

There is an old joke:

> What do you call a person who speaks three languages? Trilingual. What do you call a person who speaks two languages? Bilingual. What do you call a person who speaks one language? An American.

It may of course be necessary when doing business overseas or with international visitors to use an interpreter to enhance your ability to understand and be understood.

There are two types of interpreters:

- A *simultaneous interpreter,* who speaks at the same time as the speaker. These tend to be more expensive, and are best used for speeches and training sessions.

- A *consecutive interpreter,* who speaks after the speaker. This is the type of communication you will experience most often, and it works well for small groups or one-on-one discussions.

Remember that negotiations involving any interpreter take longer than those in which there is no language difference.

Understand the role that your interpreter should play within the culture you are visiting or hosting. In Japan, for instance, you may want to bring your own interpreter but have him play a subordinate role so as not to offend the Japanese.

Speak to the host or audience, not to the interpreter. Seat the interpreter between and slightly behind the principals.

When using an interpreter, you will have to adapt your speech so that you can communicate courteously through this intermediary. We've listed four keys to using interpreters successfully:

1. *Use an experienced interpreter.* A professional interpreter is not a colleague who happens to speak the language. Just because a person is bilingual does not mean he can interpret.

Meet with the interpreter ahead of time. Give him the information in English and ask him to explain it back. Does he grasp the concept? Does he translate the essence of the information? The person must have good pronunciation in both languages and also understand the correct use of inflection.

Get to know the person and let him know your voice and mannerisms. When preparing for simultaneous translation of our international course, Spanish interpreters asked for both an audiotape and a videotape of Barbara Pachter to become familiar with her style.

2. *Use an interpreter who is familiar with your profession.* A Hong Kong dentist once advertised "Teeth extracted by the latest Methodists."

Brief your interpreter on any special terminology or concerns you might have about communicating. Provide the relevant details of a meeting. Give him any written copy of what you are saying.

Remember that there may not be an equivalent word for something in another language, and the interpreter may have to use the English expression. When our international training manual was translated into Spanish, the word "chopstick" remained in English.

It's generally a good idea to use your own interpreter: be cautious with those provided by the other side. It may even be best to use more than one interpreter. Some experts suggest replacing interpreters every half hour.

3. *Speak clearly and use short sentences.* Speak slowly, but not so slowly that it's insulting.

Do not go more than two minutes—about three or four sentences—without pausing for translation.

Keep your sentences simple, without extra clauses and qualifiers. Avoid jargon and buzz words. Avoid humor.

To avoid possible confusion, be specific: "Wednesday" vs. "as soon as possible."

There have been some famous—make that infamous—translation errors that we're including here to remind you of the difficulty of accurate translations:

"Come alive with Pepsi" became "Pepsi brings your ancestors back from the grave" in Chinese.

"Federal Express is the leader in the air express industry" became "Federal Express is the goose of the air express industry" in German.

"Body by Fisher" became "Corpse by Fisher" in Flemish.

4. *Debrief the interpreter after the meeting.* When the meeting is over, go over what was said, and what you might have missed as you strove to keep the discussion

going. It's an opportunity to find out about what was not said or to discuss the nonverbal signals.

We heard this story:

> One American man received polite applause for his speech to a group of businessmen in Japan. He sat down to listen to the next presentation, which was in Japanese. The audience interrupted that presentation many times with applause. To be polite, the man thought he should join in. After he had done so for a few minutes, a Japanese man seated next to him said, "Please restrain yourself—he's translating your speech."

ELOQUENT NONVERBAL COMMUNICATION

International travelers sometimes assume they can rely on pantomime or gestures in situations in which they don't speak the language, but that approach has many potential pitfalls. The language of gestures is far from universal, with uses varying dramatically across cultures. Everything from the distance people stand apart when conversing to the amount of eye contact to the significance of a finger snap or nod is determined by the country's culture.

You need to understand the international implications of your body language when doing business overseas or with international visitors, and act in accordance with prevailing customs.

KEEPING YOUR DISTANCE:
Space, Touch, and Posture

An American woman was talking cordially with her male South American friend as they sat on her couch. Although her South American counterpart was not harassing her, he did have a habit of moving closer to her, just as she reflexively put distance between them. By the time the conversation was over, the woman realized that she had moved completely from one end of the couch to the other.

One of the most immediately observable differences between countries is the amount of physical contact between people. Some countries, such as Italy, are known for their warm embraces, while others, including Germany, are characterized by their reserve. Failure to respect these differences can be a serious faux pas.

Space

There's a joke in Latin America that in the United States, the elevators are always bigger because of the American need for more space between individuals.

When approaching someone for a conversation overseas or dealing with an international counterpart in the United States, be aware of your proximity to the person. There is no single international "average distance" that people stand apart when conversing. In some situations, the American standard of 24 to 36 inches will be too close, in others, too far away. Violating either "boundary" is considered to be ungracious. It's best to conform to local standards, even if you find them to be initially awkward.

As a general guideline, the farther north you are, the more distance there is between people when communicating. Among those who typically stand closer than in the United States are people in the Middle East, Latin America, Italy, Russia, France and Spain. Arabs may stand as close as two to three inches! If you back away from them, it's insulting.

Keep Your Distance: Space Differences Around the World

Closer than USA
   Between 2 and 24 inches

Middle Easterners, Latin Americans, Latin Europeans (including Italians, French, Spaniards) and Russians

USA
   Approximately 24-36 inches

North Americans and Western Europeans.

Farther than USA
   More than 36 inches

Asians.

During the Gulf War, many Americans had difficulty becoming accustomed to the close physical distances. When Saudi and American officers would meet to discuss strategy, Saudis would be, from the American perspective, "in their face," making it hard for the Americans to listen. In that case, the differences could have had life-death consequences, so it was vital that Americans overcome their inclination to withdraw.

A nurse in an American hospital told us she noticed that by the end of the second year, Arab medical students had learned to stand further back, even though no one had said anything to them.

It might help to understand that such closeness is made possible by the culture's view on the relationship between the person and his or her body. The Arab view, for example, is that the person—what we might call the spirit, or soul—exists deep down inside the body. As a result, there is more intense eye contact, more touching and breathing on each other, without it being seen as an intrusion.

Interestingly enough, in countries where people stand farther apart than in the United States, that's also considered a sign of respect for the individual. There may even be a practical purpose in locations such as Japan—where bowing is common—to prevent people from bumping heads.

Touch

We've discussed some issues of touch in Chapter Sixteen, "Greetings with a Foreign Flair," including considerations regarding embraces and pats on the head. However, we reiterate the need to be cautious about touching people from other cultures in any circumstances. The interpretations of touch can be as volatile as those involving casual male-female physical contact in the United States. It's best to avoid a contact that could lead to a conflict.

On a relative scale, North Americans are not touch-oriented—we don't hug casual acquaintances. Asians and the British also tend to resist being touched. The Japanese, though, have what might be characterized, from an American perspective, as an aversion to casual body contact—they shun it.

In some Hispanic and Middle Eastern cultures, there can be appropriate touching. Arabs will bump you on the street and touch you during conversation. Latin Europeans and Latin Americans may tap your chest or touch your arm as they talk, with no sexual implications or any attempt to physically "dominate" you. You need to understand these gestures as what they often are: an attempt to treat you equally, even to show that you are accepted.

Posture

American children are taught to stand up straight and to sit up straight as a sign of respect. That's true in other countries, such as Germany, where erect posture is also important. In addition, however, posture can be an important sign of submission.

In India, for instance, an appropriate posture is to stand with your hands behind your back. In Thailand, a suitably submissive position is with your hands in front.

In most of the Middle East, Singapore, and Thailand, it can be an insult to sit facing someone with the soles of your shoes showing. You are psychologically placing that person "under your feet" and that is equating him with dirt.

During a training seminar overseas, Barbara Pachter asked her Arab students if that concept was still true. The younger students said, "We understand it is your practice"; however, the older and most senior of the group said simply, "Don't do it." Similarly, do not place your feet on a desk, table, or chair.

As always, observation can be your best ally in determining appropriate behavior overseas. An awareness of possible differences, combined with an alertness toward typical conduct, can help you to perform properly and not make unwarranted assumptions. When hosting international visitors, consider the person's home culture carefully before you approach or touch him.

INTERNATIONAL IMPLICATIONS
OF BODY LANGUAGE

We communicate regularly through facial expressions, eye contact, and gestures, but even in our own country, such gestures can be misunderstood. Raised eyebrows can indicate surprise, disapproval—or both. Gazing intently at someone can be a sign of deep affection or intense dislike, depending on the accompanying expression. A person who is jumping up and down and using a lot of gestures may be deliriously happy or furious.

Our ability to decipher these situations lies in many factors. We do better at understanding the significance of an action when we know the person's personality, the circumstances in which the gesture occurred, even the words that were exchanged. Without these additional clues, we may have to ask why someone is reacting the way she is: "You seem puzzled. Is there a problem?"

When doing business internationally, we may not have the advantage of knowing a person's personality or understanding the words that accompany a gesture. While we may be able to witness the circumstances, it can be difficult to interpret them accurately without adjusting our cultural "glasses." Accordingly, we need to have patience as well as perspective as we seek to communicate nonverbally with others around the world.

The Significance of Smiles

A smile is ALMOST universally accepted as a sign of friendliness and happiness, but you should remember that it is not used exclusively for that purpose around the world.

A Greek person may smile when he is angry. Asians may smile to cover up discomfort and embarrassment. In Japan, a laugh usually indicates embarrassment or shock. In China, there are many types of smiles, from a "dry smile" to "an embarrassed smile." Smiles are extremely common in Thailand, and Thais say they are from "The Land of Smiles."

We encourage you to learn as much as possible about customary facial gestures of the specific country you are visiting before your journey as well as before hosting someone from another country.

The Emphasis on Eye Contact

Eyes are the windows to the soul.

—Saudi expression

An American hospital administrator met regularly with an Asian doctor on the staff to discuss ongoing problems. After three or four months of meetings, the American expressed his frustration. "You're not taking me seriously!" he exclaimed. When asked why he thought that, the American replied, "You don't even look at me when we discuss these things." The Asian doctor responded that his failure to do so was a deliberate sign of respect. While the explanation didn't solve all the problems, it did help to clear the air.

Americans have difficulty with people who do not make direct eye contact. We have been culturally taught that lack of eye contact indicates someone who is evasive, maybe even deceptive.

But we need to consider another perspective—one that prevails in many other parts of the world. A woman from India once told us she was mystified by our ability to listen to someone while looking at him or her. She found that to be visually distracting. "If I look at the face, I get confused by the makeup, the facial structure, and the jewelry," she said. "I do not listen to the words."

It seems, then, that while many cultures use eye contact to indicate the same response—paying attention, being sincere, affording respect—there are directly opposite ways of doing so.

Eye Contact Guide

How	Where
Very direct eye contact (shows sincerity)	Middle East, Latin America, France, Italy
Direct eye contact (shows interest and that you're listening)	USA, Northern Europe, Canada
Avoid direct eye contact (shows respect)	Asia, India, parts of Africa

It's also important to understand that the appropriateness of eye contact may differ even within a country's borders based on a number of variables:

GENDER: In Islamic countries, women typically don't look at men, but men look at men.

STATUS: In Latin American and Asian countries, people from lower status generally do not look directly at someone of higher status.

DURATION: It's almost always considered rude to stare, but the length of what's considered appropriate eye contact is culturally based. In Asia, eye contact might last only two to three seconds, compared with American eye contact in the range of five to six seconds. In Japan, only an occasional glance into the other person's face is considered polite.

Gauging the Meaning of Gestures

Each culture traditionally has developed its own sign language to communicate emotion nonverbally, to emphasize or illustrate what was said, to call attention to an object or a person, and to communicate without interrupting the flow of a conversation. There are hundreds of such signals used around the world.

When doing business internationally, you need to understand that the amount of gestures, as well as their significance, varies across cultures.

GESTURE-RICH CULTURES. Some cultures express much more, and use gestures far more frequently, than others.

Marjorie Brody's daughter, Amy, had a college roommate from Japan who visited with the family during Thanksgiving. They invited another friend who had studied in Japan to attend the dinner. Both students spoke animated English during the evening, using direct eye contact, lots of gestures, and standing two to three feet away from each other. At one point, Marjorie asked the two of them to speak Japanese. Without a word, the two moved away from each other, dropped their volume, their eye contact, and their gestures. We have seen the same phenomenon happen in training classes when we do role-play in English and another language.

It can be disconcerting to communicate with someone from a culture that uses more or fewer gestures than your own. It's like a person of few words trying to talk with a chatterbox: the dialogue may seem to be one-sided. However, just as understanding in advance that an individual is on the quiet side can help to put his response in context, so can it assist you to understand whether gestures are common in a particular culture.

In the United States, relatively few gestures are used compared with the amount used in some European or Arab cultures.

Japanese speakers usually use fewer words and fewer gestures than American speakers. The Germans are generally restrained in body movements when talking. Virtually no demonstrative hand gestures are typically used in Britain, and few are used in Denmark and Holland.

The French use both more words and gestures than Americans, and Italians use many more. Many hand gestures frequently are used during conversations in Spain, and they also are more extensive in Mexico than in the United States.

Americans may find it easier to omit their gestures than to expand their gesture vocabulary, which can feel awkward and be distracting. When dealing with cultures in which gestures are used more frequently, however, remember that even if you use what feels like an excessive number, you may actually be just blending in.

AVOIDING GLOBAL GESTURE GAFFES. Typical American gestures—those that might seem to be the most "natural" to Americans—often have different meanings overseas.

It's important to be careful about what you are communicating nonverbally. Learn the differences in gestures. A July 1992 *Newsweek* Magazine cover before the Olympics featured a photo of Magic Johnson, Michael Jordan, and Larry Bird displaying three typical American gestures—the thumbs up, the V-sign, and the OK sign—all of which would have been rude to some international participants had they used them during opening ceremonies of the actual Olympic games. When in doubt, avoid the gesture, or check it out in advance with someone familiar with the culture.

Don't use your left hand for any gestures in the Middle East.

Also don't keep looking at your watch—that's a relatively well-known sign of American impatience.

We've listed some relatively common American gestures, and will discuss how they are viewed in various cultures.

"The OK sign": (The thumb and index finger in a circle, with the other three fingers extended.) This American sign of approval, or going ahead, should be avoided in many locations because of its bad connotations. In Brazil, southern Italy, and Greece, it's considered vulgar and obscene. In parts of the former Soviet Union and in Germany, it's rude. The gesture in Japan signifies money. In Southern France, it means "zero" or "worthless."

You should be careful if, when you are speaking, you hold up three fingers to illustrate three points—some people inadvertently make the OK sign in this circumstance. Instead, hold up the middle three fingers, pressing your thumb down against your little finger.

Two fingers crossed: In Europe and the USA, this means "good luck" or a wish for protection. In Paraguay, the gesture may be offensive.

V sign: The "victory" sign can be an insult in Britain and Australia if palm is facing you. It means "shove it" or worse.

Thumbs up: This very old sign—which some believe started when the Roman emperor used it to signal whether the gladiator lived (thumbs up) or died (thumbs down)—has increased in popular use in the United States, thanks to Hollywood's use of it in many movies. While it means "Good job" or "OK" or "Great" or "Good going" in the United States, it can be rude when used with an upward motion, translating to "up yours" in Australia.

Pointing: Using the index finger to point is considered impolite in most Middle and Far Eastern countries and in Asian cultures. Pointing with the index finger in Russia, though done, is considered improper. Instead, use your open hand during presentations. During a training class overseas in the Middle East, Barbara Pachter used a pointed finger to demonstrate the difference in gestures. Even though the students knew the gesture was a demonstration, one man in particular was very agitated.

Beckoning: Americans beckon to each other with an upturned finger and the palm facing the body—a gesture that is offensive to Mexicans, Filipinos, and the Vietnamese. To signal "come here" in parts of Asia and South America, they put their palm down and wag their fingers.

Nodding: Shaking your head side-to-side for "no" actually means "yes" in Bulgaria, where nodding up and down as "yes" means "no." It's the direct opposite of the gesture used in the United States. Use verbal expressions to avoid confusion.

Fingers snap: In France and Belgium, if you snap the fingers of both hands, you are sending a vulgar message.

A WORLD-CONSCIOUS WARDROBE

Clothing is a form of nonverbal communication even in the United States, where it can be used to signal respect for an occasion, social class, and professional status. The situation is much the same in other countries, although notions of appropriate attire are influenced by the climate, the religion and the overall culture. To help you determine what to wear when and where, we've developed four guidelines for international dress:

1. *Do not dress up in "native" clothing when on business.* For instance, do not wear a kimono, a sarong, an English bowler, or a Filipino barong shirt.

You are not a native, so trying to look like one may be considered laughable or unprofessional. Your clothes should reflect your company image.

Men should wear a good quality conservative suit and tie in solid, dark colors. In hot climates, you can wear lighter colors during the daytime. Suits are more appropriate than sports jackets and blazers. White shirts are still most common. Keep things out of your shirt pockets. Always wear a tie.

Lace up shoes are more business-like than loafers, and black shoes generally more suitable than brown.

In Britain, striped ties are symbolic of certain schools, so avoid them.

Women should wear a good quality conservative dress, a skirt-suit, or a skirt-blouse-sweater combination. Pant suits are rarely appropriate overseas for women in business situations. If you expect to appear on stage or in a panel setting, wear longer skirts.

A woman in a business suit would stick out in a country such as India, where the popular female attire is a sari, so wear what might be considered the American equivalent, a dress.

Don't wear spike heels or boots—they're too casual.

All your jewelry and accessories—wristwatch, earrings, bracelet, ring, pen, pocketbook, and briefcase—should be very professional and of good quality.

Most foreign businesswomen are tasteful, sophisticated, and well-tailored, especially in Europe. Select outfits that conform to those standards. Especially in Europe, do not wear costume jewelry. Wear the real thing.

In Arab countries, women should wear long dresses that are not tight fitting. Do not wear short sleeves—the arms should be covered.

In Japan, clothes are thought to reveal the attitude of a woman. Use minimal accessories and no dangling earrings or bright nail polish—you could be mistaken for an entertainer.

In Saudia Arabia, don't wear religious jewelry.

Dress can be quite formal if you are invited to attend a cultural event in Europe or in South America. Be prepared. Men should bring a tux or dark suit; for women, a black cocktail dress is a safe bet.

2. *The fabric and color of your clothing can be important.* Because of the heat and humidity in Asia, you should wear natural fabrics. Synthetics, such as seersucker, are too hot. Polyester is worn by tourists.

In Brazil, don't wear green and yellow together. They are the colors of the Brazilian flag and you will look like the flag if you do. Brazilians don't wear them.

White suits symbolize mourning in Hong Kong, so avoid them. You can wear white shirts.

In Japan, white signifies sorrow, while black is a sign of joy.

In Spain, American "power" ties in red or yellow are viewed as tasteless. Wear navy or grey ties with dark suits.

3. *In some countries, it is better to look older.* The American preoccupation with the youth culture doesn't apply universally.

In Japan, Korea, China, the Philippines, and Malaysia, residents learn from older, more experienced people—those at least 50 years old. If you are young, they will not believe you have acquired the necessary skill and experience.

Accordingly, you need not be overly concerned about grey hair, receding hairlines, and wrinkles when doing business in these countries. Women might want to put their long hair up and men might want to leave a toupee at home!

4. *Grooming is important.* You want to establish yourself as a quality person. Good grooming ensures that you present yourself to your best advantage.

Your grooming reflects both on you and your company. It's important to not look like you have been traveling—with wrinkled clothes, casual attire, unstyled hair, or visible signs of jet lag.

Make sure your shoes are polished and that there are no runs in your stockings. Do not chew gum. Do not keep your hands in your pocket.

Dress for business when boarding the plane—you might be met at the airport.

BLENDING IN

Imitation, it's said, is the sincerest form of flattery. When doing business internationally, conformity may be the most flattering of all.

Anyone who has traveled extensively knows that it isn't always a compliment to be told, "You act like an American." Despite increased international awareness and greater recognition of the need for cultural sensitivity by Americans, the stereotype of the Ugly American prevails, often supported by the glaringly ungracious actions of tourists from the United States.

When your verbal and nonverbal communication styles take the country's culture into account, you've made a giant step toward blending in with your surroundings. You may still feel like a stranger in a strange land, but you're less likely to be treated as one. Your most significant message—that you want to behave courteously according to the standards of the culture—will be clearly communicated. And when you can convey a gracious welcome to your international visitor through words and body language, you've established an important foundation for your entire business relationship.

Chapter 18

THE WAY WORK WORKS OUTSIDE THE USA

We often irritate others when
we think we could not possibly do so.

—LA ROCHEFOUCAULD

Every day throughout the wide world of business, decisions are made, supplies are ordered, information is communicated, schedules are planned and products are assembled. What's not so universal, however, is just *how* all of that happens. The influence of a country's culture permeates every aspect of business, including the significance that people place on trust and connections, the nature of boss-employee relationships, the amount of business that is transacted over the telephone, and the role that work plays in a person's life. In order to operate courteously and competitively in the global marketplace, you need to understand how business within the office is conducted outside the boundaries of the United States.

In this chapter, you'll explore the many customs of business conduct, beginning with international interpersonal skills. You'll find out:

- how different attitudes toward time impact on worldwide business schedules.

- how the language of foreign correspondence works and how to avoid committing a telephone faux pas.

- how to make an effective presentation overseas.

FINESSE IN INTERNATIONAL INTERPERSONAL SKILLS

In the United States, business sometimes can be impersonal. If there is money to be made, we will do business with almost anyone—virtual strangers, even people we don't really like. What's more, to some big companies, customers are anonymous, interchangeable and far away, so the organization is structured more toward sales volume than towards maintaining relationships with established clients. Workers may regularly change jobs, making it difficult to build enduring working relationships with colleagues or clients.

Elsewhere, though, business may have a more familiar approach. A personal and social relationship is often necessary before a work relationship can begin. In many parts of the world, including Asia and Latin America, the way you treat people is at least as important as a profitable bottom line, and sometimes more so. Friendship and business can be intertwined.

An American was to meet his Mexican counterpart at a restaurant to discuss business, but the Mexican was late. When he arrived, the American tried to make up for lost time by going over the proposal right away. The Mexican, however, did not see the need to rush or to skip what he considered the necessary preliminaries, such as providing an overview of his country and its many beautiful sights. The American's impatience and his failure to understand the importance of the trust-building process cost him the contract.

When doing business internationally, you need to allow time to develop a relationship with your counterpart. Your hosts may want to see how you handle a golf game, for instance, before they feel comfortable discussing a business arrangement with you. Or they may want to talk with you at length about seemingly unrelated matters—such as food, or music—so that they can better gauge your tastes and temperament. While Americans may see this step as a waste of time, an unnecessary expenditure of effort for a relatively simple business transaction, people overseas often see this step as an important investment that could provide mutual and long-term dividends.

In most countries outside of the U.S., trust must be established before a working relationship can occur. Europeans and Middle Easterners may not do business with you, even if they are interested in your offer, if they do not think you are reliable. In Japan, businessmen are interested in developing long-term relationships based on mutual trust, friendship, quality, and service, not just on price and other financial considerations. In Africa, trust and confidence are essential. Friendship comes before business. When establishing her first contact in South America, Barbara Pachter was encouraged to think of the process as the first step in developing a possible long-term market niche for her company.

From an etiquette perspective, this means that it's rude, as well as ill-advised, to focus exclusively on "getting the job done" when you begin an international business relationship. You need to invest the time and commitment required to establish trust. Devote yourself to demonstrating your integrity, sincerity, and respect toward your counterparts. If you appear fixated on immediate business results, it could create the impression that you are abrupt, anxious, aggressive, or greedy.

You may have heard that Americans are too informal, that they assume too much friendship or intimacy compared with their international counterparts. However, that difference concerns surface informality, for example, asking too personal questions or using first names without permission. Americans often fall short in the deeper matter of establishing the relationship between people that carries over into work.

As you work to build trust between yourself and someone from another country, you need to heed the country's customs, such as respect for professional titles or matters that are viewed as private. Just as vital, though, is that you consider relationship-building to be an essential part of business.

Trust Me: Connections Count

In many countries, connections count for a great deal. As an outsider, you will need word-of-mouth endorsements to build your business.

One American who had hosted a young Japanese girl as part of an exchange program quickly discovered the value of such a link. The American was looking for international information for a special project, and so asked the girl's parents if they could offer any assistance. Her father responded—within three days—with lots of material. He was following up on the obligation that had been established.

There are many terms for this bond: "raccomandazioni" in Italy, which means good references; "enchufado," or well-connected, in Spain; "compadrazgo," part of a network of family obligations in Mexico; "guanxi" in China. These terms imply a kind of loyalty and duty that goes beyond a typical American business network. It's important that you value and respect these connections. Once you have established a new relationship through your international counterpart, it is important to remember that your conduct also could reflect on those who recommended you.

In some locations, such as the Middle East, a trusted third party may serve as an intermediary in negotiations. Our own work in the Middle East was initially handled through a management consulting firm based in the United Arab Emirates.

The intermediary serves as a sort of matchmaker, screening would-be corporate suitors for competence and compatability. Some Americans resist using a "middleman," thinking it is an old-fashioned or an unnecessary extra step, but from the perspective of many cultures, the third party provides a valued service. The contact person makes proper introductions and knows the country's systems, saving time in building trust.

Get Smart: Charting the Organization

Basic business management practices also differ greatly around the world. Below are some of the key areas in which you may encounter distinctions:

- Employee-boss relationships
- Decision-making style
- Meeting style
- Women's role in business

- The value placed on experience and seniority
- The significance of work as part of life

While you may have been taught that the American way is the "best" way—meaning the most efficient, or most equitable, or offering the greatest opportunity—this is not necessarily true. It's important to remember that other countries have developed systems that work well for them. It would be poor manners as well as poor business practice to constantly compare another country's systems to America's—implying that the American method is the standard by which all others should be judged. Instead, understand the culture behind their practices, and respect their method as equally valid. Knowing how their system works also can help you to fit in.

Employee-boss relationships. Organizations differ in the amount of participation they encourage vs. their emphasis on the authority of those in power.

Research done by Dutch Professor Geert Hofstede shows that cultures can be placed on an international continuum with participative management on one end and autocratic leadership on the other. The U.S., Great Britain, Australia, Israel, and Scandinavian countries generally rank higher than others in participative management. In these countries, management will emphasize a working style that includes discussions and encourages employee teamwork.

By contrast, France, Malaysia, Brazil, Mexico, Arab cultures, and Turkey, among others, tend toward more autocratic systems. Employees show more deference to authorities. In Greece and India, workers typically expect their employer or supervisor to tell them what to do. In those cultures, if you don't give orders, you may lose respect.

Decision-making style. American companies pride themselves on quick decisions, but elsewhere, the emphasis is on thoroughness rather than speed. The French like to prepare for a decision, gathering lots of details. In Japan, "ringi-sho" calls for a written document on the impact of a proposal, with each person affixing his personal seal of approval. Countries also vary in the number of people who are given power to make decisions.

Meeting style. In the U.S., meetings are scheduled for a limited time, with the goal of reaching agreement on general principles. Details can be left to others to work out later. In Greece, however, meetings usually are designed to work out all the details in front of everyone. Meetings are often open-ended, continuing as long as is necessary.

Women's role in business. How involved women are in business and how much power they have in the corporation varies not only across cultures but sometimes even within a culture. When doing business internationally, you need to show respect for the host country's customs.

However, remember also that those customs may be undergoing change. The number of women working overseas is increasing, and as it becomes more common and acceptable, the old barriers are falling down.

Nancy J. Adler, co-author of *Competitive Frontiers: Women Managers in a Global Economy,* notes that when doing business overseas, women are first regarded by their international counterparts as foreigners, and only after that as women. A foreigner—male or female—is not expected to act like a local person, so a female visitor is not expected to act like a local female. For that reason, cultural rules that limit local women's access to managerial positions do not automatically apply to foreign women. In fact, many North American women sent overseas have found their gender to be an advantage, because it made them more visible and they were accorded more social status. Their foreign clients want to meet them—they assume a woman who has been chosen for an overseas assignment is highly qualified.

The problem women face when doing business internationally, however, is more often with their colleagues. North Americans may believe the myth that women won't be successful in international business. They may demonstrate their lack of confidence by defining her assignment as temporary or imposing restrictions on travel to remote regions that would not apply to a male counterpart. To ensure a successful outcome in international business, North Americans instead need to reinforce and support the female manager's role and authority when dealing with their foreign clients.

The value placed on experience and seniority. While the United States values youthful enthusiasm, other cultures consider age and experience to be undisputed assets. When visiting other countries, it's important to show respect for a senior or older person by letting him get through the door first or letting him get seated first. The age of the American making business trips also is important; it can help build trust if the person is experienced. Barbara Pachter once trained a young American man who was going to Germany. He had a master's degree and was going to supervise older people who had doctorates. Part of the training involved how he should dress and carry himself so he would look older.

The significance of work as part of life. Other countries don't always share Americans' workaholism. In France, work is not the most important part of life. In Mexico, people work to live, not live to work. In the United Arab Emirates, we heard the phrase "Every day is a holiday and every meal is a banquet." When leading seminars in the United Kingdom, we make it a point to end on time. However, in Japan, long work days and extensive after-hours work-related entertaining are typical.

Other subtle differences in working style may come into play when doing business internationally. A woman from Peru who was applying for a job in the United States found it difficult to "boast" about her impressive qualifications. She learned through coaching that this was considered acceptable conduct in an American job interview.

We suggest that you not only be aware of these general differences, but that before attempting to do business with another country, you take international management training courses and seminars to help prepare for the specific situations you may encounter.

ITAP International, located in Princeton, N.J., and Cross-Cultural Consulting Associates, in Brooklyn, N.Y. are among the companies that provide international management training for employees and their families going overseas to live and work. Their courses stress how cultural differences affect business practices, from negotiation to performance appraisals. "Culturgrams: The Nations Around US," produced by the David M. Kennedy Center for International Studies at Brigham Young University, are four-page publications that provide information on the customs, values, traditions, and lifestyles of 81 countries.

Of course, other countries perform similar services for employees who do business outside their borders. A list of tips to travelers abroad issued by the Chinese government says, "Don't squat when waiting for a bus or a person. Don't spit in public. Don't point at people with your fingers. Don't make noise. Don't laugh loudly. Don't yell or call to people from a distance. Don't pick your teeth, pick your nose, blow your nose, pick at your ears, rub your eyes or rub dirt off your skin. Don't scratch, take off your shoes, burp, stretch or 'hum.'"

EFFECTIVE TIMING TACTICS

Because the way people view time varies across cultures, understanding the prevailing sense of time and schedules can have a major impact on business. Americans tend to be inflexible with time: time is money. Work is done according to schedule. Meetings are to start and stop on time.

Not all countries are this way. When planning international business meetings, it's gracious to take these differences in attitudes into consideration and set your own clock to fit your host country's "time zone." Remember, it is the visitor who must adapt.

The days of the week that are work days. The Israeli work week begins on Sunday, with Saturday, the Sabbath, the day off. In most of the Middle East, work takes place from Saturday through Thursday, with Thursday sometimes a half day and Friday a Muslim day of rest. It is said that Hong Kong does business 24 hours a day, 365 days a year! Many cultures work part or all of Saturday. In China, business offices are open Monday to Saturday. When one of us gets a phone call at 7 a.m. on a Sunday, we know it's from the Middle East—not our mothers!

The hours of the work day. Start and stop times vary from country to country and even within countries. Americans usually work from 8:30 A.M. to 4:30 P.M. or 9 A.M. to 5 P.M., with a 30- to 60-minute lunch break. South Koreans work from 9 A.M. to 6 P.M. Italians generally work from 9 A.M. to 8 P.M., with 1 to 4 P.M. off for lunch. In Greece, the work day is from 8 A.M. to 1:30 P.M. and then from 5:30 P.M. to 8:30 P.M. In Japan, although the official time is 9 A.M. to 5 P.M., most people work longer hours.

The continuity of the work day. In many countries, as is evident from the work hours we listed above, employees work in the morning, then take a long lunch break. People may go home, have a meal, and rest. Work resumes from late afternoon to early evening.

In Latin America, although some people work from 9 A.M. to 5 P.M., traditionalists work from 9 A.M. to noon, followed by a three-hour break. In Mexico, work typically is from 9 A.M. to 2 P.M. and resumes from 4 or 5 P.M. to 7 or 8 P.M.

In the Middle East, although the work hours are from 9 A.M. to 1 P.M. and 2 to 5 P.M., Arabs will stop to pray during the work day. In the United Arab Emirates, the government works from 7 A.M. to 2 P.M.

The importance of promptness. To Americans, it's rude to be kept waiting, but lateness isn't thought of as rude in many places.

The Russians, for instance, have a more relaxed attitude toward time, which is reflected in their proverb, "If you travel for a day, take bread for a week."

In Central and South America, appointments are approximations: you may be seen in an hour, or wait "until mañana" (tomorrow). There is a saying that "Getting to an appointment on time in Mexico is not polite—it's lucky."

Greeks are usually what Americans would call late, and Arabs may be late too, but it's all relative. Saudis are not on time but expect you to be. Their sense of time has to do with *inshallah*—"If God is willing"—and also reflects that business does not come before family, friends, or religion.

In most of Europe, including Germany, Norway, Austria, Sweden, Denmark, the United Kingdom, Holland, and Switzerland, you should be on time for appointments. You may be kept waiting in Southern Europe, but you should still be on time. On the other hand, don't be offended if the person you're meeting is running late.

Asians, including the Chinese, usually are prompt and so you should be too. Asians tend to be a few minutes early to show they take the matter seriously. Filipinos, though, are usually late.

When doing business in a country where the American notion of promptness is not shared, be sure to build lots of flexibility into your schedule. Do not appear impatient while waiting. You should not feel that you are being insulted. It is not meant to be perceived that way.

The sanctity of time off. In Britain, as soon as the day is done, so is business. Running overtime is not considered acceptable. People do not "talk shop" over drinks or dinner. Conversely, in Japan, there is no distinction between the business day and the business night. Because views regarding time off vary from country to country, you need to investigate the customs of the country you are visiting before you ask someone to come in on a day off or during vacation.

Civic and religious holidays. There are many civic and religious holidays not observed in the United States. Islamic countries keep a lighter schedule during the month of Ramadan: the French leave Paris en masse in August on vacation. Europeans also value holidays and sabbaticals far more than Americans, and most probably would consider it rude if you asked them to interrupt or reschedule them. Many Europeans have four to five weeks of vacation. Some holidays fall on different dates every year, like Ramadan, Yom Kippur, Easter, and the Chinese New Year. When you develop your business schedule, check with a representative of the country you are visiting to make sure your trip does not coincide with special days off.

IMPRESSIVE GLOBAL COMMUNICATION

When doing business internationally, whether you negotiate in person, in writing, or over the telephone, the possibilities for gaffes come not just from what you say, but from how you say it. You can adhere strictly to American notions of proper phrasing and conduct, and, from the standards of other countries, be improper and inappropriate. As always, the key is to fit your behavior into the context of the culture.

Negotiation Basics: Winning Friends and Contracts

During international negotiations, you enhance your chances of business success by conducting yourself in a manner that your hosts will see as polite. Once again, the American "cut to the chase" mentality doesn't always apply. Robert J. Radway, an international lawyer based in New York City who negotiates business alliances, notes that overseas, the negotiation process often includes six steps:

1. The courtship, or "getting to know you" stage. This may appear on its surface to be a strictly social process, but actually is laying the groundwork for further steps. You need to take this step seriously and, particularly, make sure that nothing you do during this phase offends your hosts.

2. The exchange of information. This is the time to inform them of the history and track record of your company and find out about theirs. In countries where thoroughness is highly valued, this step could be time-consuming. Be patient.

3. Establishing parameters for formal bargaining. In this critical step you both present your proposals, and define the common areas of agreement. You are, in effect, identifying the range of acceptability of prices or project costs, and also identifying the major areas of disagreement. Take this step slowly and carefully, as much can be learned about the other side, and the important relationship and trust-building components can be strengthened at this time.

4. Actual negotiations or bargaining, as Americans think of it. This is the step where you engage in the testing of each other's positions, getting more information, modifying your positions where possible, making trade-offs where appropriate, and assessing where the real problems lie.

5. Resolution of differences, or coming to terms.

6. Implementation, which likely will involve negotiations about conflicts or disputes that arise as the agreement is put into practice.

From an etiquette perspective, you need to show that you respect this process, that you are not trying to "skip" to step four before the preliminary steps have been completed. Of course, during the actual negotiations, you need to demonstrate respect for your host country's customs. This could include anything from operating under that country's timeframes rather than your own to drawing up highly detailed and precise contracts.

Proficiency in Foreign Correspondence

What Edward Hall has to say about low-context and high-context societies carries over into writing between countries. Low-context societies communicate through direct, bottom-line-oriented, concise letters, while high-context cultures are more polite and elaborate.

For instance, Americans, Swiss, Germans, and Scandinavians—all low-context cultures—have what could be considered a more blunt and impersonal business writing style. They generally would not exaggerate or use colorful hyperbole, instead writing with a very straight-forward "Do this" or "Be there" approach.

Germans can appear abrupt. They typically would not say, "Thank you very much for the meeting" or even "I enjoyed meeting you." A German woman in one of our classes said she "had to learn to put in some nice words" when writing to Americans. Although both cultures are low-context, on the continuum, Germany is the lower of the two.

When writing to people in low-context cultures, it's a good idea to avoid superlatives—"best," "newest"—as well as the overuse of "I" statements.

In Malaysia, Japan, and Arab countries—high-context societies—business letters tend to be longer, more elaborate and more personal. Their tone usually will be polite and respectful, asking that you "consider doing this" or that it is "requested." A business letter we received from Malaysia closed "with warmest regards." Barbara Pachter once received a two-page letter from a hotel in Japan in response to her request to book a room. The letter mentioned that her journey would occur at a beautiful time of year, when the flowers were in bloom, and discussed the many assets of the region she would be visiting. Toward the very end of the letter, however, it stated, "Sorry that we have no room - all sold out."

We've included samples of letters illustrating these different styles. Three of them are thank-you notes and one is a follow-up letter. However, as you can see, the writer of the follow-up letter, from high-context Malaysia, was very personal, while the writers of the second and third letters, from low-context Switzerland and Germany, were formal and proper. In the case of the letter from Germany, the response was sent by an assistant, not the person who received the initial letter. In the fourth letter, from high-context Japan to Thailand, what we might consider to be the real point or purpose of the letter—the sending of the computer report—is virtually buried within a personal thank-you note.

Business Writing Styles Around the World

FROM MALAYSIA TO USA

Hello dear Barbara!

I have just been made a father of a baby boy!!!

I am so excited and busy shuttling between the hospital and the office.

Your seminar brochure will be out soon. Will air-courier some to you.

Please stay in touch.

Cheerio,

FROM SWITZERLAND TO USA

Dear Sir:

In Mr. Smith's absence, I acknowledge receipt of and thank you for your letter of 11 August.

Mr. Smith is travelling extensively at present but the contents of your letter have been relayed to him and he wishes to thank you for the photos you have so kindly forwarded to him.

Yours faithfully,

FROM GERMANY TO JAPAN

Dear Mr. Kojima,

Dr. Robert Pimental asked me to thank you for sending the beautiful calendar with the four seasons in panorama of Kyoto and Nara.

With repeated thanks and best season's greetings—also on behalf of Dr. Pimental—and with kind regards.

Judy Becker
Dr. Robert Pimental's office

FROM JAPAN TO THAILAND

Dear Jack,

I want to thank you again for the wonderful and memorable days in Bangkok. Really I was impressed by not only the exotic scenery and Buddhist surroundings but also the fresh vitality such as new buildings, highways, and attitude of the young people.

Enclosed please find photos for your memory. Every time I see those, I will remember your hospitality and beautiful country.

Also please find our computer report which is compiled by our staff....

The reason I'm sending them is I recalled when we had dinner with Tom that he was too busy to find the time to read many computer magazines.

Please read and examine the report, and if you need some articles, then I can send the full pages.

Again, thanks for your friendship, I remain.

Best wishes,

When corresponding with people in other countries, awareness of these differences can help you to crack the code of international correspondence and put a letter in context. You'll know, for instance, that a short, direct letter from Germany is not meant to be rude or that a long, personal response from Japan is typical. You need not totally adapt your own writing style to match the style of the country that you are writing to, but adjusting your tone could have some benefits including increasing your ability to get your message across.

For instance, when writing to a prospective client in Colombia, Barbara Pachter made sure to reflect what her contact had told her in a telephone conversation, expressing that she was "most interested in visiting your beautiful country." When writing to Japan, she makes sure that the letter sounds personal, beginning, "It is wonderful to hear from you. I'm delighted to be maintaining contact with you. Your letters mean a lot to me."

Here are some additional tips to keep in mind when writing international correspondence:

Use the correct salutation and closing. Use "Mr." and "Mrs.," or "Dr." in salutations, and appropriate closings such as "Sincerely" and "Very truly yours." There are some closings that Americans may not be familiar with. In Britain, if the letter starts "Dear Sir," it will close with "faithfully," or "faithfully yours." If it starts with "Dear Max (the person's name)," it will close with "Sincerely" or "Yours Sincerely."

Be cautious with abbreviations, and avoid jargon and buzz words. Abbreviations that we might consider common—ASAP or even CEO—are not universally understood. Phrases such as "the bottom line" may not appear in their English translation dictionary. The guidelines are the same as guidelines for spoken communication—when in doubt, leave it out.

Use simple and direct everyday language. What we said in Chapter Nine, "Written Communication: Write it Right!," about writing clearly applies especially in international correspondence. Basic words will be more easily understood. It's also important that you use English words correctly (such as "insure" vs. "ensure") since your correspondent will expect you to be fluent in your native tongue. Keep your sentences short. Include examples to reinforce your message.

Provide background on your company. You should not begin a relationship with a blunt offer or make statements that could be considered a hard sell. Instead, describe yourself and your company objectively, and don't knock the competition.

Keep it brief. Much material is better expressed in face-to-face discussions. For this reason, you need to plan to schedule one-on-one discussions in many countries—no matter how carefully you write, they will still need to meet with you. Understand when you are reviewing written responses from some countries, such as Mexico, that people may be afraid to put things into writing because there is always room for interpretation.

Avoid humor. It can be next to impossible to successfully communicate humor internationally—even if the words are correct, the sense of what is actually funny can vary from culture to culture. Tongue-in-cheek references and irony also should be avoided. Our clients in the Middle East were not amused when we inadvertently failed to remove from our writing manual a quotation from Andrew Jackson that said, "Only a poor mind can spell a word one way."

Make date references culturally appropriate. In some countries, the day, month, year are written in a different order than in the U.S. As a result, 5/1/98 may be May 1, 1998 or January 5, 1998. Spell it out to avoid confusion.

Address the envelope properly. When mailing a letter overseas, always write the country name in English on the last line of the envelope, preferably in capital letters. Be sure the country name always follows the postal code, or American scanners will send it to a similar U.S. zip code, if one exists.

For example:

Mr. Pierre Poulain
9 Boulevard Voltaire
Paris, 75011
FRANCE

It can be helpful when dealing with countries where English is not commonly spoken to enclose a translation of your letter. Make sure the translator is a professional.

The etiquette on sending faxes when doing business internationally is the same as what we discussed for the United States—for instance, do not send an unsolicited fax. Remember that when doing business overseas, if you send faxes at off-hours, you may save your company a lot of money.

Avoiding the Telephone Faux Pas

In the United States, we take for granted our ability to conduct business over the telephone. But outside of the United States, business generally is not discussed over the telephone with someone you have not met personally, for several reasons:

You can't always depend on the local phone service. Although international service is improving, it is still not always reliable around the world.

Telephoning, even within a country's own borders, can be expensive. If you are using your host's phone while overseas, keep the cost in mind.

Telephoning is perceived as "pushy" in some cultures. In the United States, "cold calling"—where you call someone you don't know, make a sales pitch, and ask for the sale all over the phone—is an accepted, if not always welcomed, business practice. But in many places around the world, the phone is not used for sales calls or to discuss business at length. Instead, it is used primarily to arrange future meetings.

In Latin America, deals are virtually never conducted over the telephone, usually not even by letter, but instead in person. In China, most everything is done in person.

The only real way to handle this situation is to visit the country and have face-to-face discussions, since that is the best way to develop a business relationship.

Most Europeans don't usually conduct business over the telephone with people they have not met, nor will they discuss business at length. In Britain, for example, a letter is considered much less disrupting. Once you have met each other, then it is more likely you will talk on the phone.

Here are some universal guidelines for international telephone calls:

Introduce yourself, your company, and identify to whom you want to speak. Be formal. Use last names. "This is Mary Smith from Global Engineering. May I speak to Mr. Lopez?" It can help to be able to at least say "hello" in the language of the country you are calling. Speak clearly and slowly, building in pauses if the transmission requires it. Remember that small talk may be necessary. It's part of relationship-building.

Call at the appropriate time. Keep time differences and the difference in business hours in mind when deciding when to place the call. Respect time off. Europeans complain that people call them at any hour of the day or night. Try not to call the person at home, even if he gave you his home number.

During the conversation, summarize from time to time. Plan your conversation in advance and take notes to make sure all the pertinent points are covered. Do not use jargon or buzz words. Avoid humor. Review at the end what you have agreed.

Confirm important points in a follow-up letter. It's best to at least draft these letters immediately after the conversation, when your memory is the most fresh.

MAKING A POWERFUL PRESENTATION OVERSEAS

Speakers know that the success of a speech is measured, at least initially, in its reception. By that standard, the Gettysburg Address, one of the most eloquent, moving, and enduring statements ever made, was a failure. President Abraham Lincoln's audience, which was accustomed to (and expected) hours of flowery oratory, was astonished when he spoke so briefly and simply. Many in the crowd, in fact, had just settled down to "really" listen to him when the speech came to an end. The address has endured in part because of its message, and in part because it made such a compelling *written* statement.

An American addressing an international audience wants to be a success in his own time, preferably immediately. To do so, you need to catch the audience's ear even when you might not speak its language. To empathize with your potential audience, try tuning in to a panel discussion on a foreign language television station. When you don't speak the language, even if you want to be polite, your attention may drift. Unable to comprehend the words, you might focus on superficialities, such as the dress or demeanor of the presenter. You might give more attention to charts and graphics than you would if you could understand the actual words.

Even when the audience understands your speech, an American presentation doesn't always "translate" well when presented unaltered abroad. Taking the audience into account means "speaking its language" in the examples you use, the way you give the information, and the gestures you use. We've summarized these in *Do's and Don'ts of International Presentations* on page 331. We'll discuss them in more detail, along with suggesting how to handle questions and visual aids, before outlining some presentation pointers for specific cultures.

Do's and Don'ts of International Presentations

Do	Don't
Greet audience in its language	Make fun of your audience's language, or use wrong language
Begin and end the speech with phrases, quote, or poem from their language	Start with a joke or use humor during speech
Use stories, examples, quotes from their culture	Use American sports analogies or jargon
Use written materials: a copy of speech, a translation of speech, a summary of speech, a glossary of key terms	Arrive without notes, even if you don't use them
Explain any references to American personalities, methods, locations	Mock the competition
Speak distinctly and slowly	
Write down numbers	
Allow extra time if using an interpreter	Address the interpreter and avoid the audience
Use culturally-appropriate gestures	
Use visual aids	

Organize Your Presentation for Substance, Style, and Sensitivity

The basic structure of an international presentation is the same as for one in the United States: beginning, middle, and conclusion. However, you also want to organize your presentation for substance (culture-specific references), style (a format that appeals to the host country's audience), and sensitivity (avoiding behaviors that could be considered offensive). You need to know, of course, how many members of your audience speak English, so that you can plan your presentation accordingly.

The age of the presenter may matter in high-context cultures, where wisdom is associated with age. You can select a member of your delegation to be the speaker who matches the rank and age of the important members of the audience. And while you can't change your own age, you can make sure you don't look too youthful through your grooming and attire.

When planning your speech, make sure it includes stories, examples, and references to your host country's culture. It can be especially effective to quote people from the host's country. This keeps it relevant and interesting, and also shows you care enough to find out something about their culture. For example, when teaching writing in Canada, we use Canadian writers as examples.

Do research to make sure that your examples are accurate. You do not want to refer to a controversial figure as "your great leader" or make a faulty historical reference, since this will undermine your credibility.

The flip side of this is to use American references sparingly. When you must use them, explain them in sufficient detail. If you cite Andrew Carnegie, for instance, explain that he was an American industrialist and philanthropist. You don't want to be patronizing, since people outside the United States are sometimes better versed in our history than our own citizens, but it's equally rude to assume everyone is familiar with every aspect of our development. (Quick: Can you name three important historical events in Malaysia's history? See what we mean?)

Be aware that locations and events sometimes have different labels elsewhere, just as "The Civil War" in the Northern United States is still "The War Between The States" in America's South. What Americans call the "Persian Gulf" is "The Arabian Gulf" to countries surrounding the Gulf, and the French *never* refer to the body of water that separates them from England as the *English* channel. To be culturally sensitive, try to use both terms in your speech or acknowledge that other labels apply ("What we call the English Channel and you call 'La Manche' ..."). Again, it's important that you have your American facts straight, since it would be embarrassing to be wrong about your own country.

Always specify to which country you are referring. Don't refer to "the president" without making it clear just who you mean—ours or theirs.

Do not use American sport analogies. There's no point talking about "the quarterback" in a country where that position and role may be as obscure as that of "the batsman" (in cricket) is to you. Anything that excludes people is, by definition, ungracious.

Have your speech culturally proofread in advance for possible faux pas. Our own international course was culturally proofread by an Asian, a European, a Latin American, an Australian, and an American.

Arrive Prepared with Written Materials

Since spoken language can be a barrier to understanding, bring appropriate written materials with you. (For your peace of mind, carry two copies of your speech, in separate locations, one on the plane with you.)

Distribute a written outline of the speech in advance if possible. You could even have the speech, or at least a summary of it, translated in writing into the audience's language, or provide them with a glossary of key terms at the end of the speech.

This will enhance the speech by improving comprehension and emphasizing key points.

Establish a Connection

Connect with your audience immediately by greeting them in their language. If possible, begin and end the speech with phrases, a quote or a poem in their language. You might then want to give a short explanation that you are not proficient in their language—although they may have figured that out already!

Before a presentation in Montreal, an American practiced for three weeks the French phrase she would use to greet the audience. When the actual time came, she froze. But after a few false starts, she succeeded in saying the phrase, and afterwards, added by way of explanation, "I didn't have any difficulty saying that in front of my mirror!"

Even when speaking in the language doesn't work precisely as you intended, it has positive benefits. In John F. Kennedy's famous "I am a Berliner" speech, what he really said was, "I am a jelly donut." However, he won the people's approval with his effort to communicate in their language.

Do not make fun of their language or anything about their culture, for that matter.

Use the correct language—remember, for example, that Brazilians speak Portuguese. In 1984, U.S. diplomats threw a party in Sao Paulo to promote American printing equipment, but they gave the sales pitch in Spanish.

Adjust Your Speaking Style

If you are known for your rapid-fire delivery, your flamboyant gestures, or your dramatic use of pauses, you need to evaluate whether these will work well with a global audience.

Speak distinctly and slowly. When preparing a speech, put just a few lines on each page to slow yourself down.

Avoid the American ritual of starting with a joke. Jokes are culture-specific. You may bomb, or appear to be not serious. Germans, for instance, usually don't appreciate jokes in presentations.

When using numbers, write them down. Even someone fluent in a language might have trouble making instant mental translations of calculations or figures. Remember that a comma may substitute for a decimal point in some locations.

Don't mock the competition. This is considered rude, even though Americans have come to expect it.

When comparing their country to ours, do not speak as if the American item or way is superior. If you must note differences, it's best to do so without passing judgment on them.

Bring notes. You will appear more prepared, and the audience will respect you more for that.

If you are using an interpreter, remember that the speech will take about twice as long. Make sure the interpreter has his or her own microphone. Provide a written translation ahead of time. If the interpreter translates every sentence after you say it, that will slow both of you down. Try to have a simultaneous translation or pause every two to four sentences to allow the translator to summarize. Speak to the audience, not the interpreter. (For other tips on translators, see "Communicating Across Borders: Verbal and Nonverbal Communication," Chapter Seventeen).

Pay particular attention to your visual image. It communicates your credibility.

Use Globally Appropriate Gestures

The appropriateness of your use of gestures will vary greatly with the culture.

Northern Europeans don't talk much with their hands. Try to keep such unconscious movements to a minimum when you are with them, since they are seen as distracting or rude. Keep your hands out of your pockets. Don't smoke during presentations.

In Asia, talk with your hands as little as possible and minimize facial expressions of emotion. Use very few gestures in Hong Kong.

Don't gauge your audience's response by imposing American interpretations of gestures. In China, the audience may look as though it is sleeping when it is, in fact, listening; it may even applaud. The Japanese often sit and nod their heads, which means they understand, but do not necessarily agree.

Also remember if you are conducting a training session that not all people like to participate in demonstrations. Canadians or Australians, for instance, may not like small-group or individual exercises in which they have to stand up, shake hands with their neighbor, or role play with a group. Ask your contact ahead of time. It was helpful during one of our training sessions in the Middle East that our client actively encouraged class participation when he introduced us.

Know How to Handle Questions

Don't be surprised if there are no questions after your presentation. This does not mean you have not been thought-provoking; rather it may reflect some deeply held cultural values.

In Europe, controversial issues tend to be debated in small groups at lunch or over drinks rather than in public forums. In Asia, asking questions may upstage the speaker or reveal the questioner's ignorance. In Australia, though, you may encounter questions that challenge your expertise.

If the person asks a question in English and you have a difficult time understanding him, do not admit that you don't understand. It may embarrass the person, who may feel you are attacking his pronunciation. Instead, say something like, "If I understand you correctly, you are asking about___" or "My answer would be ..."

Try to avoid waiting until the end of the speech to check for comprehension. Ask probing questions and then pause. If possible, ask open-ended questions—who, what, when, where, and why—as opposed to yes/no questions.

If possible, have them send questions in advance, perhaps based on the written materials you have sent.

Before or after your speech, let people know that you are available for them to come up to you privately. Add that an interpreter can assist with the questions.

Be aware of the cultural implications of answers. In Asian cultures, you should have answers to questions even if it is only your best educated guess. You lose face, and so do they, if you don't know. People normally expect you to be the expert and authority in the field, so don't use, "I don't know but I'll find out," as you might in the United States. Anticipate the tough questions. Be as prepared as you can be, with as much information as possible. This may not become an issue, though, because chances are, they won't ask questions to begin with.

Make Your Visual Aids Effective

Visual aids and collateral materials can be valuable assets in international presentations. They show you are prepared and also increase understanding. Customize your visual materials to the specific culture whenever possible.

Use good paper and good printing. In Italy, the quality of the presentation material may be as important as the presentation itself. The standard paper size varies. In Thailand, it's 8-by-12 inches.

Use both languages on your visuals and always read the caption, if only in English. All collateral materials—ads, price lists, catalogs—should be translated into the local language for presentation. Also be aware of spelling. When Marjorie Brody presented in England, she changed the spelling on her visuals to British English. See Chapter Seventeen, "Communicating Across Borders: Verbal and Nonverbal Communication" for examples.

Don't print the materials until they have been culturally proofread by someone who knows the country and language and can suggest possible problem areas.

Include brief biographies of your presenters in the business proposal or send them separately ahead of time.

Be culturally sensitive with illustrations and photographs. In Arab countries, don't use sexy models—they will be offensive. Do not use cartoon caricatures or stereotypical images, such as a Frenchman in a beret. In China, it is usually best to use black and white pictures, since colors have great symbolic significance.

When using an overhead projector, don't write as you go. It gives the impression that the presentation is not important enough to prepare ahead of time.

Tailor Your Presentation to the Culture

Each culture has its own learning style, based in part on methods used in its educational system. Effective presentations take each culture's information-processing methods into account.

THE UNITED STATES. American presentations generally have three parts:

- Tell them what you are going to tell them, beginning with the conclusions.
- Tell them the key selling points.
- Tell them what you have told them—sum up and go right for the close.

The basic attitude toward the audience is reflected in the KISS rule—"Keep It Simple, Speaker" and an emphasis on getting right to the point, explaining "the bottom line."

EUROPE. Be direct and logical, very detailed, and thorough. Don't come on too strong—the typical American "hard sell" will usually not work.

In Switzerland, for example, information needs to be accurate and demonstrable. Approximations are not appreciated. Avoid flamboyant statements, but putting your cards on the table is OK here.

The French allow more time for the details. Start at the very beginning, and offer a brief history of your company, your product, and the relationship of your company to theirs. They want to know your credentials. You need to argue each of your points eloquently and in great depth. The French often engage in philosophical discussion about each point. We know of a pharmaceutical company that offers a one-day training program in the United States, but when it taught the same program in France for its French personnel, it became a two-day program.

In presentations with visuals, use classy and conservative graphics. With Northern Europeans, avoid splashy colors. Be organized and meticulous. Use illustrations that tell the story. Southern Europe will tolerate livelier colors.

ARAB COUNTRIES. Western-educated Arabs may prefer the American approach, but you should generally avoid the hard sell. Use a logical and direct approach. Give the appearance of having lots of time.

You might want to offer two presentations, first with officials, then with the technical people.

Allow time for questions and for the digestion of what has been said. Expect frequent deviations from the topic, as well as lots of questions.

You may be interrupted or notice many people moving about the area. Breaks are important. Be patient. During the breaks, be sure to drink the coffee as a sign of respect.

ASIA. If possible, mail any business proposal to them for review ahead of time. Pause every ten minutes or so to let the information sink in. When making an important point, look at the key person. Don't make the mistake of thinking that the one who speaks the most English has the most influence. Be prepared to repeat yourself.

JAPAN. In Japan, an executive may open his remarks with an apology: "I am very sorry to stand before you today and bore you with this speech." So when speaking to a Japanese group, use a low-key self-introduction. Say something like, "I am very honored to be here today." Also apologize for your poor ability to speak Japanese. Compliment them on their excellent English.

Start by praising their company, the pleasure of doing business with them, and the benefits of working together.

In the middle, use persuasion, not pressure. For the visual presentation, use samples, models, charts, and tables to clarify and enhance the information. Bring lots of copies of written materials. Know that they will be shown to others. Copies of published articles about your company or products will enhance your credibility.

LATIN AMERICAN COUNTRIES. An appeal to emotion and pathos will be appropriate. Make your points dramatic, and build up to your conclusions. Use short, separate segments.

Mexicans often find the American way of presentations to be too caught up with details. They usually prefer general outlines of principles which are supported by credible personal experiences. Their speeches are dignified and eloquent.

WINNING THE GLOBAL GAME

Americans, as we've noted, have a tendency to take themselves more seriously than their international counterparts in the business arena. It can be helpful, then, to consider the global marketplace to be a giant playing field in which the rules change with the location. The way that you win the game is by playing according to the prevailing rules. It may take time to learn the new behaviors, and you may occasionally commit a foul, but you will be seen as a good sport. Effective global manners have much in common with the respect, control, and graciousness that is known as sportsmanlike conduct.

INTERNATIONAL BUSINESS OUTSIDE THE OFFICE

Tell me what you eat and I will tell you who you are.

—ANTHELME BRILLAT-SAVARIN

An Australian journalist on a job interview in Philadelphia was receiving a tour of the city from the person who would be her boss. The man insisted that she try the Philadelphia pretzels with mustard. She knew she couldn't stand the taste, but made herself eat one bite. As she swallowed, she seriously questioned whether she wanted to work in a town where this type of food was common and valued! However, she was offered the job and accepted it. Even so, she never had another pretzel, even though she lived in the city for the next fifteen years!

When you do business internationally, meals take on a special significance: what goes on at the lunch or dinner table could very well influence what happens at the conference table. In many countries, a lunch or dinner may be used to welcome you or to show off the host country's food specialties. Key get-acquainted sessions as well as important negotiations can be conducted during meals. When you host international visitors in the United States, you want the meals you share to enhance the business relationship, not detract from it.

As is the case with American business lunches, your manners count. A faux pas committed during an international business lunch or dinner can have far-reaching consequences. And in some of these situations, the setting may be stunningly unfamiliar to you. Few Americans know when to slurp and sing-along in Japan or how to eat with no utensils from a common center dish in Saudi Arabia. Within U.S. borders, you want your international guests to feel comfortable in environments they may find equally exotic, including casual fast-food lunches while driving between facilities on a company tour.

In this chapter, you'll discover some of the global differences in dining:

- when meals are served,
- who is invited to dinner,
- the advisability of discussing business during the meal,
- the significance of an invitation to a home.

You'll find out about:

- utensils including chopsticks,
- variations in place settings,
- tips on how to present proper toasts.

We'll explain the diplomacy involved in dealing with unusual dietary delicacies.

- When to tip—and when not to.
- how to entertain overseas at occasions other than meals.

PLANNING PROPERLY AROUND THE WORLD

Much of the discomfort that overseas travelers face vis-à-vis meals could be avoided if they knew what to expect. It generally will be up to the host to establish the general guidelines and even to handle most of the arrangements. However, if you know what is customary in any given country, you can at least be psychologically prepared for what you might encounter.

What you need to know in advance about a meal includes when it will be served, who is invited, whether business will be discussed, and where it will take place.

When to Eat

An American woman once casually invited her new next-door neighbors, who were from Chile, to dinner on an upcoming Sunday. When the day arrived, she stopped by their house to let them know dinner would be at 6 P.M. They were not at home. She stopped by a number of times during the afternoon, and they still were not home. She assumed they had made other plans, which was fine, because it had been a casual invitation. At 6 P.M., her family sat down to dinner. At 7 P.M., there was a knock at her door. It was the neighbors, wondering what time dinner would be served. In Chile, dinner takes place around 10 P.M.

Meal times differ around the world: American meals are often served much earlier than those elsewhere. In *When to Eat Around The World* on page 340, we've listed some typical dining times by country to give you an idea of what you might encounter.

When to Eat Around the World

LUNCH

USA	11:30 - 12:30 or 12 - 1 P.M.
Spain	1:30 or 2 P.M.
Portugal	12 P.M. to 3 P.M.
Mexico	1:30 P.M. or later
Greece	2 to 5 P.M.
France	12:30 to 3 P.M.
Israel	1 P.M.
Egypt	2 to 4 P.M.

DINNER

USA	Between 6 and 7 P.M.
France	8 P.M. or later
Spain	9:30 P.M. to 11 P.M.
Japan	6 P.M., over by 9 P.M.
Mexico	8:30 or 9 P.M.
Egypt	10:30 P.M.
Italy	8 to 10 P.M.
Saudi Arabia	5 to 9 P.M.
Hungary	7 to 8 P.M.
Ecuador	8 P.M.

The etiquette implications are rather obvious—it's impolite to eat "off schedule." For traveling Americans, this means you must switch your stomach to the time zone of your host country—hunger pangs and jet lag notwithstanding! (Remember that there is always room service to help tide you over.)

You also may need to adjust the time of day in which you eat your main meal. In Germany, Israel, Latin America, and Italy, for example, lunch generally is the "big" meal. In Mexico, lunch once was the main meal but that is gradually changing. Mexico City is too big and busy, so people can't get home for lunch. Instead, many Mexican people are now eating a big dinner "early"—from 7 to 8 P.M. To eat only a salad or a sandwich while your counterparts consume an entree, side dishes, and dessert would be awkward for everyone.

Finally, you need to conform to local standards in terms of the length of the meal—an area in which American habits are often quite different from those of their international counterparts. We not only eat early, but relatively quickly, while in other countries, routine meals can take hours. Sometimes the extra time allotted for a meal may include a siesta. However, even when it doesn't, it's usually expected that you will savour your food and leisurely partake of the conversation.

In cultures operating under polychronic time, you can even arrive late for dinner. In Peru, for instance, guests may arrive a half-hour after the time for which they were invited without unduly upsetting the host.

The key to acting graciously is, as you might expect, understanding the expectations of the culture you are visiting. Check on the timing of meals in advance, so that you can plan your schedule and food consumption accordingly.

When hosting international visitors, be sensitive to the adjustments in meal times and duration that they may be making. You can help them know what to expect by including meals in discussion of the day's itinerary, rather than assuming they know the American practice. For instance, you can say, "We'll review the production schedule before we break for lunch at 11:30." Although it is the visitor who should adapt, it is not gracious to press someone to have a large meal if he isn't hungry or to rush someone through a meal.

Figuring Out Who's Invited, Whom You Should Invite

Guessing who's coming to dinner can be tricky overseas, particularly if you are traveling with your spouse. While most American businesspersons would attempt to include a visitor's spouse in a dinner, the spouse probably would be alone for lunch. In many other countries, though, the spouse may have to fend for him or herself at dinner, just as your host's spouse may be home alone during that time. It's of course important that your spouse understand the need to adhere to cultural customs and avoid the awkwardness of being a "fifth wheel" at a business dinner.

In the Arab world, you can ask if the invitation includes the spouse. In Saudi Arabia, for instance, usually only the man is invited and if a woman is invited, she goes to another room to be with the other women. As a business woman in the Arab world, you are usually not invited home, but you may be taken out for drinks or dinner.

In Japan, you can usually assume the invitation is just for you. Spouses also are seldom invited to business dinners in Hong Kong or in Switzerland.

We encourage you to be very respectful of the dinner invitation and to virtually always accept it. The invitation can be a gesture that your host wants to continue the relationship. In many countries, entertaining is considered a large part of business. Refusing an invitation could send mixed messages about your efforts to establish a business link.

If you do the asking, you are the host, and you pick up the check, regardless of whether or not you are the visitor. It is usually best not to offer to split the bill. Arabs, for instance, do not split bills—only one party pays.

Women doing business overseas should follow the same suggestions we gave about dining out in the United States, although a woman may want to ask more than one man to lunch. If you invite, you pay, but do it discreetly because men in other countries can be even more touchy about this than American men. However, be polite. During one of our international etiquette classes, two Frenchmen stood up and said they would *never* allow a woman to pay—and that was the end of the discussion! If the man insists on paying, it's usually not worth the battle. If a woman asks someone to dinner, she should also ask the wife.

By the way, don't be surprised if you see pet dogs in restaurants in France and Austria, since that can be customary. The good news is that they are better behaved than many children.

Be careful to be inclusive in your invitations so that you don't offend by omitting someone in the corporate hierarchy. Remember that residents of other countries may be far more status-conscious than average Americans. If a banquet is given in your honor in China, you must reciprocate by giving a banquet for the Chinese team.

When hosting international visitors in the United States, make sure it is clear who is included in your invitation. Don't assume, for instance, that they will know "you" means "all of you" or "you and your spouse."

Mixing Business with Breakfast, Lunch, or Dinner

An American in Japan to discuss a proposal once was very concerned about the amount of time that had been spent in drinking and playing golf. One night over drinks, the American asked his Japanese counterpart to meet him the next day for a breakfast meeting to catch up on business matters. The Japanese man scratched his head, drew in his breath, and made a "saa" sound. The American was pleased that they would finally get some work done. However, the Japanese man did not show up for the meeting. Breakfast meetings are not common in Japan because too many workers have too far to travel. The Japanese man, however, was telling the American through his nonverbal signals—including drawing in his breath to make the "saa" sound—that he did not want that meeting.

Although meals are considered part of the business protocol in many countries, in some, it is ungracious to actually attempt to transact business during them. Meals may be seen as the time to socialize, as is the case in Mexico and Spain, and to get to know you, as in Japan. To be safe, always follow your host's lead in discussing business during meals, and tiptoe gingerly toward any extensive work-centered conversations.

An American went to lunch with a Mexican counterpart. The purpose of the lunch was to discuss a proposed price increase. Patiently, the American enjoyed the food and small talk—for two-and-a-half hours! At the end of the meal, the Mexican looked at his watch. "Oh," he said, "I have to meet my wife in a few minutes. If you must have a price increase, OK." End of discussion.

Breakfast meetings are not common outside of Singapore and the U.S. The reasons vary. In Europe, including Germany and Great Britain, the commute may be too long. Or they may be seen as an intrusion into the daily schedule, as is often the case in Latin America. One American lawyer with limited time acknowledged this difference, saying to his international counterparts, "Let's have an American breakfast meeting." If you are traveling as an American team, breakfast also can be a good time to go over your game plan for the day before meeting with your international hosts.

Business entertaining usually occurs at lunch in Europe, including Britain, but they won't usually dwell on business during that time.

In Portugal, it's often OK to discuss business at lunch, but not at dinner.

The French usually do not want to talk business at lunch or at dinner. They sometimes use the expression "business is discussed between the pears and the cheese," meaning it is discussed quickly and at the end of the meal.

Scandinavians, though, often talk shop while they eat and business lunches are becoming more common in China.

In Japan, social drinking and entertaining at night plays a large part in the business culture. Companies there spend millions of dollars a day on wining and dining clients and colleagues after work. Lunch is not the business opportunity. Business relationships are typically cemented over dinner.

When hosting international visitors, be sensitive to the differences, particularly if they are first-time visitors to the United States. You may want to use meal time to continue building the relationship.

Where to Eat Out

When Susan Ross, a new sales manager, went to Paris, she wanted to make an impression and so invited two of her French subordinates for lunch at the restaurant in her hotel. She thought she had everything well planned. Knowing that the French often proudly "defend to the death" their right to pay the bill, she gave the maitre d' her credit card as they arrived. When the meal was finished and one of her guests did inquire about the bill, Susan said, "It has already been paid."

What she didn't know, though, was that the French do not consider hotel restaurants the best places to eat. Her guests would have been more impressed if she had selected a different location.

When you are the host overseas or with international visitors, you make an impression by the restaurant you choose. The American standard of hotel restaurants as being safe, acceptable choices doesn't always apply. Besides the French, the Swiss typically do not consider hotel restaurants to be the best places to eat. In the United Kingdom, you may find yourself eating lunch standing up at a neighborhood pub. However, in Southeast Asia, Eastern Europe, and the Arab world, a lot of business entertaining is done in hotel restaurants.

This, of course, puts the burden on you to do your hospitality homework, including consulting with your hosts as to their restaurant recommendations. A hotel concierge and other American business travelers may also have suggestions. As we recommended with American business lunches, it's best that you try the restaurant in advance if time permits.

To impress international visitors in the United States, consider alternating your selection of restaurants, including both small excellent local establishments and big American hotel-style restaurants. Resist the temptation to take an overseas guest to a restaurant that serves food from his or her home country—such as taking a French person to a French restaurant—because it is unimaginative and perhaps gauche. You can go to such a restaurant if the visitor suggests it, but your guest will probably find it amusing.

What to Do When Eating at Their Place

In countries where the separation of work and family is pronounced, you cannot expect to mingle informally during meals at your international counterpart's home. It is unlikely that the British, French, Germans, Chinese, Japanese, or Thais will invite overseas guests to their homes for dinner. In Pakistan, the nearest equivalent may be an invitation to your counterpart's club.

However, residents of Israel, Belgium, Holland, and Scandinavian countries often open their homes to guests. On one trip to Sweden, when Barbara Pachter visited three plants in three different locations, she had dinner at an employee's home at each stop along the way.

Regardless of where it occurs, an invitation to someone's home is a very special privilege. Your demeanor should reflect the fact that you know you have been accorded an unusual honor. You also should bring an appropriate gift. (See Chapter Twenty, "A Global Guide to Gift-Giving.")

An international guest will be quite honored if invited into your home for a meal. It's important, though, that you not treat this situation too casually, since the compliment could be turned into an insult if you serve the guest family-style in the kitchen. A well-prepared dinner on the deck could be acceptable.

How you seat people does have an impact. One American woman we know invited several guests, including some international business visitors, to her home for Thanksgiving dinner. Because her dining room table was not large enough for all of them, she set up another table in the kitchen—a common American solution to a space crunch. However, some of the international visitors who were placed there were offended because they viewed the kitchen as a location where guests do not eat. One of the guests was so upset that she sent a letter complaining about the treatment to her boss.

PERFORMING PERFECTLY DURING INTERNATIONAL MEALS

The etiquette of eating around the world is a subject that has long fascinated anthropologists and global travelers alike. Despite the universal need to gain sustenance through swallowing nutrients, there sometimes seems to be no common method of food consumption!

Belching, for instance, is considered rude behavior in the United States but is acceptable and can be a compliment in China. Americans allow eating with your fingers only in certain circumstances with specific foods, while in many Muslim countries, hands are the preferred utensils. In the U.S., we try not to put our elbows or get bread crumbs on the table, but both are OK in France, where it's also acceptable to stack plates as you clear the table. To the Japanese, it's rude to eat while walking on the street. In Brazil, saying "I am full" is rude—but you can say "I am satisfied."

It's important to understand these differences as you travel overseas and when you host international visitors.

Despite the different customs among countries, we've managed to come up with three global dining guidelines:

1. *Don't start eating until everyone has been served.* Wait until the host starts or he tells you to start. It's ungracious, even if you are ravenous, to start eating while others are waiting. While waiting, you can comment (favorably) on the food's appearance or smell, or engage in some other form of small talk.

2. *Don't rest the hand you don't use on your lap.* Keep both hands on the table. This may be a change of pace for many Americans who were trained to keep their elbows off the table and who complied by keeping the unused hand, usually the left, in their laps. However, in Germany, Russia, France, most of Europe, Mexico, and Brazil, it's considered polite behavior to keep both hands above the table. As always, there are exceptions, and in Britain, you should keep hands below the table. Removing your hands from the table in locations such as the Middle East, where hands are used as utensils, could be considered an indication that you are through eating.

3. *If eating American style, don't cut all your food first at one time.* Cut two to three pieces at a time and eat them before cutting more. This is the preferred style in the United States as well. Outside of the U.S., most people will use the Continental style of holding the knife and fork, which naturally lends itself to cutting only a few pieces at a time.

If you smoke, don't light up before, during, or after a meal unless the host or hostess does so first or unless you ask and receive permission. In Singapore, smoking is banned in many places, including restaurants.

It's important that you understand that in some countries, presentation is a key component of the meal. In Japan, the appearance of the food is just as important as the taste.

We recommend that you send a thank-you note for a meal. A letter once you return home can be an acceptable alternative. Although a thank-you note is not always required in countries like Hungary, Mexico, Italy, or Turkey, a letter once you return home is usually appreciated.

In addition, performing properly means being conscious of cultural considerations from seating to dietary differences.

The Significance of Seating

We've included this section here, rather than under "Planning Properly" as we did in the American chapter on dining, because in most cases overseas you will be the guest who is seated rather than the host who determines who sits where. Of course, the guidelines are the same in either instance—if you happen to be the host of a dinner overseas, you'd sit in the host's spot.

In some countries, people remove their shoes before entering a home for a dinner. This generally applies in Morocco, Japan, South Korea, Taiwan, Turkey, Singapore, and in the Arab world.

The seat of honor usually goes to the guest, although the location of the seat of honor varies across cultures.

In the U.S. and China, it's usually to the right of the host. In Sweden and Denmark, it's generally to the left of the host. In Switzerland, the host is at one end of the table, the guest of honor at the other. In Japan, the seat of honor typically is in front of the Tokonoma (alcove), and the guest is seated first. Since it is a place of honor, the guest should initially insist that the host sit there. Eventually, though, the guest should give in and graciously take the seat.

Never seat yourself overseas. Always wait for your host to indicate where he would like to place you.

Mastering Utensils Around the World

All around the world, children have to be taught the locally-appropriate use of utensils, whether it is how to hold knives and forks, the correct way to use chopsticks, or the rules regarding use of one's own hands. Just as someone who had never handled a fork might not understand the method of use, so should you not expect to be able to "wing it" when it comes to using unfamiliar utensils. You want to demonstrate that you are well-versed and worldly by applying the proper protocol in your use of utensils.

CHOPSTICKS: Chopsticks are commonly used in Japan, China, and Singapore. If you are traveling to those locations, you should learn how to use them. It may take a few practice sessions at home before you become comfortable and agile with them, but the gesture of friendship will be well worth the time and effort. Many chopsticks are made of ivory, and some have sayings printed on them.

The lower stick remains stationary and rests on the third finger. The upper stick does all the moving. Hold it as you would a pencil, between the thumb and index finger, resting it on the second finger. Hold them half to three-fourths of the way up the stick.

Hold the chopsticks and the bowl close to your mouth. Scooping and "shoveling" rice into your mouth is acceptable.

When not using the chopsticks, put them on the chopsticks rest—a small, usually porcelain curve. Do not stick the chopsticks up in the rice. Also do not lick them, point, or scratch with them.

In Japan, you will usually find wooden, half-split chopsticks in restaurants. They come in a paper envelope and if there is no chopstick rest, put them on the paper when you are resting.

In China, chopsticks typically are not disposable and don't come in envelopes, but this is gradually changing.

The finished position for chopsticks is across the bowl in China, South Korea, and Japan or on the chopsticks rest in Japan.

HANDS: In the Middle East and in Muslim countries such as India, Indonesia, and Pakistan, you should be prepared to eat with your fingers if you see your host doing it. Most restaurants, though, do serve a knife and fork. In Muslim countries, eat with your right hand only!

There may be no individual plates and all may eat from the center dish. Hands are washed before and after the meal. You eat some foods with three fingers, others with five fingers—to determine which, observe your host, who will also delight in putting food on your plate with his hands.

Your hosts will consider you to have finished when you empty the plate and withdraw your hands. The bill is paid after hands are washed.

SPOON AND FORK: You will see a large spoon and a fork used in many countries, including Indonesia, Malaysia, Singapore, Thailand, the Philippines, Pakistan, and Iran. In some of these countries, you may also eat with your hands or chopsticks.

Hold the fork in the left hand and the spoon in the right. Push food onto the spoon with the fork and eat with the spoon.

The finished position is with the fork and spoon in the middle of the plate. Usually the fork is placed prongs down under the spoon, in a crossed position.

KNIFE AND FORK: Much of what we had to say in, Chapter Eleven, "Dining for Fun and Profit: The Business Lunch" applies overseas in countries where these utensils are used. The American style, in which the knife is in the right hand to cut the food and the fork in the left, but switched to the right hand to eat, is acceptable, since you are an American.

However, it would also be appropriate to use the Continental style, in which the knife is in the right hand and the inverted fork in the left, with the knife used to help push food onto the fork. The Continental style is used in Europe, including Bulgaria, Croatia, the Czech Republic, Hungary, Poland, as well as in South America, including Argentina, Brazil, Chile, and Peru.

People eating Continental style will usually hold their utensils in their hands until they're done eating. It developed this way, the story goes, because British schoolboys had to eat quickly and also had to finish everything on their plates before they could ask for seconds. They found they got more food if they didn't switch hands!

In the United States, Spain, Switzerland, and other countries where these utensils are used, the rest position is with the knife and fork in an inverted V. The finished position is when you lay your knife and fork side by side on your plate. But, as with all things, there are variations, so watch your host. In Venezuela, the finish position is with both utensils in the center of the plate.

In either style, don't rest your knife halfway on your plate and halfway on the table. If you are eating American style, you should cut just two or three pieces at a time and eat slowly. If you are using Continental style, you can use the knife to push the food onto the fork, something that you should not do if you use the American style.

In France, table bread is usually a baguette, and you tear off a piece rather than cut it with a knife. Fruits, such as apples, generally are peeled with a knife.

When in doubt about the proper use of utensils, stall for time while subtly watching your host. Then follow his or her lead.

Maneuvering Through Global Place Settings

Understanding the basics of American place settings will see you through most international situations, with a few exceptions.

UTENSILS AND DISHES: When using the knife and fork, you eat from the outside in. Your forks are to the left of the plate, while your knives and spoons are to the right. You use a new set of utensils for each course. Follow the lead of your host.

Your dishes are to the left and drink is to the right.

With a fork and a spoon setting, there may be many serving dishes placed in the middle of the table. Use the spoon in each serving dish and help yourself to a portion. If there is no serving spoon, use your spoon to take the food from the serving bowls.

GLASSES: Because a lot of liquor may be served at business meals in Europe, you may be confronted with more glasses than you are accustomed to.

The glasses are positioned above the silverware, according to size so all can be seen. The water glass, which is the largest, starts. It is above the knives.

The sherry glass is a small V-shaped glass. Sherry is served at room temperature.

The white wine glass is round-bowled and stemmed. White wine is served chilled. Hold the glass by the stem.

The red wine glass is less rounded than that for white wine, rather tulip-shaped. The wine is served at room temperature.

Do not pour the red wine into your white wine glass after you have finished with the white wine. It offends connoisseurs and destroys the taste. Instead, use the red wine glass.

There are two kinds of champagne glasses: a flat, wide-rimmed glass or a tall, long, narrow flute. Champagne is served very chilled, usually with dessert.

The Secrets of Food Finesse

Many people have strong emotional reactions to foreign foods. Even though the average American's diet has broadened considerably in the past twenty years, Americans as a group tend to be reluctant to eat exotic items. When spices, smells, and serving styles differ drastically from the traditional meat-and-potatoes American way, many people become fearful. That's not irrational—what you eat and drink can affect how you feel and function. Even so, good manners require that you be a good sport.

It's important to remember that your hosts are trying to impress you, not poison you. It's also important to remember that, barring an actual case of inadvertent food poisoning, one meal will not kill you. While the child in all of us may react by saying, "Yuck! I don't like *that*," a grown-up voice of moderation should respond, "Just try it. Just a few bites. You don't know whether you'll like it until you try it."

At best, you may be pleasantly surprised by your dietary discoveries: Barbara Pachter acquired a taste for salmon after being encouraged to try it in Ireland. At worst, you'll have a great tale to tell about courteous culinary courage when you return home. While in Holland many years ago, Barbara's host wanted to show off during a tour and insisted that Barbara try the raw herring and onions from one of the street vendors. She swallowed quickly.

What matters most is that you don't offend those who are providing the meal. We've developed three guidelines for globally gracious manners:

1. *Eat what is offered.* We're often asked if there is any courteous way to refuse something you might find unappetizing. Alas, there is not. Acceptance of food is acceptance of the host, of the company he or she works for, and of your host's homeland. In countries like China, France, Japan, and Italy, food is an art form, an emotional expression, a cultural statement, a personal labor, a means of ensuring good health. Accordingly, you cannot refuse it without insulting the host.

This situation occurs both on the grand scale—in Arab countries, for instance, with the entire meal—and in seemingly small instances: the French, for example, may offer you coffee at the end of a meal, out of the firm conviction that it helps the digestion. Refusing even that gesture can be considered rude.

The only possible reason we could suggest for refusing any food would be a genuine allergic reaction or a serious medical condition such as an ulcer or diabetes. It would of course not be good manners on your host's part to insist that you eat something that would actually sicken you. However, in that instance, we suggest that you express deep regret for your inability to partake of what appears to be a fine offering, commenting positively on its appearance, smell, the obvious time involved in its preparation—and be lavish in your praise of whatever you are able to consume. Beware of faking any strange medical condition that prohibits you only from eating escargots, for example. Any lie will undermine the trust you are attempting to establish.

For the healthy and finicky, we offer these two tips: if you don't like something, swallow it quickly. And if something tastes good, don't ask what it is!

2. *Eat what is offered, but wait until it is offered.* The American potluck "help yourself" style is usually thought rude overseas. Wait until a dish is specifically offered to you. This avoids eating foods in the wrong order, putting sauces on the wrong item and other mistakes. (We even heard of one man who helped himself to the centerpiece!)

3. *Do not salt or season food without first tasting it.* A cook may take great pride in the seasonings of a dish. What's more, appearances can be deceiving: some-

thing may only look bland while actually tasting tangy. At any rate, it's an insult to assume automatically that something needs salt. Try the dish first.

It's also often bad manners to refuse a beverage. In some cases, you will end up *hungry* as a result. We'll explain.

In the United Kingdom, "tea" can be either a cup of tea, usually served very strong and with milk, or a meal. High tea typically will consist of a full, informal meal during the late afternoon, with lots of food—hot dishes, sandwiches, pastries, and fruit cake. Afternoon tea generally is a middle-afternoon snack break consisting of tea, pastries, fruitcake, and small sandwiches. It is said that the ritual of afternoon tea began with the 7th Duchess of Bedford (1788-1861) who found the period between lunch and dinner too long.

In Australia, depending on the region of the country, "tea" may also be the evening meal, while "dinner" is what you consume at lunch time.

In Latin America, when coffee is offered at a business meeting, always accept it even if you only take a sip. It is considered an insult to refuse to drink it, especially in countries where coffee is a main source of income.

In the Middle East, coffee is more than a beverage. It's a sign of hospitality. In the Arab world, meals may have three parts: coffee, food, coffee. You will be seen as gracious for trying the coffee.

The courses of a meal do vary around the world, so be prepared when traveling to eat "out of sequence." In the United States, "entree" refers to a meal's main course, while in Australia and some European countries, it is an appetizer. Salad is served as a separate course in many countries, including France and Italy. In the middle of a meal you may also be offered sorbet, a palate refresher somewhat resembling sherbert. A consultant in Holland wrongly assumed it was the end of the meal. In some parts of Europe, cheese may be served as dessert.

The Keys to Surviving Dietary Differences

Variety is the spice of life and food variety can become the spice of many business trips. When traveling overseas, however, a gracious guest conforms to prevailing dietary rules. A courteous American host takes an international visitor's dietary restrictions into account when planning meals.

Muslims and some Israelis do not eat pork. Those on kosher diets cannot consume milk products with or immediately after eating meat or poultry. Hindus and some Buddhists do not eat beef. Even though you do not share their beliefs, it's polite to adhere to the rules. Violating them would be offensive.

If these distinctions strike you as unusual, perhaps you can empathize with the Polish woman who was appalled when she learned her American hostess planned to serve corn for dinner as a vegetable. In Poland and much of Europe, corn is considered fodder for cattle.

The most significant sign of good manners when dining internationally is a positive, receptive attitude. Be ready to try local specialties. It shows that you are open to what your hosts may consider the best of their culture. As long as you nibble politely at everything, you can discreetly fill up on more familiar foods like bread or vegetables.

To overseas guests visiting the United States, local specialties may include fried chicken, cold potato salad, and homemade pie. While in the Philippines, you may be offered lumpia, an egg roll. In Switzerland, you may be asked to dip into the cheese fondue. Mulligatawny—a curry soup—is served in India. A New Zealand and Australian specialty is vegemite, a sandwich spread. In China, one restaurant offers thirty different Jialu rat dishes, although the availability varies by regions.

Raw food is sometimes considered a delicacy. In Finland, they eat raw reindeer meat. In Japan, you may eat sashimi or sushi, dishes that include raw fish. In the Netherlands, raw herring is served as an appetizer in fine restaurants.

International Table Manners

> *They say you have to stop eating when he does.*
> *But what if he's having a snack and you're starving? Do you have to eat fast?*
> —U.S. OLYMPIC BASKETBALL STAR CHARLES BARKLEY,
> REFERRING TO MONACO'S PRINCE RAINIER

You may have to abandon your American notions of "good" table manners in order to behave appropriately in other lands. When dining with Prince Rainier, Charles Barkley should indeed have settled for a snack even if he wanted a meal.

Slurping and loud swallowing generally are expected in Japan, and slurping of coffee also is OK in Arab countries.

Do not eat anything with your fingers in Germany, including pizza or fried chicken.

In locations including China, Egypt, and Jordan, you should always leave some food on your plate—it means your host is very generous. In Russia, leave food on your plate to indicate that you have eaten well. But in Lithuania, it's impolite to leave food on the plate. To avoid confusion, observe your host!

In Japan, it's best to try to finish your bowl of rice to the last grain—it means that you have finished the meal. However, as we mentioned previously, eating on the street in Japan, as well as Korea, is considered rude.

It can be a good idea to know the appropriate greeting that will be used to start the meal. In France and the Netherlands, it's "Bon appetit" (I hope you have a good appetite) and in Germany, it's "Guten apetite" (good appetite). The Japanese say, "Itadakimasu," which means "I am going to eat now." In China, the host says, "Ch'ing" and then you may begin to eat.

Finding Finesse for Consuming Wine and Liquor

Consumption of alcoholic beverages is part of social entertainment in many locations around the world, and it's good manners to know its protocol. Of course, you need to be careful about drinking to excess. Losing control can be damaging to your business relationship in any country—you could agree to things that you'll come to regret in the morning.

However, drinking does have a different role in different cultures. Many people are surprised to learn that it was Norway which first developed the concept of the "designated driver." In Japan, drunkenness excuses almost everything—it's a way to relieve personal and professional tension. People may get drunk in order to say things they otherwise might not say. The next day, people go back to formal behavior.

The practice of toasting, some say, comes from the Greek ritual of sharing wine with the gods. One stood and looked towards the heavens, prayed aloud while lifting a glass with wine and deliberately spilled some of the liquid.

Toasts vary across cultures. If you don't know how to offer an appropriate toast in your host country's language, you could find yourself in a predicament similar to the one faced by a Chinese man who was in the United States on business. He ended his toast by thanking the host's wife for her help with the meal—specifically wishing her "a good bottoms up." To help you avoid similar embarrassment, here's a list of toasts around the world.

Germany	Prosit
England	Cheers
Scandinavia	Skol ("skoal")
China	GanBei ("gon-bay")
France	Santé/A votre santé ("sun tay")
Italy	Alla Salute
Greece	Yasou ("Yasue")
Japan	Kampai
Israel	La Chaim
Russia	Na Zdarovia ("Nah-zda-roe-vee-ah")
Mexico	Salud
Netherlands	Proost ("Prohst")
Australia	Cheers
Philippines	Mubuhay

Protocol around the world says that the host usually toasts first. If you are hosting the meal, you take the lead.

Unlike the informality of toasts in the United States, in some places including Denmark and Sweden, toasts follow a very formal pattern. There, you should never toast your host or anyone senior to you until they toast you. Nor should you touch your drink until the host has pronounced the toast.

The ritual in the Netherlands typically consists of eye contact, raising the glass, saying "proost" while taking a drink of the wine, re-establishing eye contact, raising the glass, and then putting the glass down.

In Japan, the exchanging of cups of sake (rice wine) signifies the onset of a social relationship. Refusing a cup of sake is like refusing a handshake. If you do not drink, keep your cup full, but go through the motions.

Being served Mao-tai (120 proof liquor from sorghum and wheat germ) while in China is an honor; it's usually reserved for toasting at banquets and for distinguished guests.

You, of course, should not ask for an alcoholic drink in Islamic countries, where it is against the religion, but you can accept if it is offered.

Brace yourself for brews that may differ from American bourbon, beer, or wine. Mixed drinks, for instance, are not popular in Europe. "On the rocks" is an American expression. In Europe, it is common to drink liquor "neat"—that is, without ice.

The French often begin a meal with an aperitif—a wine meant to stimulate the appetite. If you are asked if you want one, accept.

At a formal business meal in Europe, you may be served a great deal of liquor: aperitifs, white wine, red wine, and then brandy or port. Accept and pretend to take an occasional sip if you are concerned about holding your liquor.

In Britain, the preferred drinks are beer, ale, gin and tonic. In Greece, it's retsina (wine) or ouzo. In the Netherlands, people drink jenever, a cousin to gin and vodka.

Excellent white wines are often served in Chile, while in Mexico, tequila is, of course, common. Germans favor dark beer and white Rhine wine.

A few words about wine:

Never refuse wine. If you don't enjoy it, just leave it in the glass. Don't admit that you can't appreciate wine.

Be sure to sip it with appreciation—never gulp it. Also do not sniff the cork.

White wine does not need to "breathe." Red wine does only if it is ten years old.

Let the wine steward or your colleague do the ordering. When you do select, order local wine.

How to Handle International Tipping

While dining abroad, you should not automatically assume that you need to leave a tip. There are some places—including China, Iceland, Japan, and Tahiti—where tipping is an insult.

If tipping is done in Japan, it must be handled in private to avoid offending the individual. In China, it's considered thoughtful to write a thank-you note instead to the hotel manager. In Singapore, tipping is discouraged. In Australia and New Zealand, tipping is not widespread.

While all this is changing as people get used to Western ways, it's always best to ask about tipping customs in the country you are visiting. Ask at your hotel for local tipping rules. The concierge will know.

Make sure you leave the correct amount—overtipping is offensive, a sign of extravagance. Also tip in local currency. Carry small bills and coins for that purpose.

In most places in Europe and Asia, restaurants and hotels add a service charge. It is not necessary to tip when a service charge has been added to the bill. It's a good idea, though, to leave the change or a small amount, such as 5 percent of the bill. If no tip is added, leave 15 to 20 percent of the bill, just as you would in a similar American restaurant.

The tip may be included in the taxi fare in locations including Holland, Switzerland, and long trips in Italy. Otherwise, tip 10 to 15 percent of the fare.

That's Entertainment

Part of your time spent socializing overseas may include occasions other than meals. You should always accept such invitations, whether they include a tour of the local sights or a proposal to play golf. Remember that your hosts may see these as business-related get-acquainted sessions.

We recall the tale of one American executive who was quite eager to discuss a proposed deal, but nonetheless accepted when his Japanese host invited him to play golf. The next day, he accepted another request to play. When he was asked again on the third day, he said, "But when are we going to start doing business?" His host replied, "But we *have* been doing business!"

In Korea, you may be asked to sing—singing is a Korean passion. Karaoke bars—where you sing along with a pre-recorded accompaniment—are popular in Asia and now in the United States. A hostess will join your group to keep the conversation going.

In Vienna, you may be lucky enough to be invited to attend a musical performance at the wonderful Opera House.

It's important to participate—join in the singing, play the games, attend the concert. This will be considered a sign of courteous conduct.

Similarly, it's important to build in some social activity when hosting an international visitor in the United States. Philadelphians, for instance, should take their guests to see the Liberty Bell, even if they themselves have already seen it twenty-five times. You also can take your guest on a river cruise, to a live performance, or a sporting event.

AN OPEN MIND

Many culinary and social customs do not hold up very well to serious international scrutiny. If you think about it, for instance, the American penchant to serve almost every sandwich with french fries (which do not come from France) and to cover them with ketchup (which was originally developed as a fish sauce) is not logical. The reality is that many of these behaviors are acquired tastes. Gastronomic graciousness is a worthwhile skill to refine, one that you may well profit from both here and abroad.

Chapter 20

A GLOBAL GUIDE
TO GIFT-GIVING

Do not do unto others as you would that they should do unto you.
Their tastes may not be the same.

—GEORGE BERNARD SHAW

An American businessman visiting Germany got the cold shoulder when he brought red roses to dinner at a colleague's home, unaware that the flowers had romantic connotations.

A group of Americans meeting with their Japanese counterparts were unprepared when their guests presented them with gifts at their first meeting. The Americans knew they were supposed to give presents, but they had left them back at the hotel, thinking the gift exchange would occur when it was time to say goodbye.

In South Korea, an American business traveler waited, in vain, for the gift she had just presented to be opened in front of her. The Korean never considered doing so, because in his culture, opening a gift in front of the donor is considered rude.

For Americans doing business abroad, gift-giving can be an important but perplexing part of international protocol. Gifts can either contribute significantly to the development of a long-term business relationship, as is often the case in Russia, or be discouraged, as is the case in Germany. The language of gifts—what they signify to the recipient—also varies greatly from culture to culture. A gift that is joyously accepted in one country may be considered an insult in another. And even when a gift is appropriate, you may unwittingly violate another country's etiquette if you present it at the wrong time or in the wrong way.

What's needed, then, is a clear understanding of how gifts fit into the culture of the particular country you are visiting or the home country of the visitor you are hosting. Do good manners dictate that gifts be exchanged? If so, to whom should they be

355

given? What kinds of gifts are appreciated? When should they be presented? How should they be wrapped? And if you receive a gift, what's the gracious way to accept it?

In this chapter, you will find out how to walk the fine line of global gift-giving without making a gaffe. While providing a guide to the specific customs of every country is, of course, not our purpose here, you'll discover the kinds of issues that might arise with the protocol of presents. Internationally, it's not just "the thought" that counts. "Gift-giving," explained a Chinese businesswoman in the United States, "is a complicated thing!"

YOUR PASSPORT TO THE WORLD OF PRESENTS

In the United States, we make a distinction between business gifts and host or hostess gifts. These categories differ both in the types of items that are considered suitable as gifts and in the circumstances in which they are given.

Host or hostess gifts are the tokens of appreciation presented for a meal cooked at someone's home or as a thank-you for an overnight stay. These gifts are meant to express gratitude for the welcome one has received. Although the situations in which they are given are similar, more flexibility is allowed when giving a hostess gift. They can, within certain established boundaries, reflect a bit of the personality of the giver and/or the taste of the recipient. You might, for instance, bring an unusual type of cheese you have discovered or indulge the host's preference for milk vs. dark chocolates.

Business gifts, however, are professional rather than personal expressions of appreciation. They may serve as an initial ice-breaker or as a final farewell when dealing with clients. They generally are not geared toward an individual's interests, but rather reflect what is considered appropriate for the recipient's position or role. They can be standardized, so that all clients who generate the same amount of business receive the same present. They sometimes may not be handed directly to the recipient, but may instead be left at the person's place setting at a company banquet. (One of our colleagues received an expensive watch at the company's annual management meeting, as did all the other executives.) Business gifts are cordial but corporate, courteous but correct, while fitting within corporate guidelines.

In the global marketplace, however, the lines between business and host or hostess gifts may not be so clear-cut. Your international counterpart is, after all, also your host. Failure to bring the correct hostess gifts may affect the relationship and therefore business. Success at gift-giving in the international arena requires knowing your host country's gift-giving customs.

When hosting international visitors, remember that they will bring their home country's gift-giving expectations with them, and may also bring presents. You want to appear gracious and not be caught off-guard, even if the situation is one that wouldn't require a gift if you were all North Americans.

The Power of Place: Where to Give Gifts

Generally speaking, in Hong Kong and in English-speaking countries including Britain, Ireland, Canada, and Australia, business gift-giving is not a required part of the culture. They somewhat parallel the United States, where gifts between companies that do business together are rare, and where most of the business gifts are service awards given to employees within a company or holiday gifts between business contacts.

Business gifts are rarely exchanged in France, and in Spain, gifts are usually discouraged. However, while business gifts may be optional in Europe, hostess gifts are not—you usually send or bring a gift if invited to someone's home in Europe. Chocolates or flowers are often appropriate.

In China, though, gift-giving is increasing and not giving a business gift can have a negative effect on future dealings. Gift-giving also is important in the Philippines. A new friend from the Philippines presented an American with a lovely birthday gift, even though she had only known the American for three weeks.

In many countries, failure to present gifts may be seen as a major breach of etiquette. In Japan, gifts are an important factor in maintaining or establishing business rapport. When an American woman was hosting two Japanese visitors, not only did they provide presents for the woman, but when they realized she had children, they went back into their bag and presented gifts to them as well.

When the situation requires a gift, you should seriously consider the nature of the gift, its meaning, and its quality.

SECRETS OF SELECTING A GREAT GIFT

It's usually more appropriate to give something from your own country. Doing so makes the gift both more personal—by virtue of the fact that it has traveled with you—and somewhat exotic, because it may not be available in your host's country.

If you are presenting a gift as "something from the States," you need to be certain that it is, indeed, "made in America." Check to make sure it doesn't say "made in Japan" or "a product of Denmark," for instance.

Discerning what is uniquely American—especially from an international perspective—can be difficult. Americans sometimes are surprised at which aspects of our culture—from film stars to statesmen—are known outside the United States. Your host may be just as familiar with Walt Whitman as he is with Walt Disney, for instance, or be more knowledgeable about the Old West than he is about the latest Hollywood sensation. "You know you have been away from the States too long," a colleague who is stationed in Russia says, "when you rush back to watch Wyatt Earp on television."

Remember, too, that what is considered a historic artifact in the United States could be considered relatively modern in Europe or Asia. That makes it difficult to impress residents of those continents by giving them an "antique."

It can be awkward, disappointing and poor manners to present a gift that is obscure to the recipient. A photo-history of Lionel Ritchie's career, for instance, won't mean much if the recipient has no idea who he is. To be safe, be traditional. If you want the gift to be in some way linked to a well-known American, pick someone, such as Thomas Jefferson, who has stood the test of time.

Also be careful about the "patriotic" message you may be sending through the gift. Especially make sure that it doesn't subtly indicate that American products are superior. It would be clearly inappropriate and insulting, for instance, to give a bottle of California or New York state wine to a French vintner.

Americans love logos—from university emblems to corporate logos—but be cautious about giving something that might be seen as self-promotional or overly aggressive, and therefore gauche.

Items reflecting America's natural wonders—a book with photographs of the Grand Canyon, a pen-and-pencil set made with Michigan petoskey stones, or commemorative postage stamps showing California redwoods—generally are safe offerings that avoid the traps of company boosterism and American arrogance. Another choice would be well-made items affiliated with well-known American landmarks, such as a memo pad depicting the Empire State Building, the St. Louis Arch, or the Golden Gate Bridge.

If you know your counterpart fairly well, you can be thoughtful. Bring your colleague his favorite chocolates or a musical tape when visiting.

Eleven Sure-Fire Gift Ideas

1. A bottle of liquor, such as scotch (except in Arab countries). It's also usually less expensive when you buy it duty-free.

2. Pen-and-pencil sets.

3. Baseball caps and T-shirts of famous teams.

4. Toys made in the U.S. if the host has children.

5. Items from your state, for example, maple syrup from Vermont or Georgia peach preserves.

6. Books about the U.S. with scenic photographs for those who speak limited English. In China, a subscription to Reader's Digest.

7. Quality regional crafts, such as Native American pottery or weaving.

8. Good quality stationery.

9. Small electronic gadgets, such as calculators, especially in Russia and Eastern European countries.

10. Binoculars.

11. Something you've done yourself—a photograph, or craft item, provided you have genuine talent.

Also keep these guidelines in mind when determining what gifts to give international visitors to the United States. In most countries, photographs of the person taken during a visit and sent afterwards also are appreciated presents, since it is something the visitor can't acquire personally.

Questions to Ask Before You Give

Outside of the United States, gifts have many meanings that Americans may not know. Our *Gift-Giving Test* contains several items that an American might give in all innocence, only to find the gift could be considered insulting.

Gift-Giving Test

Can you match the gift with the country or countries in which presenting it would be a faux pas? For extra points, explain why it's an error. Answers on p. 360.

1. Desk clock	a. England
2. White lilies	b. France
3. An unwrapped gift	c. China
4. Yellow and white chrysanthemums	d. Japan
5. A bottle of scotch	e. Italy
6. Set of knives	f. Saudi Arabia
7. Item with large company logo	g. Germany

When selecting a gift, it's crucial that you consider its symbolic significance. Ask yourself the following questions:

Does it violate any cultural or religious taboos? Liquor and products made from scavenger animals such as pigs are forbidden to Muslims. As a result, in most of the Middle East, it's best to avoid giving alcohol or pork products. In India, avoid gifts that are made of cowhide, since you will offend those of the Hindu religion, for whom cows are sacred.

Does the color or the item itself have any unintended meaning? In France, Germany, Austria, and Switzerland, red roses are for lovers only, and to bring them implies, "I love you." In Italy, France, and Belgium, chrysanthemums are used mainly for funerals, and in Germany, yellow and white chrysanthemums are a mistake for the same reason. However, in Brazil, it's purple flowers that signify death.

The president of a local manufacturing company was preparing for a trip to China and was going to give her counterpart the company's commemorative clock. Upon checking with us, however, she realized it was not appropriate and, in fact, would have been insulting because clocks signify bad luck. Instead, she brought a book on Philadelphia, which was well received.

Is the gift appropriate to the occasion? Although many people consider flowers a universally acceptable gift when invited to someone's home, they're not. In Egypt, you bring flowers only if someone is sick. In Japan, flowers are presented when courting, or in situations relating to illness and death.

Is the amount appropriate? The Japanese associate the number four with death, so it would be bad manners to give them four of anything, such as four glasses. An odd number of flowers is generally good in the Czech Republic, Poland, Italy, Austria, Germany, because nature is asymmetric. In most of Europe, twelve flowers implies "cheaper by the dozen" and 13 is bad luck, so it's best to avoid both.

As a visitor, you must respect these traditions. Do not dismiss them as silly superstitions. Consider those times you have received a gift that may have made you wonder about the giver's intent. Was the exercise bicycle from your wife a reflection of your interest in physical fitness or a hint that you needed to lose weight? Did the cookbook he gave you mean that your meals were uninspired? You do not want to confuse the recipient of a business gift about your motives. This is bad for business and also is just not nice. Instead, you want to use the gift to help establish a business connection based on mutual trust and respect.

When in doubt, check with on-site mentors about a gift's appropriateness or ask them for suggestions in advance. You can't know everything, but you can know what questions to ask. Thinking things out ahead of time can make all the difference.

ANSWERS TO GIFT-GIVING TEST

1-c. It's a symbol of bad luck, death.

2-a. They're used for funerals.

3-d. This shows bad form.

4-g. They signify death.

5-f. It's against the religion.

6-e. It symbolizes cutting off the relationship.

7-b. It's considered to be an advertisement, in poor taste, and impersonal.

How Much Should You Spend

A big thank-you ... This is a small token of appreciation.

—A NOTE LEFT BY THE SULTAN OF BRUNEI
AFTER A FIVE-DAY STAY AT THE FOUR SEASONS HOTEL ON CYPRUS.
IT ACCOMPANIED A $170,000 TIP FOR THE STAFF

The gift you present to your international counterpart should be of high quality and, if possible, comparable in value to whatever he may be giving you. If the gift is shoddy or inexpensive, it will insult the recipient and reflect negatively on you and your company. If it is too costly and you are just establishing a business relationship, it might be interpreted as a bribe.

The gift should reflect positively on the company. It should indicate that the company knows and provides quality.

BRIBES AND QUESTIONABLE PAYMENTS: Before accepting a gift, you should, of course, consider whether there is an implied obligation if you accept it. And if the gift is very expensive, how will you reciprocate?

If your company has strict rules about what you can accept as a gift, you have two choices: try to explain your refusal to your host based on company policy, or try to explain your acceptance to your boss based on diplomacy. The solution depends on whom you most fear offending, as well as the consequences. Some companies have a policy under which you accept the gift and then turn it over to the corporate gift bank.

However, the Foreign Corrupt Practices Act, which became U.S. law in 1976, sets guidelines on acceptable conduct in dealing with foreign businesses.

According to Robert J. Radway, an international lawyer based in New York City, who negotiates business alliances, many countries operate on a "welfare system," in which salaries are low and civil servants in particular are expected to supplement their incomes through gratuities, tips, and other payments which may now fall into a category of illegal bribes.

This frequently places U.S. companies and individuals at a disadvantage vis-à-vis some foreign competition, Radway notes, and has accounted for significant amounts of lost business.

What is clearly illegal are payments made to influence the obtaining or maintaining of specific business contracts, sometimes known as "gravy payments." What is clearly legal are payments made to expedite paperwork at borders, expedite shipments at various stages, or to generally facilitate the processing or movement of goods or services for which contracts are already agreed. These are known as "grease payments." Contributions to "political parties" in foreign countries generally will be considered as influence payments or bribes.

To handle these situations, many U.S. companies have adopted codes of conduct and have clearly communicated them to their employees and foreign representatives.

When, on the other hand, a foreign customer initiates a potential extortion, the flip side of bribery, Radway notes "smart and forewarned executives immediately take an unflinching position." He suggests they tell their international counterpart, "Not only is such action illegal under strictly enforced American laws, but our company policy also forbids it and I would lose my job."

Wrapping it Up in Style

The gift that you present should be wrapped. Failure to do so can be seen as bad form. In some countries, the way the item is prepared for presentation will be almost as important as the gift itself. It can be considered an indication of your attention to detail, thoroughness, and even your sense of artistry.

Make sure that you remove the price tag before wrapping the gift.

Do not be surprised if the still-wrapped gift is examined and exclaimed upon—this can be a sign of respect toward you. In Japan, Singapore, South Korea, China, and Malaysia, gifts are not opened in the presence of the giver. Waiting shows that it is the act of giving, not the content, that is important.

When an American company presented its Chinese research manager with a parting gift, she adhered to her home country's custom of not opening it. "This is America," the director said. "Please open the gift."

Check with a representative of the country you are visiting as to their wrapping customs or taboos. Red, black, and white are considered funeral colors in Japan, while in China, red is a lucky color and white is for funerals.

In Europe, it's gauche to include a business card with a gift. Use a blank card for a handwritten note.

SELECTING RECIPIENTS TO ENSURE RESULTS

In societies in which status and class are significant, you must heed protocol in determining who will receive your gifts. If you give an underling a present and neglect his boss, it not only will reflect badly on you but could also get the underling in trouble.

If you are giving only one present, make sure it goes to the highest-ranking person with whom you've had dealings. In your remarks while presenting it, you can note that the gift symbolizes your appreciation of everyone's assistance. You can also add that it is a company-to-company presentation, rather than an individual expression. If you are uncertain about the hierarchy, make it a joint gift, presenting, for instance, a silver tray or a crystal bowl.

If more than one person will receive presents, consider making them identical for all recipients of equal rank.

If you plan to hand out presents to everyone in the group, make sure you have enough to go around.

POLISHED PROTOCOL FOR PRESENTING A PRESENT

Americans tend to be much more informal than those in other countries when presenting gifts, and this can be a liability if you do business overseas. You need to think in advance about how you will present your gift, because failure to do so appropriately can devalue the gift and sour the very relationship you are working to build. Presenting the gift in a suitable manner—with respect and dignity—shows that you have good manners.

When: Gifts are typically presented either before both parties get down to business or at the conclusion of business, but rarely while a business transaction is under way.

It is usually best to give your gifts at the end of a visit, although there are exceptions.

In Norway, a modest gift, such as alcohol or chocolates, is acceptable at the first meeting.

In Japan, gifts are frequently given at first meetings. Let the Japanese initiate the gift-giving exchange: do not surprise them with a gift. They will lose face. In China, too, small gifts may be given at the first meeting to encourage the friendship.

Gifts are usually not given on the first trip to an Arab country. However, if you meet several times during the trip, a small gift is acceptable. At the end of her first trip to the United Arab Emirates, Barbara Pachter received an Arab dress and silk robe. As a thank-you, she sent back copies of the class pictures.

Gift-giving and receiving can be extensive in Latin America, but it does not occur during business sessions. Instead, give the gift when in a relaxed social setting.

How: If you are giving gifts to more than one person, it's generally a good idea to make all the gift presentations at the same time, when all the recipients are gathered together. The highest-ranking person is usually given the first gift.

In Japan and Malaysia, gifts are presented, with two hands, to the highest-ranking person. This shows respect. He may hesitate to accept for two to three times. Continue to offer, while apologizing for the gift's unworthiness. He will eventually accept.

In China, proper etiquette also calls for the recipient to decline a gift several times. It's polite, and is done by instinct. The Chinese expect the other person to continue to offer the gift. Give the gift in private, and make it clear that it is a gift from your *company* to theirs.

A woman should make sure that any gift given to a male international business associate is not personal. Company-to-company gifts are usually best and are least likely to send any unintended message. Remember that a gift need not be a tangible object. To reciprocate for kindness shown by an international client, Barbara Pachter hosted the man's son for one week in the United States. That fulfilled the same function as a gift, which is to aid in establishing a business relationship.

What to Say: Countries differ in the amount of "speech-making" someone will expect from you when you present your gift.

If the presentation comes at the end of your stay, it will be easy for you to summarize all the reasons you are giving the gift: their graciousness in hosting you, their cooperation in the negotiations, the beginning of what you hope will be a long-term business arrangement. If you name individuals, be sure not to leave anyone out. Also respect protocol and rank. You usually want to name the most important person first and make it clear that you are *especially* grateful to him.

If you are presenting the gift at the beginning of your stay, your speech can express gratitude for the opportunity they have given you by affording you this time to work together, combined, perhaps, with a little explanation of the gift itself.

GIFTS UNDER DURESS: While you are overseas, you should be careful in general about expressing admiration for someone's possessions. In some cultures, this creates a social obligation on the owner to offer it to you as a gift.

Although this practice is no longer regularly followed in Arab countries, it once was common. One Australian diplomat's wife told the story of the time she wore her aunt's old beads to a dinner party attended by a sheik's wife. The beads were not valuable, but had lots of sentimental meaning for the woman. However, when the sheik's wife admired them, the woman knew, based on protocol, that she was obligated to give them away, even though she didn't want to. Seething inside, she graciously sent them to the Arab woman's house the next day.

Two weeks later, she received in recompense an expensive diamond and gold watch. Now, when people admire her watch, she says, "Oh yes, my dear aunt's old beads."

MAKING ACCEPTANCES AND THANK-YOU'S WORK FOR YOU

Tastes do vary across cultures. What we, as Americans, may find gaudy may be another culture's idea of beauty, and vice versa. Graciousness requires that you view a gift within its cultural setting, within the context of its genre. This is true whether you receive a gift from an international visitor or while visiting another country.

Refusing a gift may be a slap in the face to someone. Regardless of how you may feel about the gift, it's usually best to express appreciation for it and accept it. (What you do with it when you get home is your own decision—but if there's a chance the gift-giver might come to visit you, it could be wise to at least keep the gift in a drawer.)

Never joke about or make fun of a gift, or say anything that could be interpreted as doing so. This is rude. It insults the giver. Appear genuinely pleased with the present and grateful for the thought behind it. You can always find something positive to say, such as "Oh, what fine workmanship!" "Such an unusual color," "I've never seen anything quite like it!," or just "How thoughtful of you."

Remember to send thank-you notes in addition to verbally expressing appreciation. It is probably better to do so as you go along. If you wait until you get home, it may not happen.

THE JOY OF GIVING

We all know, from childhood, that there's something special about receiving gifts. It's not just that we all like new "toys" or even the attention that comes with a present, although those feelings may be part of it. However, what a gift does—regardless of what the gift may be and how we may feel about the item itself—is make emotions tangible. Here is something we can hold, something we can look at, which shows that someone was thinking about us, that someone wanted to please us. That's quite a compliment, in any language.

Part 3

THE ETIQUETTE GAME

Chapter 21

FIND THE FAUX PAS

We do take our manners seriously, but that doesn't mean you can't have some fun with them! The whole point, after all, is for courtesy to make you comfortable enough to enjoy yourself while operating effectively in the corporate realm. For your enlightenment and entertainment, we have devised an etiquette game, "Find the Faux Pas."

As we said in Chapter One, "Test Your Etiquette Awareness," etiquette in the real business world isn't a true-false, multiple-choice test, but more like a never-ending story problem. That's what you'll find here: domestic and international story problems for the etiquette-enlightened. The real situations you face will not be unlike these scenarios: filled with numerous variables, any of which could represent a potential protocol pitfall. Your daily challenge will be to try, quickly and gracefully, to do the right thing. You may recall accurately the information you have stored away, but can you apply it correctly?

One thing you should know in advance, though, is that this test will be graded on a curve. The fact that you were interested enough to pick up this book, that you had the willingness to improve your business savvy, will put you ahead of many others. When it comes to etiquette gamesmanship in the *real* business world, we expect that you will be competent, courteous—and therefore successful—players.

Where's the Faux Pas

THE DOOR DILEMMA. A man and a woman of equal corporate status walk down a corridor. She comes to the door first; however, he moves ahead to open it for her. She objects. Where's the Faux Pas?

DINNER CHEZ BOSS. You and your spouse are invited to your boss's home for dinner. Not knowing the boss's taste in wine, you decide to bring a dessert. You take your time and bake your specialty: lemon meringue pie. You get a little lost on the way, but are only five minutes late. Your spouse chats amiably with the boss's spouse, while you and the boss enjoy cocktails. During dinner, you quickly remove a fish bone from your mouth using your thumb and forefinger, placing it on the rim of your plate. After dessert, you all stroll around the grounds, where you admire the fine flower garden. Thanking both of them for a delightful evening, you head home. Where's the Faux Pas?

SCHEDULE WARS. Over the weekend, you find out that your spouse cannot take your child to the doctor for an annual checkup on Friday. If you take your child to the doctor, you will be unable to have lunch with one of your regular customers. The first thing on Monday, you have your secretary call to reschedule your Friday lunch. Where's the Faux Pas?

PROGRESS REPORT. You are talking on the telephone to a client about a proposal. You inform him that he is on the speakerphone and that there are two assistants with you. It soon becomes clear that you need to search for some additional information, and you offer to call him back. He says he'll wait.

   You leave to get the information from the marketing manager, who suggests that he return to your office with you. After entering the room, you tell the customer that the material has not been located. The customer interrupts and proceeds to criticize both the proposal and the marketing department. At this point, the marketing manager apologizes for the incomplete data. Where's the Faux Pas?

SHOPPING AROUND. Six sales representatives—five women and one man—are in New Orleans for a sales meeting. After a busy day listening to presentations, the women decide to go shopping after dinner. They know that their male colleague hates to shop, so they tell him when and where they'll meet him the following day. Where's the Faux Pas?

THE TOO-GENEROUS GIFT. Your company has a policy of not accepting gifts worth more than $25 from vendors. You receive a pen-and-pencil set on Monday. By Friday, you have realized that the value of the set exceeds the limit. On the following Monday, you ask your secretary to send the set back along with a note from you that thanks the gift-giver but makes it clear that you cannot accept it. You keep a copy of the note for your own protection. Where's the Faux Pas?

MEETING MANIA. You are to join your co-worker from another division for a 10 A.M. meeting with senior management. You have not seen your colleague in six months, although you speak regularly on the phone. She arrives at your office with just minutes to spare to get to the meeting on time. You stand and shake hands and comment favorably on her new hairstyle. You realize at that time that she has a run in her stocking and lipstick on her teeth. After a minute of other small talk, you leave for the meeting. It's then you give her feedback about her teeth and stockings. Where's the Faux Pas?

THE FREE LUNCH. You are the guest during a business lunch. The host is paying the bill. You start out with a glass of wine, then switch to iced tea. Since there is no spoon with the iced tea, you use the one from your place setting. Your host orders lobster, you order steak. You know not to offer to help with the check, but you do offer to leave the tip. After leaving the table, you pick up your coat at the coat check, where you leave a $1 tip. Where's the Faux Pas?

A STAR IS BORN. You have invited clients to attend an opening night of a theater production. The star of the show is your cousin. You bring flowers to give to her after the performance. While you are watching the show, a stranger next to you falls asleep and starts to snore. You gently shake his arm and, sounding concerned, you ask, "Excuse me, but are you all right?"

Following the show, you take the flowers backstage and hand them to your cousin, bringing your clients with you. Where's the Faux Pas?

A GOOD TIME WAS HAD BY ALL. You and your husband attend a holiday party given by your female boss, Pat Smith, and her husband, Nick Jones. It is a glittering soiree—fine food, convivial conversation and, at the end, everyone joins in singing Christmas carols. You were among the first arrivals, but stay nearly until the end. Afterwards, you send a thank-you note to Mr. and Mrs. Jones thanking them for the pleasurable evening. Where's the Faux Pas?

THE CHOPSTICK NOVICE. An American in Japan wants to try using chopsticks, so when the waiter asks if he wants a fork, he declines. After eating a little of his rice, he stops to answer a question and places his chopsticks in the rice. When he finishes talking, he continues eating his rice and is able to eat just about every grain with his chopsticks. He then puts the chopsticks back in the paper envelope they came in. Where's the Faux Pas?

CHOW, BABY. Tom Kyle and his wife Betty have been invited to dinner at the home of an Italian colleague. They arrive on time, with chocolates for their hostess. During the dinner, many courses are served. Betty tries all of them, but Tom is worried about his weight and lets the pasta appetizer pass, knowing the entree is on its way. He compliments the cook on the main dish, and also eats a lot of cheese and fruit, which is served for dessert. After the dinner concludes, Betty offers to help with the cleanup. Where's the Faux Pas?

DINNER IS AT HAND. Tom Bing is invited to dinner at a business colleague's home in Saudi Arabia. He is told to arrive at 6 P.M., but Tom is eager to make a good impression and he arrives at 5:50 P.M. This is an unusual meal for Tom—there are no individual plates and all eat from the center dish. Though left-handed, Tom refuses the offer of a spoon and uses his right hand. As the meal begins with dates and a plate of bitters, Tom asks for a glass of wine. After the meal, incense is offered. Tom waves some on himself and passes it to the person on his right. He leaves after the incense has been passed to the last person. Where's the Faux Pas?

THE KING'S ENGLISH A company executive is giving a presentation to her British colleagues. She went through her visuals and changed, when appropriate, the American spelling to the British spelling. She provided some descriptive background on those she cited in her speech—Abraham Lincoln, Thomas Jefferson, and Theodore Roosevelt. She practiced slowing down her speech so she would not overwhelm her audience. Following the presentation, she was available for questions. Where's the Faux Pas?

Answers

THE DOOR DILEMMA: The Faux Pas is her objection. He is demonstrating old-fashioned manners which are no longer appropriate in the business setting. Even though she was technically correct in that whoever reaches the door first opens it, she demonstrated poor manners by calling attention to his behavior.

DINNER CHEZ BOSS: The Faux Pas is bringing an unannounced dessert. Making your specialty might seem like a nice gesture, but if it doesn't go with the meal, you will have put the host in an awkward position as to whether it should be served anyway. You should check with the host first before bringing food. Send flowers or bring chocolates. Being five minutes late is socially acceptable, although next time you should check your directions. We're assuming cocktails were offered to the spouses, who declined. The bone removal was handled appropriately—in matters of safety, expediency supersedes etiquette.

SCHEDULE WARS: The Faux Pas is having your secretary call. You should call to reschedule because it's your conflict. You are, however, to be commended for realizing (and resolving) the conflict in advance, rather than the night before!

PROGRESS REPORT: The Faux Pas is that you never told your client that the marketing manager came back into the room with you. Had you done so, he might have tempered his remarks about the department. Leaving him on the speakerphone with the two assistants was acceptable since he agreed to it. Not having the material ready was embarrassing; you should have located the material before making the call if you were the one to initiate it.

SHOPPING AROUND: The Faux Pas is that you should always ask whether someone wants to be included, rather than automatically excluding him. This question usually is answered correctly in our seminars, but what if the situation were reversed, with five men and one woman, and the activity they all planned to attend was a sporting event such as a boxing match? The faux pas would be the same. If the group is more gender-balanced—say three men and three women—it would be courteous to attempt to find an event that everyone could enjoy together.

THE TOO-GENEROUS GIFT: The Faux Pas is the lateness of your response. You must take action within 24 hours of when you receive the gift. Delaying any longer than that can lead the gift-giver to think the item was accepted.

MEETING MANIA: The Faux Pas is telling her about her stockings, since there's probably nothing she can do about them. Of course, if you know that she always carries a spare pair in her briefcase or if you have a pair to offer her, that would change the context. Telling her about her lipstick is appropriate, since she can do something about it. However, it would have been better to let her know as soon as possible rather than right before you walked into the meeting. This would have given her time not only to correct the mistake but to recover mentally before facing senior management. (It also would have been better on her part not to have been so late.) It was quite nice of you to notice her hairstyle, which was new to you even if she'd been wearing it that way for several months.

THE FREE LUNCH: The Faux Pas is your offer to leave a tip. You can tip for your coat and car. He shouldn't have ordered lobster because it is too messy to eat, but that was his call. You acted appropriately by switching after one alcoholic drink and using the only provided spoon for the iced tea. By the way, did you remember to say thank you?

A STAR IS BORN: The Faux Pas is bringing the flowers. You should have arranged to have the flowers sent ahead of time in a vase. A performer does not need to be concerned about placing flowers nor do you need to hold them during the performance. One would hope that you selected the show *despite* the fact that your cousin was the star, unless she is a well-known success, because it could put your guests in an awkward position if she bombed. Your actions with the snoring stranger were appropriate.

A GOOD TIME WAS HAD BY ALL: The Faux Pas is addressing the envelope to Mr. And Mrs. Jones. You should use your boss's name, and, assuming you want to flatter her, should list it first on the envelope: Ms. Pat Smith, Mr. Nick Jones. (P.S.: It probably would be enlightened for the host and hostess to include songs other than Christmas carols for those of different faiths.)

THE CHOPSTICK NOVICE: The Faux Pas is placing the chopsticks in the rice. They should go in the chopsticks rest, or he could keep them in his hand while carrying on the conversation, provided he didn't wave them around. Finishing the rice was appropriate. He does get points for his efforts to blend in.

CHOW, BABY: The Faux Pas is that Tom should eat some of all that is offered. He should take a small amount of food and just leave it on his plate, if he must. Besides, we have to wonder how serious Tom really is about weight loss if he eats a lot of cheese. Betty's offer to help clean up is acceptable. Chocolates are an appropriate hostess gift.

DINNER IS AT HAND   The Faux Pas is asking for the wine, which is against the prevailing religion. Without knowing his host's religious preferences, Tom should wait to be offered wine. Arriving for dinner ten minutes early is acceptable. He is correct, and perhaps even courageous, not to use his left hand—we admire his ambidextrousness! He's a sport to stay through the incense.

THE KING'S ENGLISH: The woman should have changed her American references to British ones: Winston Churchill, William Shakespeare, and Charles Dickens, for instance. Changing the visuals was a nice touch, and slowing down the speech was a good idea.

INDEX

ABOUT THE AUTHORS

Barbara Pachter, president of Pachter & Associates, is a speaker, trainer and author known nationally and internationally for her practical, results-oriented approach to building essential communications and management skills. For more than 20 years, she has designed and delivered training programs and coached executives for major corporations, organizations and institutions world-wide. Among these are 3M, AT&T, Abu Dhabi Gas Company, Conrail, General Electric, Hewlett Packard, Johnson & Johnson, Merck and Company, Merv Griffin Resorts Academy, Prudential, PSE&G, Rohm & Haas, ServiStar Corporation, and the U.S. Department of Defense.

Barbara also regularly conducts skill-building seminars for personnel at all organizational levels. These seminars focus on today's most relevant communications and management issues including business writing, presentation skills, communication skills, business etiquette, assertiveness skills, and intercultural awareness. She also offers seminars specifically designed for women in the business world.

She is co-author of the training book *Business Etiquette* (published by Irwin Professional Publishing). Her professional affiliations include the American Society of Training and Development and the National Speakers Association.

Marjorie Brody has more than 25 years of teaching, training and coaching business etiquette and presentation skills. She has worked with over 20,000 people ranging from corporate executives to college students in the United States and abroad. She holds a BA and MA in Rhetoric and Public Address. In 1994, Marjorie was honored by the National Speaker's Association with the designation of CSP—Certified

Speaking Professional—a designation that has been given to only a handful of speakers.

Marjorie began her career teaching public speaking skills and interpersonal communications on the college level. She is currently President of Brody Communications Ltd., an international communications training corporation that specializes in oral communication workshops. Her clients include such distinguished organizations as Merck & Company, SmithKline Beecham, Princeton University, Prudential Insurance Company, Thomas Jefferson University and Hospital, University of Pennsylvania, Rohm and Haas, Rhone-Poulenc-Rorer, US Healthcare, Colgate Palmolive, Conrail Corporation, Johnson & Johnson, Price Waterhouse, Abu Dhabi Gas Company of the United Arab Emirates, and Towers Perrin.

Marjorie is co-author of *Power Presentations: How To Connect With Your Audience and Sell Your Ideas* (John Wiley & Sons, 1993) and *Business Etiquette* (Irwin Professional Publishing, 1994). She is a member of the American Society of Training Development, the National Speakers Association, the 3M Meeting Management Institute and ToastMasters International.

Betsy Anderson's work covering education, politics, religion, and the military has been recognized with several national and state writing awards. Her honors include first places in newspaper feature writing from the New Jersey Press Association and from the New Jersey chapter of Sigma Delta Chi, the Society of Professional Journalists. She also is a winner of the Benjamin Fine Award from the National Association of Secondary School Principals and was a finalist in the Penney-Missouri national newspaper feature writing competition. Anderson is a former reporter and editor for newspapers in Michigan and New Jersey. Her work as a freelance writer has appeared in nationally known magazines and newspapers including the *New York Times* and the *Philadelphia Inquirer*. She has been on the faculty of the Philadelphia Writers Conference. A native of Flint, Michigan, she lives with her husband and son in Moorestown, New Jersey.